Regional Science Techniques in Practice

Regional Science Techniques in Practice

The Case of Nova Scotia

Stan Czamanski
Cornell University

Lexington Books
D.C. Heath and Company
Lexington, Massachusetts
Toronto   London

To F. C.

Contents

List of Tables

List of Figures

Preface

The present monograph is largely the product of six years of intensive research spanning the period 1966-71. The very idea of testing and sharpening the various tools of regional anslysis, the descriptions of which are scattered in the literature, by applying them to a single region, had appealed to me for a long time. My work in Nova Scotia thus provided me with a long-sought opportunity not only of experimenting under realistic conditions with methods of analysis but of expanding a hypothesis of regional growth, focusing on locational attractiveness and investment equilibrium as significant determinants of progress.

This hypothesis was formulated many years ago. In Nova Scotia it was made an integral part of a sizeable econometric model admitting of a much more extensive exploration of its implications and usefulness in providing a conceptual framework for regional development planning. Of importance was also the related set of studies aimed at measuring the various stock variables as well as of the more elusive elements of physical and socio-economic environment. The emphasis on stock phenomena is clearly at variance with studies of national economies where flows are ordinarily more relevant.

The manifold objectives of the several research projects carried out in Nova Scotia, commissioned by unrelated agencies but focusing on a single Province, soon revealed the inadequacy of existing techniques in several areas and necessitated extensive adaptations and forging of new ones. Some of these, like the application of multivariate analysis to interindustry flow matrices, and the use of regression coefficients in linear programming studies of land uses, proved to be useful in Nova Scotia but require further extensive testing. In presenting my empirical findings I have tried to be as objective as consistent with readability, yet the order of presentation reflects a logical sequence rather than the timing of various parts of the research.

Most of the studies reported in the present volume were carried out during the six summers and part of the winter 1969 which I spent at the Institute of Public Affairs, Dalhousie University, Halifax. Others were executed during the longer teaching seasons at Cornell, while the final editing and putting together of the manuscript was accomplished mainly in 1971 at The Florida State University, in Tallahassee.

Various institutions have provided the generous financial support required. The original general survey and the development of the format of income and product accounts were financed by the Agricultural Rehabilitation and Development Administration (ARDA). Later work on income and product accounts and on their interpretation and evaluation was supported by the Nova Scotia Department of Trade and Industry, Economics and Development Division, while the econometric model of the regional economy was commissioned by the Nova Scotia Department of Finance and Economics, Voluntary Economic Planning Branch. The development of techniques for exploring the uses of input-output tables for regional planning, as well as of applications of econometric models for decision purposes were largely financed by several Cornell University faculty research grants.

Two pilot studies yielded some useful preliminary insights and are reported in the following pages. The first, sponsored by the Canadian Council on Urban and Regional Research, dealt with urban land use models; the second, financed by the Department of Regional Economic Expansion of the Government of Canada, dealt with the formation of industrial agglomerations and growth points. The major research effort involved in the exploration of the effects of existing resources and more generally of stock variables upon regional development was supported by the Canada Council, which also financed the writing of the present monograph. I am most obliged for their assistance.

Some of the findings of the research here reported were previously published in article form. I gratefully acknowledge permission to reprint material which appeared in *The Town Planning Review*, 36, No. 3, 1965, *The Annals of Regional Science*, December 1970, *Papers of Regional Science Association*, XIII, 1965, and XXVII, 1971, and Allen J. Scott (ed.): *Studies in Regional Science*, Pion, Ltd., 1969.

In the substantial amount of research work reported in the monograph I have been assisted by an outstanding group of my students at Cornell University. My debt to Mr. Malcolm C. Brown, Mr. Robert A. Lewis, Mr. John Holmstrom, and especially to Mr. Emil E. Malizia and Mr. Andrew Daurik, all of whom except for Mr. Holmstrom spent various periods with me in Halifax, is heavy. In addition, Mr. Dzurik later read carefully an early draft of the present monograph. All have since assumed independent teaching positions. In my work on the econometric model I was assisted also by Dr. Manas Chatterji, Dr. Glenn Alexandrin, and Miss Janet Wykes, who at that time were associated with the University of Pennsylvania and joined me for one summer in Halifax.

My gratitude also to Mr. Guy Henson, Director of the Institute of Public Affairs, Dalhousie University, for providing me with an organizational framework and for creating at this institution a most stimulating atmosphere and ideal environment for fruitful research. Several permanent staff members of the Institute, especially Dr. Andrew S. Harvey, Mr. K. Scott Wood, and Mr. John Palmer, provided research assistance at one time or another. The most competent editing of the innumerable drafts was the work of Mrs. Margaret Dingley, while Mr. Keith Clarridge was responsible for all figures, maps, and diagrams. The final draft was patiently typed in Tallahassee by Mrs. Suzan Sanz.

I am most obliged to Dean Kermit C. Parsons for his constant encouragement over all those years and for the broad view which he took at times of my teaching duties. Professor Lawrence L. Klein of the University of Pennsylvania and Professor Roy E. George of Dalhousie University made several helpful comments, while Professor Charles L. Leven of Washington University read through the whole draft and suggested many improvements. I am happy to acknowledge my indebtedness to them.

But my greatest thanks are due to my former teacher, Professor Walter Isard, who introduced me to the fascinating field of regional science. The present volume is largely the outcome of his suggestions and of the many discussions we have had. I am most obliged for the penetrating comments he made on an earlier draft of this book.

Finally, I am heavily in debt to my wife Franciszka for her constant encouragement, in the face of her lost weekends and summers over a number of years. In the final stages of my work on the manuscript she rushed to my aid, editing and putting together the final draft, after a long winter of despair. To her this volume is dedicated.

Regional Science Techniques in Practice

1 Introduction: Study Background

1 Objectives and Scope

Regions which have ceased to grow and are stagnating or declining, either relative to the rest of the country or in absolute terms, present a number of serious economic, social, and political problems. For purposes of analysis, the depressed or declining regions can be grouped into two broad categories. On the one hand there are the distressed industrialized areas, such as the British Clydeside, Southeastern New England, or the Pittsburgh region, where the trouble is arrested industrial growth combined with symptoms of regression, on the other there are the relatively backward regions that have never experienced real industrialization, whose period of growth and development precedes the Industrial Revolution, or that for historical reasons have grown in population without the benefit of modern technology. Such diverse areas as Appalachia in the United States, the Canadian Atlantic Provinces, or the Italian Mezzogiorno provide good examples of this class of regions.

The two types of declining regions have, of course, many symptoms of maladjustment in common. Both suffer, essentially, from obsolescence of their former viability. Both may need help in making a structural shift to a new base in response to changes that have occurred in demand, in resources availability, or as a result of competition from other areas. For both, successful transition calls for modernizing their capital and human resources, their infrastructure, and their attitudes. In both cases fundamental changes are needed to enable them to grasp effectively new opportunities provided by technological and economic progress and thus become more resilient, self-reliant, and generative.

There are, nonetheless, important differences between the two. The population of a distressed industrialized area may show no particular deficiencies in literacy and capability for productive industrial or tertiary employment. They possess substantial local resources of capital and at least some industrial know-how. Internal and external transportation and communication facilities in such an area are likely to be adequate, or better than adequate. In this group are found many coal-based industrial complexes endowed with a very rich water, rail, and road communications network, often considered as their typical characteristic. In the second group of regions, by contrast, the human, industrial, and other resources are simply nonexistent; the infrastructure is typically inadequate for a modern industrial economy, while the attitudes reflect the general hopelessness and are in themselves a major obstacle to progress.

1

Awareness of problems raised by the existence of depressed regions, of pockets of economic stagnation, unemployment, and poverty in the midst of the highly industrialized and prosperous nations of North America and Western Europe, has been gaining ground slowly. In Canada and some other countries the issues are not only moral and sociopolitical, limited in scope to the geographic areas affected, but also present an economic problem and dilemma of national dimensions. The bulk of the problem of interregional disparities in Canada resides in the four Atlantic Provinces, of which Nova Scotia forms a part. Their combined population comprises almost ten percent, and together with the adjacent depressed parts of Quebec exceeds fifteen percent of all Canadians. The sheer size of the area and magnitude of the population affected impose a serious burden upon the national economy, and may slow down its progress.

The alternatives open to the federal government are few, and none of them is entirely satisfactory either from the political or socioeconomic point of view. In a country facing numerous problems of integration, and striving to overcome the differences and divisions rooted in its past, the affected provinces and regions clearly cannot be left to their own fate, perpetuating the already discernible division into the rich and the poor. On the other hand, to facilitate the outmigration from the depressed regions to other parts of this vast country better endowed by nature and history might be financially beneficial to the migrants but in its wider implications is economically dubious and politically unacceptable. Even assuming that the potential migrants could be retrained and prepared for the intense competition they are likely to encounter in the metropolitan labor markets of Central and Western Canada, would this prevent their dropping to the bottom of the social pyramid? The experience with "push" type migrations uncomfortably points toward this possibility. More important, under this policy it might be impossible to prevent a complete collapse in the now lagging regions once the most active part of the population has left; moreover, the magnitude and value of the assets and infrastructure to be abandoned may well be staggering. The alternative of forcing economic development by heavy government investments and subsidies raises other problems. The threshold for these outlays to be effective in stimulating genuine growth and eliminating the existing disparities may be very high indeed. By diverting huge resources from their best use, it might adversely affect the whole Canadian economy for a considerable period of time.

Yet in order to be able to attack effectively the complex issues involved, policy makers and analysts alike need a comprehensive conceptual framework which so far is largely missing. The situation bears some similarities to the one prevailing in the early 1930's, when the theoretical and methodological basis for the pursuit of an effective stabilization policy was lacking, or to the one following World War II with respect to development policy to be adopted in the newly independent backward countries. The vast amount of work in the field of development economics resulted in solid progress in our understanding of the process of growth only in the last decade, although without a dramatic breakthrough similar to the "Keynesian Revolution."

Recognition has been gaining ground slowly, that problems related to depressed and declining regions in the highly developed nations of Western Europe and North America are different from those faced by the underdeveloped countries of Africa, Asia, and Latin America and cannot be handled with the models and tools appropriate to the former. Some of the numerous difficulties encountered in applying concepts and models developed at the national level to subnational regions are due to their lack of institutional and economic boundaries which, combined with the high mobility under modern conditions, not only of goods and financial capital but even to a large extent of factors of production make such concepts as capacity limits and financial or foreign trade equilibrium irrelevant. More specifically, in the long run a region may face a perfectly elastic demand curve for the majority of its products; i.e., it may be able to sell all of its output as long as it is able to produce at competitive prices. Hence, fluctuations in demand, internal or for export, are less meaningful as main exogenous variables in models dealing with regions that are not economic entities. Similarly, because of high interregional mobility of financial capital, local investments do not depend, as a rule, on local savings. The fact that savings and investments may be permanently imbalanced limits the use of models focusing on this particular problem. These differences in emphasis of models dealing with regional problems raise as their corollary the question of whether the various formats of social accounts evolved at the national level can provide, without considerable changes, a suitable framework for regional studies and the indispensable background for analysis.

Even more important, perhaps, the focus of interest in regional studies differs widely from that of the economist or analyst working at the national level. Not only is the time horizon typically much longer, but the regional scientist, at variance with the traditional economist, is interested in breaks or shifts in regional structure rather than with incremental changes. This increases the analytic importance of stock phenomena and downgrades the relevance of many flows. Location theory, when skillfully used, may go a long way toward explaining many spatial phenomena. Finally, when dealing with systems of regions, the regional scientist, transcending the bounds of traditional spaceless economics, has to consider phenomena that are lacking one or several attributes of a good, that cannot be explained by reference to the optimizing behavior of ultimate decision-makers, or that reach beyond the matrix of an exchange economy. A notion such as sunshine, for example, refused the status of an economic good and having no place in theories dealing with exchange of values among ultimate decision-makers within a given social matrix, may be useful in explaining the interregional distribution of citrus growing.

The present monograph deals with the province of Nova Scotia; yet, its objectives go beyond a mere description of the regional economy. Nova Scotia is largely treated as a case study, since it happens to have many characteristics of a wide class of depressed regions in the highly industrialized nations. The relative geographical isolation and political integration of the province offer a rare opportunity to study the phenomena involved in the process of economic decline.

The more general analytic objectives of the study are twofold. First, it develops and tries to apply a hypothesis of regional growth focusing on locational attractiveness and investment equilibrium as significant determinants of progress. The hypothesis, while based on a modified theory of comparative advantage, leans heavily on industrial location theory and on study of stock phenomena. Second, in the course of an intensive, in–depth analysis of the Nova Scotia economy most of the tools and techniques of regional science have been applied, enabling an examination of their usefulness and efficiency, both for development planning and for other often equally pressing objectives of regional and urban planning.

2 The planning problem

In Nova Scotia the symptoms of stagnation, and in many areas of outright decline, are numerous and clear. Personal income on a per capita basis is considerably lower than the Canadian average, even though it is the highest among the Atlantic Provinces. Unemployment rates are high, while labor-force participation rates are correspondingly low. The resulting outmigration produces as its corollary the well-known unfavorable changes in the age and sex structure of the remaining population. The process is highly selective in other ways, too, and affects the composition and quality of the remaining labor force from the point of view of training and education. The weakness of the industrial base of the regional economy is reflected in the fact that manufacturing accounts for only about one third of the employed labor force, although the heavy concentration of activities in the service sectors, typical of underdeveloped economies, is partly explained in Nova Scotia by the presence of the defense establishment, which is one of the main income-generating forces in the local economy.

The studies reported below were carried out over the past six years in the absence of any agreed-upon planning objectives, a situation not infrequently encountered by regional planners. The inability of the political mechanism, over a protracted time period, to generate consistent policies was a factor in arriving at a number of demonstrably highly wasteful decisions. The several to a considerable extent mutually exclusive goals that seem to have been followed include the more obvious objective of raising the provincial per capita income to the Canadian level. This goal, reasonable in view of the very considerable difference, conflicts in Nova Scotia with the widespread although somewhat mute desire to preserve the traditional ways of life and values not easily translated into dollar terms. Hence, local opposition to decisions involving drastic changes, understand-

able among some segments of society, is not without support in popular senti-
ment. It is perhaps not a mere coincidence that the few attempts at evolving
development policies for Nova Scotia were mostly the work of federal agencies
and received cool reception in the province.

The objective of raising per capita output is not only different but often
incompatible with the goal of securing a more equitable income distribution
among the various segments of society, and of eliminating existing disparities
between various parts of the province. Both are embedded in and largely superseded by the concern for the survival of local agriculture in the face of considerable odds, and the more general problem of rural poverty. But while the plight of
local farmers, fishermen, and lumbermen is undoubtedly an important sociopolitical issue, its economic significance is in fact almost marginal. The unwilling-
ness to see it in its real proportion and the inability to face squarely and assess
the problem of substantial relocations involving much of the existing obsolete
settlement pattern, is probably at the root of the potentially disastrous location
policies followed during the last decade. Simultaneously, other important problems retain much of the attention of local decision-makers without having led to
a coordinated overall plan of action. Among them the organization of space and
provision of adequate services to rural areas, preservation of recreation areas,
especially of the coastline and beaches, construction of a modern road network,
and prevention of outmigration might be singled out. Often viewed as policy
objectives in their own right they tend to make the planning processes more
difficult to integrate.

The multiplicity of objectives has been more than matched by the number
of federal, provincial, and local agencies and programs involved in the planning
process. The rural problem was attacked by a task force set up by the federal-
provincial agreement on the basis of the Agricultural Rehabilitation and Development Act (ARDA) of 1961.[a] Originally limited to nine northeastern counties of
Nova Scotia forming the so-called "pilot area," the task force soon found itself
unable to separate the rural from the urban-industrial problems and to limit the
inquiry to a rather poorly delimited study area.

The policies followed under the Area Development Agency established in
1963 amounted to providing incentives, originally in the form of tax concessions,
to industries locating in designated areas. In Nova Scotia they aimed at revitaliz-
ing the hardest hit declining centers. Halifax, probably the only potential growth
point was not included until 1967. But whatever limited impact ADA may have
had upon the province, it contributed practically nothing in terms of comprehensive study of regional problems.

---

[a]The title was changed in 1966 to Agricultural and Rural Development Act and supplemented by Fund for Rural Economic Development (FRED). For an evaluation of ARDA
and other regional policies see Brewis, T.N.: *Regional Economic Policies in Canada,* Macmillan, 1969.

Much more significant was the establishment in 1962 of the Atlantic Development Board as a federal agency charged with both evolving policies and recommending the use of federal funds for development. The work of the ADB represented the first commitment of the federal government to broad and systematic regional planning. Over the six years following its founding the ADB produced a number of studies and reports but nothing approaching a comprehensive plan or set of consistent policy recommendations. The functions of the ADB were taken over in 1968 by the new Department of Regional Economic Expansion which so far, while supporting scattered projects, has failed to evolve a comprehensive policy.

At the provincial level the half hearted attempts at regional planning were carried out by various ministries of the Government of Nova Scotia with apparently little coordination among themselves. Special mention should be made of the efforts of the Ministry of Municipal Affairs, which produced a number of studies and guidelines for developing a network of service centers and local growth points, while the Ministry of Mines explored the future development and spatial distribution of primary industries. The efforts of the Ministry of Trade and Industry and of several other agencies do not amount to planning. An interesting innovation is the Nova Scotia Voluntary Planning Board which consists of members representing industry, labor, and government and is charged with promoting voluntary cooperation without regimentation or compulsion. Yet despite some successes the Board failed to evolve a regional plan and this function was entrusted in 1968 to a new agency of the Government of Nova Scotia called the Secretariat. In turn this body became involved in strictly operational tasks without making any serious effort at planning or coordinating various development policies. Finally, mention should be made of metropolitan planning in Halifax-Dartmouth and attempts at city planning in other towns. More important for the whole province are efforts of the Atlantic Provinces Economic Council (APEC), a nonprofit, nonpolitical organization that, since its founding in 1954, has produced a number of studies and provided a forum for discussions and critical appraisal of regional policies.

Given the number of partly conflicting objectives and the multitude of planning agencies, the set of regional studies reported below had to be designed so as to provide a framework and be capable of answering a host of pertinent questions not necessarily, or not only, related to development. For ease of exposition the main problems can be grouped into several broad categories. The first would attempt to assess and measure backwardness and decline. For example: Is low per capita output a fair index of a depressed region, or should one rather focus on a per capita income? By what standards should these be evaluated, and to what compared? Are the more elusive, nonquantifiable, or only partly measurable noneconomic goods to be included in this appraisal? And which, if any? Of special importance might be questions transcending the purely economic aspects of costs, investments, relocations, or productivity, such as those dealing with education or general physical and social environment. The immediate relevance of these questions is apparent in the context of federal-provincial relations, since one of the objectives of regional studies in Nova Scotia is to serve as background to discussions relating to the extent of federal involvement in promoting development and providing subsidies.

The second set of questions would address itself to industrial development. The fundamental question is whether to try to attract new industries by investing public funds in infrastructure or by providing direct subsidies. The studies have to provide insights into which industries to promote. From the point of view of feasibility, sources of raw materials, markets, transportation costs, availability of specialized labor, services, and a host of other factors have to be considered. From the point of view of desirability, such elements as growth prospects, wage levels, capital-labor and capital-output ratios, and direct and indirect multiplier effects have to be assessed.

The third group of problems deals with locations within the province. Should or could Nova Scotia have several or only one growth point? And should spatially unbalanced growth appear desirable, what would be the cost (economic, social, and political) of ensuing relocations and resettlement? What ancillary investments in infrastructure would be required and where? What is the value of assets that would have to be abandoned?

The fourth problem would deal with costs of development, or more broadly with the means necessary to achieve the socially desirable results. Alternatively, the set of studies should be capable of providing reliable predictions of outcomes of various combinations of decisions taken by the federal and provincial governments. Many but not all of these questions are related to the very theory of regional growth, succinctly summarized in the twin question: (1) What factors determine the rate of economic advance? and (2) What is the optimal allocation of resources to promote growth?

The studies and models reported below furnish answers to some of the basic questions raised.

The present chapter deals with the spatial and temporal setting of the study. It analyzes the broad aspects of Nova Scotia's location with its attendant advantages and disadvantages; it examines its natural conditions, such as relief and climate, from the point of view of their economic usefulness; and finally, it presents a brief history of settlement.

Chapter 2 concentrates on natural and human resources and reexamines the very notion of a resource and the theoretical and practical problems involved in their valuation. While it is largely descriptive it summarizes information basic for both planners and decision-makers. It explores the basic inbalance in planning methodology resulting from lack of methods of rigorous analysis of elements of the environment, both physical and social, in economic terms. Nonetheless, many of the findings presented in this chapter are incorporated as variables in the econometric model developed in Chapter 7.

Chapter 3 quantifies the main features of the regional economy, its structure, and shortcomings. It sizes up the problem as revealed by regional income and product accounts. The findings presented proved to be immediately useful to agencies of the Government of Nova Scotia in their day to day decisions and in policy measures affecting several levels of government. They also provided a wealth of inputs into the econometric model, while the usefulness of income and product accounts was appraised in terms of insights that might be gained with their help.

Chapter 4 deals with the productive and industrial basis of the province and tries to assess the locational advantages and disadvantages of the region. Its contribution resides in new insights into the locational attractiveness of the province, enabling selection of industries likely to find in Nova Scotia a suitable environment and determination of the extent of subsidies required to overcome existing disadvantages. It examines the uses of such standard tools of enquiry as shift-share analysis, comparative advantage, and analysis of variance.

Chapter 5 examines the responsiveness of the local economy to exogenous developments with the help of an interregional input-output. It concentrates on linkages existing among the various sectors of the Nova Scotian economy, and on the various multiplier effects generated; it redefines the concept on an urban-industrial complex and tries to establish to what extent this concept is useful and capable of rigorous application in a region devoid of major clusters of industries. It reexamines the question of industries to be promoted from a wider perspective of the whole provincial economy.

Chapter 6 evaluates invested capital and infrastructure and their spatial distribution. It furnishes some partial answers to questions related to costs of massive relocations and develops an accounting framework for grouping and classifying various provincial assets. It attacks the long-neglected problem of stock variables and their role in regional studies and models.

Chapter 7 presents a simple econometric model of the Nova Scotian economy. The basic assumptions of the model, its structure, properties, and estimating procedures are described as background for a more general discussion of regional econometric models and of their place in regional planning. It contains the main analytic findings of the set of studies, and results of simulation experiments. It reports practical applications of rigorous models in developing policy recommendations.

Chapter 8 contains the main conclusions of the study, both with respect to the economy examined and to the methodological issues involved.

3 Regional Setting: Location

Nova Scotia is a long, narrow peninsula forming the easternmost projection of the North American continent. Small by Canadian standards, the province stretches in a northeast to southwest direction for a total length of 374 miles. The width ranges from 60 to 100 miles, while the total area is a mere 21,068 square miles.

Geographically the province consists of two parts. The northeastern portion is formed by Cape Breton Island, which accounts for 106 miles of the total length and which since 1955 has been joined to the mainland by the world's deepest causeway across the Strait of Canso. The mainland part is a peninsula joined to the province of New Brunswick by the Isthmus of Chignecto. The more than 4,000 miles of rugged coastline, with numerous bays and coves, borders on the Atlantic Ocean, the Bay of Fundy, Northumberland Strait, and Cabot Strait.

Only 2,500 miles distant from Britain, Nova Scotia is nearer to Europe than to Canada's own west coast. Its location in relation to the main land mass of the North American continent and to Europe has been variously considered as a more or less important economic asset. The validity of this argument and the key to its evaluation rest on the assessment of the importance of the great natural harbor at Halifax and of the links connecting it with the major Canadian agglomerations. Technical developments have combined to reduce the importance of Halifax and other Nova Scotian ports as they have increased the attractiveness of ports located on the St. Lawrence system. The opening of the St. Lawrence Seaway has allowed large vessels access to the farthest corners of the Great Lakes system and the use of icebreakers has kept open the St. Lawrence River ports during part of what was formerly their closed season. In addition, the other bypass to Central Canada via the east ports of the U.S.A. continues to prove attractive to many shippers, its superior facilities and shorter haul to the main centers of population apparently outweighing any additional cost even when there is a loss of tariff preferences. Nonetheless, sea traffic funneled through the excellent port of Halifax increases somewhat during the winter months when the Gulf of St. Lawrence is icebound. Sydney, Hantsport, Lunenberg, and Liverpool are ports of secondary importance hardly to be considered as important outlets for intercontinental trade.

Hopes for the future are largely centered on claims that the year-round, ice-free Halifax Harbor could regain its role as a natural port of entry for a large portion of North America. Historically, this circumstance was undoubtedly a factor contributing to its early development. More recently these hopes have been set on the development of a container harbor and, in time, the emergence of Halifax as terminal of a land bridge connecting the Atlantic with the Pacific. Of the two interrelated ideas, the container harbor has greater appeal.

The land bridge is predicated on the assumption that with the time factor rapidly overshadowing cost considerations, goods being transported between Europe and the Far East will cross the American continent by rail rather than by way of the Panama Canal. Rail transportation being faster than seaborne, the very length of the land haul over Canada may confer an added advantage over the shorter overland crossing in Central America or Mexico, provided, of course, that the costs of transshipments in Canada can compete with the lower labor costs farther south. Yet, it is unlikely that the volume of traffic between Europe and East and South-East Asia will assume massive proportions in the foreseeable future. Developments based on shipments of grain and other products from and to Central Canada and the Great Plains appear far more promising.

For a container harbor, regularity and ease of access for ocean-going ships ensuring short turnaround time are of the essence. Halifax, located on a protruding peninsula, seems to enjoy here an advantage not only over Montreal and Quebec but even over Saint John, New Brunswick (although here the situation is less clear-cut), and this quite aside from ice conditions. The possible future competition from Portland, Maine, is a different and far more serious matter. Whether a container harbor is likely to trigger developments similar to those associated in the past with transshipments and break of bulk is far from obvious. Owing to the novelty of the idea and lack of experience elsewhere, it is difficult to draw any definite conclusions.

Of crucial importance for the position of Nova Scotia as a potential transportation hub is the network of connections between the province and the rest of Canada. Railroad facilities running from Halifax to the west with local branches to the southern and northern parts of the province are adequate but do not compare with similar networks in the more developed parts of the continent. They are supplemented by several ferry services, operated by Canadian National Railways, Canadian Pacific Railway, and Northumberland Ferries Limited. Ferry services are available from Yarmouth to Bar Harbor, from North Sydney to Port aux Basques, from Digby to Saint John, New Brunswick, and from Caribou, Pictou County, to Wood Island, Prince Edward Island.

Road connections have been greatly improved recently. With the Trans-Canada Highway completed, Nova Scotia is connected with population and manufacturing centers of central Canada by paved roads that are good enough to allow reasonably quick movement of persons and goods. Yet the new roads that now connect the province with Quebec, Ontario, the prairies, and the United States through northern New Brunswick, together with roads serving various parts of the province, form a road system that is still rather primitive compared with the highways of central Canada or much of the United States.

Air transport, which has transformed travel patterns in the vast regions of Canada, is largely bypassing Nova Scotia. Montreal and Toronto both rank among the world's busiest airports, with frequent services to other parts of Canada, to North and Central America, and to Europe; the modern Halifax airport, while capable of handling the large jets now in service, is hardly in the same category. Yet there has been considerable progress recently, with an increasing number of transcontinental and intercontinental flights. Air Canada should soon be joined by Canadian Pacific as a trunk carrier, while local air services to the smaller airports at Sydney and Yarmouth are provided by Air Canada and Eastern Provincial Airlines.

Nova Scotia is also suffering from lack of pipeline transportation which is

used to an increasing extent to move oil and gas. Having no large concentrations
of population and being separated from the present eastern terminals of the pipeline by hundreds of miles of sparsely populated and difficult country, the
province seems unlikely to enjoy this form of transportation for many years.
How serious this deficiency is with respect to attempts to develop in Halifax a
major port of entry serving much of Canada is not immediately obvious.

Thus, even a cursory examination of the underlying facts dampens any excessive optimism, or at least adds some important qualifications. Notwithstanding
certain natural advantages and existing linkages to the outside world, the geographic situation of Nova Scotia makes it relatively less accessible to the large
markets and population centers in Canada and the United States than some other
points on the eastern seaborad of North America. This is partly conveyed by
Figure 1-1 and by a comparison of the relative locational advantages of Halifax

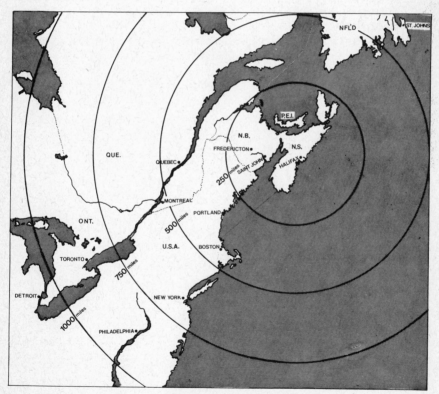

Figure 1-1. Nova Scotia in Relation to East Coast Centers.

and other ports in the northeastern part of North America, involving some generalized indexes of accessibility to the Canadian and United States markets. The analysis makes use of gravity and spatial interaction models predicated on a highly aggregate macro-approach to the location of activities. [1] Although the market potential concept differs sharply from the familiar behavioral models with which economists ordinarily work [2] and is still controversial, the gravity approach is introduced here as a crude description of the locational advantages and disadvantages of Nova Scotia.

The assumptions underlying the analysis are few but strong:

(1) The prime concern of all producers in locating a new plant or in selecting a port of entry for their raw materials is minimization of transport costs (which can be easily extended to encompass transport time).
(2) Transportation rates are equal for all commodities and proportional only to weight and distance.
(3) Only urban North American markets are considered.
(4) Demand for all consumer goods is spatially distributed in proportion to either population or volume of retail sales.
(5) Demand for all raw materials and intermediate manufacturing goods in each center is proportional only to total value added in manufacturing.
(6) No trade barriers between Canada and the United States are assumed.

In keeping with the above assumptions, three measures of market potential were used: (1) population, (2) retail sales, (3) value added in manufacturing, yielding the following Indexes of Accessibility.

$$T_{1 \cdot i} = \sum_{j=1}^{n} P_j d_{ij}; \qquad \begin{array}{l} (i = 1, 2, \ldots .7) \\ \\ (j = 1, 2, \ldots .115) \end{array} \qquad (1)$$

$$T_{2 \cdot i} \sum_{j=1}^{n} S_j d_{ij}; \qquad (2)$$

$$T_{3 \cdot i} \sum_{j=1}^{n} V_j d_{ij}; \qquad (3)$$

where

T_i = index of accessibility from the ith port of entry,

P_j = population of the jth North American urban center,

S_j = retail sales in the jth market center,

V_j = value added in manufacturing in the jth center,

d_{ij} = road, rail, or shipping distance in miles between centers i and j (shortest distance was used).

The indexes $T_{1 \cdot i}$ and $T_{2 \cdot i}$ may be considered as indicating the relative total transportation costs involved in supplying the entire North American market with consumer goods. They provide a measure of the locational attractiveness of any of the seven eastern North American harbors as a port of entry for consumer goods or, alternatively, for locating a plant producing such goods. The third index, $T_{3 \cdot i}$, refers to a producer of intermediate manufacturing goods.

The analysis was based on data pertaining to the 48 largest urban centers in Canada and 67 in the United States. In Canada these 48 centers comprise about 53 percent of the total population and 87 percent of the urban population. In the United States they account for 47 percent and 56 percent respectively. In terms of retail sales and value added both in Canada and in the United States, the selected cities covered about 60 percent of the respective totals. In addition, the urban centers considered have large suburban populations, which would raise even further the above proportions.

The results are summarized in Table 1-1. The advantages of Toronto and New York over Halifax on all three counts are net and clear-cut. Interestingly enough, even Saint John seems to enjoy a better relative location. The fact that trade barriers between Canada and the United States were disregarded (Assumption 6) does not seem to influence the results to any great extent. The introduction of the extreme assumption of no trade or transit through Canadian ports to the United States, in other words, limiting the analysis to accessibility to the Canadian market alone, does not change the relative positions of Toronto, Saint John, and Halifax, This is brought to the fore in Table 1-2.

It is easy to exaggerate the importance of these results. The indexes derived are at best generalized indicators, neither revealing the complex underlying relationships nor giving any clues to the future. A more detailed analysis, considering other factors as well, presented in Chapter 4 as part of the discussion of the industrial basis of Nova Scotia, reveals a slightly more favorable situation.

4 Physical Environment

Nova Scotia belongs to the Appalachian system extending far into the southern United States. Although lacking amplitude, the region shows considerable diversity of relief with a backbone of hills of complicated pattern running almost its entire length, and reaching about 1,750 feet in Cape Breton. [3] In terms of geology it is part of the Eastern North American region characterized by old,

Table 1-1
Accessibility to North American Market

City	$T_{1,i}=$ $\Sigma P_j d_{ij}$ (1)	Index Base: Toronto =100 (2)	$T_{2,i}=$ $\Sigma S_j d_{ij}$ (3)	Index Base: Toronto =100 (4)	$T_{3,i}=$ $\Sigma V_j d_{ij}$ (5)	Index Base: Toronto =100 (6)
Toronto	83,175,573	100	126,157,774	100	98,951,454	100
New York	84,752,499	102	127,484,568	101	102,221,302	103
Boston	97,133,634	117	146,238,913	115	117,542,179	119
Montreal	97,673,870	117	147,601,842	117	118,335,558	120
Saint John	137,308,105	165	204,829,801	162	168,315,040	170
Halifax	162,981,744	196	240,797,748	190	200,288,177	202
Sydney	187,649,262	226	275,207,908	217	230,978,971	233

Table 1-2
Accessibility to Canadian Market

City	$T_{1,i}=$ $\Sigma P_j d_{ij}$ (1)	Index Base: Toronto =100 (2)	$T_{2,i}=$ $\Sigma S_j d_{ij}$ (3)	Index Base: Toronto =100 (4)	$T_{3,i}=$ $\Sigma V_j d_{ij}$ (5)	Index Base: Toronto =100 (6)
Toronto	6,476,880	100	6,944,087	100	3,152,459	100
Montreal	7,541,387	116	7,163,947	103	3,399,361	108
New York	9,509,423	147	9,055,873	130	4,687,124	149
Boston	9,794,199	151	9,305,193	134	4,995,252	159
Saint John	12,019,410	178	11,365,489	164	6,516,813	207
Halifax	14,415,086	214	13,641,966	197	8,164,207	259
Sydney	16,730,384	248	15,872,251	229	9,738,126	309

weathered bedrock and glaciated terrain. Moraines account for rough, attractive topography with many lakes at different heights above sea level. Glaciation caused the rugged and stony shoreline, giving rise to extreme tidal fluctuations, especially in the Bay of Fundy, and the many natural harbors.

The Cobequid Mountains, although appearing as a sharp ridge from both north and south, in reality form a plateau at about 900 feet above sea level from 8 to 12 miles wide and 85 miles long. The Pictou-Antigonish Uplands, extending across both counties, slightly exceed 1,000 feet above sea level at McNeil Mountain. On Cape Breton Island there are several upland ridges trending from southwest to northeast, with the Cape Breton Highlands National Park, rising abruptly from the narrow coastal lowlands to an elevation of 1,500 to 1,700 feet.

The upland areas are all underlain by hard crystalline rocks. The lowlands, on the other hand, are found on the weaker sedimentary sandstones, shales, and limestones largely belonging to the Carboniferous system. The central feature of the structure of the whole Maritime Provinces is the broad syncline forming a depositional basin upon which the Carboniferous, or coal-bearing, rocks were laid.

The numerous rivers are very short and flow southeast or north-northwest. The longest, the Mersey, is only about 50 miles long. Only a few of the rivers are useful for navigation but, in general, they are potential sources of electric power. The territory of the province also comprises numerous lakes. The largest body of water, the Bras d'Or Lakes, is really an inland arm of the sea and almost cuts Cape Breton into two parts.

This diversity of landforms is closely related to the character of the under-lying geological structure which affects the natural environment in several ways. The land surface is generally uneven and ill suited to agricultural use. The Pleistocene ice age spread a great mixture of unconsolidated material over the bedrock. This has resulted in major changes in drainage patterns, causing swamp-land, lakes, and new river systems that divide the land into numerous small areas. Much of the land surface is dominated by bedrock. Also, much of the land that could be put to agricultural use is broken by ridges, valleys, hills, and bouldery knobs. Thus the geology and land form of the region are not favorable to exten-sive agriculture. The soils are quite good in the Annapolis Valley and there is some good grazing land around Truro, but nowhere are there large stretches of good agricultural land. Over much of the province the soils are unfertile, stony, and acid.

Climatically, Nova Scotia belongs to the environment of the Western Atlantic Ocean. Instead of being exposed to the warm Gulf Stream from the south, however, the region lies directly in the path of the cold Labrador Current sweeping down from the north and forcing the Gulf Stream farther to the east. The meeting of the two currents results in abundant fog formation as the winds blowing over the warm Gulf Stream pick up moisture and then are cooled as they pass over the Labrador Current. The fog banks quite often drift over the coast.

Their effects are particularly noticeable in summer and result in higher humidity and lower temperatures relative to inland areas. The January and July average temperatures of about 25°F and 65°F signify moderate winters and cool summers. High humidity adds to the chill factor in winter and results in a deficiency of sunshine of the order of 10 to 20 percent relative to other regions in this latitude. Precipitation on the other hand is abundant, with 55 inches evenly distributed throughout the year, about one quarter of it falling as snow.

With respect to agriculture, the growing season of between 100 and 160 days is shorter with fewer hot days than elsewhere in Canada. A deceptive feature of Nova Scotia is that surface growth generally looks green and flourishing because of the high relative humidity, even though it is in fact in poor condition. The high relative humidity and cool temperatures not only affect field crops but also reduce the length of the grazing season, thus increasing the feed requirements of livestock. These are all the harder to meet because lack of sunshine hinders harvesting and hay curing while lower soil termperatures hinder grass and fodder growth. Winter wind chill which is greater than in Central or Western Canada raises the cost of both feed and shelter and puts Nova Scotia at a disadvantage compared to areas that compete with it in beef cattle and hog production. Other forms of economic activity are adversely affected to a lesser extent. The moist, cool summers, cold seas, and lack of sunshine are detrimental to the development of a tourist industry.

5 History of Settlement

Up to 1763 the name Nova Scotia was applied to what is now mainland Nova Scotia, New Brunswick, and Prince Edward Island. In that year its area was further augmented by Cape Breton Island, ceded together with Acadia by the French in the Treaty of Paris. In 1769 Prince Edward Island broke away, followed in 1784 by New Brunswick and Cape Breton Island, but in 1820 Cape Breton was reunited with Nova Scotia, which since then has retained its present boundaries.

The original inhabitants of the region were the Micmac Indians. Although Great Britain claimed the area on the basis of John Cabot's explorations, the French were the first Europeans to settle in the province. Port Royal, established in 1603, was the earliest permanent settlement north of Florida. The inhabitants dyked and cultivated the tidal flats near the Bay of Fundy for almost a century, and called the area Acadia. Population expanded in a typical linear French settlement pattern, with houses built on both sides of a single highway. The Acadians cultivated the Annapolis Valley, although they remained on the western side of the province. By 1755, there were about 10,000 Acadians in Nova Scotia. [4]

Politically, Nova Scotia, which then encompassed the entire Maritime region, was claimed by both England and France, and soon became the battleground for these two European powers. [5] Port Royal was attacked several times between 1618 and 1654 by the British, who conquered the area more than once only to have it returned to France through treaty agreements. Political and military developments had their economic repercussions, with the area becomming alternately part of two European economies. While the English favored fishing and the French depended more heavily on agriculture, settlement in general was motivated primarily by military objectives.

The spatial pattern of settlement clearly reflected the rugged topography of the province. The deep channels and bays of its southeastern coastline, forming a hindrance rather than a help to internal transportation, the rocky terrain, the dependence of a substantial portion of the population upon activities connected with the sea, with agriculture limited to a few valleys, all combined in evolving a series of poorly connected coastal settlements. This characteristic feature of Nova Scotian colonization persisted well into the nineteenth century, with many vestiges clearly discernible to this day. As late as 1800 the roads leading from Halifax stretched for only a few miles, and not until the early part of the nineteenth century did a road network built by statute labor and a stagecoach system ensure regular if somewhat precarious connections between Halifax, Windsor, Annapolis, Truro, and Pictou. The province had to wait till 1858 for the first railroad line connecting Halifax, Windsor, and Truro.

By that time fundamental changes in the political, economic, and demographic structure of Nova Scotia had taken place. Throughout the seventeenth century the French were clearly dominant and enhanced their position with the founding of Louisbourg in 1720. While the British had unsuccessfully encouraged migration to Nova Scotia before, the Louisbourg settlement was an overwhelming catalyst for English colonization, since the population of Nova Scotia was becoming solidly French. Thus, in 1749 Halifax was founded, with many settlers coming from New England. Four years later, Hanoverian Germans established Lunenburg, which became the most prosperous location in the province. In addition, New England colonists were encouraged to settle in the Maritimes and, from 1759 to 1761, founded more than a dozen settlements.

With the treaty of Paris in 1763, all French possessions in this part of the world were ceded to Great Britain. During the preceding war and as a result of the French defeat, the demographic structure of the province underwent a drastic change from French to English, Irish, and German, with the deportation of the Acadians to Louisiana and Georgia. [6] Later in the eighteenth century, Loyalists and their slaves were evacuated from Boston and New York, and their number reached 35,000 during the period from 1776 to 1783. Except for the Irish and Scottish immigrants who slowly settled the Cape Breton area, the last significant inmigration occurred after the War of 1812. This wave was comprised of ex-servicemen who were given land grants and encouraged in various ways to settle. [7] The migration peaked in 1840 and virtually ceased thereafter.

Like many declining regions, Nova Scotia had its "golden age," which began in the second part of the eighteenth century. This corresponded to the "wood-wind-sail" economy. While during its entire prior history fishing and agriculture were the major sources of income and subsistence, sea commerce was now becoming increasingly important. Salted fish, usually cod, was exported to the West Indies and other parts of North America. Favorable trade agreements with England and the demand from the United States, especially during the "gold rush" to California and the Civil War, created boom conditions lasting almost without interruption for three quarters of a century.

Lumber was early added to the main Nova Scotian export commodities but was gradually diverted to local consumption, providing the raw material for construction and shipbuilding. The abundance of timber and thriving fisheries led to the development of a boat-building industry sustaining the colony's own mercantile fleet and supplying ships to Britain and other countries. Together, shipbuilding and the carrying trade formed the twin basis of the new prosperity. By the middle of the nineteenth century, Nova Scotia stood fourth in the world in merchant tonnage. Its population reached 275,000 in 1850. [8] Maritimers now look with nostalgia upon the period around the middle of the preceding century, which turned out to be the most prosperous in their history. The buoyant world economy, the Crimean War and the American Civil War, a world railway-building boom, and the 1854 Reciprocity Treaty in raw materials with the United States all seem to have played their part.

Nova Scotia entered the Canadian Confederation in 1867 as one of the founding members. Politically and economically it was a milestone in the development of the province. The gradual decline that now set in was not wholly unexpected, although only partly related to attempts at linking the economy of Nova Scotia to that of Canada. The ominous clouds started to gather much earlier, in the 1830's and 1840's, when the world's first railway-building boom collapsed and with it the demand for lumber for ties. The slump in demand was aggravated by the raising of lumber tariffs by the United States. Moreover, Britain allowed the United States to enter the West Indies trade, and a few years later adopted a general free trade policy, thus destroying Nova Scotia's traditionally favored position in inter-British Empire trade.

Confederation, with its emphasis on economic integration, merely reinforced the need to reorient the economy of the province, now that the favorable trade agreements, such as the Reciprocity Treaty with the United States which expired in 1866, were eliminated. Yet the national policy adopted in 1879, while seeking integration, seemed to orient the young nation away from the Maritimes and toward economic development in the central and western part of Canada. The center of power, political and economic, shifted westward. Immigration into Nova Scotia, which had reached considerable proportions during the first half of the nineteenth century, dried up, and the later waves leap-frogged over into the central provinces and the west. From housing 10 percent of Canada's population in 1961, Nova Scotia could claim only 5 percent at the outbreak of the Second World War, and scarcely 3.5 percent at present.

The adverse forces that brought the good times of Nova Scotia to an end were more fundamental than freeing of British trade or national economic policies following the political unification of Canada. The principal reason for Nova Scotia's economic decline was beyond doubt technological, the gradual undermining of the "wood-wind-sail" economy by the ever increasing use of steel and steam. A century earlier, the more profitable occupations as shipbuilding, forestry, and commerce drained labor from stagnating agriculture, shifting the entire economic structure toward the new rapidly growing sectors. Now, steamships replacing wooden sailing vessels brought an end to both Nova Scotia's carrying trade and also to its ship-building industry,[b] but no new industries developed in the province to open new possibilities and take advantage of existing skills and infrastructure.

The adverse changes which took place were fairly rapid although unspectacular. The development of refrigerated ships reduced the demand for salted and dried fish, replacing it with meat, now capable of withstanding long transportation. Although the fishing industry managed to survive by shifting from dried fish to lobster and fresh fish production, putting development of refrigeration to good advantage, competition from Britain, Norway, and Iceland cut into traditional markets, and in the inter-war period the collapse of sugar ruined the West Indian market. In spite of these vicissitudes fishing remained an important industry, and since the last war sustained demand for fish in the United States, and generous government subsidies encouraged capital investments in more efficient boats and equipment.

Agriculture, never a major asset of the regional economy, did not fare so well. At no time did it really develop beyond the stage required to supply its own domestic needs for food, meat, poultry, and dairy products. Faced with overwhelming competition from Western grain and limited by the generally low quality of the soil and rough topography, it has survived until the present, but largely as a subsistence activity carried out on small, inefficient farms, often combined with part-time fishing and lumbering. Were it not for the lavish subsidies paid by government, most of the farms would not continue at all. As it is, net income of farm operators from farming operations including subsidies represented in 1965 barely 0.79 percent of total personal income, excluding the income of hired hands. Only Nova Scotia's apples, grown mainly in the Annapolis Valley, proved a match for inland agricultural competition and remained a fairly prosperous undertaking.

Similar developments took place in lumber. The opening up of the great forests of the Northwest allowed the timber industries of those regions to develop into the world's most important producers. At the same time demand was falling off due to the end of the railway building boom and the invasion of steam. To make matters worse, the Panama Canal was opened in 1914, letting West Coast

---

[b]Ironically, the first crossing of the Atlantic on steam was made in 1833 by the "Royal William," out of Pictou, Nova Scotia.

timber through to traditional Nova Scotian markets in enormous quantities at a time when the most easily accessible forest resources in Nova Scotia were becoming depleted. Relief, and this only partial, had to await development of the pulp industry. The Nova Scotian forests yield good pulpwood, and with reasonably good management should do so indefinitely. They are, however, on a small scale compared with the enormous reserves elsewhere.

Two other industries, coal mining and primary iron and steel manufacturing, which developed largely in the nineteenth century, are at present facing serious problems. Coal mining in Nova Scotia dates from 1720, but the real development took place more than 100 years later. At one time the province's mineral wealth in the form of coal promised to become the basis of a highly developed industrial economy as well as providing a valuable export. The Canadian tariff in 1879 made it easier for Nova Scotian coal to compete in Central Canada with American coal, and the growth of the iron and steel industry at Sydney in the latter part of the nineteenth century provided an important home outlet. The American market fell away in the late nineteenth century, due to competition from its own producers, who enjoyed favorable treatment afforded by American railways with which they were often financially linked. The situation was soon reversed until competition from American coal imported into Central Canada necessitated the institution in 1928 of subventions to Nova Scotian coal mining. The easily accessible deposits are now almost exhausted, and the industry is surviving only with the help of heavy government subsidies, both direct and in the form of cheaper freight rates. This hardly compensates for the fact that the cost of coal at the pithead is about three times higher in Nova Scotia than in the United States. Recently the coal mines have been bought by the government and the operation is being phased out over a period of fourteen years.

As far as other minerals are concerned, Nova Scotia's endowments are meager compared with the bounty of other parts of Canada. Gypsum, of which it produces some 80 percent of the Canadian total, is exported as rock to the United States, and together with salt and some barites forms the more extensively mined minerals; but all of these are of the low-value variety. The mining sector of Nova Scotia provides employment to over 4 percent of its labor force, but most of it relies upon coal mining with little prospect of surviving for long.

The iron and steel industry was founded in response to a demand for steel rails and railway cars in the great railway-building period. Its original location was in Pictou County, where iron ore was discovered in 1828. The first steel ingots made in Canada were poured at North New Glasgow-Trenton, but this operation stopped in 1904 with the virtual exhaustion of the more valuable ore deposits. Prior to that a far more important plant was opened at Sydney, Cape Breton Island, based on local coal with ore and limestone imported by boat from Newfoundland, and soon reached impressive dimensions. After the Second World War it encountered increasing competition from Central Canadian and foreign steel producers and is suffering from a lack of nearby markets. The long distance to its main customers in Central Canada, as well as the high cost and low quality of local coal, puts the industry at a great disadvantage in relation to its competitors. More important, it has failed to attract iron and steel processing industries to Nova Scotia and thus trigger the development of a local industrial complex. The industry itself has reached the minimum efficient size as far as total capacity is concerned, but its equipment is obsolete. It has been underinvested for a long period of time and under present conditions could not survive without substantial government subsidies. Late in 1967, its owners decided to close the plant. Ownership has been taken over by the Nova Scotia government in order to prevent serious dislocations to the economy of the Sydney area which would follow a sudden closure, but its future is uncertain. Its fate, even in decline, is not wholly independent of the future of Cape Breton coal mining.

Other manufacturing activities include many small and rather inefficient plants, mainly those in the foods industry, oriented, except for those engaged in fish processing, toward the needs of the local market. The latter industry, comprised of numerous small plants, accounts for some 2¼ percent of total employment in Nova Scotia. Of the older industries, one should also mention ship- and boat-building and repairing, now largely limited to the construction of small vessels, and the relatively small railway car factory at Trenton. The wood industries are mainly processors of primary products, with sawmills accounting for the bulk of production. Most of the rest of Nova Scotia's manufacturing was aimed at supplying local markets with goods that could not be brought in from elsewhere easily or cheaply, such as dairy products or bread. Only a handful of firms succeeded in carving out for themselves markets in Central and Western Canada. Knitwear manufacturers, confectionery makers, and spice firms were perhaps the best examples, and in the inter-war years a pulp and paper industry did develop in the province.

This rather gloomy picture, with primary sectors stagnating and declining and with many manufacturing industries facing a very uncertain future, is partly relieved by the sprinkling of new plants recently located in the province with considerable government help. Table 1–3 illustrates the progress achieved in this direction. Of the firms employing over 100 persons, there are two oil refineries, a television manufacturer, an electronic equipment firm, a deuterium oxide plant, a polyethylene film and fiber plant, and an automobile assembly plant.

The rather weak manufacturing base of the regional economy provides employment for only about one-third of the employed labor force. The heavy concentration of activities in the service sectors, typical of underdeveloped economies, is partly explained in Nova Scotia by the presence of the defense establishment. These activities have grown in scope throughout the 1950's, and by 1961 the military establishment provided 1.6 percent of total employment while defense expenditures in the province amounted to almost 12 percent of the Gross Regional Product. If one adds to this the personal expenditures of the considerable number of military personnel stationed in Nova Scotia, it appears

Table 1–3
Number of New Manufacturing Firms Established in Nova Scotia by
Number of Employees, 1956–1967

Year	Under 5	5–14	15–49	50–99	100–249	250–499	Over 500
			Number of Employees				
1956		1					
1957	2	1					
1958	2	1	2				
1959	1			1			
1960		1	3	1			
1961		3	1	2		1	
1962	2	1	4	1	1		
1963	4		1	1			
1964	2	1	3	2	2		
1965	2	3	1	1	2		1
1966	1	4	1	3	1		
1967	3	2	4	4	1	1	1
Under construction		2	6		4		

that defense, together with other federal and local government activities, is the
real income-generating force of the local economy. Here again, however, the
future is uncertain.

Yet, notwithstanding such minor windfalls as the gold rush in the 1880's and
the development of a major defense establishment centered in Halifax during the
Second World War, Nova Scotia has been a declining province for almost one
hundred years. Even the splendid natural harbor at Halifax lost much of its
attraction, as the building of locks and canals allowed ocean-going vessels to pene-
trate deeper and deeper into the country's interior while more powerful icebreakers kept the St. Lawrence River open and much of the cargo destined for
Central Canada was attracted by the superior facilities of the East Coast ports of
the United States. Nothing illustrates this more clearly than the fact that while
in 1870 some 11 percent by value of all Canadian trade was handled by Nova
Scotian ports, by 1939 this portion had dwindled to a little over 4 percent. With
the scale of operation in sea commerce substantially increased, Halifax does not
serve a large enough economic hinterland. Its decline as an important North
American port was accompanied by the virtual disappearance at the beginning of
the present century of many ports of lesser size, scattered over the eastern shore
of Nova Scotia.

After Confederation, great efforts were made to ensure an adequate transportation link with the rest of Canada. The Intercolonial Railway was extended
through New Brunswick down to Halifax, a branch line being built into Northern
Cape Breton. The ferry service linking Digby and Saint John, New Brunswick,
provided an improved connection with Montreal. Also, within the province a few

local lines were built, bringing Nova Scotia's rail mileage to about 1,300 miles, but despite the progress achieved in communications, technological change favored large market areas for attracting new manufacturing activities, and Nova Scotia had not attained the threshold population size.

Because of its geographical position, Nova Scotia comes into its own in wartime. This was so during the First and even more so during the Second World War, between 1939 and 1945. Great strides were made toward closing the economic gap with the central provinces. Shipping, shipbuilding, and ancillary manufacturing industries, deliberately steered toward it by government action, and expansion of the great naval base were responsible for the booming economy. It proved, however, in both cases short-lived and the first few post-war years saw a reversion to the original situation. Although fishing, forestry, a few manufacturing activities, defense, education, and tourism will probably remain viable, natural seeds for economic growth seem not to exist. To make up for this situation, the Canadian government is beginning to devote more energy and public resources to the Maritime Provinces.

The present plight of Nova Scotia, the extent of which is amply documented in the following chapters, is real enough. It is hardly an isolated phenomenon and in a general sense seems to have its roots in failure to adapt to changing circumstances. Regions suffering from past or present maladjustment to technical, political, socioeconomic, or spatial phenomena are fairly numerous and are to be found in almost all countries. Severe cases affecting relatively small communities give rise to "ghost towns" which, contrary to popular belief, are neither rare nor limited to North America. In the case of larger regions the decline is rarely total or rapid. More often than not it spans many generations; with numerous, sometimes successful attempts at rehabilitation. The economic, social, and political problems involved in their decline face governments with many difficult dilemmas.

A cursory examination of the history of Nova Scotia does not provide many clues. Treated in isolation, without recourse to in-depth examination of the various trends and above all without the benefit of numerous interregional comparisons, it does not reveal regularities upon which to base a more rigorous analysis. It is submitted for what it is worth, simply as a background for an inquiry dealing with the present.

2 Locational Attractiveness: The Resource Base[1]

1 Problems of Measurement

While natural and human resources figure prominently among character-istics that distinguish the physical and socioeconomic environment of one region from another and have long played a prominent role in regional planning, attempts to incorporate them explicitly into regional models have so far been few. The evident difficulties of quantifying the important but elusive elements of the environment in a meaningful way only partly explain their omission.

Because of the considerable number of resources with at least several possible ways of measuring each one, the use of physical measures in order to quantify them is hardly feasible. An obvious alternative would be to use money values, thus providing a common measuring rod with additive properties, but progress in this direction has so far been slow. The main stumbling block seems to be the fact that the concept of value applies to commodities and services defined within a specific legal context with value depending not only on their material properties but on three elements: the object being valued, the person placing the value on it, and the sociopolitical environment. But many resources lack one or more of the basic attributes of a commodity, namely utility, scarcity, appropriability, and transferability, and some have even to be classified as free goods, becoming valuable only because they enhance the utility or productivity of other goods or services. Thus, their possible uses and marginal contributions to production have to be considered.

The three approaches to valuation of assets or wealth are: market value, depreciated past outlays or replacement cost, and capitalized future income stream. Each evolves from a slightly different time perspective. The first explores market prices at the present point in time, the second looks backward in time, cumulating investments or past costs in previous time periods, while with the third approach, the existing stocks are measured by discounting the expected returns. But even the first method using prices, which are established by the equilibrating mechanism that balances supply and demand, cannot be entirely removed from the temporal context, since price itself is a ratio of two flows. The very concept of market price when applied to a stock is conditional, and amounts to asking: What would the market price of the resource be, if it were sold in the marketplace? It implies the existence of a fairly active market with numerous transactions, and a volume of current transactions representative of the entire stock. A complementary condition would require that the market price be invariant to changes in sample size, or constant regardless of whether the entire stock or only a few items are offered for sale, implying a perfectly elastic demand curve not often met in the case of resources. Moreover, the very concept of market price cannot be of much help with respect to resources that are lacking some of the basic attributes of commodities or subject to important legal limitations and government controls.

Aside from practical difficulties, the conceptual basis for valuation of those natural resources to which the notion of scarcity does not apply (such as air or sunshine) is controversial despite their importance for explaining inter-regional differences. Ordinarily, any good supplied in excessive quantities and thus superabundant would have no value, because its marginal utility would be zero. In other words, the demand and supply curves for this good would intersect at zero price or no intersection would take place at all. This abnormal situation would rarely arise with respect to produced goods, at least under competitive market conditions, but in the case of goods supplied by nature, the mechanism to stop production of superabundant resources does not exist.

The attribute of scarcity, which affects the price of a commodity, can impair the use of value in regional studies in yet another more subtle but hardly less drastic way. The total value of a resource is sensitive to shifts in demand as well as in supply. Consequently, relative or local scarcity may (by affecting the unit price) increase the total value of a resource. For example, a comparison of two cities of equal size in terms of the number of housing units may reveal that the total value of the housing stock in one is substantially higher than in the other. The difference, however, may be due to either higher average quality of the housing units or to higher demand resulting from population pressure. Hence, interregional or intertemporal comparisons based on value cannot be made independently of fluctuations in demand. To the extent that they reflect social needs, these are obviously legitimate influences to be reckoned with, but should not be confounded with differences in absolute or potential abundance. Total value of several resources used as an index of relative attractiveness of a region may thus be sometimes deceptive.

The above discussion seems to indicate that the very heterogeneity of resources may require, for purposes of their valuation, a classification into several broad categories. A fourfold division has been applied in the case of Nova Scotia.

The first group is composed of resources such as minerals produced for national or world markets for which an infinitely elastic demand and an exogenously determined price level exist. Their unit value can thus be derived as the difference between price obtainable for the mineral at pithead and costs of mining, thus resembling economic rent. Unfortunately, it will often overestimate the value of subsoil resources because in most cases it is virtually impossible to deduct the cost of land and the opportunity costs of entrepreneurship. Subsoil resources whose potential supply is almost unlimited, present additional difficulties. In deriving their value the estimated physical quantity of such resources had to be replaced by expected long-run market demand.

Another method would view subsoil resources as capital goods supplying productive services over time.[2] Their value would be increased with new discoveries and decreased by the value of extracted resources. A slightly different approach would derive present worth by capitalizing future returns at a given discount rate, casting the analysis in the profit maximizing framework.

The second broad category would comprise living populations such as forest, game, or ocean resources. Their common characteristic is that they grow and multiply, and hence as long as the resource is not overexploited it conserves its value. Here the discounted future income stream approach is more appropriate than imputed cost calculations, but the practical difficulties attending its application are considerable, since valuation has to reflect both the ecological balance and developments in the regional economy. The relation of inter-dependence between equilibrium in the ecosystem and in the socioeconomic system has been powerfully analyzed and fused into a general framework by Isard and others [3] with the help of an extended input-output model.

The third category would comprise the fairly numerous free goods that are devoid of value within the social matrix but that may be of considerable significance in explaining interregional disparities and differences in growth rates. Their contribution to the value of capital assets or to the regional produc-tivity can at best be established only indirectly by considering differences and shifts in regional production functions. In the latter category water has to be singled out. The difficulties attendant on attempts to evaluate its contribution to regional development stem from the manifold uses which are to a large extent complementary to one another rather than mutually exclusive. Not only do water transportation, generation of hydropower, and recreation frequently represent noncompeting results of a single investment, but the subsequent use of water for residential and industrial purposes falls largely into the same category. Free, unprocessed water is rarely directly usable. Hence, one could consider water in its various forms and uses as the end product of an extremely capital intensive industry. It is here, however, that the failures of the market mechanism are most apparent. The prices charged for processed water or for the use of water facilities are not the outcome of the interplay of supply and demand. They are neither cost determined nor are they high enough in most cases to curtail some uses. Moreover, the existence of several noncompeting uses makes the allocation of production costs arbitrary.

The fourth, and last, category is concerned with human resources. The practical difficulties of valuation of human resources are considerable and obvious. In the total absence of market prices for humans, value estimates can be based either on (1) the cost approach or (2) the income approach. When applied to labor resources the two methods of valuation are unlikely, even in principle, to yield identical results. Human beings have innate abilities that would allow them to earn some income and increase their proficiency even in the absence of specific and identifiable expenditures to develop their skills; thus, valuation using the total outlays or cost approach would always tend to be slightly lower than valuation based on discounted value of future contributions to production. Either of these two approaches can be applied on a net or gross basis. On a net value basis, consumption expenditures are not added to past outlays on education and training but are deducted from the discounted future income streams, thus applying to human beings an approach similar to the one used for valuation of livestock. On a gross or total value basis, consumption outlays during the period of training (cost approach) are added but are not deducted from future incomes flowing from productive activities. Net measure reflects perhaps the value from the society's point of view, while gross or total measure, which transcends the purely economic aspects, is more relevant to the individual or social group. Total value has been used more often as a measure of human capital, but the choice between these approaches depends ultimately upon the purpose of the study. When using the cost approach, it is necessary to correct for the fact that past expenditures often differ considerably from what their present cost would be. In order to establish a uniform basis for outlays incurred at different times, price deflators have to be applied expressing past costs in terms of their present value.

Measurement of human capital [4] based on discounted future income is the more often used approach. For this purpose the population is divided into relatively homogeneous groups by age, sex, education and/or occupation, depending on the detail of available data. Assuming constancy of the relevant parameters such as death rates, labor force participation rates, existing occupational structure, and incomes, the population is aged and reduced by the repeated application of a survivorship matrix. Applying to the results the labor force participation rates and average earnings, a declining future income stream is obtained. Refinements may be introduced by making allowances for changes in average incomes, occupation, and education and for additional outlays for retraining and improving education standards of the existing population.

The data requirements are always considerable and are not easily met. The cost approach requires estimates of all past expenditures made for education and training of the existing population and, if on gross basis of past consumption, expenditures for food, shelter, and clothing as well. If the estimates are made on a net basis, the often elusive division between investment and consumption expenditures has to be made, with health expenditures particularly difficult to categorize.[a] Income forgone during education and training is sometimes added to explicit costs, [5] but whether the opportunity cost of child-rearing might

---

[a]Consumption and investment are distinguished by their results. Pure consumption satisfies needs but has no effect on productivity, while pure investment changes capabilities and future productivity without satisfying needs.

be equated to the amount forgone by a mother who could have joined the labor force [6] is an open and difficult-to-answer question.

A difficult conceptual problem is posed by the fact that part of the present population may emigrate from the region in the future. Under these circumstances it is not obvious whether their discounted future earnings should be added to the value of regional resources. Finally, a sensitive and difficult element of all valuations based on future income streams is the discounting rate to be applied, since small differences in it importantly affect the final result. Market interest rates are quite high in Canada, but it can be argued that lower discounting rates are more appropriate for measuring resources, not only because the rate of inflation should be subtracted, but also because market interest rates reflect the time preferences of individuals whose longevity is substantially shorter than the social perspective.

2 Gifts of Nature: Land and Mineral Resources

The category "gifts of nature" is composed of resources that are tangible and at some stage of processing have the attributes of a transferable commodity. All are available in finite quantities; i.e., they do not multiply or increase in total volume, although additions to some subcategories of land occur through change of use, and to subsoil resources, through new discoveries. Along with many similarities there are important differences between the two groups, for while land, whether used for agricultural purposes or serving as support for manifold human activities and artifacts, is physically indestructible, subsoil resources, valuable when brought to the surface and manufactured into goods capable of satisfying needs, are transformed or destroyed in the process.

Of all natural resources, land has longest occupied the attention of economists and been discussed most extensively. The quantity and quality of available land has long been viewed as a prime consideration in regional development, its importance being obviously related to the role which agriculture has historically played in many presently depressed areas. An attempt to assess the available land resources must be preceded by classification or grouping of all parcels of land into several broad categories. The criteria for classification vary depending on objectives of the study, and include: (1) present, or sometimes potential use; (2) chemical qualities and inherent physical characteristics such as topography and drainage; and (3) location with respect to climatic conditions, proximate man-made improvements, or accessibility. The first criterion is ordinarily preferred although it requires, in order to be relevant, a rather detailed subdivision. The second criterion has the great advantage that the characteristics used are unchanging over time even though their relative importance responds, albeit slowly, to socioeconomic developments. The difficulty of this approach resides in the very considerable number of characteristics which have to be

considered and in the uncertainties involved in weighing them. The third
criterion, rarely applied, would include socioeconomic or agro-climatic classifications.

The distribution of major land categories in Nova Scotia, in order of
decreasing intensity of use, shows that of the 13,722,200 acres of which the
province is composed, 1.16 percent was developed or urban land,[b] 6.32 percent
agricultural, 1.9 percent parks (including Indian reservations), 80.39 percent
forested land, 5.26 percent other waste land, and 4.97 percent water surfaces.

For a variety of analytical purposes a single index of the land resources
of the province would be most useful. The value of land measured in dollars
would meet many requirements but, unfortunately, valuation of land is beset by
ambiguities.[7] It depends to a high degree upon societal phenomena such as
emergence of alternative uses, accessibility, and relative scarcity, and such
rapidly fluctuating factors as business cycles or changing expectations. Not all
land is salable, but even for those areas that do at one time or another enter
the market mechanism, for which sales data are reported and assumed to be
representative of the entire land market, the market price will vary with the
conditions surrounding the transaction [8] while the existing and potential use of
land may be affected by scale factors and indivisibilities, adding another
distortion.

Table 2-1 illustrates the relative importance of various land categories in
terms of area and value.[c]

The most important component of total value of land in Nova Scotia
is developed or urban land. Its total value in 1961 was estimated at $238.2
million, the major part of it ($184.6 million) being represented by residential
land. The estimated worth of agricultural land is little over one-tenth of the total
while the vast forested areas contribute only 16.5 percent to the total value of
land resources. Even allowing for the uncertainties surrounding valuation and
estimates of the total amount of suitable farmland in the province, the general
picture is of land more appropriate for forestry than farming. Moreover,
existing farmland seems better adapted to pastures than to crop growing. The
problem, because of its sociopolitical implications, has commanded the attention
of policy-makers for a long time and has been the reason for most planning
efforts, out of proportion to its economic significance.

The basic issues are the physical characteristics of the land available, such

----

[b]This category refers to the land area of all cities, towns, and urban areas in municipali-
ties, and hence corresponds to an administrative criterion rather than to intensity of use.

[c]The value estimates were based on assessed values of real property which ordinarily
cover both land and improvements and are one of the most readily available and most often
used sources of information. This method must be treated nonetheless with care, since
assessors put values on land, for tax purposes, that are not identical to the future worth of
land. Furthermore, much land is tax exempt, and the assessed values for this land are usually
considerably lower than potential market price. For details see Appendix A.

Table 2-1
Land Uses and Values, Nova Scotia, 1961

		Area *('000 acres)*	*Value* *($ million)*
Developed or urban land		159.0	238.2
Agricultural land except farm woodlots		867.4	29.3
Parks, incl. Indian reservations		261.0	16.5
Forested land		11,031.0	
Productive land	9,668.0		
Farm woodlots	1,363.0		
Other and waste land		721.6	.5
Total land area		13,040.0	
Water surfaces		682.2	
Total		13,722.2	284.5

as topography, parent materials, drainage, climatic conditions, and natural vegetation. Topography is of crucial importance, and the uneven, at places rugged, surface of Nova Scotia does not stand comparison with other farming regions in Canada. In addition, large areas have to be excluded from machine cropping because of excessive stoniness, characteristic of the variety of parent materials derived from underlying rock formations, often crushed, mixed, and redeposited during the ice age. Drainage, which is a function of topography, is satisfactory in the upland areas with, on the whole, ample slopes for effective runoff of surface waters, but the lowlands are often poorly drained due to impervious layers in the soil profile or bedrocks lying close to the surface. The soils themselves are generally of quite low quality, largely podzolic and acidic due to the constant leaching of the soil's soluble bases by heavy rainfalls. Leaching is accelerated by the hilly nature of the terrain, which is conducive to this process except in the Annapolis Valley and in the marshlands where the land is flat and the soil of a reasonably high quality. Generally, however, the soils tend to contain insufficient quantities of the base materials, and the growing of crops requires heavy fertilizing, which makes farming more expensive than it is in Southern Ontario or farther west. The climatic environment more-over favors a forest type vegetation that is subject to a high degree of podzolization.

A comprehensive soil capability classification based on a combination of characteristics of soil, climate, and difficult-to-remove limitations for agricultural use is contained in the Canada Land Inventory [9] and summarized in Table 2-2. Its relevance for policy purposes is limited, however, by its omission of socio-economic factors influencing land use, such as demand for agricultural products, distance from markets, kind of roads, size of farms, land ownership, availability of capital and labor, or cultural patterns.

Classes I-III are considered fit for sustained production of common and

Table 2-2
Soil Classification, Nova Scotia

Soil Type	Area ('000 acres)	Percentage
Mineral soils		
Class I	–	–
Class II	417.3	3.2
Class III	2,438.5	18.7
Class IV	1,043.2	8.0
Class V	208.6	1.6
Class VI	39.1	0.3
Class VII	8,554.1	65.6
Total mineral soils	12,700.8	97.4
Organic soils	339.0	2.6
Total soils	13,039.8	100.0
Water surfaces	682.2	
Total area	13,722.0	

Based on: Nova Scotia Department of Agriculture and Marketing, various Reports;
and Canada, Department of Forestry and Rural Development, A.R.D.A., *The
Canada Land Inventory*, various Reports.

perennial field crops, while Class IV is composed of soils only marginally
capable of crop production. Class V is suitable for permanent pasture, and
Class VI only for wild pasture. Class VII covers soils and land types considered
unsuitable for either cultivated crops or pasture. Consideration of additional
factors such as adverse micro-climate, inundation by streams or lakes, excess
water, and rugged topography leads to a much more gloomy picture and the
conclusion that much of Nova Scotia's farmland is marginal at best.

Despite these natural handicaps the amount of land actually farmed was
surprisingly large. In 1966, a total 446,500 acres were used for crops and
pasture, of which 248,400 acres were operated by commercial units.[d] Table 2-3
succinctly illustrates the situation.

Assuming that most of the potentially usable agricultural land is already
farmed, this further reinforces the impression that the total endowment of
Nova Scotia is poor, even against the background of the agriculturally lagging
Eastern Canadian provinces. On a per capita basis, in 1961, Nova Scotia had .43
acre of farmland as against .79 in New Brunswick, 4.2 in Prince Edward Island,
and 1.7 in Ontario. Comparison of improved agricultural land with the total
land area is equally unfavorable, for Nova Scotia showed a ratio of .0372
as against .0358 in New Brunswick, .3180 in Prince Edward Island, and .0545

---

[d]A census farm is defined as one of at least one acre in size selling at least $50 in
produce annually. A commercial farm is a census farm which sells over $1,200 per year.
D.B.S., *1961 Census of Canada,* Agriculture, Cat. No. 96-520.

Table 2-3

Commercial and Noncommercial Census Farms, Nova Scotia, 1966

Farms	Commercial	Noncommercial	Total Census Farms
Total (number)	2,867	6,754	9,621
Total area (acres)	818,552	1,033,343	1,851,895
Total improved land area (acres)	263,822	222,037	485,859
Total improved land area under crop[a] (acres)	180,424	133,719	314,143
Total improved land area pasture (acres)	68,009	64,346	132,355

[a]Includes field, vegetable, fruit, and nursery crop land.

Source: *1966 Census of Canada, Agriculture*, Vol. III (3-4), Cat. No. 96-604, April 1968, Table 3.

in Ontario. Similarly the contribution of agriculture to the economy of Nova Scotia was less important than in the other Maritime Provinces, with farm output in 1961 accounting for only 6.3 percent of the value added of the commodity producing industries. The higher share of agriculture in New Brunswick and Prince Edward Island might, of course, also reflect the lack of a manufacturing base in the other Maritime Provinces.

The limited supply of good farmland in Nova Scotia has affected the profitability and the structure of the agricultural sector. The net value of production per farm worker in 1961 was $896 in the Maritime Provinces compared with $1,069 in Central Canada. Significantly, in 1966 only 29.8 percent of Nova Scotia farms were classified as commercial, compared with 33.7 percent in New Brunswick, 52.4 percent in Prince Edward Island, 52.3 percent in Quebec, and 64.4 percent in Ontario.[10] The poor quality of available agricultural land resulted in dairying and livestock-raising assuming a far greater importance than crop growing, although neither kind of farming is really competitive with Central Canada. The relative share of the various kinds of farming in total agricultural output is indicated in Table 2-4.

The small size of the agricultural sector necessitates heavy imports of food and results in lack of self-sufficiency of the province with respect to most food products, even of meat, the production of which is best suited to the agricultural land available. Only few food products are exported, the most important ones being apples and blueberries, while in potatoes, eggs, and chickens the province is almost self-sufficient.[11]

Geographically, the main agricultural areas are concentrated in the northern part of the Nova Scotia mainland as illustrated in Figure 2-1. The Annapolis Valley and the area as far as Truro and then northwards toward Amherst and the

Table 2–4

**Value of Agricultural Products Sold by Commercial Farms in Nova
Scotia, June 1, 1960 to May 31, 1961**

Product	Value ($'000)	Percentage
Dairy products	8,746	27.7
Cattle	4,023	12.8
Eggs	5,340	16.9
Hens and chickens	2,443	7.7
Pigs	2,264	7.2
Tree fruits	2,180	6.9
Forest products	1,660	5.3
Potatoes, roots, tabacco, sugar beets, and other field crops	1,126	3.6
Greenhouse and nursery products	1,035	3.3
Other	2,719	8.6
Total	31,536	100.0

Based on: D.B.S., *1961 Census of Canada, Agriculture*, Cat. No. 96–527.

New Brunswick border possess some of the best agricultural land in the province.
The counties of Annapolis, Kings, Hants, Colchester, Pictou, Cumberland,
and the northern part of Halifax County account for the bulk of the agricultural
production of the province, with Kings County producing well over seventy-five
percent of Nova Scotia's tree fruits, potatoes, and eggs. Possessed of the best
agricultural land in the province, the valley is free from many problems besetting
rural Nova Scotia. It has fewer small subsistence farms than other areas in the
province,[e] a phenomenon partly at least related to the orientation of Valley
farming away from dairying which, together with livestock raising, are more or
less ubiquitous in Nova Scotia.

In view of the niggardly natural endowment of Nova Scotia, the future
development of the province will almost undoubtedly involve a reallocation of
resources, notably labor and capital, away from agriculture into urban-industrial
occupations. Annapolis Valley alone may conceivably form an exception and
evolve a viable rural economy. The immediate cause pushing labor out of agriculture is ordinarily a drop in the relative prices of food products. In order to
survive, the farmer has to become more competitive by increasing the size
of his farm and by using modern equipment and machinery. The phenomenon
is often referred to as the "cost price squeeze," and results in a release of
redundant farm population. In Nova Scotia the process has not been taking
place to the same extent as elsewhere, as witnessed by the substantial number of

---

[e]Approximately 25 percent in Annapolis and Kings Counties compared with 71 percent
for the whole province.

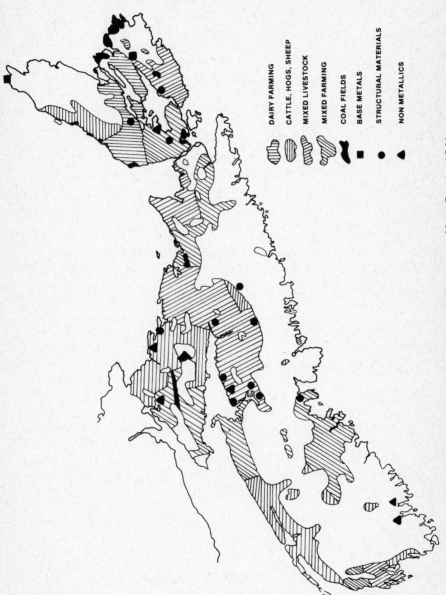

Figure 2-1. Agricultural and Mineral Resources, Nova Scotia, 1961.

noncommercial farms and the slow pace of capitalization. The amount of
capital per farm in the Maritimes in constant dollars has increased from
$4,868 in 1941 to barely $6,671 in 1961, compared to a change from $9,594
in 1941 to $14,153 in 1961 in Central Canada. Even more significant is the
relative underinvestment of commercial farms in Nova Scotia, which in 1961
commanded on the average only $18,589 compared to $36,090 in Ontario.
Admittedly, the difference in capital investment per acre of improved land was
small, with $295 in Nova Scotia against $314 in Ontario, but this conceals
rather than reveals the full competitive disadvantage of local agriculture which
resides in the lack of economies of scale, which are achievable on the larger
Ontario farms. Because capital in Nova Scotia has been applied to a basically
poorer resource, it suggests a national misallocation of capital.

The state of agriculture in the province raises serious political problems.
The main issue seems to revolve around measures necessary to speed up the
process of consolidation of farms into larger units, and the related problem of
relocation of redundant rural population,[f] which in 1966 stood at 336,495, [12]
of which over 31,000 showed incomes of less than $3,000. On the other hand,
out of 12,488 farms there were 7,174 with a capital value of less than $25,000
and with gross sales of less than $3,750. Moreover, according to Hedlin-Menzies,
"one out of two of the farms surveyed earned only about half their income
from farm sources. Viewed one way the farm was supplementing off-farm
incomes."[13] Thus the sociopolitical issues overshadowing the purely economic
ones are connected with rural poverty and embedded in the wider question of
resettlement connected with changes in the location of major nonagricultural
industries within the province.

Consideration of subsoil resources raises different problems. The mineral or
subsoil resources belong to four main groups, all of which are represented in
Nova Scotia, namely: (1) fuels, (2) base metals, (3) nonmetallics, and (4)
structural materials. Their spatial distribution and the approximate location of
mining operations are illustrated in Figure 2-1. Traditionally mining operations
have been very important in terms of income and employment and as a source
of revenues accruing to the province from other parts of Canada and from
foreign countries, accounting until recently for almost ten percent of the total
net value of commodity production, a percentage higher than those of Ontario

---

[f]The amount of surplus labor which a successful farm improvement program would
create is probably in reality quite small. The potential number of economically viable farms
in Nova Scotia is variously estimated as between 4,000 and 6,000. The consolidation which
would be involved in such an important reduction of the number of existing units would
result in the disappearance of between 6,000 and 8,000 farms in the next 10–15 years, re-
leasing a flow of labor off the farms of the order of perhaps 6,000 to 8,000. This estimate is,
however, very tenuous and probably too high, since many of the people classified as farmers
already have urban or non-farm occupations and abandonment of their part-time farming
would not imply a substantial increase in the labor supply. Furthermore, many of the farm
operators are near retirement age.

Table 2-5.
Average Value of Coal Resources, Nova Scotia, 1961 ($ per ton)

		Revenue		Average Economic Rent	
	Cost Estimates	With Subsidies	Without Subsidies	With Subsidies	Without Subsidies
J. Donald	12.0000	8.3654	3.5029	−3.6346	−8.4791
E. Malizia	7.4129	8.3654	3.5029	.9525	−3.9100

and of Canada as a whole. The position of coal mining has been, and still is, predominant despite the fact that since 1950 a serious decline has set in. The uncertain future of coal mining is a source of much concern, hardly relieved by the sharp uprise in the production of other minerals.

Two analytic approaches, complementary to one another, which were followed in order to assess the present and future impact of subsoil resources upon the regional economy, are based respectively on (1) an assessment of the total value of available known deposits, and (2) an appraisal of the various extractive industries.

The valuation of subsoil resources in Nova Scotia in 1961 was based on estimates of existing reserves.[14] For coal, which plays such an important role in the provincial economy, the two existing estimates contained in the work of Malizia [15] and in the Donald Report [16] differ considerably despite similarity of approaches. The heavy subsidies provided by the Canadian government complicated both the average revenue and the average cost estimates.[17] The two appraisals are summarized in Table 2-5. In three of four cases the resulting economic rents were negative. Malizia thus seems justified in claiming that coal was as much a liability as an asset in 1961, and in assigning zero value to the coal reserves of Nova Scotia, despite the importance of the industry to the province in terms of employment.

The above results seem to deemphasize the importance of subsoil resources, especially of coal, at variance with the significant role that they currently play in the regional economy and to point toward a serious misallocation of resources, due to sociopolitical considerations. This conclusion is reinforced by the fact that coal, traditionally the most important mining product exported in great quantities from Nova Scotia, currently faces serious problems. The 1965 output of 4.3 million tons of coal valued at $43 million generated $32 million of value added and provided employment for approximately 7,500 persons. The industry thus accounts directly for some 2.3 percent of the gross provincial product and 2.8 percent of total employment. But the true dimensions of the coal issue become more apparent when one considers the situation in Cape Breton Island, where coal mining accounted for 9.6 percent of gross regional product.

The bulk of the coal mined in 1965, or some 3.7 million tons, came from the Sydney area; about a quarter of a million tons came from Stellarton; and the balance, some half a million tons, was produced by small independent mines on Cape Breton Island and on the mainland. Of the 7,500 coal mine employees, approximately 6,500 were employed in the Sydney area. In that area the only other major industry was the closely related steel complex, so that steel and coal jointly employed a total of some 10,500 people, or about 26 per cent of the estimated male labor force on Cape Breton Island. The bleak outlook and the problematic future of Nova Scotia coal combined with the dependence of the Cape Breton economy on the mining industry came to be known as the coal problem and induced the federal government to bear the high costs of sustaining these operations.

The roots of the problem go back to the substantial exhaustion of the easily accessible deposits, their relatively poor quality, and their remoteness from markets outside the province. High labor charges and general costs are often blamed for the inability to compete with the United States coal and other sources of energy but they are, in fact, only a reflection of the basic difficulties inherent in winning coal from old mines with operations extending progressively farther out under the sea in seams with slopes of up to thirty degrees. The overall geology of the Sydney coal field is such that coal is currently being extracted from workings up to four miles out under the sea and at a depth approaching 3,000 feet below the sea bottom. This involves long uphill haulage and difficult maintenance and ventilation problems. Also, with working places from three to four miles from the pithead, about 1½ hours of the 8-hour working day is spent traveling to and from the coal faces. It is estimated that the existing Sydney mines at current rates of operation would require in, at most, fifteen years heavy new capital expenditures for equipment, new haulage, ventilation, and other services. The uncertain prospects of the industry and the unprofitable nature of the operations lead to inadequate maintenance of the pits and equipment, the cumulative effects of which are becoming progressively more obvious.

The production difficulties are compounded by marketing problems. Of the 4.3 million tons mined in 1965, 2.5 million tons valued at $24.6 million, or slightly more than one-half, were exported to Ontario and Quebec, while the Atlantic Provinces continue to absorb 1.8 million tons per year. In the Sydney area itself, where most mines are located, the market for some 500,000 tons of coking coal required by the Sydney steel plant was lost at one time to the United States, due to technological changes requiring coal of low volatility and low sulfur content. The major remaining use is the generation of thermal electric power, heating, and home consumption.[g]

---

[g]For this purpose Cape Breton coal is directly in competition with residual oil available at Atlantic or St. Lawrence ports at about 6.12 cents per Imperial gallon. The equivalent

The coal mines in Nova Scotia can thus only be kept in operation with the help of heavy government subsidies in various forms adding up to $22 million per year or almost $3,000 per employee. It is believed that without federal subventions the market for Nova Scotia coal would have been cut in half. Such a drastic reduction in markets and hence in output would have pushed the operating cost per ton to such high levels that it is doubtful if any mines could have continued in operation.

The Donald Report[h] also considered new developments taking place in the energy markets where the convenience and availability of oil have resulted in further losses of domestic and commercial space-heating markets, even in the Atlantic Provinces. In the long run, rapid progress in the use of nuclear energy in thermal electric generation facilities cannot be overlooked, Nuclear thermal power is competitive with coal or oil in plants of large capacity (300 megawatts or over) at 25 cents per million BTU. The equivalent value for Sydney coal is about $6.75 per ton. Installation of such large plants is not considered feasible in the Atlantic Provinces at present but cannot be ruled out in the not too distant future. Furthermore, the possibility of oil and gas discoveries cannot be ignored. Active exploration by major petroleum companies is proceeding on the continental shelf off the Atlantic Provinces and in the Gulf of St. Lawrence.[i] In conclusion the 1966 Donald Report recommended the gradual phasing out of coal mining over fifteen years, the acquisition by the government of the coal operations from their owners, and the organization of the Cape Breton Development Corporation. These recommendations won swift acceptance. Nonetheless, a new mine was opened in 1969 in Lingan geared to an annual production of two million tons of carbonized coal.

Other mining operations in Nova Scotia do not give rise to problems of

---

value of Sydney coal required, assuming a thermal value of 13,500 BTU per pound, is about $9.10 per ton. Imported United States coal shipped by water can be delivered at ports in the Atlantic Provinces at about $11 per ton. With Sydney coal currently costing about $12 per ton at the pithead, heavy subsidies are reauired to make it competitive for thermal electric power generation. For example, to compete with residual oil at the thermal electric power plant near Halifax, the coal must be delivered at about $9.10 per ton. This requires a gross subsidy of about $9.15 per ton at present. To supply the thermal electric power plant near Toronto, Nova Scotia coal must compete with United States coal delivered at $8.96 per ton, requiring a gross subsidy of $7.85 per ton.

[h]The problems of coal mining in Cape Breton in the face of declining markets and increasingly inaccessible seams are not new, and were investigated by the Royal Commission on Coal. *Report of the Royal Commission on Coal,* the Honorable I. C. Rand, Q. C., Commissioner, Queen's Printer, August, 1960.

[i]Cape Breton coal still accounts for some sixty percent of Canadian output, but its former importance as a reserve source of fuel for Central and Eastern Canada in an emergency has been downgraded and deemed negligible due to the use of petroleum products for all forms of transportation. Western oil and gas, due to pipeline connections, have also reduced the dependence of Ontario and Quebec upon imports of United States coal. The practice of encouraging exports of oil and gas to the United States while at the same time heavily subsidizing Cape Breton coal in Central and Eastern Canada seems contradictory.

similar magnitude. Of the base metals known to occur in the province, copper, lead, zinc, and silver have been successfully mined at Walton for several years. Partially developed deposits of lead are located at Salmon River and of zinc at Meat Cove, both in Cape Breton. There are other promising deposits of all of the above metals and of gold. Iron ore, on the other hand, can be written off except perhaps for some minor speciality output. The outlook in metallic minerals is uncertain. While it is hoped that the intensive efforts and fundamental studies and research will bear fruit in the future, the present yearly production of base metals is insignificant, with sales totaling roughly $1.5 million.

The nonmetallics consist of barite, gypsum, quartz, peat moss, salt, clay and shale, fluorspar, metallurgical and chemical grade limestone, dolomite, anhydrite, and strontium sulfate, of which only salt and gypsum are of economic significance. Sand and gravel, silica sands, stone, and cement grade limestone account for structural materials. The provincial salt production accounts for approximately five percent of Canada's output. Most of the other salt deposits are concentrated in Ontario, which supplies almost ninety percent of the national total. The basic market for salt is industry, but the domestic. demand in Nova Scotia is limited by the size of manufacturing industries, among which only fish processing stands out as an important consumer. In net terms, about seventy-six percent of the salt that moved out of Nova Scotia in 1963 by train and by ship went to Southern Quebec and Ontario, with the rest of the world accounting for the remaining twenty-four percent. Total exports of salt in 1963 amounted to 267,000 tons, valued at just over $3 million.

Nova Scotia is the most important producer of gypsum in Canada, accounting for over eighty percent of the total output. Most of the gypsum is exported in a primary form to the United States. Only one of the thirteen plants that process gypsum in Canada is located in Nova Scotia, the local consumption of gypsum products being quite small. In 1963, ninety-one percent of net exports by boat and train went to foreign ports, while the rest of Canada accounted for nine percent of Nova Scotia's export market. The value of gypsum exports began to increase steadily in 1950, primarily due to increases in physical output rather than higher prices. In 1963, 4.1 million tons were exported, valued at $6.8 million.

Other nonmetallic products are composed mainly of building materials. More recently, free sulfur bearing ore has been discovered near Truro, Colchester County, while new techniques for separating barite and fluorite ores might lead to development of the extensive deposits of those minerals in Inverness County. Silica sand is being developed on a small scale near Belmont, Colchester County, while active exploration for manganese, antimony, bismuth, tungsten, lithium, and molybdenum is taking place on Cape Breton Island. Total output, including structural materials, amounted to $27.0 million in 1967. Table 2–6 indicates the relative importance of the various operations. It is interesting to contrast the employment in coal mining, amounting to 7500, with the above

Table 2–6
Output and Employment in Nonmetallic Minerals, Nova Scotia, 1967

Mineral (Ranked in order of man-days worked)	Production ('000 tons)	Employment (Number)	Man-days Worked
Salt	494.1	232	88,703
Gypsum	3,589.7	321	77,148
Limestone	532.4	41	9,202
Anhydrite	252.6	51	8,490
Crushed Stone	457.0	39	4,695
Construction Sands and Gravels	1,092.4	100	3,996
Sandstone	12.0	11	2,145
Clay and Shale	56.6	9	1,737
Fire Clay	2.6	6	454
Dolomite	66.3	14	448
Marble	.8	3	75
Industrial Sands	6.9	2	40
Other	174.4	92	20,767
Total	6,737.8	921	217,900

Source: Nova Scotia Department of Mines, *Annual Report on Mines*, 1967, pp. 134–138.

figure of little over 900. On the other hand, value estimates of subsoil resources in Nova Scotia assign $530.6 million to nonmetalics and $151.9 million to structural materials while denying any economic rent to existing coal deposits.

Even more revealing are the trends illustrated in Figure 2-2, which indicates the extent to which new mineral production has replaced the falling output of coal in the last decade and which summarizes the hope that in the not too distant future other minerals will replace it as the main subsoil resource of the province. Since the value of existing reserves of subsoil resources in 1961 has been estimated at $766.5 million, of which coal was assigned zero value, base metals $84.0 million, nonmetallics $530.6 million and structural materials $151.9 million, the two analytic approaches based respectively on flow and stock phenomena seem to lead to similar conclusions if long-run rather than short-run trends are considered. The analysis based on the results so far obtained is pursued in greater depth in Chapter 7, where the numerical findings form part of a model of the regional economy.

3 Living Populations: Forest and Aquatic Resources

The most prominent of resources belonging to this group were forests, which in 1961 occupied over 80 percent of the land area of Nova Scotia.

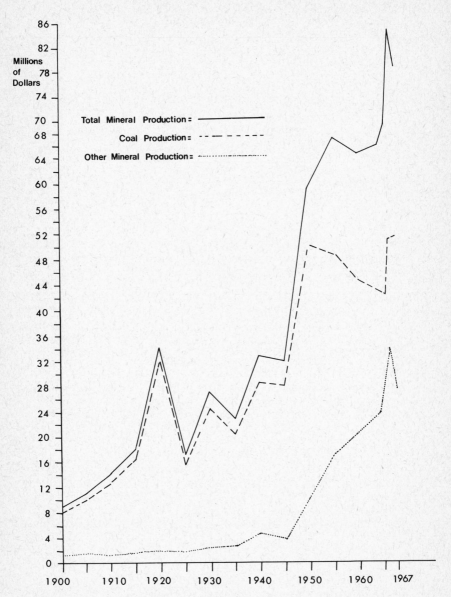

Figure 2-2. Value of Mineral Production, Nova Scotia, 1900–1967.

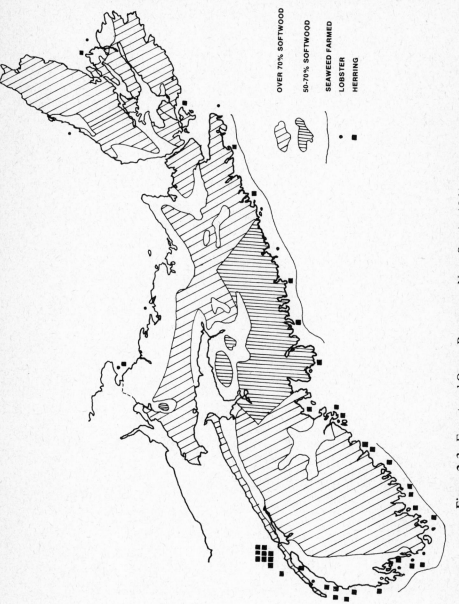

OVER 70% SOFTWOOD

50-70% SOFTWOOD

SEAWEED FARMED

LOBSTER

HERRING

Figure 2-3. Forest and Ocean Resources, Nova Scotia, 1961.

Softwoods were substantially more common than hardwoods, reflecting the geographic situation and climate of the province.[j] The spatial distribution of the two main types of forests as shown in Figure 2-3 indicates a relatively greater abundance of hardwoods in the central part of the mainland.

In order to assess the economic importance of the regional forests it is perhaps best to deal first with the contribution of trees only, and to treat other benefits derived from forested areas separately. The valuation of forests as a source of timber can be calculated by considering either the allowable annual cut or the harvest of wood that may be taken from the forest without reducing its ability to produce a sustained yield, or the total standing stock, obtained as the product of the estimated quantities by average market values. In both cases the age distribution of the 1961 stock and potential uses of Nova Scotia timber, which can be processed into (1) sawlogs, (2) pulpwood (used to make paper and paper products), (3) roundwood (used primarily in rough construction work and as telephone poles), and (4) fuelwood, form the obvious basis for valuation and discounting.[k] Total values were estimated by applying to existing stocks of standing timber the revenues from expected yields, which were often considerably lower than the current market price of harvested timber.

The value of timber should exclude the value of land in forest use. The separate treatment of the population of trees and of land on which they are growing seems the more justified as some forested land could potentially be put to other "higher" uses. Thus, in order to arrive at the value of trees, the estimated value of land in an alternative use was subtracted from the total. Moreover, only half of all forest reserves was immediately marketable while

---

[j]A more detailed description is provided by Halliday, W.E.D., *A Forest Classification for Canada,* Canada Department of Mines and Resources, Forest Service Bulletin 89, 1937, pp. 10, 36–39, and Hawbolt, L.S. and R.M. Bulmer, *The Forest Resources of Nova Scotia,* Nova Scotia Department of Lands and Forests, 1958. They place Nova Scotia in the Acadian Forest Region, with the exception of the Northeastern part of Cape Breton Island, which resembles a Boreal Forest in character. The forest cover of the province is mainly white spruce, balsam fir, yellow birch, maple, and mixed hardwoods.

[k]**Potential Use of Standing Timber, Nova Scotia, 1961**

	Size	
Wood Type	10' or more D.B.H.	4"–9" D.B.H.
Softwoods	50% sawlogs 50% pulp, fuel, and roundwood	100% pulp, fuel, and roundwood
Hardwoods	100% pulp, fuel, and roundwood	100% pulp, fuel, and roundwood

Since prices of timber used as pulpwood, roundwood, and fuelwood do not differ significantly, while timber used for sawlogs is more valuable, all standing timber was allocated for purposes of valuation into two categories only.

Table 2-7
Quantity and Value of Forest Reserves, Nova Scotia, 1961

	Sawlogs		Pulp, Fuel, and Roundwood		
	Quantity Mfbm	Value $ per Mfbm	Quantity '000 cords	Value $ per cord	Total Value $ million
Softwoods					
Spruce	2,162,000	12.50	29,667	2.25	93.8
Balsam Fir	834,000	8.50	26,720	2.25	67.1
Hemlock	556,000	8.50	2,945	2.25	11.4
White Pine	668,000	12.00	2,987	2.25	14.7
Red Pine	44,000	12.00	285	2.25	1.2
Jack Pine	2,000	12.00	39	2.25	0.1
Cedar	2,000	12.00	12	2.25	0.1
Larch	30,000	12.00	810	2.25	2.2 190.6
Hardwoods					
Poplar			1,224	0.75	0.9
White Birch			3,282	0.75	2.5
Yellow Birch			9,271	0.75	6.9
Maple			18,988	0.75	14.2
Beech			3,435	0.75	2.6
Elm			24	0.75	–
Ash			1,435	0.75	1.1
Oak			1,212	0.75	0.9
Other			106	0.75	0.1 29.2
Total Value of Timber					219.8
Less: Value of Land					14.5
Total					205.3
Less: Discount					31.1
Total Present Value					174.2

the other half was too young, maturing over an estimated period of twenty-five years, or at a rate of two percent per year. Applying a discounting rate of three percent compounded yearly yielded the results summarized in Table 2-7.[1]

Forestry was traditionally a significant provincial activity. It can be divided into the primary or extractive phase, covering logging for sawlogs, pulpwood, fuel wood, poles and piling, mine timbers, and Christmas trees, and the manufacturing phase which includes the pulp and paper industry, the sawmill industry, and other wood-using industries such as sash, door, and planing mills, wooden box factories, specialty wood products industries, and miscellaneous. Other wood-using industries such as boat building, furniture,

[1]The value of half the forest reserves which could be harvested and sold in 1961 was estimated at $102.7 million. The other half was expected to become marketable at the rate of $4.1 million per year during the twenty-five subsequent years. The discounted value of young growth at three percent compounded over twenty-five years was $71.5 million.

and some preservation plants are not resource-oriented, and do not belong in the same category.

The primary extractive phase of the forest industries of Nova Scotia experienced a substantial decline after the Second World War, and has been subject since then to strong cyclical fluctuations roughly reflecting, with a small time lag, national business cycles. Production levels have also been affected by some accidental exogenous factors such as, for example, the hurricane damage in 1954. The generally gloomy outlook of the forest industries in the 1960's was largely due to a decline in sawlog and pole production which reached approximately only one half of the level of output of the immediate post-war period. Fortunately, pulpwood production, while subject to cyclical trends with peaks in 1951, 1957, and 1962, increased gradually by about one third. Because of new manufacturing capacity, strong export demand, and generally buoyant business activity, pulpwood production not only surpassed any previous total but recently for the first time exceeded sawlog production, despite the increasing use of sawmill residue by the Nova Scotia pulp and paper industry, which effectively lowers demand for pulpwood.[m]

The demand for other forest products has declined steadily, partly as a result of improved preservation techniques that have extended the life of railway ties, and partly because of a shift to other materials, especially in the coal industry where the demand for mine timber has been greatly reduced. The exception is fuel wood, the production of which reached a low in 1958 but has since rather surprisingly strengthened. The general situation, then, is characterized by a declining total demand with a minor reversal only in the mid-1960's and a definite shift in the demand pattern toward pulpwood. In terms of value added the sector has by now lost its importance for the economy of Nova Scotia.

The recreational value of forest resources of Nova Scotia or the closely related issue of their potential contribution to the development of a tourist industry is fraught with very great conceptual and measurement difficulties. It is tackled in Section 4 together with other free goods.

Measurement and valuation of game and wildlife, on the other hand, were less involved. Their economic value can be viewed mainly as an attractive force for sportsmen and campers, both residents and visitors. Several approaches to measuring the contribution of game and wildlife to the local economy are theoretically possible but could not be carried out in Nova Scotia due to paucity of data and to the prohibitive cost, beyond the importance of the subject, of research based on a field survey. A crude estimate was made, based on the heroic assumption that the value of game and wildlife equals direct payments

---

[m]In addition to supplying the local pulping capacity, a significant proportion of pulpwood is exported, mainly to European markets. Total exports in 1965 exceeded 207,000 tons valued at over $3.1 million.

made for hunting and angling privileges.[n] This approach, followed of necessity,
almost certainly results in a gross underestimate, because the fees imposed
on hunters and anglers are institutionally determined and can hardly be considered as representing the users' valuation of satisfaction derived or the value of
the resource to the province seeking to develop its tourist industry. Moreover,
while only hunters and anglers actually deplete the resource, other individuals
including campers, naturalists, and photographers consume wildlife services
free of charge. The total worth of the 1961 game and wildlife population was
estimated to be $2.0 million by discounting the unequal revenue stream 1961 to
1967 at three percent.

Different types of problems are encountered when taking stock of marine
or, more generally, aquatic resources, since the main difficulty is not in finding
an appropriate price but in estimating quantity. In Nova Scotia, with its more
than 4,000 miles of shoreline and a population distributed near the sea, it
is not surprising that marine life constitutes an important source of livelihood.
At present, only fish and seaweeds are landed in the province, but new discoveries
and innovations are likely to lead to further exploitation of marine wealth.

At the conceptual level the problem of boundaries has to be attacked first.
The fishing grounds of the Northwest Atlantic are international waters,
accessible to fleets of many nations. This fact is becoming increasingly relevant
because the physical supply is limited and for many species the total catch is
close to the maximum permitting survival. Thus, with respect to offshore fishing,
Nova Scotia may enjoy a locational advantage, the importance of which
declines with increasing size of fishing vessels and the appearance of larger and
more sophisticated fish processing units. The problem is different with respect to
territorial waters. In those waters, only Canadian, although not necessarily
Nova Scotian, fishing vessels are allowed. The legal basis for measuring the extent
of waters denied to foreign vessels is provided by the 1964 Territorial Sea and
Fishing Zones Act.[18] The Act claimed that all internal waters belonged to
Canada and that national waters extended twelve miles from the shore.[o] The

----

[n]The amounts spent by residents and visitors for game and wildlife licenses were

Year	Revenue ($'000)
1961	337.9
1962	267.8
1963	247.2
1964	256.3
1965	279.1
1966	408.2
1967	426.4

The data are deficient since changes have been made in user fees during this period with
licenses required for a greater number of species in 1967 than in 1961.

[o]Measurement of these areas was accomplished by establishing a set of benchmarks
along the shoreline and connecting these with straight hypothetical lines. National waters

territorial sea was designated as the waters within a three-mile limit, but fishing
zones include the sea from three to twelve miles from shore. Several countries,
as parties in various reciprocity treaties, are allowed access to the fishing zones.
It has not been legally or politically decided whether resources in the territorial
sea and fishing zones are provincially or federally owned. Yet almost all
individuals harvesting within national waters adjacent to Nova Scotia are
provincial residents.

As a result of the geological structure of the sea bed and the combination
of ocean currents, the fishing grounds of Nova Scotia provide fishermen with
a wide variety of marine life. Projecting from the mainland are a series of
banks varying in depth from fifty to three hundred feet and sufficiently shallow
to permit penetration of sunlight and growth of marine life such as plankton,
upon which cod, herring, and other small fish feed. The cold North Labrador
current moves south and, being relatively dense, pushes down under the warm
Gulf Stream, stirring plankton to the surface and attracting shoals of fish.
Some sea fish and seaweeds are permanent residents of the territorial sea and
fishing zones around Nova Scotia, but these species are mobile, migrating in
search of food and comfortable water temperatures and their classification as
provincial "property" is at best ambiguous.P

The offshore or international resources are composed of groundfish,
caught largely in waters east and southeast of Halifax. The pelagic and estuarial
fish resources are superseded in importance by mollusca and crustaceans.
Finally, there are seaweeds, which grow in bands of varying width slightly off
the coast of Nova Scotia and include dulse (Rhodymenia plamata), and Irish
moss (Chondrus crispus), which is the most abundant type harvested within the
three-mile limit.

On the basis of an assessment of the quantity available in the Northwest
Atlantic, the value of accessible marine resources can be calculated by assuming
that (1) death rates and birth rates balance for each species; (2) total population
is a fixed proportion of yearly catch; and (3) the present share of Nova Scotia
in total landings in the Atlantic Provinces will remain unchanged for an
indefinite period. The results of the estimates are summarized in Table 2-8. [19]
The total value of ocean resources is of interest in itself, and as an index of
availability of a marine resource, lends itself to interregional comparisons.

Among the extractive industries, fishing represents the oldest industry but
has undergone many significant changes from the early days of seasonal fishing
stations along the Nova Scotia coast. Higher capital intensity, larger operating

---

included a "band" of ocean surrounding the shore. The twelve mile width of the band was
measured with straight lines which were perpendicular to these imaginary continuous shoreline segments.

PThe quantitative estimates supplied by the Nova Scotia Department of Fisheries and
the Bedford Institute of Oceanography distinguish fish caught inshore from offshore catches.

Table 2-8
Quantity and Value of Ocean Resources by Species, Nova Scotia, 1961

Species	Quantity Estimate (million lbs.)	Value ($ per lb.)	Total Value ($ million)	
Alewives	50.5	0.025	1.262	
Eels	0.5	0.174	0.082	
Herring	1,878.5	0.014	26.299	
Mackerel	30.5	0.047	1.432	
Salmon	1.3	0.566	0.735	
Shad	2.3	0.055	0.126	
Smelts	7.8	0.154	1.201	
Swordfish	50.0	0.387	19.350	
Total Pelagic and Estuarial Fish				50.5
Clams	9.8	0.061	0.597	
Lobsters	34.9	0.443	15.461	
Oysters	1.8	0.064	0.115	
Scallops	213.8	0.293	62.643	
Squid	0.7	0.029	0.020	
Total Shellfish				78.8
Irish Moss	59.6	0.022	1.311	
Total Seaweeds				1.3
Total				$130.6

units and changing product forms have accompanied a higher degree of processing and a vastly evolved organizational structure. Most important has been the shift from cured products, mainly dried, salted fish, to fresh and frozen production.

The total catch on the rich fishing grounds of the Northwest Atlantic amounted in 1964 to 2.95 million metric tons, but the share of the Atlantic Provinces, despite their most favorable location, was only twenty-eight percent. The size of Nova Scotia landings has increased over the years, but only slowly, with more important changes taking place in the composition of the catch. In 1964 in terms of value the main fish species were:

Lobster	$12.0 million
Scallops	$ 7.0 million
Haddock	$ 5.4 million
Cod	$ 4.8 million
Swordfish	$ 3.6 million
Small flatfish	$ 2.4 million

The total number of men employed annually in the primary fishing industry has shown a definite downward trend. The decline reached its low point in 1961 with a total employment of 12,578 persons. Since then a slight increase has

taken place. The most significant change has been in the number of full-time
offshore fishermen, although the majority of fishermen are still employed in the
inshore lobster fishery for part of the year. The efficiency of fishing has increased
in recent years. Based on three-year averages, the weight landed per fisherman
was about 34,900 pounds, while in value landed the largest gain per fisherman in
the swordfish fishery reached almost $4,000. The gains in efficiency are largely
due to new investments. The capital stock in fisheries is composed mainly of
vessels, gear, and shore installations with vessels representing two thirds of the
total. It is in vessels and gear that the industry has experienced rapid expansion.
The acquisition of larger vessels has started to show results in ground-fish
and scallop landings and has had its effects on employment. Fewer men are now
producing more fish, and more men are working a larger portion of the year,
thereby reducing to some extent the seasonality of employment.

There have also been important changes in the fish-processing industry.
Growing production has been accompanied by a changing product mix, while
the number of plants has declined as average plant size and productivity have
increased, with the net value of output per worker standing at $4,457.

4 The Twilight Zone: Free Goods and the
Social Matrix

A growing class of phenomena involved in regional studies is devoid of
some or all of the characteristics of commodities. Ordinarily classified as
social or free goods, not only are they not traded in markets but the very
concept of value is in their case inapplicable. The dominant feature of many
free goods is that while capital and labor combined in their presence yield
higher returns, their unlimited or currently unconstrained supply precludes a
straightforward application of imputed or shadow prices.

Among the free goods affecting regional development, water is the most
conspicuous one. Theoretically, one could estimate savings resulting from
the local abundance of fresh water which obviates the need to use desalinated sea
water, but even aside from the obvious difficulties of measurement, a number
of pertinent questions makes such an approach impractical. What is the maximum
cost from which savings should be measured? How should the almost infinite
number of technical possibilities for savings through recirculation be considered?
Even more important, can one assume an infinite demand for all such resources?
The major applications of water can be grouped for purposes of analysis into
the following broad categories:

(1) Residential, including consumption by households and for municipal
    purposes;
(2) Industrial, comprising numerous applications: as raw materials (for example,
    in beer production), conducting processes in liquid state (for example,

dyeing, many food-processing operations, and, in fact, most chemical
processes), washing of raw materials and finished products, cooling, transport of heat, humidifying, steam and power generation, and transportation
of solids in water streams;

(3) Irrigation;
(4) Generation of electricity, in both thermal and hydro power stations;
(5) Transportation, on both fresh and salt water;
(6) Fishing or, more generally, as a source of aquatic life;
(7) Recreation.

Almost every one of these manifold applications imposes different
constraints on quality,[q] acceptable cost, and regularity of supply. Because of
its numerous uses, differences in quality, price, and temporal availability,
water cannot be treated as a homogeneous commodity. The fact that water
may cause damage (flooding) or adversely affect the environment (standing
water or flows of polluted water) and thus require heavy investments in preven-
tive measures is also of economic significance. Since several uses of water are
complementary rather than competing with one another,[r] the contribution of
a major water investment to each is often hard or impossible to separate, thus
increasing the difficulty of assessing its marginal value. The supply and demand
for water have to be balanced within relatively small areas because, though
there are few technical restrictions on transporting water over long distances,
the costs involved are forbidding and preclude the utilization of water hauled
from remote sources for most purposes. Hence, the very notion of region-wide
abundance or scarcity is meaningless, except in cases in which the study area
corresponds to a water supply region. Moreover, estimates of total requirements
for water covering its various uses remain elusive, while demand often turns
out to be price inelastic.

The evaluation of total supply is just as uncertain as that of total demand.
The total supply of water could be defined as a stock or as the sum of surface
water contained in lakes and estuaries plus groundwater reserves. Alternatively,
total water supply could be defined as the annual flow of surface and groundwater available under normal climatic conditions. The first definition would
be relevant for such purposes as measuring water available for recreational uses
or as a potential source of power; however, the total stock of fresh water
usually forms only a fraction of yearly circulation, or even of residential and
industrial consumption. Hence, the availability of fresh water is often measured
with the help of flow phenomena. The average annual supply of fresh water or
water surplus potentially available for human use corresponds to the difference

---

[q]Quality refers not only to the broad distinction between fresh and saline waters but
to such characteristics as mineral content, presence of organic substance, temperature, and
color.

[r]For example, the construction of a dam may ensure a regular water supply, prevent
flood damage, create an energy source, and enhance recreational facilities and fishing.

between precipitation in the catchment area and evapotranspiration and runoff. To the extent that the study region does not correspond to the catchment area, surface and underground flows have to be accounted for.

Total supply of fresh water does not determine the quantity available unambiguously. Water used for residential and industrial purposes is often recycled and reused – in some areas up to twelve or fifteen times – before being finally discharged into the sea or used for irrigation. It is not obvious whether the processing of water (economically not very different from the purification of sewage) should be treated as part of making the supply available. In other words, should supply be defined as supply of untreated and hence ordinarily not usable fresh water or as supply of water ready for use? In the latter case, because of recycling, quantity will often exceed that supplied by nature. The situation bears little similarity to the one discussed with respect to coal underground and coal at the pithead, since frequently the available supply of unprocessed water is (technically at least) unrelated to total use.

Since untreated water is seldom usable for residential and industrial consumption, water may be considered as the product of a highly capital intensive water purification industry, the relative abundance or scarcity of untreated water being reflected in differences in returns of the water purification plants operating in different regions. In principle these differences could be capitalized to yield an index of the regional availability of water, but measurements are so far too crude to lead to useful results. Moreover, such an approach would encounter also serious theoretical objections. The demand for water is a function of, among other factors, the existence of closed loop systems in the local water-using industries, the installation of which is ordinarily forced upon industries by local authorities and not by market forces. Generally, water has many properties of a public good, with its price as a rule unequal to either cost or marginal utility, and demand price inelastic. Neither the supply nor the demand curves for water are well behaved; both have kinks and do not respond to price changes. As with other natural resources, the low value of local water resources may be the result of lack of demand as much as of abundant supply. In depressed regions especially, water is sometimes potentially superabundant and hence commands zero value. This, however, may be taken as a positive characteristic, making the region attractive for water-consuming industries. Of interest to a regional analyst would be an index indicating the distance from the threshold beyond which water would have a positive value or, still better, a supply curve.

Nova Scotia does not face water supply problems in the near future. The relationship between precipitation and run off in five Canadian regions, indicated in Figure 2-4, forcefully illustrates the relative abundance of water in the Atlantic Provinces compared to other Canadian regions. The impression of abundance is further reinforced when quantities of water available per capita are considered.

The total water surplus in Nova Scotia in 1961 was estimated at 37,000,000

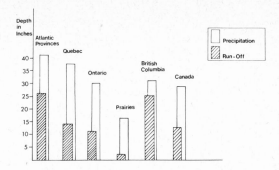

Figure 2–4. Precipitation and Runoff in Settled Regions of Canada. Based on Cass-Beggs, D.: "Water as a Basic Resource," *Resources for Tomorrow*, Vol. 1, Queen's Printer, 1961, pp. 180–181.

acre-feet per year, [20] of which roughly 10,000,000 acre-feet were represented by groundwater and 27,000,000 acre-feet by surface water. Total precipitation, falling upon 21,000 square miles of surface area, amounted to forty-five inches per year, of which it was assumed that nine inches, or 0.75 feet, of precipitation became available as groundwater, making its water supply one of the most abundant in the country.

The water distribution systems existing in Nova Scotia were mostly started in the late 19th and early 20th centures, [21] at a time when the tendency was to avoid pumping because of its comparatively high costs and to rely on surface supplies and transmission by gravity. Lakes in which the region abounds, were generally preferred as sources of supply even in places in which the available quantities were small and the advantages involved dubious. Under modern circumstances, the cost factors have changed to such an extent that water obtained from lakes is more expensive than pumped groundwater or river supplies. As a result, about two-thirds of all towns and villages in Nova Scotia are now dependent upon groundwater supplied from fairly recently constructed wells. In the long run the situation is, however, far from satisfactory because only in twelve locations would the potential groundwater supplies suffice for a substantially augmented consumption, associated with industrial activities. Hence, further consumption will have to be increasingly covered by river waters, which require treatment facilities well beyond the simple chlorination applied at present.

The economically significant feature of the water situation in Nova Scotia is that untreated water is superabundant, with, according to expert opinion, average annual supply approximately twice as great as foreseeable demand. Therefore, despite its considerable potential importance, the present marginal utility of water and hence its value may be deemed to be zero. Analytically this conclusion largely begs the question and leaves the problems of valuation unsolved.

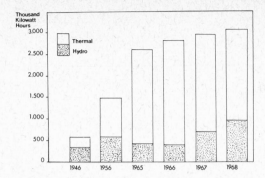

Figure 2-5. Total Electrical Energy Generated Nova Scotia. Source: D.B.S.: *Electric Power Statistics, Vol. II, Annual Statistics*, Cat. No. 57-202, 1967, 1968.

Among other largely complementary uses of water, generation of hydro-power commands increasing interest. Over the past four decades a vast change has occurred both in the total demand for power and in the relative shares of various sources of energy. Not only have oil and natural gas largely replaced coal and wood, by accounting for over 77 percent of thermal power, but water power provided already in 1960 11 percent of total energy supply in Canada. While nuclear, solar, and tidal power do not yet amount to much they hold out considerable promise for the near future. These developments are of consider-able relevance to the economy of Nova Scotia, not only because of possible discoveries of commercial quantities of oil and natural gas as a result of the extensive explorations taking place now but also because of possibilities of harness-ing the tidal power of the Bay of Fundy. The two counties of Cumberland and Colchester both possess favorable sites for power stations and the project might affect their economies. The construction would involve considerable investments, yielding power far beyond the needs of the local electricity market, and is not likely to take place in the near future. Hence, for some time to come, coal and hydropower are likely to remain the main resources used. Despite the fact that of the forty-seven generating stations in Nova Scotia thirty-seven are hydro stations and only seven thermal, the electricity generating system is dominated by the few large thermal power stations. Figure 2-5 shows the relative unimpor-tance of hydropower to Nova Scotia in terms of total generated energy.

The undeveloped hydro resources in Nova Scotia, though not fully explored, are not considered to form a significant part of the existing energy reserves. Even in the long run, thermal plants are expected to continue to supply the base load, with hydro resources contributing only in the field of peaking capacity.

Finally, a discussion of provincial water resources would be incomplete without considering some more elusive aspects and advantages connected with its geography. The Atlantic coastline of Nova Scotia consists basically of drowned river valleys. This has left a wealth of natural harbors extending along virtually the whole of the Atlantic seaboard, with offshore islands and long inlets providing shelter from storms. Water deep enough to permit fishing craft and all but the largest tankers to dock can be found in most inlets, while some inlets have enough water to permit the docking of the latest giant vessels. Combined with these advantages is the important factor that the area has only light ice to ice-free conditions throughout the year.

The economic value of the coastline configuration with respect to shipping and fishing has greatly declined with modern technology, but the many coves and bays, combined with the generally mild climate, numerous beaches, camping and fishing facilities, and the rugged landscape constitute a major tourist attraction. Much of Nova Scotia's scenic beauty is related to the sea, from the dramatic tides of the Bay of Fundy to the grandeur of the Cabot Trail in Cape Breton.

Any attempt at evaluating these natural assets would have to begin by disaggregating provincial data on tourism, but such an analysis has never been carried out. It is impossible to evaluate how many of the estimated 706,000 visitors to the province in 1962 were attracted by natural beauty and how many came for other reasons. Generally the intensity of use of the forests, lakes, and beaches of Nova Scotia for recreational purposes is not only a function of their intrinsic qualities but of ancillary on-the-spot facilities, access roads, and accommodations.

5 Human Resources [22]

In 1961, the year of the latest available census, the population of Nova Scotia was estimated to be 737,007, barely 4.0 percent of the national total, which then stood at 18,238,274. This ratio, marking an all-time low, declined even further in the following years as indicated in Table 2-9.

With one exception, the Canadian growth rate was considerably higher than that of Nova Scotia in all time intervals, with the latter even becoming negative between 1921 and 1931, marking an absolute decline in population. The decreasing share of Nova Scotia in the national population was not due to a difference in the rate of natural increase, but to migrations. A perusal of Canadian and Nova Scotian rates of population change indicates that during the past thirty-two years the levels and fluctuations in the crude birth and death rates closely paralleled those prevailing in Canada as a whole, and since the early 1960's Nova Scotia's crude birthrates have actually been slightly above the Canadian rates [23] despite the relatively smaller number of females in child-bearing age. The slight lead in fertility was the outcome of two closely discernible conflicting trends: a long-run tendency toward childbearing at younger ages and a post-war tendency toward lower fertility, despite an acceleration in family formation. The rate of natural increase has declined considerably since the post-war peak, especially after 1961, partly because of a leveling off of death rates around 1954 and partly because of the relative constancy, and more recently decline, of birthrates.

Table 2-9
Population of Nova Scotia, Relative to Canada, 1901-1966

	Nova Scotia		Canada		
Year	Population	Average Yearly Rate of Increase (%)	Population ('000)	Average Yearly Rate of Increase (%)	Nova Scotia as Percentage of Canada
1901	459,574		5,371		8.56
1911	492,338	.71	7,207	3.42	6.83
1921	523,837	.64	8,788	2.19	5.96
1931	512,846	- .21	10,377	1.81	4.94
1941	577,962	1.27	11,507	1.09	5.02
1951	642,584	1.12	14,009	2.18	4.59
1956	694,717	1.62	16,081	2.96	4.32
1961	737,007	1.22	18,238	2.68	4.04
1966	756,039	.52	20,015	1.95	3.78
1967	757,000[a]	.13	20,405	1.95	3.71
1968	760,000[a]	.40	20,744	1.66	3.66

[a]Intercensal estimates.
Based on: D.B.S., *1961 Census of Canada*, Cat. No. 92-539; D.B.S., *1966 Census of Canada*, Cat. No. 92-610; D.B.S., *Canadian Statistical Review*, Cat. No. 11-003, April 1969, pp. 5-10; D.B.D., *Vital Statistics*, Cat. No. 84-202.

Among the demographic characteristics of a region the age-sex distribution of population is of fundamental importance. Comparisons between the Nova Scotian and Canadian age-sex structures revealed by Figure 2-6 are most instructive.

In a country unaffected by violent past upheavals, wars, or major migrations, the proportion of the population in its several age groups declines smoothly as one passes from the bottom to the top of the pyramid. Both the Canadian and to a much larger extent the Nova Scotian data are marked by depletions and indentations caused by population movements and periods of low wartime fertility. Both show, also, protuberances signaling past periods of high fertility or large immigration. The irregularities move gradually from the bottom of the pyramid toward the top, disappearing only when the age groups affected finally die off. The cycles in the age-sex pyramid are likely to be discernible in the following generation because of their effects upon the crude birthrate. Indentations in the age group 20-34 in Canada are marked, but far less pronounced than in Nova Scotia. They are at least partly explained by the abnormally low birthrates during 1931-45. But in Nova Scotia the 15-19 years age group is also below its normal size, a circumstance likely to have some short-run repercussions.

An examination of the age-sex distributions in 1951 and 1966 points toward a progressive deterioration in terms of the relative strength of the

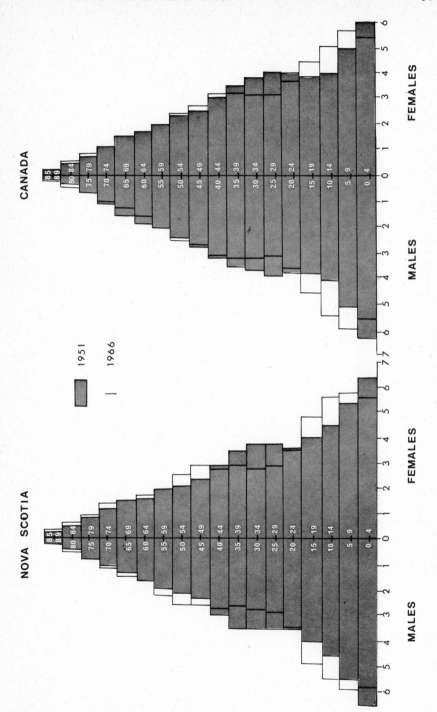

Figure 2–6. Age-Sex Structure of Population, Nova Scotia and Canada, 1951 and 1966.

economically active and dependent age groups. In both Nova Scotia and Canada the gaps in the age groups 20–44 become deeper, with Nova Scotia leading Canada. In 1961 Nova Scotia also displayed weaknesses in the active population groups between 45 and 64 relative to the rest of the country, although in 1966 this was no longer true. Furthermore, between 1951 and 1961 a decline occurred in the active age–sex groups 20–39, relative to Canada. Thus in all three censuses, 1951, 1961, and 1966, Nova Scotia had a smaller percentage of persons than Canada in the age groups forming the active population. As illustrated in Figure 2–7, if Canada distribution is used as a benchmark, Nova Scotia has a relative shortage of population in the most economically active age groups and a surplus in the dependent portion of the population.

The dichotomy into active and dependent population highlights the fact that the latter groups tend to consume more than they produce, and hence have to be partly supported by the active population. Yet the dependent population is not homogeneous with respect to several important characteristics; hence the classification into "active population," "dependent children," and "dependent aged" is sometimes preferred because, while the relative surplus of older people increases the burden carried by those in active age, children influence in addition the demand for educational facilities. Nova Scotia contains a larger proportion than Canada of people both under fourteen and above fifty years, although numerically the difference is not very pronounced, the ratio of total population to those of productive age being 1.74 in Nova Scotia as against 1.68 in Canada as a whole.

The main factor in the relative decline of the population of Nova Scotia compared to the rest of the country was undoubtedly outmigration, which in some years even exceeded natural increase. A lesser factor was the unattractiveness of the Atlantic provinces for new immigrants from overseas who, because of the prosperity of areas farther west, settled in relatively smaller numbers. Moreover, many of the immigrants who arrived in Nova Scotia seem to have used it merely as a jumping-off place, since of about 18,900 who were destined for the province between the two censuses, only 11,738 were present in mid-1961.[24] It has been calculated that between 1946 and 1962 Nova Scotia received immigrants in numbers which could have increased its mid-1946 population by 5.6 percent, had they remained in this region.

More important, Nova Scotians born in the province were seemingly drifting away in considerable numbers. Net outmigration between 1951 and 1961 was almost 32,000 persons. Allowing for the arrival during the same period of new immigrants from abroad (of whom approximately 11,700 were still living in the province in 1961) the number of residents leaving Nova Scotia exceeded new arrivals by some 44,000. The age and sex composition of migrants from and to Nova Scotia is a matter of speculation, as no direct records exist. In fact, the very number of migrants entering and leaving the province each year is only an estimate. Indirect evidence suggests, however,

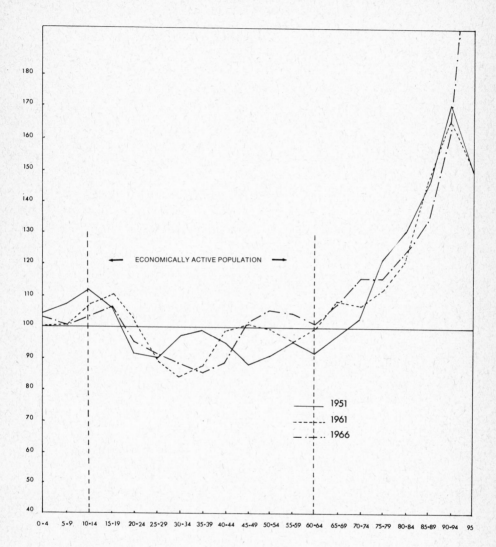

Figure 2-7. Age Structure of Population, Nova Scotia as a Percentage
of Canada, 1951, 1961, and 1966.

that the outmigrants are mainly in the productive age bracket, while the immigrants are often older people, perhaps Nova Scotians returning home to retire.[s]

The causes of interregional migrations are difficult to establish in a form enabling rigorous testing. Wage-rate differentials and employment opportunities, the two most often quoted factors, are not independent of one another. According to Phillips, [25] and Bowen and Berry, [26] the rate of change of money wages responds negatively to both the level and the change in unemployment rate, but this need not be true at the regional labor market level because of the possibility of substantial migrations. Bell [27] has tested the Phillips hypothesis for the State of Massachusetts using the following three forms:

$$\frac{W_t - W_{t-1}}{W_{t-1}} = \underset{(2.037)}{-2,621} + \underset{(.3284)}{.7324} \left(\frac{U}{N_o}\right)_{t-1} ; \qquad \begin{array}{l} R^2 = .276; \\ d = 2.42; \end{array} \qquad (1)$$

$$\frac{W_t - W_{t-1}}{W_{t-1}} = \underset{(.587)}{1.595} - \underset{(.3852)}{.7204} \left[\left(\frac{U}{N_o}\right)_t - \left(\frac{U}{N_o}\right)_{t-1}\right]; \quad \begin{array}{l} R^2 = .212; \\ d = 2.57; \end{array} \quad (2)$$

$$\frac{W_t - W_{t-1}}{W_{t-1}} = \underset{(2.371)}{-1.583} = \underset{(.3946)}{.5477} \left(\frac{U}{N_o}\right)_{t-1} - \underset{(.4431)}{.3890} \left[\left(\frac{U}{N_o}\right)_t - \left(\frac{U}{N_o}\right)_{t-1}\right];$$

$$\begin{array}{l} R^2 = .320; \\ d = 2.49; \end{array} \qquad (3)$$

where

W = real wages
U = unemployment
N_o = labor force
d = Durbin-Watson statistic.

The results of the tests were clearly negative. The first equation shows a positive relationship between movement in real wages and unemployment, with a barely significant coefficient at the five percent level. Equations (2) and

_____

[s]This conclusion is reinforced by observing that in 1951 Nova Scotia had relatively more people in the 10–19 years age groups than Canada. The fact that ten years later, in 1961, the 20–39 years age groups are relatively less numerous can be assumed to be a direct consequence of a considerable amount of outmigration in the intervening period. The phenomenon is quite common in regions experiencing substantial outmovement of population because migrants are typically recruited from among persons in their prime productive age, with males outnumbering females.

(3) have correct negative signs but the regression coefficients are not significant even at the five percent level. In the third equation the unemployment rate has again a positive sign. Studies by Bell [28] in Detroit, and Ross [29] in eighty-four S.M.S.A.'s confirm that unemployment has no impact on wages. The results of tests carried out in Nova Scotia confirming the positive relationship between employment opportunities and migrations are reported elsewhere.[30]

The economic effects of migration upon both regions involved are manifold and easy to point out but difficult to quantify. Depopulation is bound to bring about a drop in investment activity or even negative net investment and thus ordinarily further reduces the possibilities for productive employment, while the increased burden of the upkeep of social, educational, and other facilities results, to the extent that transfers from other regions are not forthcoming, in higher taxes. Moreover, migrations due to economic motives are a highly selective process involving not only a high proportion of persons in prime productive age but the most highly skilled, educated, and energetic. The loss of these people, who are lured away first when local opportunities falter, is particularly undesirable because of their potential contributions to regional output and income. There is evidence that in areas of declining job opportunities there is a potential core of workers who are unable or unwilling to move, even though the existence of this core of immobility may be obscured by a high rate of total outmigration.

In spite of the numerous negative effects of outmigration, the positive side should be mentioned too. Whenever a basic change in industrial structure causes high chronic unemployment in an area over a long period of time, out-migration may be the only factor preventing poverty and social disintegration. There is a strong presumption that when the marginal productivity of labor is zero or very low, emigration is likely to increase the region's per capita income.[31] Even in such extreme situations, however, the waste of social capital involved may justify attempts to attract new industries and employment to a declining region. The inflow of migrants from a depressed region may by itself be a mixed blessing for the receiving economy. A substantial sudden inflow of low quality labor may lower average output per worker, canceling the positive influence of the rise in the proportion of population in the labor force. The new investments required, both for new productive facilities and for infrastructure, may severely tax the existing resources. In addition, to the extent that the migrants are ill-prepared for the metropolitan labor market, they are often found at the very bottom of the social scale.

The economic importance of the human resources of a region is primarily a function of the size and quality of the labor force[t] of which the region is

_____

[t]D.B.S., *1961 Census of Canada: Labour Force* defines as labor force, "all persons 15 years of age and over, who were reported as having a job of any kind, either part-time or full-

possessed. In a modern economy with machines performing routine physical
tasks the demand for human resources is rapidly becoming highly selective,
with increasing requirements for specialized occupations accompanied by
a decline of demand for unskilled workers. Thus the skilled and the unskilled
not only do not compete for the same jobs but also differ markedly in terms
of productivity, earning power, and probability of being employed.

As illustrated in Table 2-10, the occupational distribution of the labor
force in Nova Scotia does not differ greatly from that of Canada or Ontario,
although Nova Scotia has a fractionally higher proportion of unskilled workers,
compensated by a seemingly small deficiency in relative numbers of managers
and technicians. These peculiarities are undoubtedly related to the present
industrial structure of the regional economy, with its inadequate manufacturing
base, but may have important implications for future developments. The direction of causation is in this case by no means clear.

More significant, but at the same time more difficult to unravel, is the
level of skills of persons in various occupation groups. While formal education or
educational attainments are imperfect indicators of skills, a higher education
level often signifies greater mobility in response to structural change and a
higher income level. An educated labor force is often a factor attracting new
industries. In Figure 2-8 the educational levels of the labor forces of Nova
Scotia, Canada, and Ontario,[u] are compared, conveying the impression that
while Nova Scotia is somewhat deficient in educational standards, particularly
in jobs requiring by their very nature higher educational attainments, the
differences are less pronounced than might have been anticipated. Despite some
significant exceptions, for a depressed region with substantial outmigration,
Nova Scotia seems to have been able to preserve a remarkably high proportion
of its skilled labor force. The damaging differences are mainly discernible in
the educational standards in the key occupations of professionals, managers,
technicians, and skilled workers. It appears that in the sensitive category of
managers Nova Scotia shows a lower educational level than Ontario and Canada.
In both Ontario and Canada, the second and more important mode occurs
at four to five years secondary education, while in Nova Scotia the distribution
is unimodal, indicating a length of formal education roughly three years shorter
than the Canadian and Ontario averages. Only in the semiskilled category are
the Nova Scotia standards equal or superior to Canada and Ontario, which, in
view of the numerical strength of this group, is of considerable social, if not

---

time (even if they were not at work) or were reported to be looking for work, during the
week prior to enumeration."

[u]Ontario statistics are used in this analysis for purposes of comparisons. While the
Province of Ontario is the most industrialized region of Canada its use as a benchmark raises
some questions since taken as a whole it includes, besides the manufacturing core of the
Canadian economy, considerable areas of an entirely different socioeconomic character. For
details see Appendix C.

Table 2-10
Labor Force by Socioeconomic Status, Nova Scotia, Canada, and Ontario, 1961

Occupation	Nova Scotia		Canada		Ontario	
	Number	*Percentage of Labor Force*	*Number*	*Percentage of Labor Force*	*Number*	*Percentage of Labor Force*
Scientists	732	.31	23,873	.37	8,112	.34
Professionals	11,744	4.96	319.756	4.94	116,626	4.87
Managers	18,217	7.69	542,383	8.38	210,826	8.81
Technicians	12,999	5.49	397,711	6.14	160,594	6.71
Skilled Workers	41,183	17.39	1,241,901	19.19	415,676	17.37
Semiskilled Workers	103,033	43.51	2,707,915	41.84	1,076,699	44.98
Unskilled Workers	48,911	20.65	1,238,311	19.14	404,482	16.92
Total	236,819	100.00	6,471,850	100.00	2,393,015	100.00

Based on: D.B.S., *1961 Census of Canada.*

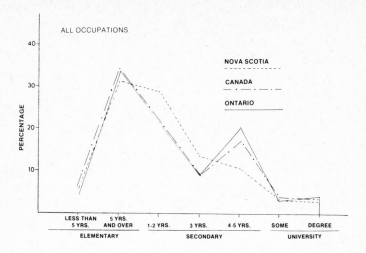

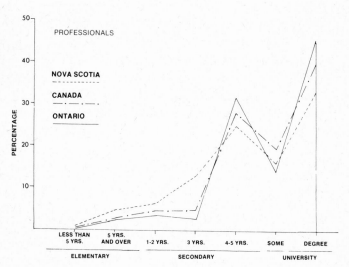

Figure 2–8. Labor Force: Educational Levels, 1961.

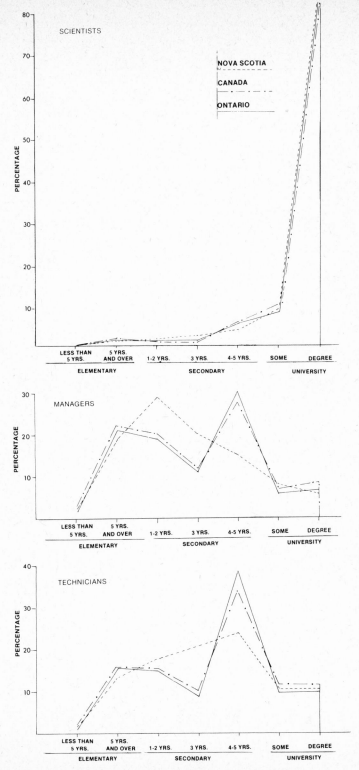

Figure 2–8. Continued.

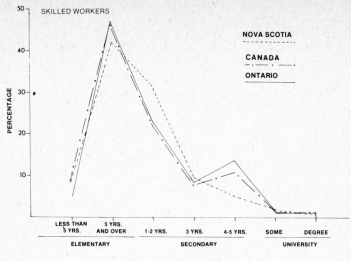

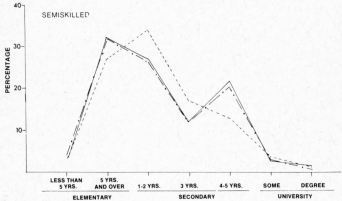

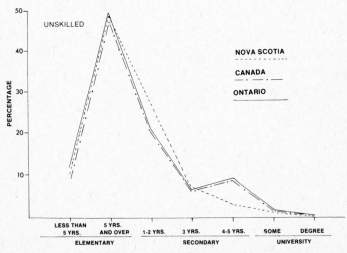

66   **Figure 2-8.** Continued.

economic importance. Even here the lack of a second mode in the distribution, indicative of workers with substantial secondary education, is ominous. The advantage conferred by slightly higher education levels of semiskilled workers in Nova Scotia seems insufficient to secure the outmigrants jobs in the highly competitive markets of Central Canada. Moreover, this category of employees does not constitute an important factor capable of affecting the economic progress of the province.

The distribution of the labor force by educational standards both in Canada and in Ontario, but not in Nova Scotia, shows the presence of two modes in all occupations except scientists. For all occupations together, the first mode occurs at five years of secondary education. While direct evidence is lacking, it can be hypothesized that the first mode represents older workers and the second the younger generation. Thus, the peculiar age and sex structure of Nova Scotia, with relatively higher concentration in the older age groups, is partly responsible for the higher proportion of people with uncompleted secondary education. This fact has some implications for the future that are unfavorable to Nova Scotia, for, while in Canada and Ontario it can be expected that the educational level of the labor force will be raised as the older workers retire and those with four to five years secondary education become more typical, in Nova Scotia, due to persistent outmigration depriving the province of the younger and better-educated inhabitants, the promise of a change is considerably smaller.

The rather bleak outlook is partly, at least, relieved by the presence and influence of the expanding academic center at Halifax, producing each year a substantial number of graduates and capable of attracting by its very existence skills and talents from elsewhere. A pertinent question, however, is to what extent the graduates of the various local educational institutions remain in Nova Scotia and to what extent they simply reinforce the skilled labor force elsewhere. The experience with training and research facilities in most depressed regions is that they tend to support economic growth in other, better-endowed parts of the nation.[v]

Several analytic objectives could be served by the introduction of a single index of human resources. Since as a rule the prime objective of such studies has been to make labor and capital directly comparable, correcting the asymmetry in the treatment of these two components of the aggregate production function, the problem has been largely conceived as an extension of wealth or capital accounting, with labor measured as a stock expressed in money terms.

---

[v]An examination of the occupational distribution of the labor force and of its educational standards ought to be supplemented by an inquiry into the levels of skills of employees of the various sectors. The sectoral structure of employment, cross-classified by occupations and educational levels, has not been developed, however, due to lack of data. Its construction in the form of labor converters translating anticipated sectoral expansion into requirements of particular occupations and skills is an important task in view of their usefulness as planning and analytic tools.

The human resources of Nova Scotia have been evaluated by four methods: (1) the present value of future gross income, (2) the present value of future net income (net of consumption expenditures), (3) the cumulated value of past outlays on, and incidental to, education and training, and (4) the cumulated net value of past investments in education and training. Each of these methods yielded different estimates, with the range of results so wide as to raise some fundamental questions. All four approaches are based on the following assumptions:

(a)   The 1961 residents will remain in Nova Scotia. Actually the weaker assumption, that net future balance of migrations will leave the population size and educational levels unchanged, is sufficient.
(b)   The basic 1961 demographic and socioeconomic characteristics of the population, such as mortality rates, labor force participation rates, and occupational structure, will remain unchanged.
(c)   Real average incomes will remain unchanged in the future.

The model, based on 1961 population and labor force statistics, is straightforward. The first part, based on the income approach, corresponding to methods (1) and (2) consisted of the following major steps:

(1)   The survivorship rates were calculated for each five-year age–sex cohort on the basis of Canadian mortality rates and summarized in two survivorship matrices on the subdiagonals. Raised to the appropriate power, the matrices were used to calculate the size of each age–sex cohort at any future time.[32]
(2)   Employment probabilities for each age–sex cohort were computed on the basis of both Nova Scotian and Canadian labor force participation rates, with the latter introduced in order to offset the effects of underregistration. The results were summarized in four matrices, covering the employment probabilities by age groups, separately for males and females, and according to Nova Scotian and Canadian labor force participation rates.
(3)   The occupational structure of the population in 1961 was used to compute the proportion of males and females in each age cohort belonging to a particular occupation. The results were recorded in two matrices, for males and females, setting occupations in rows and age groups in columns.
(4)   The two population vectors, for males and females, were premultiplied successively by the survivorship, employment, and occupational structure matrices, yielding the employment size by occupation in each future year.[w]
(5)   Mean gross and net income figures for males and females in each occupation were calculated. Gross incomes were available from published statistics [33]

---

[w]Eighty-four years was the time horizon used.

Table 2-11
Value of Human Resources: Cost Approach

Participation Rate	Income Basis	Discount-ing Rate	Discounted Value (in millions of dollars)		
			Males	Females	Total
Nova Scotian	Gross	.04	17,929.7	3,110.4	21,040.1
	Gross	.06	13,455.6	2,313.3	15,768.8
	Gross	.08	10,617.8	1,812.5	12,430.3
	Net	.04	1,391.3	− 103.7	1,287.6
	Net	.06	1,002.7	− 118.9	883.8
	Net	.08	763.5	− 121.2	642.3
Canadian	Gross	0.4	18,568.7	3,787.8	22,356.5
	Gross	0.6	13,930.7	2,825.1	16,755.8
	Gross	0.8	10,992.0	2,218.6	13,210.7
	Net	0.4	1,456.4	− 34.6	1,421.8
	Net	0.6	1,051.2	− 66.7	984.4
	Net	0.8	801.7	− 79.8	721.9

and had only to be adjusted by appropriate weighting to account for changing proportions of family heads and of persons not in families. In order to arrive at mean net incomes by occupation, consumption was deducted. In the absence of data regarding consumption by occupation, it had to be assumed that net income forms a fixed proportion of gross income. For each future year within the time horizon, employment by occupation was multiplied by mean gross or mean net income and added up over all occupations, yielding estimates of total gross or total net income of present population still working in that year. Since both Nova Scotian and Canadian labor force participation rates were used, four estimates were derived.

(6) The last step was to estimate the present worth of the four income streams, by using discounting rates of four, six, and eight percent, yielding a substantial range of present values. For reasons discussed already the lower rate seems relevant. Table 2-11 illustrates the results.

Three aspects of these results deserve comment. First, the total values of human resources are rather large as compared to other types of regional wealth. Second, the range of values is tremendous, due mainly to differences in the discounting rate used, a phenomenon not uncommon when evaluating future income streams. Third, the negative values obtained for net income of females suggest the need for imputations to account for their contributions as housekeepers and in raising and socializing children. The derived negative value of females can be interpreted as reflecting the fact that investments made in Nova Scotia females for education and training are greater than the expected amount of revenues generated by this group through their savings and tax payments.

In order to apply the cost approach, investments in human capital had to be operationally defined as expenditures for formal elementary, high school, university, and other higher education; adult education and vocational training; and on-the-job training.[34] In the face of paucity of published data and with limited research resources, a method involving accumulation of past expenditures made on the 1961 population required at least three additional assumptions, namely:

(1) The age-specific educational participation rates recorded in 1961 prevailed also in the past.
(2) The 1961 average cost of education and training were representative of the real costs of comparable services in the past.
(3) On the average, that part of the 1961 population of Nova Scotia not born in the province attained educational standards requiring the same quantity of outlays as those characteristic of the native born.

The procedure involved in estimating investments in human capital is best illustrated with the help of Table 2-12. First, the number of people in each year, starting with 1881, who were still living in 1961 was calculated and recorded (column 2). Next, the elementary and higher education outlays on people living in 1961 were estimated by computing for each five-year interval the fraction of population being education (column 3) and the average cost per pupil (column 4), and then multiplying by the population. That is, the total costs were recorded (column 5) as a product of population, fraction being educated, and average cost $[(2) \times (3) \times (4) = (5)]$. The fraction of population being educated (3) was estimated by applying 1961 age-specific participation rates to the respective age–sex distributions in each five-year interval. Costs per pupil were estimated and expressed in 1961 dollars. Outlays on elementary and high school education (5), university and higher education (6), adult education and vocational training (7), and on-the-job training (8), were added to yield total net outlays on education (9). Next, per capita consumption in each time interval was estimated (10) and multiplied by surviving population (2) to yield total consumption for each five-year period (11). Adding total net outlays on education (9) and total consumption (11) yielded estimates of total gross investments in surviving population (12).

According to this approach, the net value of human capital in 1961 was $724.4 million, and the gross value $14,864.1 million. These values compare well with estimates derived by following the income approach, assuming the Canadian rather than Nova Scotian labor force participation rate and an eight percent discount rate. This discount rate is admittedly too high, and hence one has to conclude that the income approach results in higher estimates in line with theoretical considerations discussed above. Any comparisons between results obtained with the help of these two approaches rest on the

Table 2-12
Cumulated Investments in Population[a]

Year (1)	Number of Population Surviving Until 1961 (2)	Elementary and High School Education			University and Higher Education ($ millions) (6)	Adult Education and Vocational Training ($ millions) (7)	On-the-Job Training ($ millions) (8)	Total Net Outlays on Education ($ millions) (9)	Consumption per Capita (10)	Total Consumption ($ millions) (11)	Total Consumption and Investments in Education ($ millions) (12)
		Fraction of Population Being Educated (3)	Cost per Pupil ($) (4)	Total Cost (5 yrs. in $ millions) (5)							
1881	12,200	.00	48	0	0	0	0	0	86.1	5.3	5.3
1886	24,700	.28	63	2.2	0	0	0	2.2	133.5	16.5	18.7
1891	42,100	.30	54	3.4	0	0	0	3.4	133.2	28.0	31.4
1896	63,400	.33	90	9.4	0	0	0	9.4	245.3	77.8	87.2
1901	87,000	.30	69	8.9	0	0	0	8.9	201.6	87.7	96.6
1906	114,300	.26	61	9.0	0.5	0	0	9.5	313.5	179.2	188.7
1911	149,000	.21	59	9.1	0.5	0	0	9.6	304.0	226.5	236.1
1916	190,000	.21	52	10.5	1.5	0	0	12.0	293.5	278.9	290.9
1921	234,700	.21	72	17.5	3.5	0.5	0.5	22.0	363.0	426.0	448.0
1926	279,800	.22	86	26.4	5.0	0.5	1.5	33.4	480.7	672.5	705.9
1931	323,200	.22	107	37.3	8.0	1.0	0	46.3	515.2	832.6	878.9
1936	367,100	.21	123	47.1	9.5	0.5	1.0	58.1	547.6	1,005.1	1,063.2
1941	416,400	.19	110	43.2	10.0	1.5	4.5	59.2	587.6	1,431.6	1,490.8
1946	480,700	.17	125	41.7	10.8	1.6	6.0	60.1	981.4	1,887.0	1,947.1
1950	480,700	.17	170	14.0	2.8	0.5	1.4	18.7	855.0	411.0	429.7
1951	561,000	.17	160	15.3	2.9	0.5	1.4	20.1	801.5	449.6	469.7
1952	561,000	.17	167	16.0	3.3	0.7	2.4	22.4	864.8	485.2	507.6
1953	561,000	.17	157	15.0	3.5	0.8	2.5	21.8	895.4	502.3	524.1
1954	561,000	.18	169	16.8	2.8	0.5	2.0	22.1	928.1	520.7	542.8
1955	561,000	.18	172	17.1	2.5	0.8	1.8	22.2	947.9	531.8	554.0
1956	645,800	.22	197	27.9	4.4	0.8	3.0	36.1	968.7	625.6	661.7
1957	645,800	.22	209	30.0	4.8	0.9	3.3	39.0	1,000.9	646.4	685.4
1958	645,800	.22	219	31.0	5.0	1.0	3.6	40.6	1,009.2	651.7	692.3
1959	645,800	.23	238	34.8	3.9	0.9	3.2	42.8	1,052.7	679.8	722.6
1960	645,800	.23	250	36.5	4.7	1.1	3.0	45.3	1,053.1	680.0	725.3
1961	737,007	.24	262	47.3	6.9	1.5	4.1	59.8	1,086.7	800.9	860.7
Total				566.8	96.8	15.6	45.2	724.4		14,139.7	14,864.1

[a]All costs refer to preceding time interval, which was five years until 1950, and after that, one year.

implied assumption that there is a close functional relationship between formal education and earning capacity, which in turn is used in order to measure the value of an individual to society.

6 Composition and Utilization of Labor Force

Slightly different problems are involved in the examination of the size, composition, and sectoral and spatial distribution of the labor resources of the region. Their underutilization is a function of both inherent characteristics of local labor and of developments in the provincial economy upon which they exercise in turn a powerful influence.

The numerical strength of the labor force depends upon two dichotomies: the first, dividing total population into those in the working age and those not in the working age, and the second, the working age group into those in the labor force and those not in the labor force. The latter category therefore singles out persons fifteen years old or over who are not members of the labor force, and should in principle be confined to housewives, retired and seasonal workers, students, physically and mentally disabled, inmates, and a few other categories. In depressed regions, however, this category is often underreported, because persons persistently unemployed do not register as such. The general hopelessness leads them to doubt the effectiveness of manpower centers in providing jobs and destroys motivation to register and be counted as members of the labor force. An additional reason is social customs affecting women in rural areas. Quantitative estimates of underreporting are very uncertain, yet the phenomenon is bound to affect statistics of potentially available labor force.

The total population of Nova Scotia in 1966 was composed of 501,485 persons in the working age group (fifteen years of age or over) and 254,554 persons not in the working age group. The working age group represented, thus, 66.3 percent of the population, compared to 67.1 percent in Canada as a whole, but the apparently close agreement of the two rates was hiding important differences in the age structure of the province and the nation, especially within the working age groups. The Nova Scotia labor force in 1961 was composed of 178,559 males and 58,260 females, totaling 236,819. Table 2-13 illustrates the relatively slow growth of this labor force in recent decades compared to the rapid changes taking place in Canada.

Over the four decades 1921-1961, the Nova Scotia labor force increased by 52,551, or 28.5 percent, compared with an increase in the Canadian labor force of 105.4 percent. The major growth in the regional labor force occurred during 1931-1941, when the province experienced a more rapid rate of increase than Canada, but in the decade 1951-1961, the Nova Scotia labor force increased by only 7.4 percent compared with the 22.4 percent increase in Canada. The share of females has been increasing at an accelerating rate from 15.5 percent in

Table 2-13
Growth of Labor Force, Nova Scotia, 1921-1961

	Male		Female				
Census Year	Number	Percent-age of Total	Number	Percent-age of Total	Total	Rate of Increase	Canadian Rate of Increase
1921	155,740	84.5	28,528	15.5	184,268		
1931	155,632	84.6	27,811	15.4	180,443	- 2.1	24.3
1941	177,285	82.7	37,057	17.3	214,342	18.8	15.1
1951	178,087	80.7	42,719	19.4	220,806	2.9	17.3
1961	178,559	75.4	58,260	24.6	236,819	7.4	22.4
1921- 1961						28.5	105.4

Based on: D.B.S., *Census of Canada*, 1921-1961.

1921 to 24.6 percent in 1961. This is still considerably less than the 27.3 percent registered for Canada as a whole and 28.9 percent for the most industrialized Canadian province of Ontario. There are important differences in the age distribution too, since the fifteen to twenty-four years age group accounted for the unusually high 22.7 percent of the Nova Scotia labor force, in excess of any other age group. On the other hand, relative to Canada and Ontario, Nova Scotia had considerably fewer persons in the labor force between the ages of twenty-five and forty-four.[35]

Part of this difference is due to the substantially lower Nova Scotia labor force participation rates.[x] In 1961 the provincial rate was 49.27 percent against 53.72 percent for the whole country. The difference is substantial, and translated into absolute terms means that the provincial labor force of 236,819 would have been increased by 24,745 persons or by 10.4 percent had it enjoyed the Canadian participation rate. By 1966 the situation seemed to be improving, even though the participation rates were still short of Canadian averages. The data are summarized in Table 2-14.

The low labor force participation rates, compared to Canada, are partly due to a different age-sex structure of the population, which is unfavorable to Nova Scotia, although Nova Scotia was lagging behind Canada in all age groups and especially with respect to females.[36]

In order to analyze the separate contributions of the different factors involved, Ontario may provide a better yardstick than Canada, which is composed

---

[x]Because of the ambiguities of the notion "labor force participation rate," which refers to the ratio of persons in the labor force to population fifteen years old and over and hence depends upon the age structure of the latter, "total population participation rate," which diresgards temporal or interregional differences in age structure, is sometimes used.

Table 2-14
Labor Force Participation Rates

	Nova Scotia 1961	Canada 1961	Nova Scotia 1966
1. Total population	737,007	18,238,247	756,039
2. Population 15 years[+]	480,679	12,046,325	491,485
As percentage of total	65.22%	66.04%	65.00%
3. Labor force			
(a) Male	178,559	4,705,518	179,818
(b) Female	58,260	1,766,332	70,269
(c) Total	236,819	6,471,850	250,087[a]
4. Participation rate based on			
(a) Total population	32.13	35.49	33.07
(b) Population 15 years[+]	49.27	53.72	50.88
5. Labor force at Canadian participation rate			
(737,007 x 35.49)	261,564		
6. Actual labor force	236,819		
Difference [(6) – (5)]	–24,745		
Difference as a percentage of actual labor force	10.4		

[a]According to Nova Scotia Voluntary Planning Board, *1967 Annual Report and Economic Review*, p. 103, the Nova Scotia labor force in August 1966 stood at 248,000 only.

Based on: D.B.S., *1961 Census of Canada*; and D.B.S., *1966 Census of Canada*.

of very heterogeneous provincial economies. Table 2-15 presents the results of an analysis of differences in labor force participation rates.

In terms of both males and females, the major part of the difference is clearly due to deviations in participation rates rather than to a different age–sex structure. In the case of females, almost the entire difference is accounted for by participation rates. Whether this phenomenon is due to local industries that, because of their nature, predominantly employ men or to social custom is not revealed by the above analysis.

The labor force participation rates did evolve somewhat over the past fifty years, but Nova Scotia has experienced lower labor force participation rates than Canada over long periods of time and the situation shows signs of slowly deteriorating. The trend toward lower male and higher female labor force participation rates is clearly discernible in both Nova Scotia and Canada, but the decline in the male rates was faster in the province than in the rest of the country and the increase in the female rates considerably slower.[37]

From the purely economic point of view the relatively low labor force participation rate, a characteristic that Nova Scotia has in common with the other Atlantic Provinces, suggests the existence of a potentially available pool of labor. At the same time it has a depressing effect upon the level of real incomes

Table 2-15
Analysis of Labor Force Participation Rate, 1961

	Total	Male	Female
(1) Nova Scotia labor force 1961	236,819	178,599	58,260
(2) Nova Scotia labor force at Ontario participation rate and age-sex structure	282,841	201,033	81,808
(3) Total difference [(2) – (1)]	46,022	22,474	23,548
(4) Percentage difference, total difference as a percentage of actual Nova Scotia labor force	19.43%	12.59%	40.42%
(5) Nova Scotia labor force at Ontario participation rates but Nova Scotia age-sex structure	267,469	190,183	77,286
(6) Difference due to deviations in participation rates [(5) – (1)]	30,650	11,624	19,026
(7) Percentage difference due to participation rates [(6) ÷ (1)]	12.94%	6.51%	32.66%
(8) Nova Scotia labor force at Nova Scotia participation rates but Ontario age-sex structure	249,154	188,698	60,456
(9) Difference due to deviation in age-sex structure [(8) – (1)]	12,335	-10,139	2,196
(10) Percentage difference due to age-sex structure [(9) ÷ (1)]	5.21%	5.68%	3.77%
(11) Total accounted for [(6) + (9)]	42,985	21,763	21,222
(12) Interaction effect [(3) – (11)]	3,037	711	2,325

Based on: D.B.C., *1961 Census of Canada.*

and, as a symptom of a high, persistent unemployment, generates a general feeling of hopelessness.

The second important indicator of the extent and efficiency with which existing labor resources are being used is the absolute and relative number of wage earners. In 1961, wage earners usually associated with the presence of modern industries numbered in Nova Scotia 203,3222, or 85.86 percent of a total labor force of 236,819.[y] Their spatial distribution was very unequal, with heavy concentrations in and around the major metropolitan and manufacturing centers such as Halifax, Sydney, New Glasgow, Truro, or Amherst, where they represented a high proportion of the total labor force. Self-employment was a relatively more important source of income in rural subdivisions than in urban areas, a phenomenon obviously partly related to the nature of rural economy

---

[y]D.B.S., *1961 Census of Canada,* special tabulations. The census classified as wage earners "persons who work for others for wages, salary, tips, or piece rates, or who work for others in non-family enterprises for payment in kind." Salesmen on commission are to be reported as wage earners if they work for only one company.

but also partly due to the exceptional lack of job opportunities outside cities
and towns in Nova Scotia. The range of job opportunities is illustrated by
such examples as New Waterford, where wage earners reached 93.6 percent of
the local labor force, and Inverness, where they amounted to 48.7 percent only.

The problem of utilization of labor and the related issue of partial unemployment has to be considered in the context of spatial organization of the province,
because it is also a function of its geographic distribution in relation to centers
of economic activity. The existing settlement pattern of Nova Scotia is mainly
the product of historical developments during the period of its rapid growth
and is largely unsuited for a modern economy. Hence, a revitalization of
the provincial economy will almost certainly have to be accompanied by
massive relocations. Because of the tiny area of the province (only 20,402
square miles) the average density of 36.16 inhabitants per square mile is much
higher than the Canadian average of 5.12. By itself, this index is not very
significant, because it fails to take into account important aspects of population
distribution such as the emptiness of the Canadian northern territories or the
noticeable differences between coastal settlements and the sparsely populated
interior of Nova Scotia. More important, the notion of density becomes obsolete
in view of the modern clustering of population in a few major urban areas.
The degree of urbanization of Nova Scotia is well illustrated by the fact that in
1961, 54.3 percent of the total population lived in urban areas, as opposed
to 69.6 percent in Canada as a whole. The relative size of the rural population,
especially when considered against the background of a weak, uncompetitive
agriculture, has obvious implications for such diverse phenomena as birthrate,
consumption habits, transportation facilities, income distributions, and taxation.
Table 2-16 illustrates changes in urbanization occurring over time and compares
them with developments in Canada, although by being limited to national totals
it fails to bring to the fore the significant differences between provinces.

There are three relatively minor (by North American standards) urban-
industrial agglomerations, namely: (1) Halifax-Dartmouth, accounting alone for
25.0 percent of the total population in 1966. (2) Sydney-Glace Bay-New
Waterford-Sydney Mines-North Sydney-Dominion, accounting for a further 12.1
percent and (3) New Glasgow-Stellarton-Pictou-Westville-Trenton, accounting
for 3.7 percent. Of the remaining towns, only Truro and Amherst exceed
10,000 inhabitants while Yarmouth, with 8,300 and some vestiges of industry,
has perhaps some claim to the status of an urban center. Other agglomerations
are simply small service centers or fishing villages. To what extent they fulfill
the role of nodes organizing their respective hinterlands and how far they are
simply relics of the past, leading an existence independent of the rest of
the province, is an open question. The size distribution of cities and towns does
not provide any evidence of a hierarchical system.

Significantly, over the decade 1951-1961 and up till 1966 Nova Scotia
did not register any progress in urbanization, the percentage of urban population

Table 2-16
Urban and Rural Population, Nova Scotia and Canada

	1951		1956		1961		1966	
	Population	Percentage	Population	Percentage	Population	Percentage	Population	Percentage
Nova Scotia								
Urban	355,348	55.30	399,094	57.45	416,791	56.55	438,907	58.05
Rural	287,236	44.70	295,623	42.55	320,216	43.45	317,132	41.95
Non-farm	177,038	27.55	200,242	28.82	238,959	32.42	271,881	35.96
Farm	110,198	17.15	95,381	13.73	81,257	11.03	45,251	5.99
Total	642,584	100.00	694,717	100.00	737,007	100.00	756,039	100.00
Canada								
Urban	8,817,637	62.94	10,714,855	66.63	12,971,927	71.12	14,726,759	73.58
Rural	5,191,792	37.06	5,365,936	33.37	5,266,320	28.88	5,288,121	26.42
Non-farm	2,433,506	17.29	2,734,349	17.00	3,028,749	16.61	3,374,407	16.86
Farm	2,769,286	19.77	2,631,587	16.37	2,237,571	12.27	1,913,714	9.56
Total	14,009,429	100.00	16,080,791	100.00	18,238,247	100.00	20,014,880	100.00

Source: D.B.S., *Census of Canada*, 1961, Cat. No. 92–536; and D.B.S., *Census of Canada*, 1966, Cat. No. 92–602.

remaining virtually stationary in striking contrast to general Canadian experience.
The simultaneous sizable shift among the rural population from farm to non-
farm is difficult to explain. The magnitude of the phenomenon is illustrated by a
decline in farm population from 17.1 percent in 1951 to 6.5 percent in 1966
and by a concommitant increase in the rural non-farm population from 27.6
percent in 1951 to 36.6 in 1966. A sharp change from farm to non-farm population is not uncommon in highly urbanized areas where it is due to suburbaniza-
tion or extension of areas of metropolitan dominance, but in a province lacking
large urban-industrial agglomerations its causes are not obvious.

In a much broader geographic frame of reference, however, a trend toward
progressive concentration of population in counties possessing growing urban
centers is clearly discernible. The fastest growing counties in the present century
were Halifax, Cape Breton, Kings, Colchester, and Pictou, although only the
first two exceeded the Nova Scotia average rate of growth. With the exception
of Kings, all have had some urban-industrial development. The increase in the
population of Kings County is related to agricultural activities in the fertile
Annapolis Valley. The timing of the growth processes deserves notice since of
the five counties which registered growth, only Halifax, Kings, and to a lesser
extent Colchester, were growing since the last war; the growth of Cape Breton and
Pictou took place largely in the early part of the twentieth century. Counties
lacking a strong economic base and limited employment opportunities registered
an outflow of population.

Archaic settlement patterns unresponsive to shifting locations of economic
activities are one of the main causes of persistent total, partial, and seasonal
unemployment, with all its economic and sociopolitical implications. Labor
utilization has as a rule to be examined within a rather narrow spatial context
because of the limited range of commuting. Availability of jobs outside the place
of residence of the unemployed or beyond the commuting radius involves
relocations, with considerable attendant investment outlays for housing and
infrastructure.[z] In relative terms unemployment displays a pattern reflecting the
economic development of various areas of the province, with heavy concentrations in parts of Cape Breton Island, Northern Nova Scotia, and along the
South Shore. The number of unplaced female applicants exceeds the share of
females in the labor force, partly as a consequence of the industrial structure of
the province with its lack of light industries, while the concentration of unemployment in the age group 20–44 exceeds the share of this group in the total labor
force.

Partial unemployment, or employment during less than forty weeks per
year, is related mainly to seasonal variations in demand for labor and results in an

---

[z]Unfortunately, the Canada Manpower Centers in Nova Scotia do not correspond to
labor market areas because quite often a substantial volume of commuting takes place between Local Office Areas.

Table 2-17
Wage Earners by Weeks Worked per Year, Nova Scotia, 1961

Weeks Worked	Males	Females	Total
0	658	2,124	2,782
1–13	8,626	5,344	13,970
14–26	12,414	4,074	16,488
27–39	15,958	4,436	20,394
40–52	108,320	36,176	144,496
Not stated	3,733	1,459	5,192
Total	149,709	53,613	203,322

Based on: D.B.S., *1961 Census of Canada*, special tabulation.

important underutilization of existing human resources, the magnitude of which may even surpass losses due to structural unemployment. The magnitude of the problem is illustrated in Table 2-17.

Seasonal and partial unemployment, by lowering labor income and creating a sense of uncertainty, provides an incentive for outmigration. The phenomenon is very unevenly distributed; Inverness County is hardest hit, while in industrialized areas and urban communities with some manufacturing industries it is less widespread. Seasonal unemployment reaches its peak in February and declines rather rapidly till the trough in September–October. The yearly amplitude in employment is considerable. The seasonal index of unemployment in 1965–68 is illustrated in Figure 2-9.

The employment conditions in Nova Scotia, with massive hidden unemployment and high seasonal fluctuations are reflected in the relative wage levels prevailing in the province. In 1967 the average weekly earnings in Nova Scotia were, at $77.37, the lowest among the Canadian provinces, as shown in Table 2-18.

In percentage terms, the differences between Nova Scotia and other provinces are very pronounced, amounting in the case of British Columbia to 46.3 percent. Equally important differences, both with respect to wage rates and average wage earnings per capita, exist between various parts of the province and between rural and urban areas.[aa]

Close scrutiny of the present and potential value of existing natural and human resources thus leads to rather gloomy conclusions. The important role

---

[aa]The two concepts are obviously far from synonymous, for while wage earnings per wage earner show the returns to labor related to the marginal productivity of labor, per capita wage earnings indicate the importance of wages in contributing to the maintenance of the population and, indirectly, the degree of industrialization. Per capita wage earnings are frequently used as a social indicator, since their level depends largely upon the concentration of wage earners characteristic of manufacturing and urban centers.

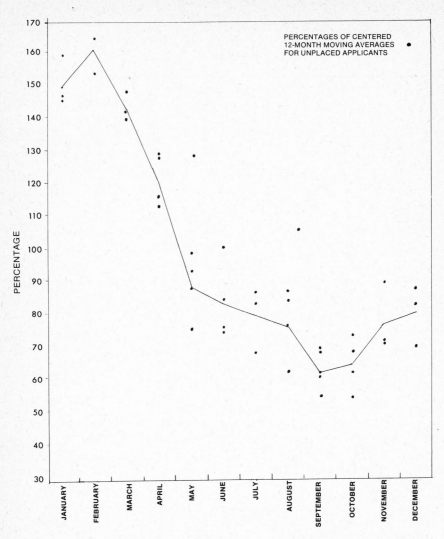

Figure 2-9. Index of Seasonal Unemployment, Nova Scotia, 1965-1968.

that natural endowment has played in the history of Nova Scotia is unlikely to extend into the future while the weakness of the economic base does not afford many opportunities to the valuable local human resources. Yet, to be accepted these general impressions have to be substantiated by rigorous analysis. This is reported in Chapter 7, where the findings and numerical results derived so far form the necessary building blocks of an econometric model

Table 2-18

Average Weekly Hours and Earnings on Hourly-Rated Wage Earners, 1965-67

Province	Average Weekly Hours			Average Hourly Earnings			Average Weekly Wages		
	1965	1966	1967	1965	1966	1967	1965	1966	1967
Newfoundland	41.5	41.0	40.8	$1.73	$1.90	$2.06	$71.73	$ 77.69	$ 84.01
Nova Scotia	40.7	40.6	39.8	1.77	1.85	1.94	72.01	75.11	77.37
New Brunswick	41.6	41.9	41.1	1.75	1.86	2.00	72.78	77.70	82.28
Quebec	41.8	41.8	41.1	1.88	2.02	2.16	78.62	84.25	88.81
Ontario	41.2	40.7	40.3	2.24	2.37	2.52	92.35	96.41	101.58
Manitoba	40.3	40.0	39.5	1.84	1.94	2.14	74.17	77.72	84.44
Saskatchewan	40.2	39.8	39.6	2.18	2.29	2.47	87.70	90.99	97.82
Alberta	40.2	39.9	39.5	2.14	2.27	2.45	86.13	90.37	96.83
British Columbia	37.9	37.7	37.7	2.62	2.78	3.01	99.50	104.93	113.20

Source: D.B.S., *Canada Year Book*, 1969.

of the regional economy. Together with findings of several other partial analyses they are fused into an analytic framework used to validate hypotheses concerning the forces operating in the local economy and likely to shape its future.

3

Structure of the Regional Economy: Contribution of Income and Product Accounts

1 Role of Accounts in Regional Studies

During the past fifteen years, in most advanced industrial nations, regional applications of various types of social accounting have become commonplace. Official government agencies still rarely assume the responsibility for publishing regional accounts, but considerable research work has been accomplished by private organizations, often within the scope of regional planning and sometimes as an integral part of it. The institutional and organizational framework within which regional social accounting is carried out is of considerable importance since it affects the scope, methodology, and format of the accounts. This has recently been the subject of extensive discussions.[1]

In itself, social accounting represents little more than a way of recording and summarizing economic information as it relates to the aggregate economy rather than to individual economic entities. It is ordinarily applied in order to measure macroeconomic variables and relationships, which are subsequently used in quantitative economic analysis.[2]

The primary attraction of the accounting framework is that of placing money values on economic events while at the same time introducing some discipline in reporting data. Its internal consistency is mainly a function of the double-entry nature of the framework, with flows measured as revenues or expenditures, as income or outgo, as sales or costs, and stocks measured assets or liabilities. The ability to collect information in a double-entry framework reduces measurement errors by revealing gaps in existing data, identifying inconsistencies, and providing checks on results.[3] When applied over time, social accounts help to establish consistent time series.

Five main types of social accounts have been proposed and used at the regional level at one time or another; namely,

(1) Income and Product Accounts,
(2) Balance of Payments Accounts,
(3) Moneyflows, or Flow-of-funds Accounts,
(4) Interindustry Accounts or Input-Output Accounts, and
(5) Wealth Accounts.

Four of these accounts deal with flows and one with stock phenomena. They differ widely in the level of aggregation, in the way in which the economy

83

is divided into sectors, in the degree of netting and consolidation, in the amount of imputing, and in coverage.

A serious problem is presented by the conceptual framework — the theory or set of theories — within which the accounts are developed. Statistical summaries of economic data not based on theory can hardly prove fruitful; nor are they feasible [4] since, although perhaps only implied, some kind of fundamental theoretical idea underlies any collecting of numbers. Thus, according to this view social accounts can only be meaningful within the framework of a specific theory or model.

The role that data and quantitative estimates play in the social sciences and in the political decision processes is often overrated. Our basic understanding of socioeconomic phenomena as well as most political decisions is qualitative and and not quantitative in nature. The quantitative aspects which figure so prominently in the recent development of modern economics and of the other social sciences constitute the means toward gaining new insights but are not a purpose in themselves.

This brings to the fore another limitation common to all types of social accounts. They are not powerful tools for estimating externalities, which seem to play an ever increasing role in regional economics. Similarly, they are not a powerful tool for assessing social benefits or costs whenever these diverge from private ones. Furthermore, it is only in the realm of economic interaction and in a market of willing buyers and sellers that the price mechanism can be used to articulate subjective preferences. No similar quantifying mechanism is available in the field of social or political relationships that could provide a means of measuring noneconomic values.[a]

An important feature of Income and Product Accounts is that they are limited to final goods and services,[b] while intermediate goods are eliminated and dealt with in Input-Output Accounts. The rise of Income and Product Accounts at the national level received considerable impetus during and immediately after the great depression. Because of increased interest in income analysis, this

---

[a]Social accounts as developed at the national level are, in fact, economic accounts. Hardly any variables other than economic ones were ever included in those accounts. The word "social" in the name means that they refer to society as a whole to distinguish them from business accounts in which the business firm is the basic unit. Attempts have, nonetheless, been made to generalize from economic relationships and the price mechanism to all types of social interaction. Exchange theory in sociology is one example. See, in this connection, Homans, George Caspar, *Social Behavior: Its Elementary Forms*, Harcourt, Brace & World, 1961.

[b]The criterion discriminating between final and intermediate goods is intended use. Final goods and services are defined as those produced in order to be sold to ultimate users and not for resale. Intermediate goods are those produced for further processing and transformation or as ingredients in other productive processes. The conceptual problems involved in the dichotomy of final versus intermediate goods as well as differences between various types of accounts have been extensively treated in the literature. See, for example, Ruggles, Richard, and Nancy D. Ruggles, *National Income Accounts and Income Analysis*,

type of social accounts has evolved as a framework for estimating the macro-economic variables considered most critical by Keynes and his successors. In most countries their primary function is to provide data for short-run macro-economic models focusing on effective demand phenomena.

Developments in the national economy are closely watched by economists with the help of the major aggregates[c] that are obtained as a by-product of Income and Product Accounts and provide guidelines for general fiscal and monetary measures taken by the national government. Although some concepts and methods applied in developing the accounts are still open to question, the basic approach has been widely accepted at the national level.

Income and Product Accounts, enormously useful for purposes of business cycles analysis and for guiding policy at the central level, are quickly becoming an indispensable tool of regional studies and regional planning. Their use has paralleled the adoption of macroeconomic analysis and its application to regional problems.

There is, however, a wide gap between the theories of business cycles, with reference to which Income and Product Accounts were originally developed, and theories of regional growth and development, to which they are being applied with only slight modifications.

Models, independent of their form, describe the behavioral relations or assumed reactions of transactors − persons or institutions − to changes in circumstances. They have to be based on and supplemented by a set of economic identities that are given statistical content in social accounts. Taken by themselves, these identities are not more than a framework for a consistent description of economic activities of which they cannot provide any explanation.

So far, a single widely accepted regional growth theory is lacking, which raises the question whether it is at all possible to develop a unique system of regional social accounts that would satisfy all or even the majority of the needs of regional analysis.[d] The question is far from rhetorical. Many regional economists have doubts and prefer to use a separate format for each study.

McGraw-Hill, 1956, pp. 107–120; Rosen, Sam, *National Income, Its Measurement, Determination, and Relation to Public Policy*, Holt, Rinehart & Winston, 1963, pp. 65–98; Peterson, Wallace C., *Income, Employment, and Economic Growth*, W. W. Norton, 1962, pp. 55–67; Isard, *Method of Regional Analysis*, pp. 8–121; Leven, Charles L., *Theory and Method of Income and Product Accounts for Metropolitan Areas, Including the Elgin-Dundee Area as a Case Study*, Ames, Iowa, 1958 (mimeographed); and Czamanski, Stanislaw, *Regional Income and Product Accounts of North-Eastern Nova Scotia*, Institute of Public Affairs, Dalhousie University, 1966.

[c]Gross National Product, Net National Product, National Income, Personal Income, Personal Disposable Income, along with consumption, investments, savings, exports, imports, taxes, and a few others.

[d]The issue is further complicated by the fact that regional social accounts not only are used in connection with problems of growth and development but also serve as framework for transportation and land use studies, analyses of housing markets, and studies of intrametropolitan location of retail and various other facilities.

Many of the difficulties encountered in applying the National Income and Expenditure Accounts format at the regional level are a reflection not only of the much greater and rather obvious data difficulties but also of basic differences that exist between regional planning and national economic planning, especially in the following areas:

(1) Scope and objectives,
(2) Policy instruments,
(3) Availability of data for specialized research, and
(4) Methods of analysis.[5]

Again, a set of persistent conceptual doubts is raised by the analytic uses to which Income and Product Accounts are often put at the regional level. Regional planning takes place at a much more disaggregated level than national economic planning, and hence the macro approach represented by the accounts is not always the most effective one.

Moreover, a number of activities do not have any clear-cut spatial meaning. Most federal government expenditures and undistributed corporate profits illustrate well the familiar situs problem. The division of responsibilities between the federal, provincial, and local governments and the integration of regional with Income and Product Accounts are additional examples of the largely unresolved issues encountered.

Despite these problems, some of which are common to other types of regional social accounts, Income and Product Accounts are widely used because of the relative ease and low cost with which they can be prepared. Their main applications are to be found in

(1) provision of a set of data useful for a variety of purposes, especially for operational decisions affecting the regional economy,
(2) preliminary exploration of the regional economy with the purpose of identifying its main problems or leading issues on which future research should concentrate, and
(3) development of reliable data to be incorporated into quantitative analytical or planning models at a later stage.

2 Format of Nova Scotia Accounts

In our society the organization of basic economic processes such as production, consumption, and investment is entrusted to, or at least takes place through, the self-regulating market mechanism. It is thus natural to look for indexes of performance of the regional economy in exchange phenomena.

Production, distribution, and consumption can all be estimated by the volume of transactions taking place in a time unit, subject to only two important adjustments. On the one hand, the imputed value of those commodities and services that are both produced and consumed without entering the market mechanism has to be added. This group comprises such diverse elements as products of subsistence farming, free food and shelter provided to some classes of employees, and those financial services not explicitly charged to users. On the other hand, transactions that do not correspond to new production, such as sale of nonreproducible and second-hand assets, have to be eliminated. Meaningful aggregates describing the performance of the economy as a whole can thus be derived by consolidating the trading records of primary economic units, be they producers or consumers.

The practical difficulties in constructing Income and Product Accounts, both on the national and subnational levels, are largely due to the fact that many, perhaps most, primary units do not keep records of their transactions. Even in cases where such records exist their format is not uniform, they are ill adapted for social accounting purposes, and they are often subject to nondisclosure.

Practical and conceptual difficulties have resulted in the development of fairly numerous systems and formats of Income and Product Accounts. The differences between the various methods in use relate to

(1)   number and definition of sectors,[e]
(2)   extent to which legal and decision-making units are preserved,
(3)   classification of transactions between different accounts,
(4)   degree of netting and consolidation[f] present,
(5)   extent and nature of imputations,
(6)   type of aggregates presented as part of the accounts.

Other differences have to do with some key definitions such as investments or consumption, with methods of collecting basic data, and so on.

The accounts of Nova Scotia [6] rely heavily upon benchmark data available in Dominion Bureau of Statistics publications and in the National Accounts of Canada. This makes the adoption of a format closely following that of the National Income and Expenditure Accounts almost mandatory despite the various disadvantages and difficulties involved because of the important differences in scope and objectives of social accounting at the national and

---

[e]Some systems treat sectors as aggregates of similar economic units, while other prefer the functional approach, viewing sectors as aggregates of similar transactions. These differences are sometimes reflected in names of sectors, such as Producers and Consumers as against Enterprises and Households.

[f]By netting is meant the elimination of identical but opposite flows between pairs of transactors so that only the balance are shown. By consolidation is meant the elimination of flows between transactors belonging to the same sector.

subnational level.[g] The changes in the basic layout of the Nova Scotia Income
and Product Accounts were minor, although seven rather than six sectors
were adopted. This resulted from splitting the Government Revenue and
Expenditure Account into Local Governments Revenue and Expenditure
Account, and Local Operations of Nonlocal Governments Account. Thus, the
following Sectors were used:

(1) Personal Income and Expenditure Account,
(2) Local Government,[h] Revenue and Expenditure Account,
(3) Local Operations and Nonlocal Governments Account,
(4) Business Operating Account,
(5) Nonresidents' Revenue and Expenditure Account,
(6) Investment Income Appropriation Account, and
(7) Regional Savings Account.

The way in which the various primary economic units and transactions
were grouped is illustrated in Figure 3-1 and the transactions matrix for 1965 in
Table 3-1. The first sector, covered by the Personal Income and Expenditure
Account, groups transactions pertaining to resident households and private and
some public nonprofit organizations in their capacity as final consumers and
owners of factors of production.

Military personnel stationed in the area are considered as residents to the
extent that during the 1961 census they declared their place of residence to
be Nova Scotia. Other members of the military forces are treated in the accounts
in much the same way as tourists. Their pay is thus indirectly considered in the
accounts as invisible exports.

The inclusion of nonprofit organizations in Personal Income and Expenditure Account, justifiable to a certain extent on theoretical grounds, is not
particularly desirable for purposes of regional analysis. It would be preferable
to group private nonprofit organizations with local governments because their
behavior appears to follow more closely that of public administration bodies
rather than households. However, the procedure of the National Income and
Expenditure Accounts has been followed.

The Income side of the Personal Income and Expenditure Account adds up
to total personal income, composed of amounts accruing to owners of factors
of production, and of transfers. Wages, salaries, and supplementary labor income
alone account for more than 62 percent of the total. They are broken down

---

[g]The Canadian system of National Income and Expenditure Accounts is somewhat
similar to the one in use in the United States until 1957. It has six sector accounts, as
against five in the present United States system. More important, at variance with the
United States system, the major aggregates are not derived directly as part of the sectoral
accounts.

[h]The term "Local Governments" is used here to include both provincial and municipal
Governments (as distinct from federal) and certain public bodies as well.

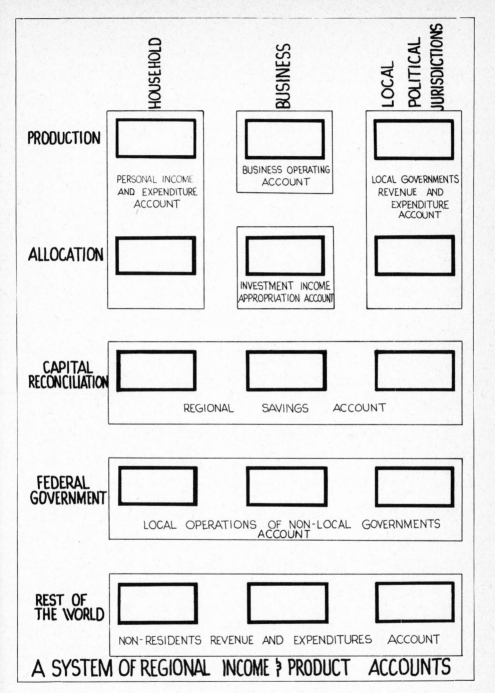

Figure 3-1. A System of Regional Income and Product Accounts.

Table 3–1

Income and Product Accounts, Nova Scotia, 1965 (in current dollars)

	Personal Income and Expenditure Account 1	Local Governments Revenue and Expenditure Account 2	Local Operations of Nonlocal Governments Account 3
Wages, salaries and supplementary labor income			
from business	486.4		
from local governments	87.2	87.2	
from nonlocal governments	87.0		87
from households	38.1	38.1	
from nonresidents	6.3		
Employer and employee contributions to social insurance and government pension plans	–31.8	13.1	18.7
Military pay and allowances	35.3		70
Net income received by farm operators from farm production	9.0		
Net income or non-farm unincorporated business	110.0		
Interest, dividends and net rental income of persons	104.0		
Transfer payments			
from local governments	39.0	39.0	
from nonlocal governments	135.0		135
charitable contributions by corporations	.4		
transfers from nonresidents	24.1		
Personal direct taxes			
income taxes	66.1	12.2	53.9
succession duties and estate taxes	2.7		3.0
miscellaneous	6.2	6.2	
Purchase of goods and services			
from business	918.0		
expenditures abroad	32.5		
Personal net saving	66.4		
Direct taxes from corporations		3.8	13.2
Indirect taxes		92.7	112.7
Sales of services		4.0	
Investment income			
interest		7.5	
profits of government business enterprises		14.4	
Transfers from non-local governments		68.2	68
Purchases of goods and services			
from business		68.8	
capital accumulation		31.7	

Business Operating Account 4	Nonresidents' Revenue and Expenditure Account 5	Investment Income Appropriation Account 6	Regional Savings Account 7
(millions of dollars)			
486.4			
	6.3		
35.2			
9.0			
110.0			
		104.0	
		.4	
	24.1		
	.3		
918.0			
	32.5		
			66.4
		17.0	
205.4			
4.0			
		7.5	
		14.4	
68.8			
31.7			

Table 3–1 cont.

	Personal Income and Expenditure Account		Local Governments Revenue and Expenditure Account		Local Operations of Nonlocal Governments Account	
	1		2		3	
Transfer payments						
interest			24.7			
subsidies			.5			
to nonlocal governments			1.0		1.0	
Surplus or deficit on transactions relating to income and product accounts			−30.8			
Direct taxes from persons – miscellaneous					5.6	
Investment income						
interest					6.3	
profits of government business enterprises					9.9	
Purchases of goods and services						
from business						40.9
capital accumulation						37.4
Transfer payments						
interest						28.0
Subsidies to business						31.5
Surplus or deficit on transactions relating to income and product accounts						−274.6
Business gross fixed captial formation						
new residential construction						
new nonresidential con- struction						
new machinery and equipment						
Sales to nonresidents (exports)						
Travel expenditures						
Investment income						
Capital consumption allowances and miscellaneous valuation adjustments						
Purchases from nonresidents (imports)						
Payments to nonresidents by business in respect of interest and dividends						
Surplus or deficit on current account with nonresidents						
Interest and dividends from nonresidents						
Undistributed corporation profits						
Residual error of estimate						
Total	1,130.0	1,130.0	222.1	222.1	224.3	224.3

Business Operating Account	4	Nonresidents' Revenue and Expenditure Account	5	Investment Income Appropriation Account	6	Regional Savings Account	7
(millions of dollars)							
				24.7			
.5							
						-30.8	
			5.6				
					6.3		
					9.9		
40.9							
37.4							
				28.0			
31.9							
						-274.6	
50.9							50.9
75.8							75.8
105.4							105.4
283.8			283.8				
26.0			26.0				
	130.4			130.4			
	155.5					155.5	
	559.1	559.1					
		24.2			24.2		
		-260.6					-260.6
			9.1	9.1			
					8.5	8.5	
	46.5					46.5	
1,706.3	1,706.3	355.2	355.2	192.2	192.2	-28.5	-28.5

according to origin into wages and salaries received from business, local governments, nonlocal governments, other households, and nonresidents. This item is treated as income accruing to households rather than as total cost to business and other employers of obtaining the services of labor. Hence, employer and employee contributions to social insurance and government pension plans are deducted. Military pay and allowances, although similar in nature, are singled out as a separate entry.

The next group of estimates deals with incomes accruing to other factors of production, such as net income received by farm operators from farm production; net income of non-farm unincorporated business; and interest, dividends, and rental income of persons.

Finally, the account contains an estimate of unilateral transfer payments received by households and private nonprofit organizations, again broken down into those originating from federal and local governments, corporations, and nonresidents.

The Expenditure side contains an estimate of personal direct taxes paid by resident households and nonprofit organizations, broken down into income taxes, succession duties and estate taxes, and miscellaneous direct taxes. This item deducted from the total personal income yields personal disposable income.

The other entries show how personal disposable income was divided between consumption and personal net saving. Consumption was assumed to be identical to purchases of goods and services by households and nonprofit organizations. The estimates of purchases are broken down into those from business, direct services (the couterpart of this item is to be found in the same account), and expenditure abroad. Personal net saving is the balancing item and thus contains the residual error of estimate involved in all the items enumerated above.

The second sector, covered by the Local Governments Revenue and Expenditure Account, groups only those transactions of the Provincial Government of Nova Scotia, the various municipal governments operating in the area, and other local authorities having welfare significance. It thus differs from the totals of the budgets of the relative governments and their agencies and affiliated institutions.

The Revenue side contains estimates of amounts accruing to local governments. They fall into three major categories. The first group contains direct taxes (both from persons and from corporations) and indirect taxes and represents revenues that depend upon the power of local governments to tax. The second group contains estimates of revenues derived from sale of services, investment income, and employers' and employees' contributions to social insurance and government pension funds. The dividing line between these two categories is in part tenuous because the differences between some types of indirect taxes and some government services are elusive. Finally, transfers from nonlocal governments are singled out as a third category, although in fact they represent a grouping of very heterogeneous amounts.

The Expenditure side contains estimates of exhaustive government expenditures.[i] They comprise current expenses in the form of purchases of goods and services from business and payments of wages and salaries, and investments, shown as capital accumulation. The nonexhaustive government expenditures are shown as various transfer payments. The balancing item, surplus or deficit on transactions relating to Income and Product Accounts, is derived as a residual and hence contains the total error of estimate.

The third sector, covered by the Local Operations of Nonlocal Governments Account, is limited in scope to those operations of the federal government, its agencies, and emanations of the Crown that influence the regional aggregates forming part of the Income and Product Accounts. The approach followed purports to measure the impact of federal government upon the economy of Nova Scotia and not the benefits derived by local residents from the various activities of the federal government. The federal government and its agencies are in effect treated in the context of regional Income and Product Accounts in much the same way as the rest of the world.

The structure of both the Revenue and Expenditure sides of this account differs from Local Governments Revenue and Expenditure Account only in details.

The fourth sector, covered by the Business Operating Account, contains transactions without direct welfare significance because business enterprises are neither final consumers nor ultimate owners of factors of production. The usefulness of the account resides in grouping and balancing various items in a meaningful way.[7]

The Revenue side of the account contains estimates of income of local business according to source. Sales are grouped by purchasing sector and comprise the following major categories: sales to residents in their capacity as ultimate consumers; investments, divided into three categories and recorded as sales to business; sales to local and federal governments, both for current consumption and for capital formation; and exports of goods and services, with sales to nonresident military personnel and tourist expenditures singled out. Finally, the Revenue side contains subsidies from both nonlocal and local governments.

The Expenditure side of the account is composed of costs incurred in production of goods, the sales of which are recorded on the Revenue side.

---

[i]By exhaustive government expenditures are meant those that compete for scarce resources with other uses. The nonexhaustive government expenditures are those which simply recirculate or redistribute the claims to the national product. An illustration of an exhaustive government expenditure might be the construction of a fighter plane using up raw materials, labor, etc., that could find alternative uses in production of consumer goods. On the other hand, veterans benefits, for example, simply withdraw the money (claim on goods) from one section of the population (taxpayers) and give it to another (veterans).

The first group of costs refers to factor costs such as: wages, salaries, and supplementary labor income; net income received by farm operators from farm production; and net income of non-farm unincorporated business. Payments accruing to other factors of production are dealt with in the Investment Income Appropriation Account, to which the relevant balance is transferred from the Business Operating Account. Expenditures also include the numerically significant imports and other costs of production such as indirect taxes, payments or services of local government agencies, capital consumption allowances, and miscellaneous valuation adjustments. The balancing item transfers the residual error of estimate to the Regional Savings Account.

The fifth sector, covered by the Nonresidents' Revenue and Expenditure Account, groups transactions between residents (and other economic units domiciled in Nova Scotia) and the rest of the world.

The Receipts from Nova Scotia side is composed of imports of goods and services; travel expenditures abroad by Nova Scotia residents; and payments to non-residents in the form of interest and dividends for services of their capital invested in Nova Scotia. The surplus or deficit representing net disinvestment in the rest of the world resulting from current transactions relating to Income and Product Accounts is transferred to the Regional Savings Account.

The Payments to Nova Scotia side of the account contains an estimate of exports and travel expenses of tourists and other visitors made in Nova Scotia. The next two items, interest and dividends and wages, salaries, and supplmentary labor income (mainly of out-commuters), refer to factor payments to Nova Scotia residents earned outside of the province. Other estimates comprise unilateral transfer payments to Nova Scotia residents and payments collected by local governments from nonresidents in respect of various (mainly property) taxes.

The sixth sector, covered by the Investment Income Appropriation Account, may be viewed as part of the Business Operating Account showing in some detail the allocation of income.

On the Source side are grouped investment income (or difference between revenues and costs transferred from Business Operating Accounts) and interest and dividends received from nonresidents and from local and nonlocal governments by both local business and local households. Interest received from governments is not considered part of the Gross Regional product.[j]

The Disposition side shows the division of total investment income between residents and nonresidents. The share of residents is composed of

---

[j]The reason usually advanced is that the bulk of federal debt has been contracted in order to finance the two World Wars and during the "great depression." Interest paid in respect of it is thus not considered as payment for the use of borrowed capital (factor of production) but rather as a charge against social product. Whatever the arguments for or against this approach may be, the practice is long established in national social accounting in Canada, the United States, and many other countries.

interest, dividends, and rental income of persons; charitable contributions made by corporations; items accruing to local governments, such as interest and profits of local government business enterprises; and undistributed profits of local corporations.[k]

The share of nonresidents is composed of interest and dividends paid by business to nonresidents, interest derived from Nova Scotia by nonlocal governments, profits of nonlocal governments' business enterprises, and corporate income taxes.

The seventh sector, covered by the Regional Savings Account is analytically the most significant. The Source side indicates the origin of the investment funds available in the province and comprises personal net saving; undistributed corporation profits and capital consumption allowances and miscellaneous valuation adjustments, together forming business gross saving; local governments' surplus; and nonlocal government surplus. These last two items were negative throughout the period covered by the Nova Scotia Accounts. In addition the Source side contains the residual error of estimate.

The Disposition side comprises business gross fixed capital formation, subdivided into new residential construction, new nonresidential construction, and new machinery and equipment, and surplus on current account with nonresidents. During the period covered by the accounts, this last item was persistently negative. The significance of surplus or deficit on current account with nonresidents resides in the fact that combined with the balance of Local Operations of Nonlocal Governments it indicates the volume of investments or disinvestments of residents outside the region.

3 Main Aggregates

One of the main objectives of constructing Income and Product Accounts is the derivation of aggregates which form one of the main tools of macroeconomic analysis. Historically, the single figure aggregates preceded the evolution of modern Income and Product Accounts and were actually largely responsible for their present form. [1] The five main aggregates presented and analyzed in order to monitor the progress of the Nova Scotian economy closely parallel the aggregates used at the national level.

(1) *Gross Regional Product at Market Prices* (GRP) is the market value of the gross output produced during each year by factors of production owned by Nova Scotia residents.

---

[k]These undistributed profits are actually accruing to stockholders whose place of residence is unknown. In regional social accounting the practice has been followed of allocating these amounts to the region in which the corporation has its headquarters irrespective of place of residence of ultimate owners or of where the actual operations take place.

Because of the double-entry nature of the Income and Product Accounts, Gross Regional Product at market prices can be derived in two ways:

(a) by summing the incomes accruing to owners of the various factors of production and adjusting the total to market prices by the addition of indirect taxes less subsidies; or

(b) by summing the expenditures — that is, the shares of the product allocated to consumption by households, exhaustive government expenditures, capital formation, and exports.

Both methods have been used, and are presented in the summary tables entitled Regional Product and Regional Expenditures. Actually, a third method is sometimes applied in regional studies: one could sum up the value added produced by industrial establishments and other economic agents and adjust it so that it corresponds to the share accruing to factors of production owned by local residents.

The fact that GRP is derived in "gross" terms means that the total has been calculated without taking into account the value of capital goods that have been consumed in the process. This omission is of little consequence because the relative value of capital consumption does not vary appreciably over time. On the other hand, it greatly facilitates interregional comparisons and, above all, comparisons with other countries whose economies use different technologies and apply different approaches to depreciation.

(2) *Net Regional Product at Market Prices* differs from Gross Regional Product at market prices by the amount of capital consumption allowance and miscellaneous valuation adjustments. Thus, the main refinement of Net Regional Product consists in taking into account the value of capital goods that have been used up in the production of goods and services forming the Gross Regional Product. Capital consumption allowance is largely composed of, though not identical to, depreciation. It includes in addition accidental damage to fixed assets and an adjustment for capital outlays charged by business firms to current expenses.

A practical difficulty arises from the fact that depreciation has a different meaning to the owner of the means of production from whose records the totals are derived, to the tax collector, and to the economist. The concern of the producer is to keep his capital intact; to society, it is largely the notion of keeping intact the physical productivity of the economy that matters. This distinction comes to the fore, for example, in case of a new invention which may induce an entrepreneur anticipating obsolescence to apply a quicker rate of depreciation; for society, on the other hand, it could justify a slower one because technical progress is likely to lower the capital-output ratio. Putting it otherwise, the existing machinery would not produce less because of the new invention, but the need to install new equipment would be more remote and more limited.

On other scores, too, the problem of keeping capital intact is highly controversial in economic theory. For example, should depreciation be imputed where none is claimed, thus creating a new flow? Depreciation of owner-occupied residential housing is a case in point, with the amounts involved by no means negligible. In this, as in several other instances, a more or less arbitrary solution has to be adopted for purposes of constructing social accounts.

Valuation adjustments, which also form part of the difference between GRP and NRP, are numerically unimportant. They result from attempts to derive a uniform valuation of end of the year business stocks despite the fact that several different legitimate methods are used by business firms.

(3) *Regional Income, or Net Regional Product at Factor Cost*, differs from Net Regional Product at market prices by the amount of indirect taxes, less subsidies. The difference between the two aggregates represents that part of the market value of goods and services not accruing to factors of production. Thus, amounts that may vary unsystematically with changes in the volume of production are eliminated from the index describing the performance of the regional economy.

Sales taxes are a typical example of producers acting as tax collectors. Unfortunately, the treatment of indirect taxes involves the controversial question of incidence of taxation and presents, both conceptually and operationally, a complicated problem. The accepted practice is to deduct from Net Regional Product those taxes that are not charges attributable to the use of the factors of production or that do not fall upon any specific factor of production.

By a parallel extension of this reasoning, subsidies are treated as amounts accruing to factors of production without which the price of the end product would have to be higher. Whether they are necessary corrections of the market mechanism, bridging the gap between costs and revenues in order to elicit the services of factors of production, or whether they are simply transfer payments deriving from the play of political forces is a relevant but difficult-to-answer question. The first assumption is usually made, and they are deducted from indirect taxes.

Like the other two aggregates, Regional Income can be measured in two ways. When measured as income accruing to the owners of factors of production, it is called Net Regional Income, or simply Regional Income, while, when viewed as a product, net of capital consumption allowance and adjusted for indirect taxes and subsidies, it is referred to as Net Regional Product at Factor Cost. It is unfortunate that the widely used term Regional Income is particularly confusing in the context of social accounts, dealing as they do with different types of "regional income."

The next two aggregates, Personal Income and Personal Disposable Income, are, at variance with those so far discussed, not measures of the performance of the local economy but of the means of payment at the disposal of residents of the region.

(4) *Personal Income* differs from Regional Income by the deduction of

earnings accruing to but not paid out to households – such as undistributed corporation profits, employers' and employees' contributions to social insurance, various forms of forced savings, and amounts that accumulate in the hands of the local governments. On the other hand, unearned payments to local households, such as government tranfers and other unilateral payments, which do not form part of aggregates measuring the level of operation of the economy, are added.

The bulk of unilateral transfers originates from the federal and local governments but in some depressed regions with heavy outmigration an important (but difficult to estimate) part may be due to transfers from former residents.

(5) *Personal Disposable Income* differs from Personal Income only by the deduction of personal direct taxes. It thus provides an estimate of the amounts available for consumption or saving.

The interrelations between the five major aggregates and their components in terms of flows are illustrated in Figure 3-2, from which some minor flows have been removed for the sake of clarity. The arrows indicate the direction of equivalent money flows rather than movements of goods and services. The four major components of aggregate demand – consumption by households, investments, exports, and exhaustive government expenditures – are indicated at the extreme left. Together they form Total Resources, not considered to be one of the major aggregates. The rest of the figure is self-explanatory.

The aggregates so far discussed refer to the economy of Nova Scotia viewed as a collection of residents. In regional studies it is customary to look also at economic phenomena taking place within specific geographic boundaries irrespective of the place of residence of owners of factors of production.[9]

A useful measure often applied in this connection is Gross Domestic Product. It differs from Gross Regional Product at Market Prices by the fact that it measures not so much the total value of goods and services produced by factors of production owned by residents of the region as the total value of production taking place in the region. Hence, it is primarily a geographical concept. Its great advantage is that it avoids some of the ambiguities surrounding measurement of phenomena that do not have any clear-cut spatial meaning. The remaining conceptual and operational difficulties are, nonetheless, considerable.

In order to derive Gross Domestic Product, one would have to adjust the Gross Regional Product at Market Prices for the wages of in- and out-commuters, interest and dividends earned by Nova Scotia residents from the rest of the world, and interest and dividends paid to nonresidents. This subject has been discussed at length in literature, and all the arguments involved need not be repeated here.[10]

Transformation of 1965 Gross Regional Product into Gross Domestic Product would involve the following adjustments:

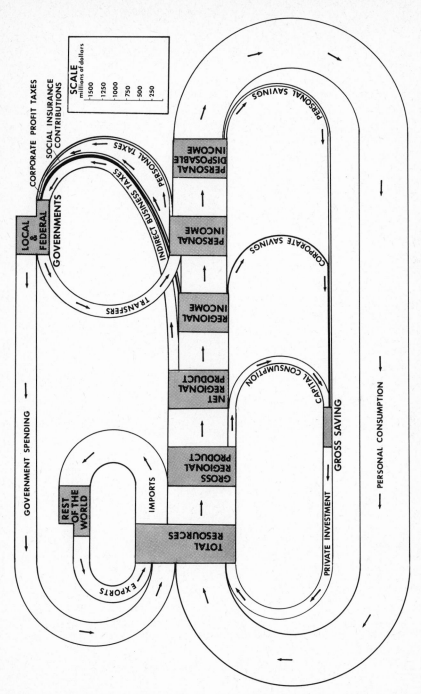

Figure 3-2. Flows in the Nova Scotia Economy, 1965.

	$ Million
Gross Regional Product	1,378.3
less: Wages earned by out-commuters	6.3
less: Interest and dividends accruing to residents	
from investments in the rest-of-the-world	9.1
plus: Interest and dividends paid to nonresidents	24.2
Gross Domestic Product	1,387.1

Wages earned by in-commuters should be added too, but they form part of total imports and are not readily available.

Actually, no reliance can be placed on the above aggregate. Flows of interest and dividends over provincial boundaries are among some of the weakest estimates in the regional Income and Product Accounts of Nova Scotia, and it does not seem to make sense to adjust for these very uncertain quantities. Gross Domestic Product is a very useful concept when derived as a summation of value added in sectors and basic economic units. This method has not been followed in Nova Scotia.

But while conceptually the use of Gross Domestic Product is attractive, it hardly removes the basic difficulties surrounding the treatment of corporations. The latter do not enter directly into the major aggregates derived from Income and Product Accounts because they are intermediaries and neither final consumers nor ultimate owners of factors of production. Hence, all that is needed for consistent derivation of GRP is the place of residence of stockholders. This is known in terms of income accruing to residents of Nova Scotia out of dividends of corporations wherever located.[11] However, in terms of GRP the real difficulty arises in connection with other items pertaining to corporations, namely:

(1)   undistributed corporate profits,
(2)   corporate income taxes, and
(3)   corporate investments.

The difficulty is not only due to lack of data but is primarily conceptual. In reality, these items form incomes of stockholders whose place of residence is unknown. No satisfactory treatment is currently available and hence, customarily, all three items are allocated to the region where the headquarters of the corporation are located. That this is inadequate is glaringly obvious [12] but numercially these flows are rather unimportant.

The first of the above items, undistributed corporate profits, seems to be very nearly zero in Nova Scotia. As far as corporate income taxes are concerned, reliable published sources of information do exist, [13] presented, it is true, according to the place where the headquarters of the corporations are located, which is equivalent neither to the place of actual production nor to the place of residence of stockholders. Finally, the third item, corporate investments in Nova Scotia, is part of the fairly reliable figures covering business investments. To be stressed, of course, is the fact that dealing with the problem on a geographic basis and deriving GDP instead of GRP does not solve the basic difficulty.

4 Performance of the Economy

The various flows and major aggregates as well as their development over time furnish the basic numerical material upon which to build or against which to confront hypotheses concerning the regional economy.[14] Yet, a vast collection of numbers such as Regional Income and Product Accounts can yield meaningful and relevant qualitative insights into the working of the economy only in terms of comparisons with other magnitudes. The following remarks are based on a critical examination of three types of juxtapositions:

(1) Interregional comparisons between similar flows or aggregates in Nova Scotia and in other provinces or regions;
(2) Structural comparisons between various flows within the Nova Scotian economy; and
(3) Temporal comparisons between magnitudes of flows and aggregates in Nova Scotia at various times.

The first problem to which Income and Product Accounts have traditionally been applied is an assessment of the general operation of the economy. Gross Regional Product at Market Prices is widely considered to be the best indicator of the overall performance of the economy. In 1965 the GRP in Nova Scotia amounted to $1,378.3 million. Compared to the Canadian GNP for the same year of $52,109 million, it indicates that the share of the economy of Nova Scotia in the national output was only of the order of 2.6 percent.

This is much less than the share of the province in national population, and the significance of the ratio is brought to the fore by reducing both figures to per capita terms. The per capita GRP of Nova Scotia in 1965 amounted to $1,811, compared to the Canadian per capita GNP of $2,662. Hence, in terms of per capita performance the economy of Nova Scotia reached only 68.0 percent of the Canadian average, indicating a serious disparity between the province and the more prosperous parts of the nation.

A pertinent question is whether a long-run trend is discernible and whether it points toward a closing of the existing gap. Between 1950 and 1965 the GRP of Nova Scotia increased from $526.4 million to $1,378.3 million. This represents an average yearly growth of 6.7 percent, which does not compare favorably with the corresponding Canadian average of 7.4 percent.

In order to assess the true significance of the growing disparity, it is necessary to conduct the comparison in terms of constant dollars, even though there is no reason for assuming that fluctuations in the purchasing power of the dollar in Nova Scotia differ from those in the Canadian economy as a whole. In terms of constant (1957) dollars the progress of Nova Scotia, as brought out in Table 3-2, was somewhat less impressive. The growth of GRP amounted to $508 million, increasing from $676 million in 1950 to $1,184 million in 1965 at an average yearly rate of growth of 3.87 percent. Understandably, this again does not compare favorably with the Canadian average yearly rate of increase of GNP during the same period of 4.56 percent.

This gloomy picture is somewhat relieved when comparisons are made on a per capita basis. During the entire post-war period Canada experienced a much faster rate of population growth than Nova Scotia. Consequently, calculated on a per capita basis, the Canadian GNP in real terms rose from $1,686 in 1950 to $2,288 in 1965, or at an average yearly rate of growth of 2.11 percent. During the same time-span the Nova Scotia per capita GRP in real terms increased from $1.059 to $1,556, or at an average yearly rate of growth of 2.65 percent. As a result, the ratio of per capita GRP of Nova Scotia so the Canadian GNP improved somewhat, from 62.8 percent in 1950 to 68.0 percent in 1965. The slight progress in terms of per capita figures may have some positive welfare implications. Yet this fact cannot overshadow the poor performance of the economy as a whole, which did not grow sufficiently to lead to the significant economies of scale upon which its future development depends to a very large extent.

A detailed examination of developments over time yields some additional insights that tend to reinforce the general impression of a lack of real progress. While in terms of average indicators covering the whole period 1950-1965 the total output of the economy, whether measured in current dollars or in real terms, was lagging behind the national with the gap between the two widening, Table 3-2 and Figures 3-3 and 3-4 indicated that the trend was far from persistent. Significantly, Nova Scotia seemed to be catching up with the national economy in 1954-1955 and again in 1960-1961, during periods of relative or absolute slowdown in Canada. In fact, its relative position was better during the 1959-1963 period than at present.

Similarly, in terms of real per capita performance, where Nova Scotia registered overall gains compared to Canada as a whole, the progress was far from steady. In 1961 its real per capita output reached a peak of 72.2 percent of the Canadian figure. From then until 1965, the last year for which GRP estimates are available, it has been declining slowly but perceptibly. The per capita figures are, moreover, slightly deceptive. They hide the significant lack of population growth comparable to that registered in other parts of the country. This in itself is the result of the growing retardation that made the province unattractive to new immigrants.

The gains registered by Nova Scotia during minor recessions in the national

Table 3–2
Gross National Product and Gross Regional Product, 1950–1965 [in constant (1957) dollars]

	Total (in millions of dollars)					Per Capita (in dollars)				
	Gross National Product		Gross Regional Product		Ratio	Gross National Product		Gross Regional Product		Ratio
Year	Absolute	Rate of Growth	Absolute	Rate of Growth	of GRP to GNP	Absolute	Rate of Growth	Absolute	Rate of Growth	of GRP to GNP
	1	*2*	*3*	*4*	*5*	*6*	*7*	*8*	*9*	*10*
1950	23,114		675.7		2.9	1,686		1,059		62.8
1951	24,531	6.1	675.8	0.0	2.8	1,751	3.9	1,051	-0.8	60.0
1952	26,514	8.1	753.6	11.5	2.8	1,837	4.9	1,154	9.8	62.8
1953	27,525	3.8	768.3	1.9	2.8	1,862	1.4	1,159	0.4	62.2
1954	26,714	-2.9	773.1	0.7	2.9	1,758	-5.6	1,149	-0.9	65.3
1955	29,018	8.6	844.2	9.2	2.9	1,846	5.0	1,236	7.6	67.0
1956	31,508	8.6	895.6	6.2	2.8	1,959	-6.1	1,289	4.3	65.8
1957	31,909	1.3	872.0	-2.7	2.7	1,921	-1.9	1,244	-3.5	64.8
1958	32,284	1.2	897.1	2.9	2.8	1,890	-1.6	1,265	1.7	66.9
1959	33,281	3.1	934.3	4.1	2.8	1,904	0.7	1,299	2.7	68.2
1960	34,200	2.8	976.2	4.5	2.9	1,914	0.5	1,343	3.4	70.2
1961	35,081	2.6	1,023.9	4.9	2.9	1,924	0.5	1,389	3.4	72.2
1962	37,429	6.7	1,057.0	3.2	2.8	2,016	4.8	1,419	2.2	70.4
1963	39,352	5.1	1,073.5	1.6	2.7	2,083	3.3	1,420	0.0	68.2
1964	41,886	6.4	1,125.6	4.8	2.7	2,178	4.6	1,481	4.3	68.0
1965	44,773	6.9	1,184.1	5.2	2.6	2,288	5.1	1,556	5.1	68.0

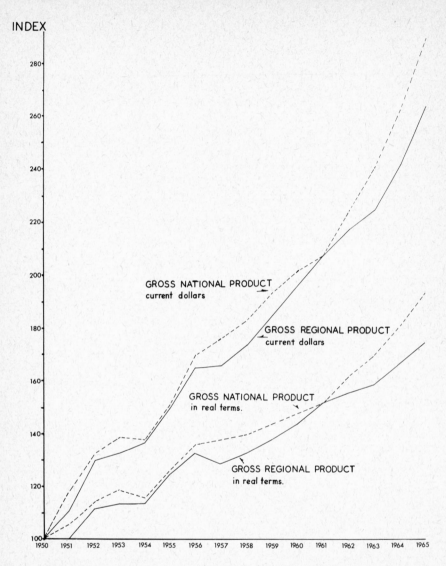

Figure 3–3. Gross National Product and Gross Regional Product, Nova Scotia, 1950–1965.

economy provide meager evidence pointing toward a greater degree of immunity of the regional economy from cyclical fluctuations. It may, perhaps, be due to lower specialization and greater orientation toward services or, more likely, to the importance of federal spending both on the defense establishment and in the form of transfer payments. This hypothesis will be explored in greater depth below.

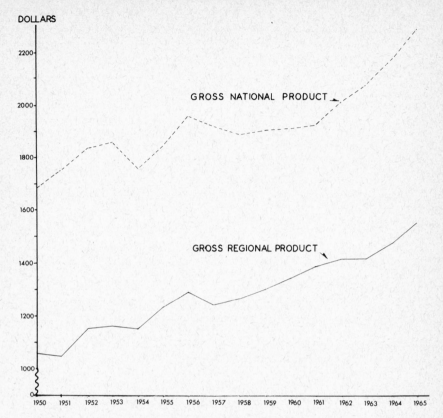

Figure 3-4. Gross National Product and Gross Regional Product, per Capita, 1950-1965.

A study of the other two major indicators of the performance of the regional economy, Net Regional Product and Regional Income, in both total and per capita terms, is illustrated in Figures 3-5 and 3-6. Their movements appear to follow closely those of the GRP. Nonetheless, there is a barely discernible widening of the gaps between them. The slowly growing differences between GRP and NRP indicate an increase in capital consumption allowance, to be expected in view of the buildup of invested capital. The insignificant increase in the difference between NRP and RI implies simply an increase in indirect taxes.

5 Income and Consumption

We now switch our attention from indicators of the general performance of the regional economy to those dealing with welfare. The first to be considered

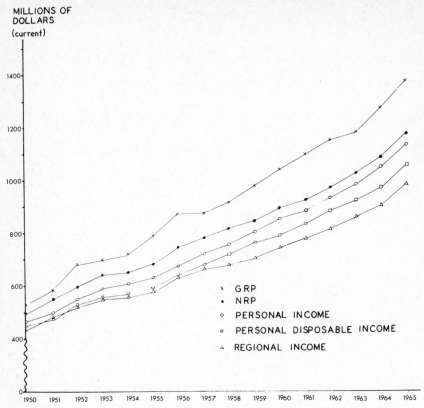

Figure 3-5. Major Aggregates, Nova Scotia, 1950-1965.

is Personal Income since its level comes close to being an index of the well-being of residents of Nova Scotia.[1] In 1965 it amounted to $1,130.0 million, a figure which does not compare favorably with the corresponding national aggregate even on a per capita basis, since the Nova Scotia per capita income of $1,485 reached only 74.70 percent of the Canadian average of $1,988.

Nor does a comparison with the Canadian average fully portray the plight of Nova Scotia. Figure 3-7 illustrates the relative position of Canadian provinces

---

[1]Personal income is, of course, an imperfect measure of welfare for, as The Royal Commission on Canada's Economic Prospects observed in its Final Report, (Queen's Printer, 1957), p. 403, "many people in the Atlantic region would not exchange on any terms their more peaceful way of life and the comparative ease and quiet that goes with it for the noise and bustle and the tenseness which are associated with living in large metropolitan areas."

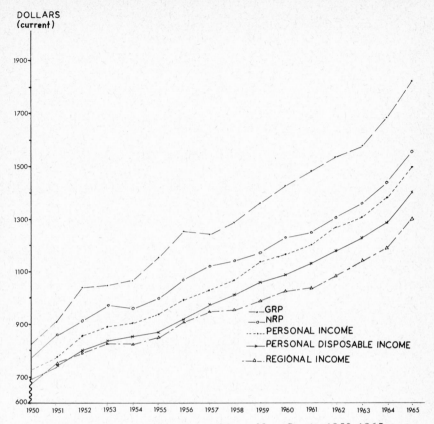

DOLLARS
(current)

1900

1700

1500

1300

1100

900

700

600

1950 1951 1952 1953 1954 1955 1956 1957 1958 1959 1960 1961 1962 1963 1964 1965

GRP
NRP
PERSONAL INCOME
PERSONAL DISPOSABLE INCOME
REGIONAL INCOME

Figure 3–6. Major Aggregates, per Capita, Nova Scotia, 1950–1965.

and territories in terms of per capita personal income. A rather significant break in the middle seems to indicate that the various parts of Canada divide into distinct subgroups. Nova Scotia clearly belongs among the poorer regions although in its subgroup it registered a higher per capita personal income than the other three Atlantic Provinces. Because of their small population, no particular importance can be attached to the fact that Yukon and Northwest Territories ranked above Nova Scotia.

The relative position of Nova Scotia remains unaffected if per capita personal disposable income is considered instead of personal income, although the differences between provinces and territories are somewhat scaled down due to progressive taxation.

Even more revealing are structural comparisons between various aggregates describing the economy of Nova Scotia. A highly significant feature is the fact

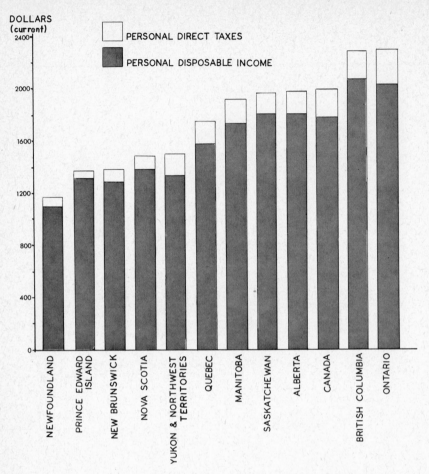

Figure 3-7. Personal Income, per Capita, Canada and Provinces, 1965.

that personal income in Nova Scotia was persistently greater than regional income throughout the period 1950–1965; see Figures 3-5 and 3-6. In 1965 the difference amounted to $146.9 million, with personal income of $1,130.0 million exceeding regional income or Net Regional Product at factor cost of only $983.1 million. The difference of 14.9 percent remained almost unchanged in relative terms during the 16 years covered by the accounts. This phenomenon is typical of depressed regions, where even personal spending often exceeds the earnings accruing to the factors of production owned by local residents. Something similar could be observed on the national scale in the United States and other countries during the great depression. At that time it was largely, though not exclusively, due to increased government transfer payments in the face of mass unemployment and to generally increased government spending related to efforts to boost the economy.

A scrutiny of components of personal income in Nova Scotia indicates that the relative share of income accruing to households in their capacity as owners of factors of production was below the Canadian average.

| | 1965 Percentage of personal income | |
	Nova Scotia	Canada
Wages and salaries	62.4	66.9
Net income of non-farm unincorporated business	9.8	7.4
Interest, dividends, and rental income of persons	9.2	10.6
	81.4	84.9

The overall difference of 3.5 percent is not very large. Curiously enough, the share of net income of non-farm unincorporated business in Nova Scotia exceeds the corresponding Canadian figure. Whether this is related to the smaller average size of Nova Scotia business enterprises or to greater prominence of services is not immediately obvious.

The Income and Product Accounts indicate that in 1965 wages and salaries in Nova Scotia amounted to $705 million or 2.7 percent of the $26,033 million which Canadian employees earned during that year. This is considerably below the 3.8 share of Nova Scotia in total population.

The considerable variations among provinces both in terms of total and of components of personal income are brought to the fore in Table 3-3 and Figure 3-8. In this connection particular interest attaches to wages and salaries, which may be viewed as a crude index of industrialization and of social change. The share of wages and salaries in total personal income in Nova Scotia is relatively high and exceeds that of the agricultural provinces of Manitoba, Alberta, Prince Edward Island, and Saskatchewan. Nova Scotia ranks, however, behind the manufacturing provinces of Ontario and Quebec, as well as behind Newfoundland, British Columbia, and New Brunswick.

Moreover, during the 16 years 1950-1965 covered by the Income and Product Accounts the share of wages and salaries in personal income of residents of Nova Scotia was declining slowly but steadily. This trend is clearly illustrated in Figure 3-9, while Table 3-4 points toward some of the causes. The table shows wages in Nova Scotia as growing during the period 1950-1965 at an average yearly rate of 6.18 percent compared to the Canadian rate of 7.71 percent. The corresponding per capita figures are slightly more favorable to Nova Scotia, which registered over the same period a growth rate of 4.93 percent compared to 5.19 percent for Canada, but it still left Nova Scotia with per

Table 3-3

Components of Personal Income, Per Capita, Canada and Provinces, 1965 (in current dollars)

	Personal Income 1	Personal Disposable Income 2	Wages and Salaries 3	Net Income of Non-farm Unincorporated Business 4	Interest, Dividends, and Net Rental Income of Persons 5
Newfoundland	1,173	1,104	819	104	62
Prince Edward Island	1,370	1,315	648	157	102
New Brunswick	1,376	1,283	880	122	109
Nova Scotia	1,485	1,386	926	145	137
Yukon and Northwest Territories	1,500	1,325	1,350	75	25
Quebec	1,755	1,578	1,221	118	178
Manitoba	1,919	1,738	1,162	166	201
Saskatchewan	1,966	1,809	850	166	178
Alberta	1,976	1,813	1,188	167	187
British Columbia	2,281	2,063	1,584	191	246
Ontario	2,295	2,030	1,609	156	272
Canada	1,988	1,788	1,330	.147	211

Based on: D.B.S., *National Accounts, Income and Expenditure, 1966*, (Catalogue No. 13-201), Tables 30-34.

capita wage earnings of only 69.6 percent of the corresponding Canadian figure. The slower regional growth rates during 1950-1965 illustrated in Figure 3-10 resulted in an almost uninterrupted decline of the ratio of Nova Scotia to Canadian wage earnings.

Per capita wages and salaries provide no information about wage rates or wages and salaries paid per employee or per man-hour. A comparison of those figures reveals that in 1965 an average wage earner in Nova Scotia earned $3,079, or only 81.2 percent of the Canadian average of $3,794. This is somewhat better than the per capita ratio but in other respects even more disturbing.

While from the social and political point of view low wage rates are unambiguously negative, their economic significance is more difficult to assess. Low wage rates may induce or, at least, stimulate outmigration, with its numerous detrimental effects. On the other hand, they may act as a force attracting new industries. The desirability of attracting industries that depend on cheap labor presents a complex problem from the long-run point of view. Moreover, the analytically relevant relationship is not the ratio of total wages and salaries to total number of employees but comparison of the wage rate with the marginal productivity of labor. This comparison can hardly be made on the basis of data derived from Income and Product Accounts alone.

A preliminary step for such an analysis would be to disaggregate the accounts by sectors. Several of the numerically important industries such as coal mining and iron and steel production would have to be eliminated altogether because their levels of employment derive from sociopolitical considerations and are not correlated with levels of output. Consequently, earnings accruing to their employees are partly at least in the nature of transfer payments. This circumstance makes the derivation of production functions and the calculation of marginal productivities of labor in those sectors extremely difficult.

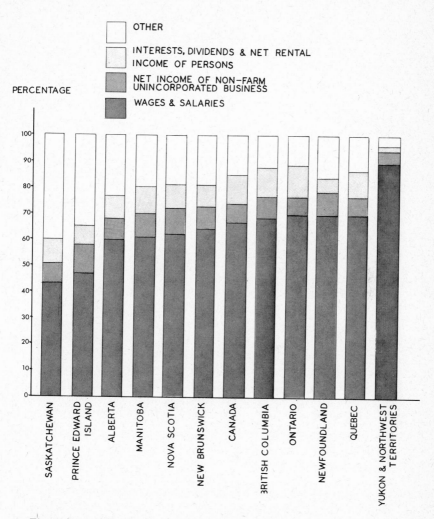

Figure 3-8. Distribution of Personal Income, by Components, Canada and Provinces, 1965.

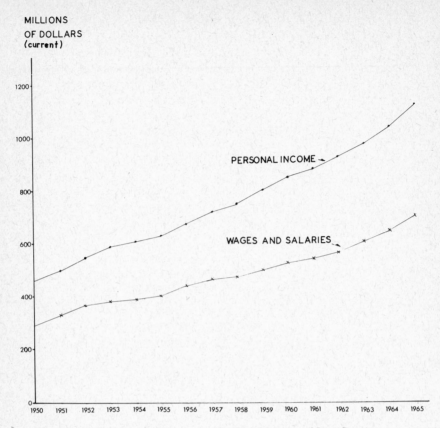

Figure 3-9. Wages and Salaries and Personal Income, Nova Scotia, 1950-1965.

Turning next to an examination of the distribution of personal income in terms of its allocation to various uses, direct personal taxes have to be deducted first, leaving personal disposable income to be apportioned between consumption of goods and services and savings. In 1965, personal disposable income in Nova Scotia amounted to $1,055.0 million, out of which $988.6 million were allocated to consumption and $66.4 million were saved. Thus, of the total disposable personal income 93.7 percent was consumed and 6.3 percent represented savings.

The percentage distribution was very similar to the one derived for Canada as a whole. In 1965 total personal disposable income in Canada amounted to $34,990 million, out of which $32,063 million were consumed and $2,927 million were saved. This means that in relative terms the shares of consumption and savings were 91.6 and 8.4 percent respectively. The slightly higher share of

Table 3-4
Wages and Salaries, Canada and Nova Scotia, 1950–1965 (in current dollars)

Year	Total (in millions of dollars)					Per Capita (in dollars)				
	Canada		Nova Scotia		Ratio of Nova Scotia to Canada	Canada		Nova Scotia		Ratio of Nova Scotia to Canada
	Absolute	Rate of Growth	Absolute	Rate of Growth		Absolute	Rate of Growth	Absolute	Rate of Growth	
	1	2	3	4	5	6	7	8	9	10
1950	8,629		289		3.3	629		453		72.0
1951	10,103	17.1	331	14.5	3.3	721	14.6	515	13.7	71.4
1952	11,208	10.9	367	10.9	3.3	777	7.8	562	9.1	72.3
1953	12,110	8.0	384	4.6	3.2	819	5.4	579	3.0	70.6
1954	12,432	2.7	390	1.6	3.1	818	-0.1	579	0.0	70.8
1955	13,223	6.4	405	3.8	3.1	842	2.9	593	2.4	70.4
1956	14,890	12.6	440	8.6	3.0	926	10.0	633	6.7	68.4
1957	16,018	7.6	465	5.7	2.9	964	4.1	663	4.7	68.8
1958	16,521	3.1	475	2.2	2.9	967	0.3	670	1.1	69.3
1959	17,463	5.7	500	5.3	2.9	999	3.3	695	3.7	69.6
1960	18,245	4.5	528	5.6	2.9	1,021	2.2	726	4.5	71.1
1961	18,996	4.1	542	2.7	2.9	1,042	2.1	735	1.2	70.5
1962	20,233	6.5	572	5.5	2.8	1,090	4.6	767	4.4	70.4
1963	21,547	6.5	605	5.8	2.8	1,140	4.6	800	4.3	70.2
1964	23,433	8.8	647	6.9	2.8	1,218	6.8	851	6.4	69.9
1965	26,033	11.1	705	9.0	2.7	1,330	9.2	926	8.8	69.6

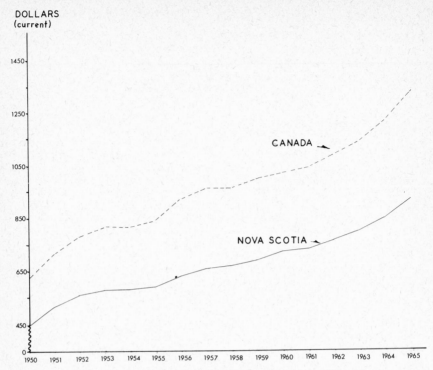

Figure 3–10. Wages and Salaries, per Capita, Canada and Nova Scotia, 1950–1965.

consumption in Nova Scotia is easily understandable as a function of the lower per capita disposable personal income.

Analytically more significant is the excess of consumption over regional income or income accruing to owners of factors of production residing in Nova Scotia. Figure 3–11 reveals that, while there was some oscillation during 1950–1957, beginning in 1958 consumption never declined below the level of regional income. This fact is again typical of depressed regions supported to some extent by transfer payments. Transfer payments, both from government and from nonresidents, were relatively high in Nova Scotia, amounting in 1965 to $198.5 million, or 17.61 percent of personal income, as against $4,546 million, or 11.7 percent of personal income, in Canada as a whole.

6 Investments

Investments are among the most analytically significant components of Gross Regional Product. Their importance derives from their impact upon (1) the short-run equilibrium of the economy, and (2) the productive capacity and long-run growth. The first finds its simplest analytic expression in the relations between savings and investments on the one hand and foreign investments and balance of foreign trade on the other; the second, in the relation between the rates of capital accumulation and growth of labor force and output.

In regional economic studies, with their emphasis on long-run growth, the various studies focusing on investments can be classified into those analyzing forces responsible for the level of investments, and those examining the effects of total regional investments or of their components upon employment and

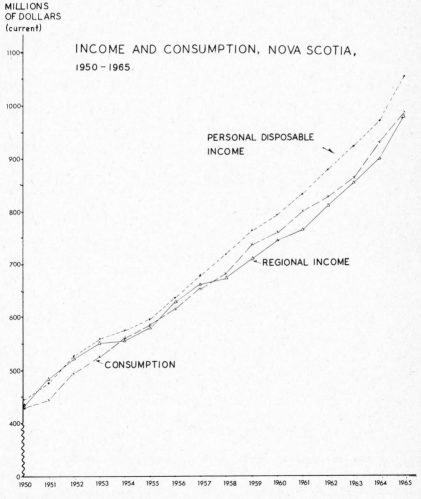

Figure 3-11. Income and Consumption, Nova Scotia, 1950-1965.

Table 3-5
Investments, Nova Scotia, 1950-1965 (in constant (1957) dollars)

Year	Total	Government Investments[a]	Business Gross Fixed Capital Formation		
			Total	Residential Construction	Non-residential Construction	Machinery and Equipment
	1	2	3	4	5	6
		(millions of dollars)				
1950	172.5	52.3	120.2	11.2	54.8	54.8
1951	157.2	41.6	115.6	13.2	41.2	61.4
1952	165.6	53.9	111.7	22.1	33.4	56.1
1953	187.3	65.2	122.1	27.5	33.9	60.7
1954	180.3	60.7	119.6	30.5	34.6	54.4
1955	179.4	43.2	136.2	33.9	44.9	57.4
1956	194.9	53.8	141.1	30.8	49.8	60.6
1957	196.3	62.0	134.3	33.0	40.3	61.0
1958	180.4	51.3	129.1	31.3	39.2	58.4
1959	210.7	58.0	152.7	50.9	44.6	57.0
1960	229.4	65.3	164.1	48.2	57.1	58.5
1961	215.2	55.2	160.0	44.9	51.6	63.3
1962	204.8	52.2	152.6	39.0	56.1	57.3
1963	208.7	47.1	161.6	37.9	59.1	64.5
1964	226.3	42.8	183.5	38.1	59.5	85.9
1965	250.8	64.8	186.0	39.4	60.2	86.5

[a]Implicit price indexes based on D.B.S., *National Accounts, Income and Expenditure, by Quarters,* 1947-1961 (Catalogue No. 13-519), Table 19; and D.B.S., *National Accounts, Income and Expenditure,* 1966 (Catalogue No. 13-201), Table 6. No implicit price indexes are available prior to 1960. A crude extrapolation was used of the form

$$PGI = 6.49 + 0.79 \, PGE;$$

where

PGI = implicit price index of government investments, and
PGE = implicit price index of total government expenditures.

production. In both types of studies ample use is made of comparisons with corresponding national magnitudes.

Investments can be disaggregated according to their character into machinery and equipment, nonresidential construction, residential construction, and government investments. The first two refer largely to productive capacity, whereas the latter form part of the physical infrastructure. In terms of its components investments in Nova Scotia did not grow at a steady rate. Disaggregation helps to pinpoint which investments were responsible for the peaks and troughs in the level of total investments. Table 3-5 and Figure 3-2 show the relative importance of the various components.

For purposes of analysis, either net or gross investments may be used. Net investments provide a measure of the increase in the stock of real capital assets and thus represent additions to the productive capacity of the economy.

Gross investments, on the other hand, include both new and replacement capital. While replacement investments would seem to do no more than maintain intact a given stock of capital with respect to size, quality, and value, financed automatically from depreciation allowances, the distinction between new and replacement investment is, in reality, not a clear-cut one. Because of constant shifts in such factors as technology, prices, and costs investment expenditures even when financed from depreciation reserves rarely represent a simple replacement of capital assets that have become worn out or obsolete. Hence, the usual analytic treatment of investment concentrates on gross rather than net investments.

Another important distinction is between autonomous and induced investments. Induced investments are those which can be determined and explained statistically from within the economy, being usually linked in some way to current output or demand, while autonomous investments are considered to be exogenous, or independent of current operation of the economy. In what follows, investments in Nova Scotia are largely treated as induced.

Attempts to pinpoint and explain statistically the factors influencing investments, even at the national level, are fraught with great difficulties. Precisely what these factors are is by no means as clear as it is for the consumption or production function. Nor is the relationship of an investment function to a production function obvious. In some macroeconomic models an investment function seems to be a substitute for a production function, while in others both an investment and a production function are included as complementary to one another.

The factors which are thought to influence investments fall into three or four categories. First, there are the relationships between the price or cost of assets and the expected future flow of net yields. Irrespective of the specific form of this relation, under appropriate market conditions the rate of return should be equal on the margin to the rate of interest. The main difficulty in practical applications of this relationship is a technical one and pertains to the difficulty of estimating the rate of return on assets.

The second group of variables is related to the demand for the product. In one-factor macroeconomic models demand is often represented by aggregate income. In those models net investments depend upon the aggregate level of income, upon its rate of change, or sometimes on both.

The third group of variables in trying to measure factors affecting investments relates them functionally to profitability of production. In macroeconomic terms these factors may be represented either by the rate of profit on invested capital (rather than by the level of profits) or by the rate of change of profits.

Finally, the three sets of factors may be treated as interrelated.

Application of these concepts to the study of the economy of Nova Scotia has to contend with several complicating circumstances that are in some respects due to the role and importance of government investments. The

efforts of governments to stimulate the provincial economy assume a variety of
forms. Some are directed toward the economic overhead capital and infrastructure, and are of late beginning to assume sizable dimensions. Analytically
more significant is the fact that business investments in Nova Scotia depend to
a considerable extent upon overt or covert government subsidies and are not
necessarily a function of economic considerations alone.

Investments in Nova Scotia have been increasing at a rapid rate. Table 3-5
and Figure 3-12 show yearly business gross fixed capital formation rising in
terms of constant (1957) dollars from $120.2 million in 1950 to $186.0
million in 1965, while during the same period total capital outlays including
government investments increased from $172.4 million to $250.8 million.

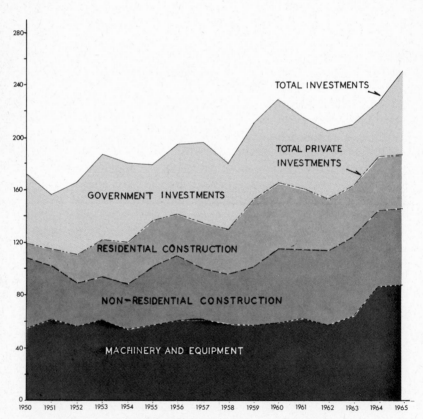

Figure 3-12. Investments, by Type, Nova Scotia, 1950-1965.

Total investments also show a steady increase over time, with the level of government investments through the 1950-1965 period significantly high. While the trend seems to be generally linear, there are two interesting peaks, one during the 1956-1957 period and the second in 1960. It is difficult to establish whether the increase in the volume of investments that started in 1964 represents a radical change in the rate of growth of investments or whether it is simply due to yet another developing peak. The 1960 peak in total investments seems to have been due largely to increased government investments and investments in nonresidential construction. The increase in nonresidential construction was followed in 1961 by increased outlays on machinery and equipment. The developing 1965 peak seems to be due to simultaneous increase in investments in machinery and equipment and government investment.

Relating a complex phenomenon such as investments in a highly aggregate form to one or two causal factors at a time involves a severe and hardly acceptable simplification of reality. Hence, the following remarks are in the nature of a preliminary exploration. A deeper analysis based on a broader data basis and more rigorous econometric formulation is presented later. Attempts at statistical explanation of investments are rendered considerably more difficult in Nova Scotia because simple regression techniques are likely to yield spurious results due to the presence of time trends in several of the series examined.[m]

Of the several factors that may possibly cause fluctuations in the level of investments, usually the first to be attacked are anticipated yields of assets and profitability of production, but they cannot be examined on the basis of data available from Income and Product Accounts alone. Some of these factors are not directly obtainable from the accounts in their present aggregate format, while the accuracy of quantities derived as differences between estimates of much larger magnitudes is open to doubt.

The second set of factors which might explain fluctuations in gross business capital formation is demand for commodities and services produced with their help. In the absence of better and more detailed data, GRP is often taken as an index of aggregate demand. It is usual to conduct such analysis in terms of constant dollars, thus eliminating the effects of fluctuations in purchasing power of the money. Figure 3-13 indicates the erratic and inconclusive nature of this relationship.[n]

---

[m]In the case of private investments a strong linear trend is present, of the form

$$I_p = 1.43.2 + 4.63t; \quad r = .94; \quad s_r = .09; \quad \text{Student's } t = 10.4;$$

where
I_p = business gross fixed capital formation and t = time.

[n]Nonetheless, a linear two-variable least squares regression of the form

$$I_p = 16.07 + .14 \text{ (GRP)}; \quad r = .95; \quad s_r = .08; \quad t = 11.88;$$

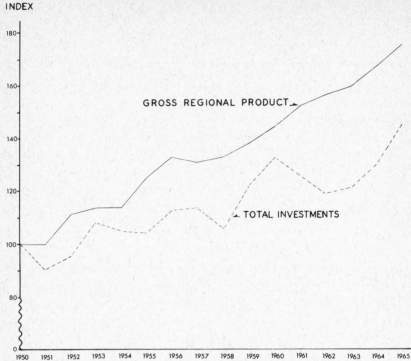

Figure 3-13. Gross Regional Product and Total Investments, Nova Scotia, 1950-1965.

The relationship between business gross fixed capital formation and private savings is considered fundamental to the internal equilibrium of the national economy. The conceptual basis of this approach in the case of a small regional economy is questionable. It is not at all certain that regional industries have to depend upon local private savings for their sources of financing. It may well be that under modern conditions of high mobility of investment capital, productive investments in a region forming a small part of the national economy simply follow the general investment trends modified by factors related to local attractiveness. Hence, a relevant study would perhaps consider locational factors

---

is statistically significant although the high correlation is probably spurious, partly due to the presence of strong time trends in both series. The more meaningful analysis in terms of first differences leads in Nova Scotia to statistically insignificant results. Assuming a constant marginal capital-output ratio $\Delta K/\Delta Y = k$ involves the familar relationship $\Delta K = I = k\Delta Y$, or $I_t = k(Y_t - Y_{t-1})$. Simple least squares regressions fitted to those data without lags and with a one year lag yielded insignificant results.

$$I_{p(t)} = 135.89 + .26 (\text{ GRP})_{(t)}; \quad r = .31; \quad s_r = .26; \quad t = 1.19;$$
$$I_{p(t)} = 141.34 + .17 (\text{ GRP})_{(t-1)}; \quad r = .21; \quad s_r = .28; \quad t = .75;$$

Table 3-6
Savings and Investments, Nova Scotia, 1950-1965 (in current dollars)

Year	Personal Net Saving 1	Business Gross Saving 2	Total Private Saving 3	Business Gross Fixed Capital Formation 4	Local Savings as Percentage of Private Investments 5
			(millions of dollars)		
1950	13.4	75.6	89.0	88.6	100.45
1951	33.0	68.2	101.2	96.6	104.76
1952	30.9	64.2	95.1	96.6	98.45
1953	31.6	70.7	102.3	108.4	94.37
1954	15.0	70.6	85.6	107.0	80.00
1955	8.1	88.0	96.1	124.9	76.94
1956	21.0	96.3	117.3	136.3	86.06
1957	24.0	92.1	116.1	134.3	86.45
1958	35.7	80.2	115.9	131.9	87.87
1959	27.0	104.4	131.4	160.5	81.87
1960	31.2	119.1	150.3	176.2	85.30
1961	31.1	124.4	155.5	173.3	89.73
1962	50.5	134.4	184.9	169.8	108.89
1963	58.1	146.3	204.4	185.3	110.31
1964	42.3	160.9	203.2	219.6	92.53
1965	66.4	164.0	230.4	232.1	99.27

affecting various industries, but this is clearly beyond the scope of simple analysis of data derived from Income and Product Accounts.

However that may be, Table 3-6 and Figure 3-14 bear witness to the fact that total private savings and business gross fixed capital formation were closely balanced in Nova Scotia throughout the period 1950-1965. The relevant linear correlations were statistically highly significant.

The second set of factors to be examined are the effects of investments upon the productive capacity of the Nova Scotian economy and its rate of growth (particulary as compared to the expansion of the labor force). They are not amenable to simple analysis without considering simultaneously such important and closely related phenomena as formation of urban-industrial complexes or growth poles, and creation of economic overhead capital and infrastructure. Both are capable, in time, of becoming an attractive force for new investments, thus changing the whole economic structure of the region. But while the importance of these phenomena is well recognized, they are most difficult to tackle and so far defy any rigorous analysis.

A simple comparison between the growth path of investments and GRP conducted in real terms (see Figure 3-13) reveals that despite the steady growth of investments the real GRP has been expanding more rapidly. Moreover,

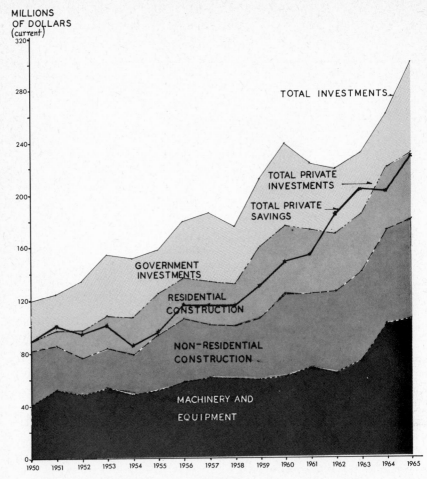

Figure 3-14. Investments and Savings, Nova Scotia, 1950–1965.

peaks and troughs in investments do not seem to be accompanied or followed by similar changes in the GRP.

Comparisons with developments in the national economy carried out in Table 3-7 and Figure 3-15 bring to the fore the interesting fact that Canada as a whole seems to invest a higher proportion of its resources than Nova Scotia. In 1965 total business gross fixed capital formation (in terms of 1957 dollars) amounted in Nova Scotia to $186.0 million, representing 15.7 percent of GRP. It does not compare favorably with the Canadian figure $8,534 million, which represented 19.1 percent of GNP. To be noted is the fact that in Canada

Table 3-7
Business Gross Fixed Capital Formation, Canada and Nova Scotia, 1950–1965 [in constant (1957) dollars]

Year	Canada			Nova Scotia		
	Business Gross Fixed Capital Formation 1	Gross National Product 2	Business Gross Fixed Capital Formation as Percentage of GNP 3	Business Gross Fixed Capital Formation 4	Gross Regional Product 5	Business Gross Fixed Capital Formation as Percentage of GRP 6
	(millions of dollars)		(%)	(millions of dollars)		(%)
1950	4,543	23,114	19.7	120.2	675.7	17.8
1951	4,736	24,531	19.3	115.6	675.8	17.1
1952	5,146	26,514	19.4	111.7	753.6	14.8
1953	5,628	27,525	20.4	122.1	768.3	15.9
1954	5,340	26,714	20.0	119.6	773.1	15.5
1955	5,682	29,018	19.6	136.2	844.2	16.1
1956	7,014	31,508	22.3	141.1	895.6	15.8
1957	7,335	31,909	23.0	134.3	872.0	15.4
1958	6,825	32,284	21.1	129.1	897.1	14.4
1959	6,562	33,281	19.7	152.7	934.3	16.3
1960	6,231	34,200	18.2	164.1	976.2	16.8
1961	6,125	35,081	17.5	160.0	1,023.9	15.6
1962	6,254	37,429	16.7	152.6	1,057.0	14.4
1963	6,618	39,352	16.8	161.6	1,073.5	15.1
1964	7,606	41,886	18.2	183.5	1,125.6	16.3
1965	8,534	44,773	19.1	186.0	1,184.1	15.7

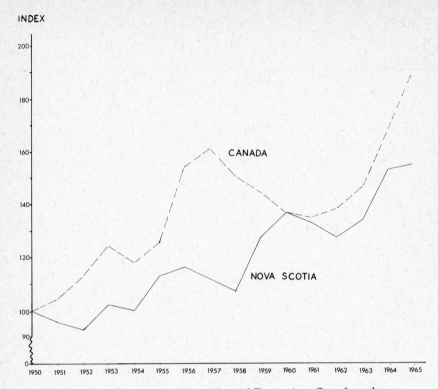

Figure 3-15. Business Gross Fixed Capital Formation, Canada and Nova Scotia, 1950-1965.

but not in Nova Scotia relative increases in investments exceeded at times the rate of increase of GNP. (see Figure 3-16). Even on a per capita basis investments in Nova Scotia, including government investments, were below the Canadian average, amounting in 1965 to $330 as against $542 in Canada as a whole. Admittedly, this may be a result of lower per capita income, but it does not auger well for the future.

7 Demand Analysis

An essential characteristic of Keynesian economics from the simple multiplier to the complete model of short-run equilibrium is that income determination is based firmly on aggregate demand defined by the flow conditions of the product market. Extensions of this model to long-run equilibrium and its applications to the theory of growth of industrialized nations all stress the central role of effective demand.

There are four main components of aggregate demand: consumption by households, investments, foreign trade, and government spending. Thus, aggregate demand can be described symbolically by the basic accounting identity distributing the gross regional product.

$$Y \equiv C + I + G + (E - M);$$

where

Y = GRP (gross regional product),

C = consumption of goods and services by households,

I = total private and government investments,

G = exhaustive current government expenditures,

E = exports of goods and services,

M = imports of goods and services.

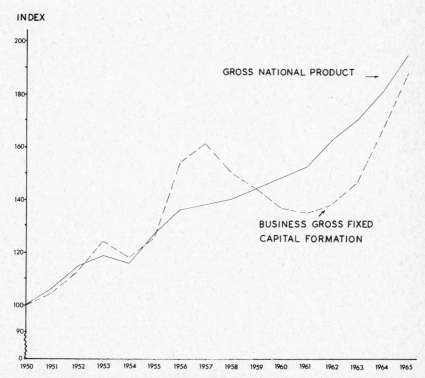

Figure 3-16. Business Gross Fixed Capital Formation and Gross National Product, Canada, 1950-1965.

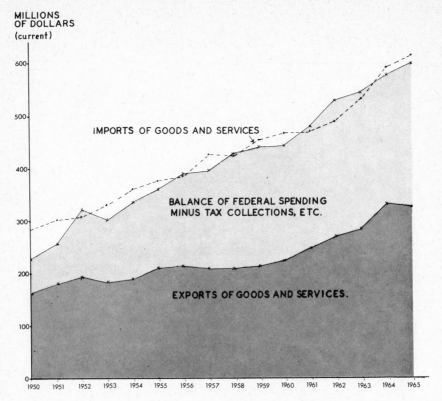

Figure 3-17. Balance of Trade, Nova Scotia, 1950-1965.

Of the four, consumption of goods and services by households forms easily the largest component and is widely used as the main endogenous variable in simple multipliers, but foreign trade has traditionally formed the basis of many regional models. Hence, it might be appropriate to analyze the foreign trade of Nova Scotia first.

In 1965 exports of goods and services from Nova Scotia amounted to $325.2 million, or 23.59 percent of GRP, with imports reaching $615.8 million, or 44.68 percent GRP. These are substantial magnitudes but, given the small size of the regional economy, they appear rather low. The relatively low exports are probably a result of the generally low volume of production.

Far more significant is the size of the trade deficit. In 1965 it amounted to $290.6 million, or 21.09 percent of GRP. Figure 3-17 indicates that between 1950 and 1965 the gap between imports and exports has been steadily widening both in absolute and in relative terms.

Foreign trade deficits may or may not be accompanied by an unfavorable balance of payments. The divergence between the balance of foreign trade and balance of payments may be substantial, due mainly though not exclusively to the following three factors, or a combination of them:

(1) Investments made in the area by nonresidents;
(2) Growth of indebtedness of the region toward nonresidents;
(3) Selling out of fixed assets by residents.

In Nova Scotia not only does the size of the foreign trade deficit exceed total investment made in the region, but another conspicuous factor has to be considered. Throughout the period 1950–1965 the huge gap between imports and exports was covered by the excess of federal government spending over taxes collected in the region, bringing the foreign trade of Nova Scotia into balance.

In 1965 the federal government deficit on transactions relating to Income and Product Accounts amounted to $274.6 million. The size of this item and the role which it plays in balancing the regional economy warrants a closer scrutiny. Part of it is undoubtedly due to transfer payments. In recent years an increasing share may originate in various expenditures connected with efforts to boost the local economy. Yet another substantial component is formed by exhaustive spending of the federal government, part of which is directly or indirectly related to the military establishment in Nova Scotia. Whether the very existence and size of the military base is dictated by defense considerations or whether and to what extent it has a welfare character or forms part of federal-provincial compromises is difficult to determine, let alone to quantify.

Before turning to an examination of the stability of these flows over time and to their role in the economy of the province, let us briefly consider internal consumption. Two features of household consumption in Nova Scotia have already been mentioned; namely, the low per capita personal income and, related to it, the relatively high propensity to consume. The low per capita personal income is by far the more important of the two, with the result that per capita consumption in Nova Scotia amounted in 1965 to only $1,299, lagging considerably behind the corresponding Canadian average of $1,638.

It is customary to relate household consumption to income, using for this purpose the notion of average propensity to consume (c). $c = C/Y$.[o]

With the help of this ratio the basic product identity can now be transformed into:

$$Y = cY + I + G + (E - M); \text{ or}$$

---

[o]GRP rather than personal income is used here in order to avoid the necessity of introducing into the equation transfer payments, retained earnings, capital consumption allowances, etc.

$$Y = \left(\frac{1}{1 - c} \right) [I + G + (E - M)];$$

where $1/(1 - c)$ is the average demand multiplier. It indicates the impact upon total output or income of exogenous changes in the remaining components of aggregate demand.

In 1965 the average propensity to consume in Nova Scotia amounted to $c = .7173$, yielding a value of the average demand multiplier $1/(1 - c) = 3.5373$. The corresponding values for Canada as a whole were $c = .6153$ and $1/(1 - c) = 2.5994$.

The difference between the rather high value of the multiplier in Nova Scotia compared to that in Canada as a whole is easily explained by the much higher propensity to consume in Nova Scotia.

Any analytic uses of this concept and the very validity of the approach depend obviously upon the stability of the multiplier. Table 3-8 and Figure 3-18

Table 3-8
Average and Marginal Propensities to Consume,[a] Canada and Nova Scotia, 1950-1965

Year	Canada		Nova Scotia	
	Average Propensity to Consume 1	Marginal Propensity to Consume 2	Average Propensity to Consume 3	Marginal Propensity to Consume 4
1950	0.67		0.82	
1951	0.64	0.45	0.76	0.24
1952	0.62	0.47	0.72	0.50
1953	0.62	0.79	0.75	1.91
1954	0.65	−3.91	0.78	1.57
1955	0.64	0.54	0.74	0.39
1956	0.62	0.42	0.71	0.37
1957	0.63	0.94	0.75	1.67
1958	0.65	1.19	0.75	0.65
1959	0.65	0.66	0.76	0.88
1960	0.65	0.70	0.74	0.40
1961	0.65	0.78	0.73	0.68
1962	0.64	0.47	0.72	0.47
1963	0.63	0.55	0.73	1.03
1964	0.63	0.55	0.73	0.73
1965	0.62	0.51	0.72	0.56

[a]Average propensity to consume is defined as the ratio of consumer purchases of goods and services to gross product, and marginal propensity to consume by the ratio of increments in consumer purchases of goods and services to increments in gross product.

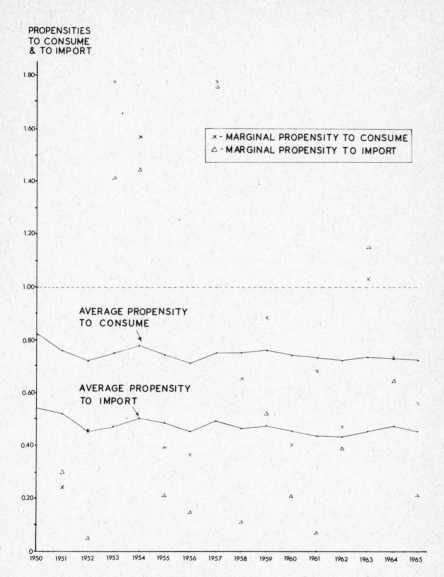

Figure 3–18. Average and Marginal Propensities to Consume and to Import, Nova Scotia, 1950–1965.

illustrate the fact that the average propensity to consume has been remarkably stable over the period 1950–1965.

Taken by itself, however, this multiplier may be slightly misleading. It fails to account for important "leakages" due to the extreme "openness" of Nova Scotia economy. Hence, a second multiplier taking into account the effects of imports has been derived.[15] For this purpose the average propensity to import (m) has been defined as

$$m = \frac{M}{Y};$$

Inserting this into the basic identity yields

$$Y = cY - mY + I + G + E;$$

or

$$Y = \left(\frac{1}{1 - c + m} \right)(I + G + E);$$

where $1/(1 - c + m)$ is the modified multiplier.

Its value in Nova Scotia in 1965 was 1.37 compared to 1.61 in Canada as a whole. The heavy dependence of Nova Scotia upon imports comes to the fore here, resulting in a considerably smaller value of this important indicator.

The size of the multiplier indicates the effects of a unit change in the remaining elements of aggregate demand (investments, exhaustive current government spending, and exports) upon the level of operation or GRP of the Nova Scotian economy. Its relatively low value simply means that a considerable part of the anticipated multiplier effects of new investments or heavy government spending may be felt in other parts of Canada or even abroad. This finding has obvious, though not unexpected, implications for efforts to boost the local economy with the help of government spending or induced business investments.

The conclusion is again based on the assumption that average propensities both to consume and to import will remain stable over time. Table 3–9 seems to bear it out, but whether the average propensity to import, and consequently the multiplier, would remain stable in case of major structural breaks in the regional economy such as might be caused by important new investments, introduction of new industries, import substitution, or formation of an industrial complex, is open to doubt. Moreover, the value of the multiplier might also fluctuate among the various components of aggregate demand divided into investments, government spending, and exports. It is difficult to imagine that the average propensity to import is the same in case of current government spending, production for export, and investments involving purchase of plant and machinery.

Table 3-9
Demand Multipliers,[a] Canada and Nova Scotia, 1950-1965

	Canada			Nova Scotia		
Year	Average Propensity to Consume (c) 1	Average Propensity to Import (m) 2	Demand Multiplier = 1/(1-c + m) 3	Average Propensity to Consume (c) 4	Average Propensity to Import (m) 5	Demand Multiplier = 1/(1-c + m) 6
1950	0.67	0.25	1.72	0.82	0.54	1.39
1951	0.64	0.27	1.59	0.76	0.52	1.32
1952	0.62	0.23	1.64	0.72	0.45	1.37
1953	0.62	0.23	1.64	0.75	0.47	1.39
1954	0.65	0.22	1.75	0.78	0.50	1.39
1955	0.64	0.24	1.67	0.74	0.48	1.35
1956	0.62	0.25	1.59	0.71	0.45	1.35
1957	0.63	0.24	1.64	0.75	0.49	1.35
1958	0.65	0.23	1.72	0.75	0.46	1.41
1959	0.65	0.23	1.72	0.76	0.47	1.41
1960	0.65	0.23	1.72	0.74	0.45	1.41
1961	0.65	0.23	1.72	0.73	0.43	1.43
1962	0.64	0.22	1.72	0.72	0.43	1.41
1963	0.63	0.22	1.69	0.73	0.45	1.39
1964	0.63	0.23	1.67	0.73	0.47	1.35
1965	0.62	0.24	1.61	0.72	0.45	1.37
Average	0.64	0.24	1.68	0.74	0.47	1.38

[a]Average propensity to consume is defined as the ratio of consumer purchases of goods and services to gross product, and average propensity to import by the ratio of imports to gross product.

Analytically, far greater importance would attach to marginal multipliers of the form

$$\Delta Y = \frac{1}{1 - \bar{c} + \bar{m}} \ \Delta(I + G + E);$$

where

$$\bar{c} \ = \ \frac{\partial C}{\partial Y} = \text{marginal propensity to consume}$$

$$\bar{m} \ = \ \frac{\partial M}{\partial Y} = \text{marginal propensity to import.}$$

An examination of the marginal propensities to consume and to import recorded in Tables 3-8 and 3-9 and Figure 3-18 show very great fluctuations. The magnitude and persistence of these fluctuations makes their application in order to derive the multiplier useless. These fluctuations may be only partly related to real causes. The greater part is probably simply due to the fact that marginal propensities are based on differences between successive estimates of GRP, consumption, and imports as recorded in the Income and Product Accounts. The total estimates contained errors commensurate with the magnitudes of the quantitites involved and hence acceptable, but these errors become overwhelming when referred to the much smaller yearly changes.

As far as average multipliers are concerned another possible refinement would consist in splitting government expenditures into those which can be manipulated in order to induce regional development and those more or less rigidly tied to various given factors. Should it prove possible to estimate this second part as a constant function of GRP, an improved multiplier could be introduced, perhaps of the form

$$Y = \frac{1}{1 - c + m - g_c} (I + G_d + E);$$

$$g_c = \frac{G_c}{Y};$$

where

g_c = average propensity of ordinary government expenditures,

G_c = ordinary government expenditures,

G_d = government expenditures aimed at regional development.

Because of the size of government expenditures, this would by itself greatly improve estimates of the impact of the remaining exogenously determined elements of aggregate demands. The existing data basis and format of Income and Product Accounts does not allow implementation of such an improved multiplier.

8 Subregional Accounts

The attempt to develop Income and Product Accounts for subprovincial units such as counties or groups of counties is novel and difficult. The general paucity of data is aggravated by the lack, even for the census year 1961, of several benchmarks of fundamental importance for constructing provincial accounts. Hence, an analysis and conclusions based on this somewhat shaky numerical foundation must of necessity be considered tentative. The significance of the attempt resides in the fact that a province, even of the size of Nova Scotia, is too large to be homogeneous enough for purposes of analysis and planning, while important policy decisions with far-reaching effects for the whole province are often taken with a view of eliminating intraregional disparities.

A rigorous delineation of meaningful regions for planning of regional policies represents a major research effort in its own right. In the absence of such a study for Nova Scotia, subprovincial Income and Product Accounts have been developed for five subregions into which the eighteen counties of the province have been divided. Each of these subregions, although far from ideal, displays characteristics of its own sufficiently at variance with the remaining portions of the province to allow it to be considered as a unit.[P]

The first subregion covers Cape Breton Island, which is a more or less distinct geographic entity with its own problems and a past history of independent administrative and political existence. The island consists of four counties: Inverness, Victoria, Cape Breton, and Richmond. Besides the cluster of towns around Sydney with the problematic coal-mining and primary iron and steel center located in their midst, it includes a picturesque coastline and the rural countryside.

The second subregion, Northern Nova Scotia, is composed of five counties: Cumberland, Colchester, Pictou, Antigonish, and Guysborough. It is poor and declining although the recent industrial developments in the Canso Strait area seem to provide a faint glimmer of hope.

The third subregion is Halifax County, at the center of which are located the two cities of Halifax and Dartmouth and the magnificent Halifax harbor. It is the only really prosperous part of the province and differs sharply in many ways from other parts of Nova Scotia.

[P]The various criteria which, either singly or in combination, may be used in order to define regions can be grouped into several broad categories:

(1) Physical features either natural or artifacts,
(2) Sociodemographic factors,
(3) Economic factors,
(4) Political factors.

Various techniques may be used in order to define a region if more than one criterion is applied. They range all the way from simple, common-sense tracing of boundaries to very sophisticated mathematical techniques, among which some types of multivariate analyses are often applied.

The selection of appropriate criteria to be used depends ordinarily upon the purpose of the study. In the case of regional Income and Product Accounts, which may have to fulfill several, perhaps conflicting, demands, the task becomes complex. The units selected would have to be small enough to be free of marked socioeconomic differences among parts, enabling a region to be treated as an entity, yet not so small as to make many economic concepts and aggregates meaningless. For purposes of regional planning and analysis the size should ideally be small enough so that a change of employment within the region does not necessitate a change of residence involving heavy private and public investments in housing and infrastructure. Another reason for selecting small, relatively stable over time, basic units for constructing social accounts is the inability to predict all their present and future analytic uses. Hence, the need for units capable of being combined into regions suitable for the particular purpose at hand.

Table 3-10
Population, By Subregions and Counties, Nova Scotia, 1961

Subregion	Population	
Cape Breton Island	169,865	
Inverness		18,718
Victoria		8,266
Cape Breton		131,507
Richmond		11,374
Northern Nova Scotia	143,616	
Cumberland		37,767
Colchester		34,307
Pictou		43,908
Antigonish		14,360
Guysborough		13,274
Halifax County	225,723	
Halifax		225,723
Annapolis Valley	90,840	
Hants		26,444
Kings		41,747
Annapolis		22,649
Southern Nova Scotia	106,963	
Digby		20,216
Yarmouth		23,386
Shelburne		15,208
Queens		13,155
Lunenburg		34,998
Nova Scotia	737,007	

Source: D.B.S., *1966 Census of Canada, Population*, (Catalogue No. 92-603), Table 9.

The fourth subregion, Annapolis Valley, comprises three counties: Hants, Kings, and Annapolis. Some of the best agricultural land in the province is to be found in this area, which enjoys a fairly prosperous agriculture.

The fifth and last subregion is Southern Nova Scotia, composed of five counties: Digby, Yarmouth, Shelburne, Queens, and Lunenburg. Despite a few small urban agglomerations, it has the dubious distinction of being the laggard among the subregions of a generally depressed province.

Table 3-10 shows the distribution of population among the five subregions. The distribution of Gross Regional Product among them deviates from the population distribution in several respects and amply confirms the existence of important regional disparities.

Among the five subregions the dominant position of the Halifax-Dartmouth metropolitan area is well established and is vindicated by the fact that in 1961 Halifax County accounted for 48.3 percent of the total Nova Scotian GRP even though it accounted for only 30 percent of the population. Considering that

Halifax County, outside of Halifax-Dartmouth, is little more than the area of its metropolitan dominance, one is led to conclude that Halifax-Dartmouth represents the economic heart of the province. Its position and prosperity are at least partly due to the concentration of noncivilian activities. In addition to the Naval Station for Atlantic Command, Halifax-Dartmouth metropolitan area also garrisons substantial army and air force units. A fairly active harbor, government services connected with its role as a provincial capital, and the fact that it is a minor university center add some vitality to the area. Small as it is, the twin city is easily the largest urban agglomeration east of Quebec City. Its relative well-being and buoyancy in the midst of the general decline depends heavily upon defense spending, which may be facing an uncertain future and which, at any rate, makes the economy vulnerable to forces and decisions beyond local control.

Cape Breton Island contains the only other urban-industrial agglomeration of any consequence. It, however, is ridden with difficult-to-solve socioeconomic problems. The local economy is based to an alarming extent on an old, under-invested, and by now largely written-off steel mill and no-longer-competitive coal mines in the process of being phased out. The lack of any sound foundation for continued existence is bound to convey a gloomy picture. The share of Cape Breton Island in the provincial GRP of only 16.8 percent is in keeping with its economically undistinguished position. This statistic by itself does not reflect the full seriousness of the situation of the Sydney center, which may be threatened with economic collapse in the not far distant future. Annapolis Valley represents an entirely different socioeconomic landscape, with its thriving agriculture and fruit growing. Two other subregions, Northern Nova Scotia and Southern Nova Scotia, comprising between them the greater part of the land area of the province and the hard core of agricultural decline, represent one of the problem areas of Canada. The relative share of the five subregions in the provincial economy in terms of GRP is illustrated in Figure 3-19.

A study of aggregates dealing with incomes accruing to inhabitants of the five subregions is equally revealing because of some striking differences that it brings to light. Not unexpectedly, it turns out that Halifax County, with 1961 per capita personal income of $1,583, is far ahead of the Nova Scotia average of $1,197. In fact, in that year it approached, without quite reaching it, the national average. Halifax metropolitan area registered an even higher per capita personal income, comparing faborably not only with the Canadian but also with the urban average.

On the other hand, the depressed position of the industrial cluster on Cape Breton Island can be read from the fact that per capita personal income on Cape Breton Island, comprising, it is true, some very poor agricultural territory, stood at a paltry $1,024. Given the overwhelming weight of the population of Cape Breton among the four Cape Breton Island counties, the conclusion to be drawn is that even the urban centers there did not enjoy a level of prosperity reached elsewhere.

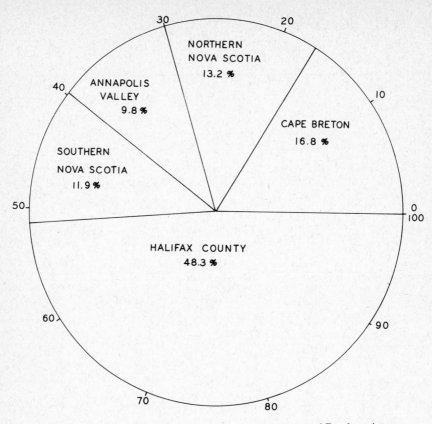

Figure 3-19. Percentage Distribution of Gross Regional Product Among Subregions, Nova Scotia, 1961.

The Annapolis Valley per capita personal income was very close to the Nova Scotian average and fractionally higher than the corresponding Cape Breton Island figure.

Both Northern and Southern Nova Scotia registered in 1961 per capita incomes below $1,000, placing them among the poorest areas of Canada. The income levels of the residents were almost as low as the Prince Edward Island and Newfoundland averages, which are the lowest in the nation. These figures are concisely presented in Table 3-11.

A scrutiny of the main components of personal income reveals that wages and salaries were relatively high in two of the five subregions into which Nova Scotia has been divided. Understandably Halifax County, with its concentration of metropolitan functions, and Cape Breton Island, with its mining and manufacturing, differed sharply from the rest of the province. In Southern Nova Scotia wage incomes did not even contribute half of total personal incomes. The prominence of incomes derived from non-farm unincorporated business activities

Table 3-11

Personal Income, By Subregions, Nova Scotia, 1961

Subregion	Personal Income 1	Per Capita Income 2	Per Capita Income as Percentage of Nova Scotia Per Capita Income 3
	$ million	$	%
Cape Breton Island	174.0	1,024	85.5
Northern Nova Scotia	142.4	992	82.9
Halifax County	357.3	1,583	132.2
Annapolis Valley	104.5	1,150	96.1
Southern Nova Scotia	103.8	970	81.0

does not fully explain the very low share of wages and salaries. The real causes are to be found in agricultural incomes accruing to subsistence farmers and, perhaps more important, in unilateral transfers. The situation is well illustrated in Figure 3-20

The relationship between regional income, personal income, and consumption provided some significant insights for the province as a whole. In Figure 3-21 this is analyzed on a subregional basis. It turns out that in Halifax County not only were all three aggregates the highest in Nova Scotia but their relative magnitudes conformed to the national pattern. In the remaining subregions, with the exception of Annapolis Valley, consumptions exceeded regional income. Hence, the phenomenon of consumption exceeding income accruing to factors of production, characteristic of the Nova Scotian economy as a whole, is actually due to its persistence in three of the five subregions; namely, Cape Breton Island, Northern Nova Scotia, and Southern Nova Scotia. In Cape Breton Island a contributing factor is the fact that the subregion combines two very heterogeneous parts: a declining and impoverished manufacturing center and an agricultural countryside comprising a fairly substantial segment of subsistence agriculture and fishing.

The relative health of the economy of Halifax County manifests itself not only in the fact that it is the only subregion in Nova Scotia with regional income exceeding consumption but also in the relative size of regional and personal incomes. While even here personal income exceeds regional income, the difference is relatively much smaller than in Nova Scotia as a whole.

9 Some Methodological Issues

An accounts system must be able to handle transactors in all aspects of their economic activities as producers, consumers, and accumulators or investors. The necessity to reduce the number and variety of transactors and transactions

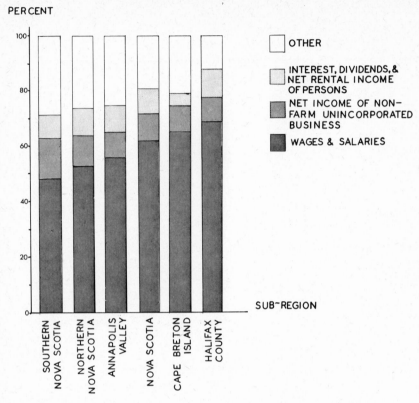

Figure 3-20. Percentage Distribution of Personal Income, by Components and by Subregions, Nova Scotia, 1961.

to manageable and meaningful dimensions makes grouping unavoidable, but the classification adopted must single out relevant transactions and be able to meet various analytic demands with which the accounts may be faced.

What conclusions can be drawn from the modest attempts at analytic interpretation of the Income and Product Accounts of Nova Scotia so far discussed?

The overriding conclusion is that they are too aggregate to be applicable to models dealing with regional growth and development. A disaggregation increasing the number of sectors would, however, of necessity involve first of all a change in format of the accounts and a transition to the matrix form. More specific changes of a substantial nature are related to the various accounts of which the present system is composed.

The first sector, Personal Income and Expenditure Account, is analytically most significant and numerically so large that it should be split into several groups of transactions affecting households in their capacity as consumers and as owners of factors of production. The numerous and heterogeneous transactors, both physical and institutional, included in this sector can hardly be expected to

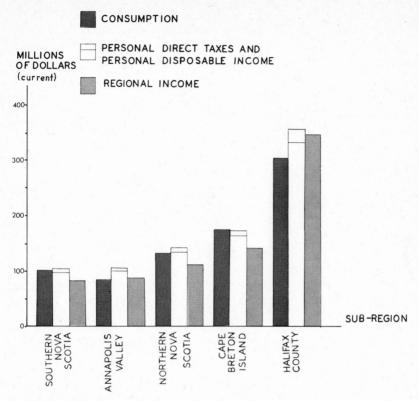

Figure 3-21. Regional Income, Personal Income, and Consumption, by Subregions, Nova Scotia, 1961.

react uniformly to changing situations, making the derivation of stable behavioral relations extremely difficult. As a first step, a disaggregation according to such criteria as level of income, profession of head of household, or position in life cycle might prove meaningful for several types of analyses. Even more important would be to single out and exclude from this sector transactions pertaining to nonprofit organizations.

The following two sectors, Local Governments Revenue and Expenditure Account, and Local Operations of Nonlocal Governments Account, should be reorganized. In the light of analytic experiences available, the splitting of government transactions relating to Income and Product Accounts between these two sectors proved to be virtually irrelevant. Yet it would be highly significant to classify transactions of various government bodies, according to the character of the operation, into those largely oriented toward development, those incapable of being influenced by considerations of regional growth, those pertaining to defense, and so forth.

The Business Operating Account and Investment Income Appropriation

Account should be disaggregated into several sectors, preferably following the standard industrial classification. The flows between sectors thus defined could be eliminated, leaving only primary inputs and final consumption, providing sufficient information for determining value added by industry or for constructing standard production functions.

The Regional Savings Account should contain government investments instead of having them covered by the Local Governments Revenue and Expenditure Account and Local Operations of Nonlocal Governments Account.

Finally, the question of developing standard regional converters should be examined. In applied work it is ordinarily easier to collect information on transactions in terms of commodities traded rather than in terms of producing sectors. Moreover, in some cases it is important to preserve the organizational structure of the decision-making units. Hence, a second kind of converters, connecting sectors with decision-making units, would have to be developed.

As far as government expenditures are concerned, grouping according to type of expenditure independent of the nature of the commodity or supplying sector would be analytically meaningful and operationally easier to handle. In order to achieve this, a new set of converters connecting both commodities and sectors with types of government expenditures and receipts should be developed.

4

The Industrial Basis: Contribution of Location Analysis

1 The Problem

The rapid, often spectacular growth of modern industrial nations seems to be largely associated with an increase in tertiary activities. The division of activities into primary, or extractive; secondary, or manufacturing; and tertiary, or service industries, is somewhat ambiguous. The terms primary, secondary, and tertiary were first used by Allan G. B. Fisher, [1] who defined primary activities as comprising agricultural, pastoral, forest, fishing, and hunting industries; secondary as comprising manufacturing, electrical power production, mining, building, and construction; and tertiary as all other activities. Two other classifications achieved great prominence. P. Sargant Florence [2] classified industries into heavy and light on the basis of such characteristics as weight of materials per operative, ratio of weight of materials to value of product, installed power per operative, percentage of men in the labor force, and share of materials in total production costs. Alfred Weber, [3] with entirely different objectives in mind, grouped all activities into five strata, namely (1) agricultural, (2) primary industrial, (3) secondary industrial, (4) central organizing, and (5) central dependent. These concepts have hardly been rigorously formulated and applied in official statistics. Consequently, the division into extractive, manufacturing, and service industries does not provide a basis for a quantitative analysis.

But, while a precise delimitation of the notions presents serious difficulties, it is an observable fact that agriculture, mining, and even manufacturing often expand at a slower rate than services and, in terms of employment, may even register a decline. Several factors, all of which are related to the progress of modern technology, may provide an explanation. Primary and secondary sectors are often composed of numerous activities in which a considerable proportion of operations are repetitive and capable of being mechanized and eventually automated.[a] Hence, if growth is measured in terms of employment, the spectacular gains in productivity, far exceeding increases in output, provide a rather obvious explanation for their relatively slower expansion.

---

[a]Automation is difficult to define or to distinguish from mechanization. According to L. Landon Goodman, *Man and Automation*, Penquin Books, 1957, pp. 19, 23, and 29, the principal components of an automated plant are mechanical handling and processing, sensing, and automatic control. Automatic control devices, which are widely considered as

143

More important, under the impact of technical progress each unit of raw material is subject to an ever increasing amount of processing, thus reducing the relative importance of the primary or extractive stages of production. By the same token, the growing sophistication of the industrial structure of modern society tends to increase the weight of the organizing or tertiary activities. Last, but not least, the primary and secondary stages of production ordinarily require less specialized skills, have lower wage rates, and are being increasingly displaced from the highly industrialized to the less developed countries. This process seems to parallel, on a vastly increased scale, the gradual displacement of certain manufacturing operations from the largest metropolitan areas.

It is, nevertheless, doubtful whether the rapidly expanding tertiary or service activities can generate growth in depressed open regions in the absence of a strong manufacturing base. Even at the national level, progress in tertiary activities is accompanied by an expansion in manufacturing output, although the widespread use of the readily available employment statistics may, by concealing the effects of rapidly increasing productivity, convey a distorted image. The road to progress still seems to lead through expansion of the manufacturing base, which alone can generate economies of scale and agglomeration essential for a center capable of supporting and attracting tertiary activities. Nova Scotia, relatively remote from the industrial centers of Canada and the United States, can hardly hope to develop as a concentration of tertiary activities serving far-away urban-industrial agglomerations.

This brings into sharper focus the importance of the local secondary industries. Here the situation is far from encouraging. The manufacturing base of Nova Scotia is poor and its share in total national output and employment insignificant. Table 4-1 illustrates the position of Nova Scotia among other Canadian provinces in absolute and relative terms. Not only is Nova Scotia far behind industrialized Ontario and Quebec, but even among the largely agricultural western provinces and the depressed Atlantic region its position is undistinguished. Other summary indicators reinforce this impression. In 1965 the total value added in manufacturing in Nova Scotia amounted to only $231.5 million, representing 17.1 percent of provincial Gross Domestic Product at market prices. The corresponding figures for Canada as a whole were $15,785.3 million value added in manufacturing, representing 28.2 percent of Gross Domestic Product. The situation appears even more serious if one considers the plight of the most significant Nova Scotia industry, namely, primary iron and steel.

---

the most significant attributes of automation, have been in use for a very long time; for example, in 14th century clocks, 17th century steam safety valves, and 19th century Jacquard looms. The word "automation," however, was first introduced in 1936; its meaning has continually expanded without becoming more precise.

Table 4-1
Value Added and Employment in Manufacturing, Canada and Provinces, 1965

Province	Value Added			Employment		
	Value Added by Province ($ million)	Percentage of Total	Value Added Per Capita by Province	Employees by Province ('000)	Percentage of Total	Employees as Percentage of Provincial Population
Ontario	8,421.7	53.35	1,239.6	774.4	49.33	11.40
Quebec	4,516.7	28.61	793.5	499.2	31.79	8.77
British Columbia	1,280.2	8.11	704.2	119.8	7.63	6.59
Alberta	500.6	3.17	344.3	45.5	2.89	3.13
Manitoba	380.4	2.41	396.3	46.4	2.95	4.83
Nova Scotia	231.5	1.47	304.6	32.1	2.04	4.22
New Brunswick	205.5	1.30	328.9	25.1	1.60	4.02
Saskatchewan	146.5	0.93	153.8	15.0	0.95	1.57
Newfoundland	86.5	0.55	172.7	10.4	0.67	2.08
Prince Edward Is.	13.9	0.09	128.6	2.2	0.14	2.04
Yukon and N.W.T.	1.6	0.01	65.4	0.2	0.01	0.65
Canada	15,785.3	100.00	801.1	1,570.3	100.00	7.97

Source: D.B.S., *Canada Year Book*, 1968; and D.B.S., *Canadian Statistical Review*, June 1967.

An analysis probing into the causes underlying the present weakness of
the industrial basis of Nova Scotia, with the concommitant heavy reliance of the
economy on government spending, has to encompass several factors. First,
in an examination of the sectoral composition of existing activities, the presence
or absence of modern fast-growing industries may furnish some preliminary
insights. Second, the distribution of activities by size of plants and the related
issue of spatial agglomerations may reveal the capacity to generate economies of
scale, of juxtaposition, and of urbanization that seem to play a central role
in regional development. Third, an investigation of existing capital resources
and investment trends may help to evaluate the physical basis of the regional
economy. Fourth, a more detailed scrutiny of the comparative cost structure and
of cost differentials between Nova Scotia and other parts of Canada might
provide some specific clues concerning future trends.

2 Sectoral Composition

One of the most significant aspects of a regional economy is the sectoral
structure of its productive activities. Few theories and models are nowadays
limited to a treatment of economic processes centered on aggregate production
and consumption functions. Almost as a matter of course, the industrial structure
is emphasized and the technical and behavioral differences between sectors
brought to the fore. But while disaggregation looms large in regional studies,
there is no universally adopted definition of industry or sector. Among the
several definitions in use, two are of special importance. The first designates as
industries aggregates of plants using similar technology, while the second
calls sectors aggregates of plants characterized by similar structure of inputs
and outputs. The two related but not identical notions respond to slightly
different analytic needs. Any economic theory or hypothesis has to be predicated
on the assumption of uniformity of characteristics and behavior of basic units
such as households, firms, or organizations, but it is by no means clear that
the groupings are the same for purposes of various studies. Depending upon the
problem studied, sectors or industries based on similarity of behavior in business
cycles, for example, may be more relevant than those defined by the criterion
of similarity in the use of factors of production or of inputs. In regional
studies, aggregates based on similarity in the main locational factors would
assume great significance, and their omission in official statistics presents a major
difficulty in the quantitative testing of hypotheses dealing with space. Clearly,
no definition could satisfy all requirements, but because of the nature of the
numerical data available, it is useful to begin the analysis in terms of sectoral
structure defined according to the standard industrial classification. A perusal of
the industrial employment reveals substantial similarity between Nova Scotia
and Canada in 1961. In Table 4–2, the provincial economy appears to be almost

Table 4-2
Employment by Industry, Nova Scotia and Canada, 1961

Industry	Nova Scotia			Canada	
	Employees	Percentage of Total	Index of Specialization	Employees	Percentage of Total
Agriculture	12,038	5.08	4.82	640,786	9.90
Forestry and logging	4,296	1.81	-0.13	108,580	1.68
Fishing and trapping	7,493	3.16	-2.60	36,263	0.56
Mines, quarries, oil	10,105	4.27	-2.39	121,702	1.88
Manufacturing industries	34,081	14.39	7.32	1,404,865	21.71
Construction industries	15,524	6.56	0.10	431,093	6.66
Transport, communication, and storage	20,403	8.62	-1.04	490,354	7.58
Utilities	2,427	1.02	0.06	70,504	1.08
Trade	36,763	15.52	-0.20	991,490	15.32
Finance, insurance, and real estate	5,652	2.39	1.15	228,905	3.54
Services	44,953	18.98	0.54	1,263,362	19.52
Government	38,948	16.45	-8.33	525,353	8.12
Miscellaneous	4,136	1.75	0.70	158,593	2.45
Total	236,819	100.00	±14.69	6,471,850	100.00

Based on: D.B.S., 1961 Census of Canada, Labour Force, Catalogue No. 94–518.

an exact replica of the national, the most significant difference being a lower
share of manufacturing in Nova Scotia, compensated by a relatively higher
employment in government services. In both cases the deviations are of the
order of seven to eight percent, but they point toward the importance of federal
(perhaps largely noncivilian) employment in the province.

A simple yet useful analytic device for assessing the extent of deviations is
the index of industrial specialization [4] shown in Table 4-2. The index is
calculated by adding up positive and negative differences between the percentage
shares of various industries in total employment in Nova Scotia and Canada,

$$
I_s = \sum_{i=1}^{n} \left| \frac{E_i^{NS}}{E^{NS}} - \frac{E_i^C}{E^C} \right| \Bigg/ 2 \ ;
$$

where

$\quad I_s \qquad$ = index of industrial specialization,

$\quad E_i^{NS} \quad$ = employment in the ith industry in Nova Scotia,

$\quad E^{NS} \quad$ = total employment in Nova Scotia,

$\quad E_i^C \qquad$ = employment in the ith industry in Canada,

$\quad E^C \qquad$ = total employment in Canada.

The value of the index for Nova Scotia in 1961 of 14.69 has to be considered very low. The use of this crude measure in Canada raises more serious
doubts than would be the case in a more diversified, self-contained country like
the United States. Due to the specialized nature of the national economy, the
implied assumption of comparing the productive activities of a region with its
consumption is not fulfilled. A visual illustration of this last point is amply
provided in Figure 4-1, which shows the localization curves of Nova Scotia and
Canada. The deviation of the curve from the 45° line indicates the extent to
which the distribution of industries, measured in terms of employment, differs
from an equal distribution of activities among the thirteen sectors examined. The
curve is not very meaningful by itself but becomes useful for purposes of interregional comparisons.[b]

---

[b]It was constructed by plotting the cumulative percentage distribution of employment
in each of the thirteen sectors, ranked in decreasing order, on the vertical axis. The
thirteen sectors were marked on the abscissa at equal intervals from the origin in accordance

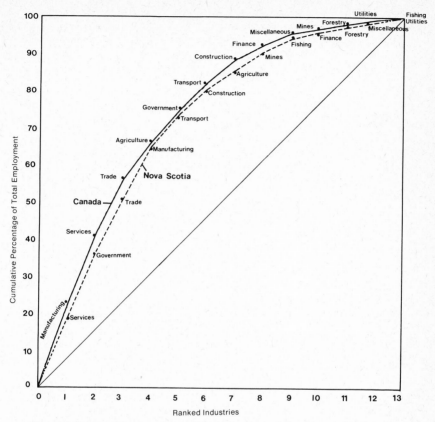

Figure 4–1. Localization Curve, Nova Scotia and Canada, 1961, Total Employment.

Comparison of the curves for Canada and Nova Scotia reveals the striking fact that the national economy was more specialized than the provincial, however slightly. This strange and rarely encountered result is due, at least in part, to the fact that, despite its far greater size, the Canadian economy is strongly oriented toward production of staples, while Nova Scotia seems to be largely bent on satisfying local needs. it is especially noteworthy in connection with the role of manufacturing, which does not achieve the same prominence in Nova Scotia as in Canada. There can be little doubt that this lack of specialization in a small regional economy is a highly negative phenomenon. The related issue of low productivity may also be reflected in the results.

When dealing with several regions, it is often convenient to use, instead of a

---

with their ranking. Their elevation, marked on the ordinate, corresponds to their cumulative percentage share of total employment.

curve, a summary coefficient derived by taking the ratio of the area bounded by the localization curve and the main diagonal to the maximum area that could be bounded if employment were concentrated in one industry only. The derivation of this coefficient (C_e) is straightforward. It is illustrated in Appendix D.

The relative coefficients for Nova Scotia and Canada were .4756 and .5218 respectively, confirming the conclusions reached previously. Although crude, the comparisons enable some valid conclusions to be drawn, subject only to two important limitations. The first refers to the use of employment as a measuring rod. Employment is frequently found to provide an inadequate basis for comparisons because of the differences in efficiency of labor. The use of employment instead of value added has been dictated by the difficult problems raised by non-disclosure rules. In the present case, *Census of Population* data were used; these refer to the place of residence of employees rather than the place of employment, a circumstance further limiting the validity of conclusions. The second limitation of the analysis so far presented is due to the use of very broad groupings of industries that often conceal many important and interesting effects of specialization within some of the groups.

The crude indexes and summary statistics discussed so far all point toward manufacturing activities as the area in which some of the main economic problems of Nova Scotia are concentrated. In 1966, employment in manufacturing stood at 33,533, indicating that its share of total employment was significantly lower than in the nation at large. Employment statistics by themselves, however, do not reveal much of the problematic nature of manufacturing in Nova Scotia beyond its relatively small size.

An examination of output, or value added, provides some additional insight. For, while in terms of employment the province's share in manufacturing activities amounted to 2.04 percent of the national total, in terms of value added it hardly reached 1.48 percent, thus furnishing a clear indication of the lagging productivity and lower wages of the local labor force. Moreover, according to Table 4-3, the considerable progress achieved over the past forty years in terms of increased productivity, or value added per employee, did not result in narrowing the gap between Nova Scotia and the rest of the country. In 1966 the average value added per employee in the province represented 72.7 percent of the corresponding national figure, against 72.2 percent in 1924.

Summary statistics alone cannot uncover the manifold causes of the significant gap in productivity. For this purpose it is necessary to examine more closely the structure of manufacturing. Low productivity may be partly at least due to the lack of specialization and to the closely related issue of the size of plants in which the bulk of manufacturing activities in Nova Scotia is carried out. A superficial perusal of the relevant data indicates that, for the tiny size of the economy, the Nova Scotia manufacturing sector was insufficiently specialized. Comparisons with the national economy in terms of both employment and value added are provided by Figures 4-2 and 4-3.

Table 4-3
Development of Manufacturing, Nova Scotia and Canada, 1924–1966

Year	Nova Scotia			Canada		
	Employees ('000)	Value added ($ millions)	Value added per employee ($)	Employees ('000)	Value added ($ millions)	Value added per employee ($)
1924	16	26	1,593	488	1,075	2,206
1931	15	30	1,990	529	1,252	2,368
1932	12	20	1,674	469	956	2,039
1933	12	20	1,637	469	920	1,962
1934	14	24	1,706	520	1,087	2,092
1935	15	26	1,761	557	1,153	2,072
1936	16	28	1,743	594	1,290	2,170
1937	18	33	1,833	660	1,509	2,285
1938	17	31	1,866	642	1,428	2,225
1939	18	36	2,036	658	1,531	2,326
1940	21	47	2,210	762	1,942	2,548
1941	25	51	2,088	961	2,605	2,710
1942	31	64	2,031	1,152	3,310	2,873
1943	37	85	2,268	1,241	3,816	3,075
1944	38	93	2,470	1,223	4,016	3,284
1945	33	84	2,524	1,119	3,564	3,184
1946	30	72	2,414	1,058	3,467	3,277
1947	30	85	2,804	1,132	4,292	3,792
1948	30	96	3,156	1,156	4,939	4,273
1949	29	102	3,490	1,171	5,331	4,551

Table 4-3 cont.

Year	Nova Scotia			Canada		
	Employees ('000)	Value added ($ millions)	Value added per employee ($)	Employees ('000)	Value added ($ millions)	Value added per employee ($)
1950	28	98	3,433	1,183	5,942	5,022
1951	31	119	3,916	1,258	6,941	5,516
1952	33	131	4,110	1,288	7,444	5,777
1953	32	128	3,992	1,327	7,993	6,121
1954	30	130	4,383	1,268	7,902	6,232
1955	30	140	4,621	1,298	8,753	6,741
1956	31	160	5,166	1,353	9,605	7,099
1957	32	176	5,572	1,341	9,822	7,325
1958	29	177	6,101	1,273	9,455	7,429
1959	28	161	5,732	1,288	10,154	7,885
1960	29	175	6,111	1,275	10,371	8,131
1961	28	165	5,945	1,353	10,932	8,082
1962	29	179	6,106	1,390	11,987	8,627
1963	29	193	6,745	1,425	12,875	9,032
1964	30	218	7,232	1,491	14,247	9,554
1965	32	232	7,212	1,570	15,785	10,052
1966	34	255	7,619	1,646	17,260	10,486

Based on: D.B.S., *Canada Year Book*, various issues, Cat. No. 11–202; D.B.S., *Manufacturing Industries of Canada, Atlantic Provinces*, annual, 1957–1962, Cat. No. 31–204; and D.B.S., *Manufacturing Industries of Canada*, Summary, annual, 1962, Cat. No. 31–203.

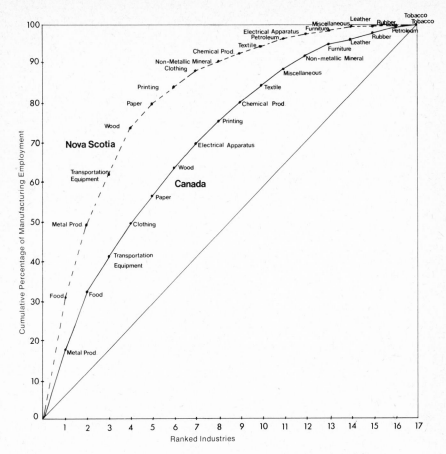

Figure 4–2. Localization Curve, Nova Scotia and Canada, 1961 Manufacturing Employment.

In view of the tremendous disparity in size of the two economies, it is remarkable how little the Nova Scotia curve deviates from that of Canada. An index of specialization in terms of employment shows that the extent of concentration amounted to barely 25.74 in 1961. In 1966 this generalized indicator stood at 33.06 in terms of employment and at 25.12 in terms of value added, but the calculations for 1961 and 1966 are not exactly comparable, those for 1966 being based on the *Census of Manufacturing*.

The low value of the Nova Scotia index is undoubtedly due to the considerable specialization of the Canadian economy. Compared to the more diversified United States economy in terms of distribution of employment, the Nova Scotia index of specialization stood at 37.90 in 1961.

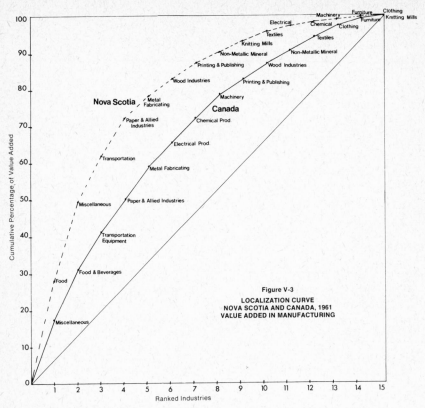

Figure 4–3. Localization Curve, Nova Scotia and Canada, 1961 Value Added in Manufacturing.

A closer examination of the data in terms of the relative importance of various industries, as revealed by Tables 4-4 and 4-5, shows a concentration of employment in the somewhat problematic sectors like fish processing, wood industries, and transportation equipment. Yet these statistics conceal the serious situation existing in the primary iron and steel industry that forms part of the metal products group. They also fail to reveal the related and highly significant absence of a strong geographic concentration, which may be an important contributing factor because economies of agglomeration, of localization, or of spatial juxtaposition may go a long way in replacing economies of scale.

For purposes of analysis, the Standard Industrial Classification used so far may not be adequate, in view of the special conditions existing in Nova Scotia. Among the various other criteria applicable, four appear particularly useful: (1) size of plant, (2) age of plant, or period of construction, (3) main destination

Table 4-4
Employment in Manufacturing Industries, Nova Scotia and Canada, 1966

Industry[a]	Nova Scotia				Canada		
	Employees	Percentage Distribution	Rank	Index of Specialization	Employees	Percentage Distribution	Rank
Food and beverages	10,651	32.30	1	-18.50	227,221	13.80	1
Tobacco products	—	—		0.62	10,177	0.62	20
Rubber	—	—		1.69	27,821	1.69	17
Leather	99[d]	0.30[d]	18	1.68	32,589	1.98	16
Textile	504	1.53	12	3.16	77,248	4.69	10
Knitting mills	1,329	4.03	8	-2.60	23,609	1.43	18
Clothing	286	0.87	16	5.19	99,708	6.06	7
Wood	2,482	7.53	4	-1.94	91,937	5.59	8
Furniture and fixtures	362	1.09	14	1.56	43,598	2.65	15
Paper and allied	2,232	6.77	5	0.33	116,840	7.10	5
Printing, publishing and allied	1,467	4.45	7	0.53	81,996	4.98	9
Primary metal	3,176[e]	9.64[e]	3	-2.74	113,645	6.90	6
Metal fabricating[b]	1,969	5.97	6	2.75	143,311	8.72	3
Machinery[c]	464	1.41	13	3.17	75,451	4.58	11
Transportation equip.	5,117	15.52	2	-6.59	146,932	8.93	2
Electrical products	983	2.98	9	4.58	124,498	7.56	4
Nonmetallic mineral products	762	2.31	10	0.92	53,189	3.23	14

Table 4-4 cont.

Industry[a]	Nova Scotia				Canada		
	Employees	Percentage Distribution	Rank	Index of Specialization	Employees	Percentage Distribution	Rank
Petroleum and coal products	537[d]	1.63[d]	11	−0.69	15,403	0.94	19
Chemical and chemical products	292	0.89	15	3.56	73,317	4.45	12
Miscellaneous	258	0.78	17	3.32	67,534	4.10	13
Total	32,970[f]	100.00		±33.06	1,646,024	100.00	

[a]Based on the revised standard industrial classification and new establishment and total activity concepts.
[b]Except machinery and transportation equipment industries.
[c]Except electrical machinery.
[d]Data for 1961. Data for 1966 for these industry groups are confidential.
[e]Estimated.
[f]This differs from the published D.B.S. total of 33,533 because it includes 1961 data for leather and petroleum and coal products and an estimate for 1966 for primary metals; it is not possible to estimate figures for any other groups for which information is confidential and not disclosed.
Based on: D.B.S., Canada Year Book, 1969.

Table 4-5

Value Added in Manufacturing Industries, Nova Scotia and Canada, 1966

Industry	Nova Scotia Value Added		Index of Specialization	Canada Value Added	
	Absolute ($'000)	Percentage		Absolute ($'000)	Percentage
Food and beverages	71,855	28.125	13.647	2,498,537	14.478
Miscellaneous	54,158	21.198	4.113	2,948,940	17.085
Transportation equipment	34,051	13.328	3.205	1,747,178	10.123
Paper and allied	25,277	9.894	1.336	1,477,123	8.558
Metal fabricating	13,496	5.283	-3.096	1,446,240	8.379
Wood industries	13,197	5.165	1.058	708,883	4.107
Printing and publishing	12,137	4.751	-.003	820,512	4.754
Nonmetallic mineral	7,778	3.044	-.801	663,685	3.845
Knitting mills	6,629	2.595	1.765	143,283	.830
Textiles	5,035	1.971	-1.420	585,232	3.391
Electrical products	3,962	1.551	-5.489	1,215,149	7.040
Chemical products	3,869	1.514	-5.519	1,213,859	7.033
Machinery industries	1,688	.661	-4.698	925,008	5.359
Furniture	1,357	.531	-1.317	319,054	1.848
Clothing	997	.390	-2.782	547,574	3.172
Total	255,485		±25,124	17,260,256	

Based on: D.B.S., *General Review of the Manufacturing Industries of Canada*, annual, 1966, Cat. No. 31–201.

of products whether for export or for the local market, and (4) factors influencing the plant's original location, such as the presence of natural resources or developments taking place in the regional economy. Classifications based on these four criteria are not independent of one another. Actually the following classification into three major categories of manufacturing activities satisfies, to a certain extent, all four criteria.

The first group is composed of predominantly old and largely problem-ridden industries. It is by far the largest. The plants composing it are, with very few exceptions, large by Nova Scotia standards. Their original location in the province and later growth were motivated by the existing advantages of the physical endowment of the region and were not due to any artifacts or human factors. Their rise to national importance was largely independent of the simultaneous developments taking place in the provincial economy, upon which they exercised a profound influence.

The second group consists of numerous smaller establishments, oriented mainly toward supplying the local market with products that either cannot be transported over long distances or cannot bear the cost of long hauls. Economically they differ little from service industries.

Finally, the third group consists of a sprinkling of new industries established rather recently, invariably with the help of heavy government subsidies. Plants belonging to this group were not in operation in 1961, the year to which most statistical data refer. This development took place largely in the Canso Strait area in connection with attempts to foster a growth pole there. The crude sectoral breakdown for which statistical data are available obviously cuts across these categories. For example, a good deal of metal products and transportation equipment actually belongs to two of the groups defined above.

In the first group, which forms the real manufacturing core of the province, the sector posing the most serious threat to the stability of the provincial economy is primary iron and steel, dominated by the huge Sydney steelworks. Based on the Cape Breton coal mines, the plant developed rapidly during the railway era at the turn of the century, supplying steel rails and some of the steel required by the rolling stock industry. Part of its later undoing was its failure to diversify when the railway boom terminated before the First World War. Some modest efforts at widening the range of products were made in the 1950's and 1960's, but the results were not always judged favorable. Its output consists of steel ingots, rods, bars, billets, wire nails, and rails, with particular emphasis on the latter.

Despite substantial amounts of money invested during the post-war period the plant has to be rated as underinvested. Although steel ingot capacity in Sydney has increased since the war from 750 thousand to one million net tons a year, production is not technically efficient. Employment, which because of important social and political considerations is not always directly related to output, stood at 3,918 in 1961. This represents a sharp reduction from the peak of roughly 5,800 in 1952.

Such efforts as were made at modernizing and making the plant more
efficient were greatly hampered by its isolated position relative to the major
Canadian centers. Its markets are predominantly domestic, although steel rails
and some other products are exported in considerable quantities. But the
fabricated steel products plants, the main processors of Nova Scotia steel
(as well as Sydney's chief domestic competitors) are located in Quebec and
Ontario. Thus, as a highly integrated but strictly primary steel producer,
the Sydney center is confronted with high transportation costs in marketing
its output, with high cost local coal, and with iron ore inputs shipped from
Labrador. The fact that the plant has been unable to attract significant steel
processing industries to Nova Scotia is an interesting example of spatial maladjustment and a major factor in the present economic plight of Cape Breton
Island.[5] Faced with closing, the plant has been taken over by the Government
of Nova Scotia, but its future is still uncertain despite proposals for heavy
investments of public funds.

Ship- and boat-building and railroad rolling stock industries are the two
major components of the transportation equipment industry group. They
differ greatly in several respects. Ship- and boat-building has a long tradition in
Nova Scotia dating back to wooden sailing vessels, and it developed into a
major industry during the Second World War. Wartime conditions created
a very strong demand, with costs assuming a secondary role. The first destroyer
constructed in Canada during the war was built by Halifax Shipyards. Cessation
of hostilities brought about a rapid decline in employment, but the outbreak
of war in Korea in 1950 sparked another surge of activity, followed by a
gradual decline from the mid-1950's to the end of the decade. In recent years
employment has stabilized between 2,000 and 2,500, with 2,651 recorded
during the 1961 census. The bulk of the work carried out by the industry has
become less defense oriented, and now consists chiefly of repairs, with orders
of commercial fishing vessels assuming increasing importance. The lesser
dependence of the industry on government contracts has been, alas, accompanied
by an increased reliance on various federal government subsidies, which form
part of a policy apparently based largely upon security considerations and
are perhaps aimed at maintaining shipbuilding facilities at various points
throughout the country.

The railroad rolling stock industry consists of the Trenton works, developed
prior to the First World War in response to a heavy demand for railway equipment during the "golden age" of railroad construction. With the exception of
brief surges of activity during cyclical expansions of the economy, it has not
regained its buoyancy since that era came to an end. In the years immediately
following the Second World War, employment increased rapidly due to pent-up
requirements of the railways, which had postponed major investment programs
during the war. The 1950's saw a return to the traditional pattern, with tremendous fluctuations in output and employment following national business cycles,
and with employment in the census year 1961 at only 399.

Among the other industries belonging to the first group, the fish products industry is easily the most important. It has the distinction of being based on a local resource and is largely export-oriented. In 1961 it employed 5,275 persons, but its many fish processing plants were small, scattered, and largely inefficient. Knitting mills were mainly represented by one fairly modern factor supplying the national market. In 1961 this sector employed 852 persons. Finally, pulp and paper mills, with an employment of 1,549 persons in 1961, and sawmills and sash, door, and planing mills, with an employment of 3,463, are both relative newcomers that owe their recent growth, partly at least, to government efforts. They are, nonetheless, primarily attracted to Nova Scotia by the availability of a natural resource rather than by subsidies, incentives, or man-made advantages.

The second major group of manufacturing industries comprises numerous industries that may be called urban-oriented because they are, as a rule, either attracted toward consumers or typically found in urban agglomerations due to other advantages to be found there. Among those deserving special attention on account of their potential contribution to the formation of an urban-industrial complex are the oil refining operations in Dartmouth, which employed 531 persons in 1961. The new oil refinery now being constructed in the Canso Strait area may play an important role in the formation of a growth pole on Cape Breton Island. Oil refining is not, however, typical of the second category of industries, to which it belongs only by virtue of being strongly consumer- and harbor-oriented. The large food and beverage group, employing 10,626 persons in 1961, may be at least partly harbor-oriented, while such industries as metal fabricating and transportation equipment may be partly defense-oriented.

Printing, publishing, and allied industries on the other hand follows commercial and population developments, and must be rated as a typical urban-oriented industry. In 1961 it employed 1,776 persons. Its modern outlook in Nova Scotia may be a function of the developing research and academic center in Halifax. Even more modern is the electrical apparatus industry, which was added to the secondary manufacturing sector in Nova Scotia after the Second World War. The three firms of which this group is composed were employing 522 persons in 1961. The first to locate in the province was a British branch plant designing electronic equipment. It was attracted to Nova Scotia in 1949 by the possibility of obtaining defense contracts, and considerably expanded in 1959 and 1962. The other two, specializing in wire and cables and batteries, rspectively, began production in 1960.

3 Economies of Scale and Agglomeration

In modern developed nations a slowly changing spatial pattern of industrial settlement displays two clearly discernible trends. Within a geographically broad frame of reference, a progressive concentration of economic activities

and population in a few areas covering a small portion of the national territory
is gaining momentum; simultaneously, on a much narrower scale a dispersion
of population and of industrial activities takes place within existing agglomerations. The nature of the centripetal and centrifugal forces behind these changes,
which act on such vastly different scales, forms the central, most important
focus for studies dealing with the interrelations between society and societal
processes and the physical environment.

In the United States and Canada, the areas experiencing the most rapid
development are confined to the urbanized eastern seaboard from Boston,
Massachusetts to Norfolk, Virginia (to which the term megalopolis has been
applied); the industrial belt between the Atlantic Coast and Chicago, with the
adjoining "golden triangle" in Southern Ontario and extensions toward Montreal
and Quebec; Southern California; parts of Florida; the area in British Columbia
around Vancouver; a few scattered points in the Prairies; and a portion of the
Gulf Coast.[6] Together they account for only 7.7 percent of the contiguous
area of the two countries but generate over fifty percent of their combined
income and seventy percent of industrial employment, house seventy percent
of those listed in *Who Is Who*, claim an overwhelming majority of registered
patents and publications, are the hub of rail, road, and air traffic, and form
in effect the economic and political core of the continent.

Attempts have been made to explain theoretically the phenomenon of
progressive spatial concentration and to use it for regional development
policy. The original ideas associated with the concept of "growth points" or
"growth poles" were first developed by François Perroux.[7] They stand
out sharply from the older central place theory and from the premises underlying the British "new towns" policy. The literature concerning growth points is
still rather scanty despite the considerable influence the concept has had upon
regional planning in Europe.[8]

According to Perroux the Casselian statistic equilibrium concept is not
really useful in describing the phenomenon of economic growth. The observed
facts indicate that an important characteristic of growth is structural change,
which manifests itself in the emergence of new industries, the disappearance of
some old ones, and changes in the relative importance of various flows and
in the rates of growth of industries. Economic growth, therefore, does not
appear everywhere at the same time, but is often concentrated in certain sectors
that form growth poles of varying intensity. From there it is transmitted by
a system of channels until its effects engulf the whole economy.

In this connection, it is important to note the role of industries that have
a rate of growth higher than the national average. Due to the interrelations
existing in a modern economy, their growth is transmitted to other sectors by a
process that has been called "external economies." Thus, in addition to its
own contribution to the total product, the effect of an industry upon the
national economy is also composed of induced effects that may extend beyond

the simple input-output relationships, and even beyond the purely economic phenomena. It may bring about changes in the legal and political institutions that form the framework within which the economic system operates, in addition to numerous intangible effects. In any articulate economic structure, certain industries are more likely than others to grow and to induce change. From this point of view one may distinguish "progressive" industries, which are capable of inducing growth in other sectors, and the remaining industries. Among the "progressive" industries an important group is formed by the "cornerstone" industries, which may be defined as those whose growth causes indirect effects exceeding their direct contribution in terms of volume of production.

The substance of Perroux's argument is, thus, that natural economic growth is unbalanced and that development policies should capitalize on this fact. This highly controversial issue is taken up in some detail later. Here, it is sufficient to stress the striking feature of his exposition of the concept, with its emphasis on the institutional aspects of the phenomenon and with only incidental references to spatial manifestations. His brief discussion of the significance of industrial complexes in economic growth processes concentrates largely on the role of key industries and sees the primary role of space in an urban-industrial complex as that of intensifying interaction among activities due to proximity and to human contacts. The spatial concentration thus affects consumption patterns, stimulates the demand for progress because of intensification of collective needs, and creates an atmosphere of progress by the interaction of individuals, while inducement to develop is provided by the very fact of increasing spatial disparities. Such a pole of growth, once started, transforms its immediate environment and, if it is strong enough, may affect the whole national economy.

These ideas reached North America and began to influence the thinking of planners and public officials after a lag of several years. Soon, however, they achieved official status,[c] with several significant implications. It is worth noting, however, that the American formulation is more restrained than the French, to the point of avoiding the more interesting but potentially more dangerous designation "growth point" or "growth pole." The main purpose in designating development centers seems to be the desire to avoid spreading the available resources too thinly, while it is recognized that in order to realize full returns public investments have to be placed within the framework of comprehensive

---

[c]In the United States, both the "Appalachian Regional Development Act of 1965" (Public Law 89–4) and the "Public Works and Economic Development Act of 1965" (H.R. 6991) direct investments to "areas where there is significant potential for future growth." The Public Works Act goes even further by stipulating that the proposed "economic development districts" eligible for investment help shall "contain one or more redevelopment areas or economic development centers . . . having sufficient size and potential to foster the economic growth activities. . . ."

planning. The name "growth pole," freely used elsewhere, implies that it may be sufficient to concentrate investments spatially in order to have a growing community transmitting growth to the surrounding community.[d]

In Nova Scotia the Voluntary Planning Board of the Department of Finance and Economics, embracing somewhat similar ideas, recommended establishing local concentrations of three types: [9]

(1) Industrial development centers large enough to support a diversified industrial base capable of generating self-sustained economic growth over time,
(2) Service centers satisfying the demand of the surrounding countryside, and
(3) Resource centers based on concentrations of primary industries.

The classification is a curious combination of Perroux's ideas related to theories of unbalanced growth and Christaller's [10] central place theory rooted in static equilibrium. Potentially more dangerous is the very attempt at applying abstract theoretical concepts to a situation entirely unlike the one portrayed by the hypothesis and without trying to analyze the mechanism involved. For, while Perroux quoted as an example of a growth pole the Ruhr Valley, an immense complex with highly diversified and sophisticated industrial structure, the planners in Nova Scotia had in mind centers of a few thousand inhabitants with relatively small or even nonexistent industries, without apparently giving much thought to the possible effects of the staggering difference in scale.

Analytically, three questions of utmost importance for assessing the validity of the concept have to be examined: (1) the nature and extent of advantages enjoyed by a plant locating in an agglomeration; (2) the critical size beyond which these advantages can be reaped by a significant number of industries, thus providing the impetus for self-sustained regional growth; and (3) the ability of a growth pole to transmit and cause growth in the surrounding areas. [11]

The problem of economies of agglomeration is part of a much broader question of economies of scale that, for purposes of analysis, can be divided into:

(1) Economies of large scale production, referring to the size of the plant in which production takes place,
(2) Economies of large scale organization, referring to the size of firm, and

---

[d]The danger seems real enough. There were recently several attempts in the United States and Canada at defining growth centers without trying to understand the underlying causes of regional growth or decline, and without even indicating the magnitude and type of required investments. See, for example, "Litton Study" (Litton Industries, Development Division, *A Preliminary Analysis for an Economic Development Plan Called*

(3) External economies, among which economies of localization derived from grouping of plants producing similar or complementary commodities, and economies of urbanization that accrue when unlike industries are grouped together may be distinguished.

In a plant, the advantages of large-scale production derive mainly from the principle of multiples, or from the fact that certain types of machinery and of highly skilled personnel are subject to important indivisibilities. Additional advantages are due to the massing of reserves, savings in storage space and capital outlays, and, frequently, the bargaining power of a huge purchasing and marketing organization because of similar economies reaped by the other party. Economies of scale usually increase with size up to a point, after which they level off or even decrease. The reason is frequently to be found in impaired flexibility, for the most pronounced savings are gained by using specialized equipment that attains its highest efficiency when applied to repetitive operations. Plants in fashions industries, where versatile rather than more efficient specialized equipment is of great importance and where rapid obsolescence due to changing styles is an additional consideration, do not attain huge size. Similar considerations apply to industries subject to strong seasonal or cyclical fluctuations and to industries experiencing rapid technical progress. In extreme cases, subcontracting, involving marginal plants using obsolete equipment, is typical. In a time of recession these plants are laid off first. More generally, industries with highly specialized products and/or unstable markets tend to be composed of small plants because of the premium on flexibility and originality.

The size of plants is often limited by the very complexity of some modern technical processes, making not only coordination of production but also other managerial functions, such as control and supervision, exceedingly involved. Efficient discharge of these functions may limit the size of the firm, which in turn becomes a factor constraining the dimension of plants of which the firm is comprised.

Economies of scale realized in large plants and firms have sometimes to overcome limitations imposed by the market size. In such cases both plants and firms may grow in scope rather than in size. This phenomenon is often referred to as integration. The number of ways in which integration can take place is almost unlimited. The traditional dichotomy into horizontal and vertical integration may be replaced for purposes of regional analysis by the following fivefold classification: [12]

(1) Integration based on related production techniques quite common in

the *Appalachian Region*, Report to the Appalachian Regional Commission, Contract No. C–181–65 (NEG), U.S. Department of Commerce, Area Development Administration, November, 1965).

many industries, and in some so widespread that the various processes are classified as one industry.

(2) Integration based on related production inputs; it refers to cases in which identical or related raw materials are converted into two or more different products. Two different types of this kind of integration may be distinguished: (a) alternative products manufactured from the same raw material, and (b) by-products that have to be produced in technically fixed proportions.

(3) Integration based on successive stages of production; it corresponds to vertical integration and represents, perhaps, the most common type. In some processes the material may be subject to a series of improvements while preserving its identity; in other cases vertical integration may involve production of complementary materials that undergo transformation in a subsequent process, or of complementary parts entering into an assembling process.

(4) Integration based on related markets; until recently the domain of the merchant. It refers to concentration of processes using different production techniques, different raw materials, or both; for example, the production of heating and air-conditioning apparatus, or paper cups and dispensers, or non-alcoholic beverages and ice cream.

(5) Integration based on unrelated processes and markets; again more typical of a firm or locality than of a plant. The advantages reaped may be financial or may simply result from the splitting of risk.

Considerable economies of scale may be realized in a large organization because of savings in such functions as management, accounting, supervision, research facilities, merchandising, and transportation, and of the power in negotiating with suppliers, customers, and labor unions. Limitation of risks may be an additional consideration. Large organizations, whether they take the form of decision-making units or simply represent commercial groupings such as joint ventures, trading or producer associations, and cartels, frequently obviate the need for large plants, so that these two forms of concentration are not complementary to one another.

Whether and to what extent economies of agglomeration can be reaped through spatial proximity of plants and firms, conserving their legal and decision-making identity, is a more controversial question, since the relations among them are bound to be very complex. Some spatial agglomerations may yield few genuine economies to the units located in close proximity. Obviously, processes using the same raw material are likely to show similar locational patterns if the material is bulky but the resulting proximity need not result in economies of integration, because each might be simply transport cost oriented to the source of the raw material.

Very often spatial agglomerations are due to historical developments, but they may also result, for example, from diversification prompted by the desire to use otherwise redundant female labor by locating textile mills in mining centers, or to use farm labor unemployed in winter by locating manufacturing industries in agricultural areas.

Economies of localization and urbanization are the two typical forms of external economies. The term external economies was first introduced by Alfred Marshall, and refers to economies accruing not because of factors such as size of plant or scale of production but because of activities of others. Many elements of production cost depend upon these elusive elements. According to Scitowsky, [13] the growth of industry A may affect the profits of industry B, which buys the products of industry A; of industry C, whose products are complementary to those of A; of industry D, whose products are substitutes for factors used by A; and of industry E, whose products are consumed by households whose incomes have increased as a result of the expansion of industry A. This may not exhaust the notion of external economies, which transcends phenomena related to growth.

External economies, which often make specialization in small plants possible, may be divided into (1) special economies referring to specific factors and industries, such as existence of a qualified labor pool or presence of auxiliary industries or facilities, and (2) general economies referring to all industries. The limits to economies of agglomeration are usually set by an excessive concentration, which brings with it transportation difficulties both internal and external, and increased social costs, sometimes reflected in such elements as the cost of land and wage rates.

The advantages of spatial agglomeration reaped by plants locating in an urban center are mainly those of specialized auxiliary servicing, existence of a trained labor pool, and for smaller firms, the possibility of obtaining services at short notice. When successful, locational integration combines some of the economies of large-scale production with the flexibility and versatility of small plants and firms.

The second analytic question, crucial to the validity and applicability for development planning of the concept of growth points, relates to the problem of critical mass beyond which an agglomeration would enjoy self-sustained growth. In the absence of comprehensive and conclusive studies only tentative answers are possible, but there is some evidence suggesting that the cut-off point is at the level of 800,000 inhabitants. A study carried out some years ago [14] had as one of its objectives the determination, on the basis of analysis of United States data, of the relative strength of various factors affecting the locational decisions of entrepreneurs. Of the seventy-four industries examined, it was found that a substantial number were attracted toward urban agglomerations with a force significantly more than proportionately increasing with the size of the center. It thus lent some credence to the view that the locational pull exercised by larger cities is qualitatively and not only quantitatively different from that of smaller centers. Population size is, of course, only an index of the various facilities an entrepreneur might find in a place, and to the extent that those facilities might exist in a smaller agglomeration the index is not valid.

Industries for which the presence of an urban agglomeration was the prime locational consideration, to the exclusion of other factors, were called urban-oriented industries. The statistical analysis was based on a sample of 232 cities in the United States, divided into four size groups; namely, 50,000-100,000 inhabitants, 100,000-300,000, 300,000-800,000, and over 800,000. The procedure actually applied was analysis of variance. There is no need here to discuss the general principles on which it is based. Essentially, the hypothesis tested has been set up as follows:

Each of the subgroups of cities could be regarded as a sample, having its own mean and standard deviation or variance. These variances could be regarded as independent estimates of the unknown universe variance, provided that the universe would be homogeneous and the division not germane to the problem investigated. In other words, if the division had no bearing on the problem one would expect the variances to be the same within sampling limits. Otherwise, one would have to conclude that the division was meaningful. This hypothesis has been tested by the F-ratios,[e] where

$$ F = \frac{s_1^2}{s_2^2} \; ; $$

The results proved that from the point of view of the aggregate effect of various locational factors on urban-oriented industries there is a qualitative as well as a quantitative difference between cities belonging to various size groups. The effect appears to be so strong that any conclusions or parameters derived from an array including cities of very different sizes have to be viewed very carefully; in fact, there are good reasons to believe that they would not be valid. On the other hand, tests based on two other classifications were negative; that is, they did not influence the results. Whether still other classifications based on a criterion different from city size would exert any influence is difficult to say, but it appears unlikely because of the very strong effect of city size. Thus, on the basis of this study, one would have to con- clude that, if the main location factor of an industry is the existence of a city, size of the city is the primary consideration in choosing a location. Other characteristics of cities, such as nearness to other urban centers or rate of growth, do not seem to affect the attraction that a community may exercise on urban-oriented industries. Furthermore, regression and correlation analyses

---

[e] F = Snedecor's F-ratio

that were carried out suggest that, with increasing city size, the effects on location of urban-oriented industries tend to become more stable, or less subject to variations between individual cities.

Another important outcome of correlation analysis was that the number of industries classified as urban-oriented increased with city size,

City size	Number of cities	Number of urban-oriented industries
50–100,000	126	37
100–300,000	70	38
300–800,000	26	41
800,000 +	10	52

Among the industries classified as urban-oriented in cities of 800,000 and more inhabitants but not in smaller centers were miscellaneous wood products, furniture and fixtures, apparel and other fabricated textile mill products, chemicals and allied products, glass and glass products, and air transportation. The increased number and the importance of urban-oriented industries seem to indicate that the locational pull of the largest cities may have reached a level that ensures their continued rapid growth even in the face of other adverse forces.

The third analytic question concerning the usefulness of the concept of growth points is their ability to stimulate economic progress and transmit their momentum to the surrounding countryside. Faced with a surprising lack of studies bearing on this important problem, one can only speculate about the nature of spatial economic relations. It can be postulated that the spatial economic links of an urban industrial agglomeration are related to the functions that it fulfills toward itself and the rest of the world. Four types of spatial interaction can be distinguished.

The first type is based on functions that the urban economy performs toward itself, partly in response to internal demand. These functions give rise to various types of multipliers, but spatially are confined to the agglomeration itself.

The second type refers to links between the urban economy and the surrounding countryside, whose characteristic feature is that their intensity declines with increasing distance from the city. The area over which the very proximity of a metropolis exerts a significant influence impinging on the economic and social structure of the countryside has been called the area of metropolitan dominance.[15] The elements typically affected by the new role that the countryside begins to play as the suburban or hinterland area of the agglomeration are density of settlement, land use patterns stressing gardening and recreation instead of extensive agriculture, presence of technical

services and noxious industries displaced from the center, and so on. It is
not immediately apparent whether the progressive and sometimes rapid
spillover of marginal urban functions from major urban-industrial agglomerations and the accompanying displacement of traditional agriculture from
the tributary areas represent economic progress for the latter. Generally, the
downgrading of the agricultural countryside to the status of a tributary area
of an agglomeration affects positively some key socioeconomic indicators
normally interpreted as growth. Some such areas may even register a higher
growth rate than the core of the agglomeration.

The third type of link is characterized by permanent spatial relationships
that do not decline with increasing distance. For example, the shipments of
automobiles from Detroit are unchanging as regards destination and yet
do not decline with increasing distance, Chicago being a more important
customer than Ann Arbor.

The fourth type of link would correspond to spatial relationships
changing over time as to their direction and being unrelated in their intensity
to distance, corresponding to production for world markets.

The second and third type of linkages, connecting points in geographic
space and stressing the role of distance, are at the heart of the theories of
spatial organization due to Christaller [16] and Loesch [17] and have been
applied by planners dealing with location and development of regional service
centers. The urban growth theory implied in the writings of Christaller and
more forcefully expounded by Loesch forms part of a theory of spatial
equilibrium and is probably more applicable to an agricultural than to a
contemporary industrialized society. The centers belonging to the lower
echelons of the hierarchy of cities are declining in many modern nations.
Their establishment or forced development in Nova Scotia, perhaps otherwise
desirable, would not be tantamount to the starting of new growth poles.
The two categories de-emphasizing distance correspond to urban growth
theories stressing (1) external demand, such as the economic base theory,
(2) local supply base, such as staples theory, stages theory, or sector theory
or (3) locational attractiveness of cities.

Some theoretical considerations seem to indicate that the effects of a
growing urban-industrial agglomeration beyond its tributary area, or sphere
of metropolitan dominance, are small and essentially negative. Myrdal [18]
classified the induced impacts of expansion in a prosperous region into spread
and backwash effects. The first refer to positive repercussions of expansion
in the nodal center upon the surrounding areas due to gains from increasing
outlets for agricultural products, technical stimuli, and so forth. These effects
may also benefit quite distant regions, even to the extent of stimulating
not only industries supplying the nodal center directly but even local production of consumer goods. But Myrdal argues that the beneficial effects will
be outweighed by adverse backwash effects, causing migration of skilled

Table 4-6
Size of Plants, Nova Scotia and Canada, 1962

Industry	Average Number of Employees Per Establishment	
	Nova Scotia	*Canada*
Extractive		
Dairy Factories	28	22
Fish Products	33	43
Feed Manufacturers	10	9
Sawmills	7	5
Sash, Door, and Planing Mills	16	33
Manufacturing		
Bakeries	12	12
Soft-drink Manufacturers	17	26
Other Food and Beverages	58	66
Clothing Industries	34	57
Other Wood Industries	7	18
Printing and Publishing	36	43
Other Printing and Publishing	9	16
Household Furniture	2	12
Other Furniture Industries	31	23
Machine Shops	11	11
Other Metal Fabricating	54	41
Transportation Equipment Industries	63	99
Miscellaneous Manufacturing Industries	3	6

Based on: D.B.S., *Manufacturing Industries of Canada*, 1962, special tabulations.

labor, capital, and services to the prosperous regions at the expense of the poorer. The deflection of savings and managerial talent toward the rich centers where returns are higher and risks lower and the change in trading patterns all work to the detriment of the underdeveloped areas and tend to accentuate the divergence. Hirschman [19] and Friedmann [20] both concur, although for slightly different reasons.

To what extent the present plight of Nova Scotia is due to lack of economies of scale in its industries is not immediately obvious from a perusal of such raw data as are available. Certainly, in terms of economies of scale due to average size of its plants it does not appear to be lagging far behind the rest of Canada. This is indicated in Table 4-6, which reveals no fundamental disparities in average employment per plant. The more relevant comparison in terms of output could not be carried out for lack of data, but in view of the lower productivity of Nova Scotia workers, it is likely to reveal more tangible differences. The more detailed analysis presented in Table 4-7 underlines the basic similarity in size distribution of plants in Nova

Table 4-7

Manufacturing Establishments Classified by Number of Employees, Nova Scotia and Canada, 1965

Number of Employees (1)	Nova Scotia			Canada			Index of Concentration (6) − (3) (8)
	Number of plants (2)	Percentage Distribution (3)	Cumulative Percentage (4)	Number of Plants (5)	Percentage Distribution (6)	Cumulative Percentage (7)	
Under 5	365	38.71	38.71	11,387	34.18	34.18	+4.53
5 to 14	258	27.36	66.07	9,173	27.54	61.72	−0.18
15 to 49	206	21.85	87.92	7,138	21.43	83.15	+0.42
50 to 99	62	6.57	94.49	2,592	7.78	90.93	−1.21
100 to 199	21	2.23	96.72	1,573	4.72	95.65	−2.49
200 to 499	24	2.55	99.27	1,009	3.03	98.68	−0.48
500 to 999	5	0.53	99.80	296	0.89	99.57	−0.36
1,000 to 1,499	1	0.10	99.90	78	0.24	99.81	−0.14
1,500 or Over	1	0.10	100.00	64	0.19	100.00	−0.09
Total	943	100.00		33,310	100.00		∓4.95

Based on: D.B.S., *Canada Year Book*, 1968, Tables 17 and 18, pp. 715–716.

Scotia and Canada. The index of concentration of size of plant, parallel to the one described in Section 2 of this chapter, amounted in 1965 to only 4.95. The index was defined as

$$I_c = \sum_{u=1}^{9} \left| \frac{N_u^{NS}}{N^{NS}} - \frac{N_u^{C}}{N^{C}} \right| \bigg/ 2 \; ;$$

where

I_c = index of concentration,

N_u = number of plants of size u,

N = total number of plants,

and where the superscripts NS and C refer to Nova Scotia and Canada respectively. The coefficient of concentration by size of plant in manufacturing industries amounted in Nova Scotia to 0.7072 as against 0.6593 for Canada, thus showing only a slightly higher relative employment in smaller plants in Nova Scotia than in the nation.

An analysis of external economies, especially economies deriving from spatial agglomeration, is all the more pertinent since these are often decisive in regions not particularly well endowed by nature. A direct study based on detailed production patterns and cost structures was not feasible because of data limitations; hence, an indirect method was used, with Ontario selected as a basis for comparisons.

The most obvious and probably decisive difference between the two is the magnitude of the two economies. In 1965 the Gross Regional Product of Nova Scotia amounted to $1,378 million as against Ontario's $22,550 million. The significant differences in terms of manufacturing activity in 1965 are vividly illustrated by the following statistics:

Manufacturing	Nova Scotia	Ontario
Production and related workers	24,800	543,500
Total manufacturing employment	32,100	774,400
Value of shipments	$563 million	$27,676 million
Value added	$232 million	$ 8,422 million

These figures speak for themselves, but spatial distribution, especially of manufacturing activities, is of primary importance as far as economies of agglomeration are concerned.

As a measure of relative concentration, the concept of standard distance developed by Bachi [21] has been used. The analysis was based on data pertaining to sixteen cities and towns in Nova Scotia and thirty-six in Ontario. For purposes of the present analysis each agglomeration was weighted by its share in the provincial output or in value of shipments of manufactured products. The measure was defined as

$$\delta = \sqrt{\frac{\sum\limits_{i=1}^{n} \sum\limits_{j=1}^{n} V_i V_j d_{ij}^2}{2 \left(\sum\limits_{i=1}^{n} V_i \right)^2}} = \sqrt{\frac{\sum\limits_{i=1}^{n} V_i I_i^2}{2 \left(\sum\limits_{i=1}^{n} V_i \right)}} \quad ;$$

where

V_i, V_j = value of shipments from centers i, j

I_i = relative accessibility index or

$$I_i = \sqrt{\frac{\sum\limits_{j=1}^{n} V_j d_{ij}^2}{\sum\limits_{j=1}^{n} V_j}} \quad ;$$

The values of the index for Nova Scotia and Ontario calculated for 1961 were 143.7 and 155.6 respectively. [22] Manufacturing thus appears relatively more concentrated in Nova Scotia than in Ontario. The spatial distribution of economic activities and population is illustrated in Table 4-8 and Figure 4-4. Several considerations, however, tend to limit the significance or even the validity of this conclusion.

According to Bachi, [23] the value of δ is affected in a general way by the influence of the following factors:

(1) Territory, its size and shape;
(2) Population, its size and distribution pattern; differences in patterns of distribution may be due to several factors, namely
    (a) dispersion of population over parts only or over the whole territory,
    (b) geographical distribution within the inhabited parts of the territory,
    (c) inequality in size of the population of inhabited places,

Table 4-8
Population and Labor Force of Industrial Centers, Nova Scotia, 1961

City or Town	Total Population	Labour Force by Industry					
		Extractive[a]	Manu-facturing	Con-struction	Services[b]	Unreported[c]	Total
North Sydney	8,657	134	235	88	1,950	55	2,462
Sydney Mines	9,122	951	136	72	1,218	53	2,430
Sydney	33,617	172	3,536	450	6,841	148	11,147
Glace Bay	24,186	2,712	436	219	3,486	99	6,952
New Waterford	10,592	1,613	67	62	1,099	28	2,869
Truro	12,241	79	834	248	3,432	76	4,669
Springhill	5,836	118	78	67	810	211	1,284
Amherst	10,788	74	955	287	2,375	48	3,739
Dartmouth	46,966	109	2,157	855	12,767	249	16,137
Halifax	92,511	135	3,699	1,420	35,799	674	41,727
Stellarton	5,327	194	244	83	912	45	1,458
New Glasgow	9,782	89	614	183	1,724	394	3,004
Yarmouth	8,636	87	644	157	1,716	278	2,882
Halifax C.M.A.	183,946	382	7,472	3,373	60,583	1,143	72,953
Sydney–Glace Bay Area[d]	106,114	7,376	5,064	1,155	16,921	429	30,945

[a]Consists of agriculture; forestry; fishing and trapping; and mines, quarries, and oil wells.
[b]Consists of transportation, communication, storage and other utilities; trade; community, business and personal services; and public administration and defense.
[c]Consists of persons not reporting industry.
[d]Consists of Sydney, Glace Bay, Dominion, New Waterford, North Sydney, Sydney Mines, Indian Reserves, and part of Cape Breton Municipality.
Source: D.B.S., 1961 Census of Canada, Labour Force, Vol. III, Part 2, Cat. No. 94–519 to 94–522; and Population, Vol. I, Part 1, Cat. No. 92–517.

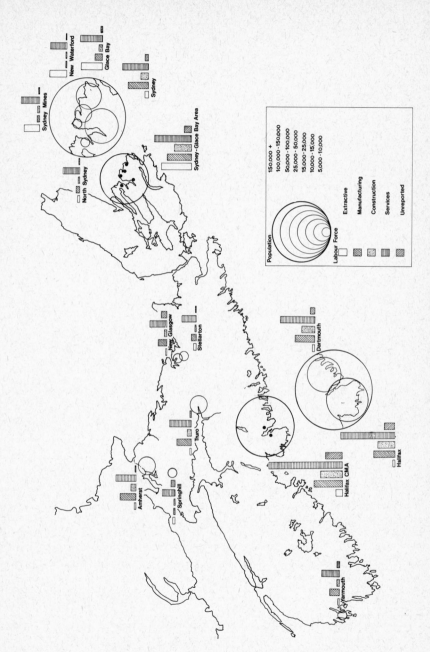

Figure 4-4. Industrial Centers, Nova Scotia.

(d) geographical distribution of places with different sizes of population;
(3) Boundaries of the areas for which δ is calculated.

The influence of size and shape of the territory occupied by the industrial agglomerations in each province can be eliminated by a simple formula, but actually this is the factor of greatest interest. Population size and distribution pattern, on the other hand, do not affect results in the present case because a relative rather than absolute measure of industrial output was used in calculating δ. Far more serious is the influence of boundaries, which in the case of Ontario are quite arbitrary with respect to Quebec and to the important industrial agglomerations just across the United States border. The industrial centers in the United States undoubtedly shaped the existing spatial pattern of manufacturing in Ontario in the past and are strongly influencing it at present Finally, cast in relative terms, the index fails to reveal the important and perhaps even overriding effects of differences in size of output. The higher spatial concentration of manufacturing in Nova Scotia is simply the result of the smaller size of the province compared even to the densely settled parts of Ontario.

The validity of the index may be questioned on other grounds as well. It is not at all certain that the effects of a spatial concentration comprising several adjacent centers are equivalent to those of a single urban agglomeration. It might well be that some types of economies do not arise if the various plants are located in different, even neighboring cities; in this case a single large agglomeration would have to be viewed as a qualitatively different phenomenon from a cluster of centers. The essence of economies of spatial juxtaposition is so far a matter for speculation and a highly controversial issue. It is undoubtedly affected by the changing impact of friction of space as a result of developments in modern transportation technology.

Friction of space can be thought of as being composed of three elements:

(1) Transport of goods. Here the cost and time involved in obtaining supplies is important.
(2) Transport of persons. Besides cost and time (the latter usually more important than the former), the discomfort involved in traveling, which often sets the upper limit to commuting, has to be considered.
(3) Transport of ideas. Cost and time involved are not negligible, but communications over space are less than perfect and do not completely replace face-to-face contacts.

Should easy and frequent face-to-face contacts be the main reason for the continued existence of downtown financial and administrative centers, several smaller agglomerations could hardly replace a single one.

The most important features of the spatial organization of Nova Scotia are the lack of strong nodal points capable of generating growth and the rather diffuse road network illustrated in Figure 4-5. Whether, and to what extent the antiquated settlement pattern of the province evolved in the 18th and 19th centuries and adapted to the technological and economic needs of a less sophisticated society is a significant factor in retarding or even preventing growth is a highly pertinent question. At any rate, the government policy, which until rather recently has been one of fostering industrial developments in a multitude of centers, has done nothing to remedy it. The more recent policy manifestations are the doubling of hardboard producing capacity at Chester, the location of the two proposed tire factories at Bridgewater and at Abercrombie Point in Pictou County, and the location of the thermal power plant at Trenton. All of these involve very heavy government financing and participation. From the point of view of improving spatial organization and promoting overall economic development of the province this policy seems to involve waste of scarce investment resources, the extent of which is difficult to establish. The long-run economic considerations were in any case probably irrelevant in arriving at these decisions because of the overriding sociopolitical pressures underlying the decisions.

The present policy seems to concentrate on developing growth points in Sydney, in Yarmouth, and in the Canso Strait area around Port Hawkesbury. Halifax has, surprisingly, been added to the list only recently and seemingly with some hesitation. Yet it is somewhat doubtful whether Nova Scotia will have the resources in the foreseeable future to develop even one urban-industrial complex capable of generating economic growth, let alone several such complexes.

The motivation for trying to channel investment funds to Sydney is clearly predicated on the desire to prevent relocations that would be costly both in economic and, above all, social terms. Whether the currently contemplated heavy investments of some $100 million in the iron and steel plant and some smaller manufacturing ventures will do more than prevent further decline is doubtful. It is, of course, conceivable that an increase of steel output by twenty-five percent to well over one million tons, or perhaps as high as 1.5 million tons, combined with a new world interest in Canadian coal and coke, may put a new light on the future of the coal industry by drastically increasing demand. The future output of coal and coke will be affected by the new Lingan mine, scheduled to enter production in 1974-5 at an investment cost of at least $23 million, and by the contemplated modernization and expansion of existing coking capacity, which stands at present at 625,000 tons. Other investments in manufacturing in the Sydney area are more modest and have not fared well so far, mainly due to labor unrest.

The rationale behind the very heavy investments in the Canso area is less obvious. It is true that the Canso causeway created a magnificent year-round ice-free natural harbor, that the area has some minor mineral deposits like celestite and salt and some hopes that the massive search for oil and

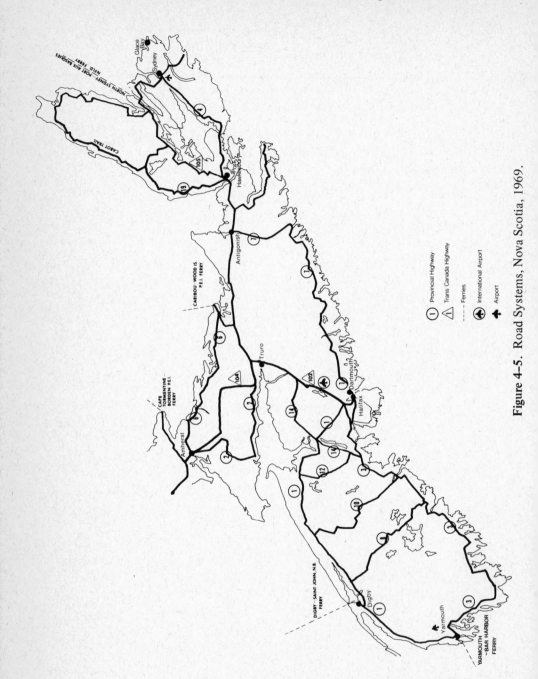

Figure 4–5. Road Systems, Nova Scotia, 1969.

natural gas on the continental shelf will soon be crowned with success; yet all this seems insufficient to justify the dispersion of investments either largely financed by the government or directly owned by the province. Besides the pulp plant, a fish processing plant, and two heavy water plants, a new refinery is nearing completion, salt and celestite mining operations are being started, while several small manufacturing units are in the project stage. Because of its distance from the Sydney area, beyond the range of easy commuting, the developments around Port Hawkesbury are unlikely to offer much relief to the hard-pressed communities at the other end of the island.

Investments in the Halifax Metro area are so far more modest and do not enjoy strong government support. The container terminal on Halifax Harbor and the Tufts Cove thermal power plant are among the most significant ones, but they are supplemented and largely overshadowed in terms of financial outlays by construction of university and office buildings and of new housing units.

Yet Halifax, probably more than the other centers currently being developed, holds out some hope of reaching a size and vitality likely to influence the growth patterns in the rest of the province. It houses a population of 198,000, is the seat of provincial administration, boasts several institutions of learning (including a significant medical center), has an important harbor, a naval base, and a highly developed infrastructure, which together add up to a list of assets not matched east of Quebec City.

According to some estimates, [24] however, even Halifax is unlikely to reach a population of 500,000, let alone 800,000, within the next fifteen to twenty years. The constraints examined in the study were employment in certain key industries, investment funds (both public and private), and construction capacity.

For the hypothesized population levels of 350,000 and 500,000 for 1986, total required employment was calculated by assuming 39.5 percent labor force participation rate, a four percent structural unemployment rate, and 10,000 in-commuters. Aggregate employment in the service and urban-oriented industries was projected, based on the "minimum requirements" [25] approach and existing employment patterns in cities of similar size and character; the remaining required employment was assumed to be mainly in manufacturing.

The possibility of attracting various industries to Halifax was carefully examined and the required investments for the most likely combination of industries were calculated. The total business investments excluding housing and local services would have to reach, for the period 1970–1986, $720 million for an agglomeration of 350,000 and $1,495 million for one of 500,000. This does not appear impossible in view of the fact that such investments are likely to reach $156 million in 1970 in the whole of Nova Scotia. They have been rising rapidly over the past nine years, increasing

Table 4-9

Estimated Total Net[a] Investment Required for the Population Growth of the Halifax Metro Area to 350,000 and 500,000 by 1986

Type of Investment	City of 350,000	City of 500,000
	(in millions of dollars)	
Business investment		
Services	156	298
Urban-oriented industries	97	202
Manufacturing	467	995
	720	1,495
Housing and local services		
Housing	1,139	2,279
Local services (local water and sewer connections)	124	247
	1,263	2,526
Public administration		
Schools	38	76
Hospitals (backlog of $7.0 million)	44	81
Fire	2	3
Police	1	1
Roads	120	240
Bridges	9	9[b]
Parks and recreation	2	4[b]
New water supply, trunk sewers and treatment plant	10	20
	226	434

[a]Depreciation of existing investments and housing is not included.

[b]Rough estimates for which no background information was gathered.

on the average by 8.5 percent per year compared with five percent nationally, although a large part of the total was invested outside the Halifax Metro area. Table 4-9 indicates total requirements for investment funds. The main problem here, therefore, seems to be the ability to attract entrepreneurs and to provide inducements capable of outweighing the disadvantages inherent in locating in the Maritimes, rather than the availability of financial resources.

The capacity of the construction industry to cope with the rapid growth of the Halifax Metro area and the availability of investment funds for housing is a different and more complex matter. According to calculations by Lewis, a population of 350,000 would require over 65,000 new housing units, or rather more than 4,000 per year, while in the second alternative, construction of over 130,000 units or well over 8,000 per year would be required. In both cases, replacements of units currently in existence have been disregarded. These figures far exceed the present construction rate as illustrated in Table 4-10 and Figure 4-6.

Table 4-10
Housing Completions, Including Replacements, Halifax and Nova
Scotia, 1961-1967

Year	Halifax	Nova Scotia
1961	1,365	3,932
1962	1,590	3,427
1963	1,660	3,491
1964	1,680	3,127
1965	1,655	3,471
1966	1,133	3,588
1967	997	2,581

It should be noted that about forty-two percent of the units constructed during 1962-1966 were replacements of existing units, while the projections are limited to net additions.

The financial outlays required also far exceed those available currently or in the foreseeable future. Taking into account the not inconsiderable funds required for ancillary investments and infrastructure, it appears that housing and public services may present a real constraint on the rapid development of an urban complex constituting a growth pole in Nova Scotia.

4 Development Trends

Study of the sectoral composition can be instrumental in providing an explanation of temporal changes taking place in a regional economy. In very broad terms, the growth of a regional economy can be attributed to a combination of the following three factors:

(1) The national growth effect, due to developments in the national economy of which the region forms part. Economic progress achieved in the nation can exercise manifold influences upon the regional economy, such as sustained demand for its products, improved supply of raw materials and intermediate products at lowered prices, abundant flow of investment funds, or technical and organizational innovations.

(2) The industry mix effect, which refers to the presence or relative weight of the fast-growing modern industries as against the older stagnating or declining ones. The industrial mix can help explain a higher growth rate in regions having relatively more fast-growing industries than the nation as a whole.

(3) The competitive effect, which is treated as a residual and refers to the numerous and often ill-defined influences that cause an industry to

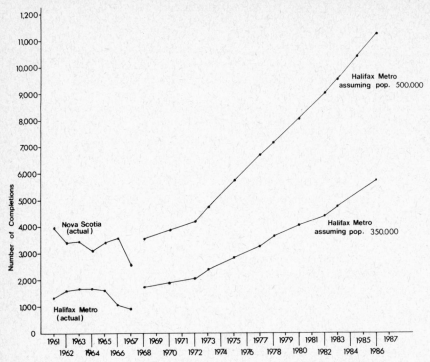

Figure 4-6. Housing Requirements for Alternative Future Sizes of Halifax Metro. Actual Number of Completions Includes Units Needed for Replacement, Whereas Future Requirements Refer to Net Additions.

grow in a specific region faster or slower than the average national rate. Differences in technology, quality of local management and labor force, and economies of scale and agglomeration are among the factors responsible for this effect.

An interesting although somewhat crude tool used for analyzing total growth in terms of its main components is shift analysis.[26] It is ordinarily computed on the basis of employment data, covering a time period spanned by censuses because of the abundance of employment statistics available. In order to probe into the developments in Nova Scotia, the decade 1951–1961, covering the interval between two decennial censuses, and the years 1961–1965 have been used.

The results of shift analysis covering the periods 1951–1961 and 1961–1965 are summarized in Figure 4-7, which shows that during the first period

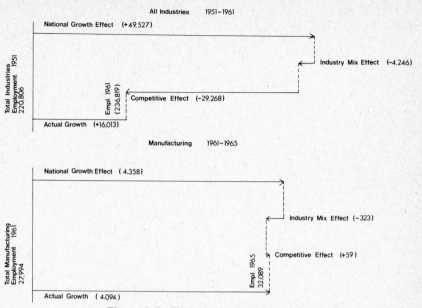

Figure 4-7. Shift Analysis: Nova Scotia.

the actual growth in employment in Nova Scotia amounted to about
16,000 persons. Had the Nova Scotian economy grown at the national rate
of growth of 22.43 percent, however, the increase in employment would have
amounted to 49,500.[f]

One of the causes of this unsatisfactory performance was the proportion
of slow-growing industries operating in Nova Scotia, which was higher than
in the nation as a whole. Yet the industry mix effect, although umistakably
negative, was rather weak, accounting by itself for a deficiency of approximately 4,200 jobs compared to what Nova Scotia could have attained had the
national growth rate prevailed. The highly negative competitive effect was
far more important, being responsible for a deficiency of about 29,300 new
jobs that might otherwise have been generated.

During the subsequent five years, growth at the national growth rate,
still higher than the regional, would have resulted in barely 4,400 new jobs,
due undoubtedly to the slower pace of national economic expansion. The
still perceptible weak industry mix effect reduced this figure further by about
300 jobs, but the competitive effect seems to have disappeared or even reversed
itself, resulting in a total actual growth of approximately 4,100 jobs.

------

[f]Details of calculations are given in Appendix G.

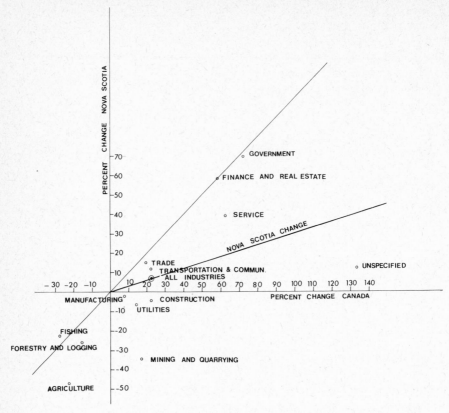

Figure 4–8. Shift Analysis: Changes 1951–1961, Major Industry Groups.

These general conclusions have to be supplemented by a more detailed analysis, with the first objective being to determine which groups of industries were responsible for the relative lack of progress in Nova Scotia. Such an analysis yields new insights into the sectoral structure of the regional economy, and might even have some policy implications. In Figure 4-8 the percentage changes in employment during the intercensal period 1951–1961 are marked for Canada on the horizontal axis and for Nova Scotia on the vertical axis. Each industry is represented by a dot describing its rate of change in the nation and in Nova Scotia during the 1951–1961 period.

The interpretation of the figure is straightforward. Industries found above the horizontal axis were growing in Canada. Hence, industries growing in both the nation and the province are located in the positive quadrant; those growing in both the nation and the province at the same rate are located on the 45° line. Finally, a point has been added showing the growth of Nova Scotia as a whole. For purposes of easier identification a line has been drawn through that point. It's position below the 45° line clearly demonstrates that the Nova Scotia rate of progress was much slower than that of Canada as a whole.

An examination of the figure shows that, on the whole, industries growing in the nation were also growing in Nova Scotia (upper right quadrant) and those declining in the nation were also declining in the province (lower left quadrant). Yet the growing industries were often growing in Nova Scotia at a slower rate and those declining were declining more quickly. Moreover, four industries (namely, mining and quarrying, utilities, construction, and manufacturing) growing in the nation registered declines in Nova Scotia. No industries were growing in the province faster than in Canada as a whole, but two (namely, finance and real estate, and government) were located on or near the 45° line, indicating identical rates of growth in both the nation and the region. Thus, Nova Scotia not only had a larger proportion of the slow-growing or declining industries than the nation as a whole but, a fact of far greater concern, those industries growing in the nation at a higher than average rate did not prosper in the province. Almost universally, the competitive effect seemed to work against Nova Scotia.

The first obvious, although crude, policy implication is that, *ceteris paribus*, the region should try to attract industries with high rates of growth in the nation, those located as far to the right as possible or at least to the right of the average national rate of growth of roughly twenty-two percent.

The analysis can be carried a step further by dealing separately and in greater sectoral detail with heavy and light manufacturing. Figure 4-9 presents the situation in heavy manufacturing. Again, several types of heavy manufacturing activities that were growing in the nation as a whole either registered outright and serious losses in Nova Scotia or at best their progress was much less pronounced. This is especially true of the railroad rolling stock industry, cement manufacturing, stone products, petroleum and coal products, and several others, marked in the lower right quadrant. The situation in heavy industries, however, is actually more serious than is revealed by shift analysis because, whereas in Canada and other developed nations the labor force is being drawn away from heavy industries to other occupations, a significant part of the population of Cape Breton Island depends upon those very industries.

Industries growing rapidly in Nova Scotia, in fact more rapidly than in the nation as a whole, included aircraft and parts, asbestos products, other machinery, and boiler and plate works, while concrete product manufacturing grew at a very fast rate both in Nova Scotia and in the nation as a whole.

Light industries were not prominently represented in Nova Scotia in 1961. Consequently, there are few notable features revealed by this part of the analysis, as shown in Figure 4-10. Of interest is the rapid growth of other electrical products, ornamental metal products, and chemical products, all

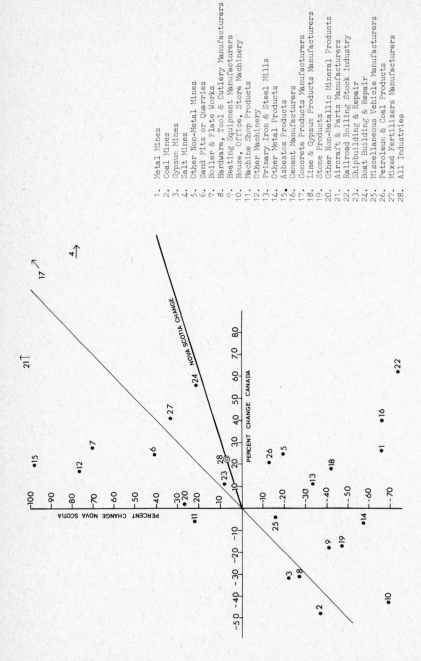

Figure 4-9. Shift Analysis: Changes 1951–1961, Heavy Industries.

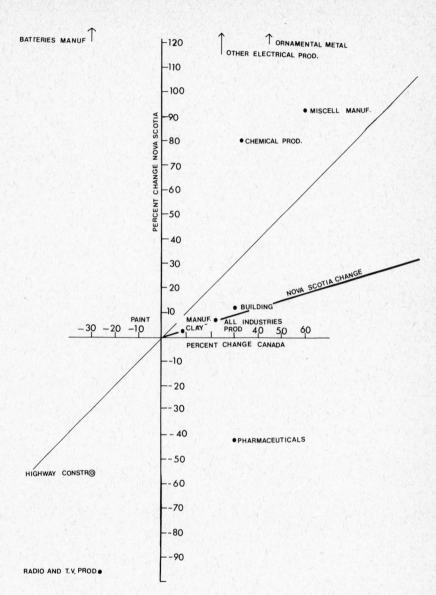

Figure 4–10. Shift Analysis: Changes 1951–1961, Light Industries.

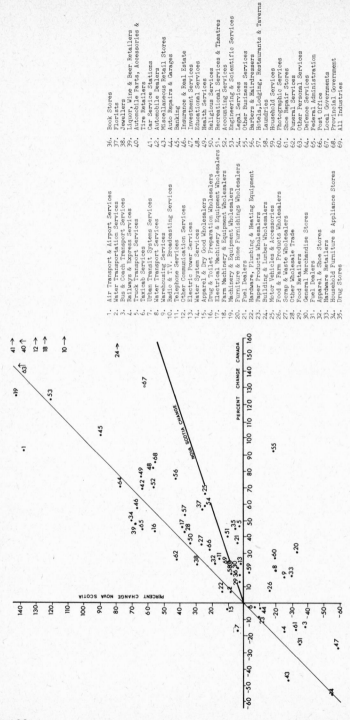

Figure 4-11. Shift Analysis: Changes 1951–1961, Services and Trade.

1. Air Transport & Airport Services
2. Water Transportation Services
3. Bus & Coach Transport Services
4. Railways & Express Services
5. Truck Transport Services
6. Taxicab Services
7. Urban Transit Systems Services
8. Water Transport Services
9. Warehousing Services
10. Radio & T.V. Broadcasting Services
11. Telephone Services
12. Other Communication Services
13. Electric Power Services
14. Water System Services
15. Apparel & Dry Good Wholesalers
16. Drug & Toilet Preparation Wholesalers
17. Electrical Machinery & Equipment Wholesalers
18. Farm Machinery & Equipment Wholesalers
19. Machinery & Equipment Wholesalers
20. Furniture & Home Furnishings Wholesalers
21. Fuel Dealers
22. Hardware, Plumbing & Heating Equipment
23. Paper Products Wholesalers
24. Building & Lumber Wholesalers
25. Motor Vehicles & Accessories
26. Food & Farm Products Wholesalers
27. Scrap & Waste Wholesalers
28. Other Wholesale Trade
29. Food Retailers
30. General Merchandise Stores
31. Fuel Dealers
32. Apparel & Shoe Stores
33. Hardware Retailers
34. Household Furniture & Appliance Stores
35. Drug Stores

36. Book Stores
37. Florists
38. Jewellers
39. Liquor, Wine & Beer Retailers
40. Automobile Parts, Accessories & Tire Retailers
41. Car Service Stations
42. Automobile Dealers
43. Miscellaneous Retail Stores
44. Auto Repairs & Garages
45. Banking
46. Insurance & Real Estate
47. Investment Services
48. Educational Services
49. Health Services
50. Religious Services
51. Recreational Services & Theatres
52. Accounting Services
53. Engineering & Scientific Services
54. Legal Services
55. Other Business Services
56. Barbers & Hairdressers
57. Hotels,Lodging, Restaurants & Taverns
58. Laundries
59. Household Services
60. Photographic Services
61. Shoe Repair Stores
62. Funeral Services
63. Other Personal Services
64. Defence Services
65. Federal Administration
66. Post Office
67. Local Governments
68. Provincial Government
69. All Industries

188

of which may have some future in the province. On the other hand, in the area of pharmaceuticals and even in highway construction, the record of Nova Scotia during 1951–61 was uninspiring.

The tertiary activities are analyzed in Figure 4–11. High hopes are often attached to the development of these sectors, although it appears that, in a region located far from major industrial agglomerations, services, even of an advanced type, cannot be the prime movers of progress and development. Increases in tertiary activities in Nova Scotia have been going on at roughly the same pace as in the nation as a whole. It is, nonetheless, disturbing to see the very highest growth rates associated with such industries as personal services and some types of retailing that are not prominent in modern growing economies. In services connected with mechanical equipment, such as trucking, fuel dealers, and electric power services, the progress of Nova Scotia was far below the nation as a whole.

Another way of presenting the results of shift analysis, yielding a slightly different perspective, is to display them in relative terms, with the 1961 figures shown as a percentage of the corresponding 1951 total. Figure 4–12 illustrates the results.

The first quadrant refers, as before, to those industries that registered growth both in the nation and in the province. The second quadrant indicates those industries which declined in the nation and grew in the province. The third quadrant indicates industries which declined both in the nation and in Nova Scotia. Finally, the fourth quadrant indicates those industries which grew in the nation but declined in the province. It is interesting to note that in this last category are to be found petroleum and coal products, storage, leather industries, and metal mines, the last a reflection of the rapid growth of metal mining elsewhere in Canada.

Shift analysis brings forcefully to the fore the relative attractiveness of the region to industries the growth rates of which show wide variations. While a region with a high or increasing share of the traditional, slow-growing sectors faces obvious difficulties, the explicit introduction of growth rates as an element in selecting industries for promotion often poses a dilemma to decision makers, since the fast-growing sectors often lack other desirable characteristics such as high output/capital, or labor/capital ratio. While admittedly crude, shift analysis is often used in simple models of regional growth, serving as a useful link between national sectoral growth forecast and regional predictions.

5 Comparative Costs

The flow of private investments, particularly into the secondary or manufacturing sectors of Nova Scotia, does not compare well with develop-

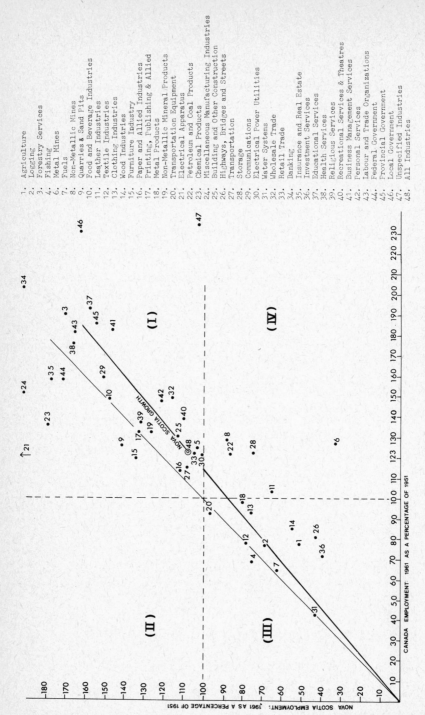

1. Agriculture
2. Logging
3. Forestry Services
4. Fishing
5. Metal Mines
6. Fuels
7. Non-Metallic Mines
8. Quarries & Sand Pits
9. Food and Beverage Industries
10. Leather Industries
11. Textile Industries
12. Clothing Industries
13. Wood Industries
14. Furniture Industry
15. Paper and Allied Industries
16. Printing, Publishing & Allied
17. Metal Products
18. Non-Metallic Mineral Products
19. Transportation Equipment
20. Electrical Apparatus
21. Petroleum and Coal Products
22. Chemical Products
23. Miscellaneous Manufacturing Industries
24. Building and Other Construction
25. Highways, Bridges and Streets
26. Transportation
27. Storage
28. Communications
29. Electrical Power Utilities
30. Water Systems
31. Wholesale Trade
32. Retail Trade
33. Banking
34. Insurance and Real Estate
35. Investment Services
36. Educational Services
37. Health Services
38. Religious Services
39. Recreational Services & Theatres
40. Business Management Services
41. Personal Services
42. Labour and Trade Organizations
43. Federal Government
44. Provincial Government
45. Local Government
46. Unspecified Industries
47. All Industries

Figure 4–12. Shift Analysis: 1961 as Percentage of 1951.

CANADA EMPLOYMENT: 1961 AS A PERCENTAGE OF 1951

NOVA SCOTIA EMPLOYMENT: 1961 AS A PERCENTAGE OF 1951

190

ments in some other parts of Canada. The causes are hardly to be found in the low rate or small volume of local savings, since the high interregional mobility of investment capital makes access to national or international financial resources easy. A more plausible explanation is probably the low attractiveness of the province for investors, the most obvious expression of which is likely to be found in lower rates of return on invested capital.

The possibility of analyzing this phenomenon by short-cut methods is severely limited because of data deficiencies and the conceptual ambiguities surrounding the measurement of capital. More important, the validity of conclusions drawn from interregional comparisons based on aggregate analysis is often further circumscribed by fundamental differences in product mix, technology, and a myriad of other factors, some of which are only transitory in nature. Therefore, an analysis of marginal rates of return on invested capital, though theoretically valid, appears to be too risky. Table 4–11 shows the huge differences in average rates of return on capital invested in manufacturing industries in Nova Scotia and in Ontario, the most industrialized Canadian province. For purposes of comparison, "returns" have been defined as the difference between (1) the value of shipments and (2) wages of production and related workers, cost of fuel and electricity, and cost of material and supplies. Total investments in manufacturing, including replacements, have been cumulated over a period of sixteen years. Neither depreciations nor fluctuations in the price level of investment goods could be taken into account, due to lack of data.[g] The implied assumption is that the average life span of manufacturing investment capital is sixteen years, which is rather short as far as buildings are concerned, although it compares well with the criterion adopted by D.B.S. for most industrial equipment.[27]

The results of this admittedly very crude comparison seem to indicate that a dollar invested in manufacturing in Nova Scotia yields on the average 31.3 cents gross per year as compared to 62.6 cents in Ontario, a difference too big to be dismissed simply by reference to the inadequacy of data or of approach. Moreover, the two provinces do not display such spectacular differences in terms of rate of return per dollar of shipments. For all manufacturing activities, the average ratio of returns to shipments $(\Sigma\Pi_i/\Sigma S_i)$ in 1966 was 0.2362 for Nova Scotia compared to 0.2820 for Ontario.

There is no dearth of explanations for the relative unattractiveness of Nova Scotia to investors. Most of them are, however, subject to considerable controversy, for while some analysts point to the relatively low quality of the labor force, the lack of competent management, the underinvested infrastructure, the remoteness of the region devoid of major urban-industrial

---

[g]The derived total is far from equivalent to the notion of invested capital. The method, which is essentially a crude variant of the Perpetual Inventory Method, has been described elsewhere.

Table 4-11

Average Return Per Dollar of Investment in Manufacturing Industries, Nova Scotia and Ontario, 1966

Industry	Nova Scotia					Ontario				
	Cumulated Investments[a] $K_i = \sum_{t=1951}^{1966} I_{i_t}$	Value of Shipments S_i	Cost of Shipments C_i	Total Returns $\pi_i = S_i - C_i$	Return per Dollar of Investment $\lambda_i = \frac{S_i - C_i}{K_i}$	Cumulated Investments $K_i = \sum_{t=1951}^{1966} I_{i_t}$	Value of Shipments S_i	Cost of Shipments C_i	Total Returns $\pi_i = S_i - C_i$	Return per Dollar of Investment $\lambda_i = \frac{S_i - C_i}{K_i}$
	(in millions of dollars)				(cents)	(in millions of dollars)				(cents)
Food and beverage	96.2	191.1	148.7	42.4	44.1	975.1	2,928.0	2,131.5	796.4	81.7
Textiles	10.5	9.6	6.1	3.6	33.8	369.9	561.9	429.0	132.7	35.9
Knitting and clothing	4.8	15.7	11.8	3.9	80.8	81.2	393.7	299.3	94.5	116.3
Wood and wood products	15.9	28.4	20.9	7.6	47.6	214.7	567.9	414.8	153.1	71.3
Paper and allied	128.2	51.6	34.8	16.7	13.1	821.7	1,101.8	786.3	315.5	38.4
Printing, publishing, and allied	8.6	15.5	7.0	8.6	99.8	272.9	638.6	351.0	287.6	105.4
Transportation	19.2	80.1	65.8	14.3	74.3	1,007.1	3,405.4	2,707.8	697.7	69.3
Electrical products	6.6	16.6	14.9	1.6	24.7	431.9	1,503.7	1,043.6	460.2	106.5
Nonmetallic mineral products	18.6	13.2	8.3	4.8	26.0	493.7	551.5	359.1	192.4	39.0
Chemical products	47.2	7.4	4.2	3.2	6.8	1,084.1	1,314.9	765.3	549.6	50.7
Others	105.9	183.3	145.4	38.0	35.9	4,670.2	6,485.2	4,677.5	1,807.6	38.7
Total manufacturing	461.7	612.5	467.8	144.7	31.3	10,422.5	19,452.6	13,965.3	5,487.3	52.6

[a]Cumulated investment figures for Nova Scotia were provided by D.B.S., Business Finance Division, Capital Expenditures Section.

Note: K_i = cumulated investments in industry i
I_{i_t} = investments in industry i in year t
S_i = value of shipments in industry i

C_i = costs of fuel and electricity, of materials and supplies used, and wages of production and related workers in industry i
π_i = total returns in industry i
λ_i = returns per dollar of investment in industry i

Based on: D.B.S., *Canada Yearbook 1969*, Table 15, pp. 710–712; Department of Trade and Commerce, *Supplement to Private and Public Investment in Canada: Outlook, Regional Estimates, 1953–1960* and *Private and Public Investment in Canada: Outlook and Regional Estimates, 1961–1968.*

agglomerations, others contend that the local labor force is, on the average, second to none in Canada, that Nova Scotia has long been famous for its entrepreneurial talent, which it exported to other parts of North America, and so forth. A massive effort to disentangle and quantify the various factors at work by examining the individual components of production costs was undertaken recently by George.[28]

The first problem to be attacked was the relative cost of labor. This is straightforward and easy to obtain when analyzing the labor components in the cost bill of a single commodity produced in different places using equivalent technological procedures. At the level of a whole economy, however, only crude comparisons are possible. For this purpose George analyzed the average cost of labor in manufacturing industries in Nova Scotia in selected years between 1946 and 1962 and compared it with similar figures for Quebec-Ontario. The data were standardized in order to eliminate the differences due to such obvious factors as product mix and average number of working hours.

The average annual wages and salaries per employee in Nova Scotia in 1962 amounted to 78.7 percent of those paid in the Quebec-Ontario region.[h] This figure does not, however, reveal the true extent of the discrepancy, a substantial part of which was due to a different mix of low-wage and high-wage industries in the two regions and to a different male-female composition. Moreover, in 1962 Nova Scotia employees worked on the average 99.7 percent of the working hours of their Quebec-Ontario counterparts. The following succinctly summarizes George's calculations.

In order to allow for differences in industry mix, average wages and salaries in Nova Scotia were computed assuming the same employment distribution as in Quebec-Ontario, the pattern region, the implied formula being:

$$A^{NS} = \frac{\Sigma(r_i^{NS} \cdot E_i^{Q-O})}{\Sigma E_i^{Q-O}} \; ;$$

where

A^{NS} = average manufacturing wages and salaries in Nova Scotia standardized to the Quebec-Ontario employment pattern,

r_i = wage rates in the ith industry,

E_i = employment in the ith industry,

---

[h]A substantial part of the difference was due to the very low wages and salaries paid in Nova Scotia outside Halifax. In Halifax itself, average wages and salaries in 1962 represented 89.5 percent of those paid in the Montreal-Toronto metropolitan areas.

and where the superscripts *NS* and *Q-O* refer to Nova Scotia and Quebec-Ontario respectively.

Expressing average standardized Nova Scotia manufacturing wages and salaries as a percentage of those in Quebec-Ontario, one could write

$$\frac{A^{NS}}{A^{Q-O}} = \frac{\Sigma(r_i^{NS} \cdot E_i^{Q-O})}{\Sigma(r_i^{Q-O} \cdot E_i^{Q-O})} \; ;$$

The difference between the unadjusted and adjusted wage rates in percentage form, or the standardization factor, is then

$$S = \frac{\Sigma(r_i^{NS} \cdot E_i^{NS}) \cdot \Sigma E_i^{Q-O}}{\Sigma E_i^{NS} \cdot \Sigma(r_i^{Q-O} \cdot E_i^{Q-O})} - \frac{\Sigma(r_i^{NS} \cdot E_i^{Q-O})}{\Sigma(r_i^{Q-O} \cdot E_i^{Q-O})}$$

$$= \frac{\Sigma(r_i^{NS} \cdot E_i^{NS}) \cdot \Sigma E_i^{Q-O} - \Sigma(r_i^{NS} \cdot E_i^{Q-O}) \cdot \Sigma E_i^{NS}}{\Sigma E_i^{NS} \cdot \Sigma(r_i^{Q-O} \cdot E_i^{Q-O})} \; ;$$

According to these calculations, this factor amounted to + 7.9 percent in 1962. A similar calculation was made to standardize for the lower percentage of employed women in Nova Scotia, leading to a correcting factor of –3.7 percent.

While earnings thus adjusted might provide interesting insights into the relative welfare of manufacturing employees in the two regions, from the investor's point of view they have to be cast against the background of performance. Value added per manufacturing employee would appear to be an obvious measure of performance. In Nova Scotia in 1962 it amounted to only 68.2 percent of the Quebec-Ontario figure. This is, nonetheless, a somewhat weak surrogate for an index of quality of local labor force, because it depends to a large extent upon several other factors, such as type of industry or the amount of invested capital per employee. In order to avoid some of these difficulties, George standardized the value added per employee figure for Nova Scotia for three factors to make it comparable to that of the Quebec-Ontario region; namely, for length of working week, size distribution of establishments and industry mix.

Adjustment for length of working week raised the index significantly to 68.3 percent. More important numerically was adjustment for size distribution of establishments, accounting to some extent for economies of scale in the larger Quebec-Ontario plants. In 1962 this factor accounted for 4.3 percent of the difference in value added per manufacturing employee. While average size of plants accounts for some economies of scale, the potentially more important economies of agglomeration completely elude this scrutiny. The last adjustment, accounting for difference in industry mix, raised the Nova Scotia percentage by 9.7 percent.

According to these calculations, the 1962 ratio of value added per manufacturing employee in Nova Scotia, compared to Quebec-Ontario, was as follows:

	Nova Scotia as percentage of Quebec-Ontario
(i) Unadjusted value added per manufacturing employee	68.2
(ii) Adjusted for length of working week	68.3
(iii) Adjusted for (ii) and size distribution of establishments	72.6
(iv) Adjusted for (iii) and industry mix	82.3

The above calculations disregard the effects of interaction, or assume that the various measures are orthogonal to one another, which does not seem at all plausible.

In his final computation, George arrives at the following figures for cost of labor in manufacturing industries in Nova Scotia in 1962, expressed as a percentage of Quebec-Ontario:

A)	Average annual wages and salaries per employee	78.7 percent
B)	Working hours per employee	99.7 percent
C)	Labor quality or value added per employee with the three adjustments described above under (iv)	82.3 percent
D)	$A \div B \div C$	95.9 percent
E)	Differences in wages and salaries due to industry mix	+7.9 percent
F)	Differences in wages and salaries due to male-female ratio in the labor force	– 3.7 percent
G)	Cost of labor (D + E + F)	100.1 percent

This last value oscillates little between 1946 and 1962, thus leaving the impression that from the point of view of labor costs there is little to choose between Nova Scotia and the more advanced provinces of Canada.

It is doubtful whether an extension of this type of analysis to individual industries would produce results warranting the extensive computations involved.

These results are markedly different from, and not directly comparable to, those obtained by Howland, [29] who tried to assign quantitative measures to factors responsible for the disparity in earned incomes between the Atlantic Provinces and Ontario in 1951. Aside from differences in objectives of study and in time and area investigated, the statistical techniques used also differed.

Howland's analysis begins with gross earned income in 1951, which stood at $923 million in the Atlantic Provinces. This total was adjusted for factors that were considered to affect it significantly; namely, labor force participation rate, rate of utilization of existing labor force, industry mix, and average earning rates. A fifth factor, different male-female mix in the labor force, also affected earnings, as women's average earning rates were only half those of their male counterparts in many industries. This factor was taken care of by carrying out the entire calculation in terms of male units.

Standardization with respect to labor force participation rates was based on the observation that at Ontario's rate the labor force of the Atlantic Provinces in male units and hence its earning power would be 22.8 percent greater. Similarly, the rate of utilization of the existing labor force was standardized by calculating the total income in the Atlantic Provinces, had the average number of weeks worked per year been equal to that in Ontario; i.e. had unemployment, permanent and seasonal, and work stoppages in the Atlantic Provinces been kept to the level prevailing in Central Canada.

The results of standardization are shown in Table 4–12.

The difference with respect to industry mix between these estimates and those of George is very substantial. Even more significant is the huge difference in average earning rates, which, incidentally, is one of the most striking characteristics of Eastern Canada.

Table 4–12
Standardization of Incomes in the Atlantic Provinces

	Gross earned income in the Atlantic Provinces, 1951	Increase	Increase as percentage of actual gross earned income (in male worker units)
	(in millions of dollars)		
Actual	a = 923		
Standardized for:			
Labor force participation rate	s = 1,120	$(S = s - a)$ = 197	22.8
Rate of utilization of labor force	w = 980	$(W = w - a)$ = 57	6.6
Industry mix	m = 1,029	$(M = m - a)$ = 106	12.3
Average earning rate	r = 1,323	$(R = r - a)$ = 400	46.2
			87.9

The next step was to account for the interaction among the four factors considered in the analysis. For example, an increase in average earning rates to the level of Ontario would amount to $400 million or forty-three percent of total gross earned income, while an increase in the labor force participation rate would account for $197 million or twenty-one percent.[i] If a simultaneous occurrence of both events is assumed, the total effect would exceed this sum, because the additional labor would also earn higher wages, or 43% · 21% = 9%, which would amount to $85 million over and above the sixty-four percent increase due to the two factors taken separately. Thus, taking two factors at a time yields:

	Increase Due to Interaction ($ million)
S · W	+11
S · M	+23
S · R	+85
W · M	+19
W · R	+24
M · R	-56
Total	+106

Significantly, interaction between industry mix and average earning rate is negative, because by standardizing for the poor industry mix some of the causes of lower wages are removed. While interaction between two factors corrects some of the results of standardizing for one factor at a time, the effects of interaction between three and four factors at a time might also be considered:

	Increase Due to Interaction ($ million)
S · W · M	+4
S · W · R	+7
S · M · R	-12
W · M · R	+1
S · W · M · R	-1
Total	-1

This is recapitulated in Table 4-13.

The relative significance of each factor can also be measured in a slightly

---

[i]These figures differ from those in Table 4-12 as the latter are based on male worker units.

Table 4-13
Summary of the Effects of Factor Differences on Earned Incomes, 1951

	$ Million	Percentage of Total
	(in male worker units)	
(1) One factor at a time		
S Labor force size	197	22.8
W Weeks/year worked	57	6.6
M Industry mix	106	12.3
R Average earning rate	400	46.2
	760	87.9
(2) Interaction of two factors at a time		
S · W	+11	1.3
S · M	+23	2.7
S · R	+85	9.8
W · M	+19	2.2
W · R	+24	2.7
M · R	−56	−6.5
	+106	12.2
(3) Interaction of three factors at a time		
S · W · M	+4	.5
S · W · R	+7	.8
S · M · R	−12	−1.4
W · M · R	+1	.1
	0	0.0
(4) Interaction of four factors at a time		
S · W · M · R	−1	−0.1
Total	865	100.0
(a) Actual gross earned income in the Atlantic Provinces in 1951	923	
Total gross income standardized for the four factors and interaction	1,788	

Source: Adapted from Howland, R. D., "Some Regional Aspects of Canada's Economic Development," *Royal Commission on Canada's Economic Prospects*, November 1957, Table D-VIII, pp. 248-249.

different way, yielding a different answer. One could remove the effects of all but one factor at a time; in other words, one could calculate the difference in gross earned income when the total remains unstandardized for one factor. In the present case the result would be:

Factor differences removed except:	
Labor force participation rate	36%
Rate of utilization of labor force	13%
Industry mix	11%
Average earning rate	52%

The results are obviously different but can easily be reconciled. In the first case, for example, if the labor force in the Atlantic Provinces were increased by applying Ontario labor force participation rates, the earned income would increase or the disparity would decrease by some twenty-three percent. Alternatively, it could be assumed that all factors are the same. If, under these circumstances, the labor force participation rates in the Atlantic Provinces were to decline without affecting the other factors, it would mean a reduction of earned incomes by eighteen percent, which in terms of the actual difference would amount to thirty-six percent.

Important as they are, labor costs may at best provide only a partial explanation of the relative unattractiveness of Nova Scotia for manufacturing industries. In a modern highly integrated national economy, accessibility or transportation costs on both end products and material inputs may easily turn out to be of crucial importance. An analysis of the relative attractiveness of the province with respect to transportation is complicated by the need to face two problems simultaneously: (1) the availability of transportation in the form of rail, road, water, and air facilities and services, and (2) the cost of these services compared to transportation costs in other locations in Canada.

The relative importance of the four main transportation systems linking Nova Scotia to the industrial core of Canada and to the vast areas beyond is the result of historical developments rather than of the free interplay of market forces in the recent past. Of the four, air freight is the least important, being used mainly for bringing in urgently needed machine parts or dispatching occasional rush orders. Few producers use it continuously. Coastal water transportation, by contrast, is far from insignificant, accounting for almost thirty percent of all shipments. Less than half of it (or just about 1.9 million tons) consists of manufactured goods, among which petroleum products shipped from the Dartmouth refinery to other ports in Eastern Canada (over 1.6 million tons) form the lion's share.[30] But coastal shipping can be dismissed from further consideration, since it has little bearing on the claim of Halifax to a position as a major port of entry to the North American continent.

The relative shares of road and rail transport forcefully illustrate the underdeveloped state of trucking in Nova Scotia. In 1962 road transport accounted for only nine percent of the combined rail and road haulage — that is, 265 million ton-miles, as against 2,689 million by rail. While railway transportation was important in Quebec-Ontario too, trucking accounted there for thirty-two percent of the total, and its share has been growing at a faster rate than in Nova Scotia. The scarcity of trucking services, typical of all the Maritimes, is of even greater significance. As recently as 1966 there were only three or four trucking companies in Nova Scotia operating on a regular basis, of which only two were of any size; hence, even the modest amount of road haulage in Nova Scotia was largely undertaken by vehicles owned by producers or distributors.

The existing situation is the outcome of past policies of the federal government. Until Confederation, Nova Scotia had few links with the rest of

Canada. The St. Lawrence River is frozen in winter and, prior to the construction of locks and canals, could only be used beyond Montreal by small vessels even in the warm season, while the overland transportation route was difficult and expensive. The Intercolonial Railway, completed in 1879, established a convenient connection with the territories to the west, and the policy of fostering economic unity embodied in the British North America Act resulted in freight rate advantages in the Maritimes. The preferential treatment which the Maritimes enjoyed was slowly eroded until 1923, when it had virtually disappeared. The Maritime Freight Rates Act of 1927 again restored the privileged position of the Maritimes, but by then, and even more markedly since the Second World War, technical developments resulting in the decline of the relative importance of transportation costs compared to production costs blunted the impact of preferential treatment with respect to railway rates. An increase in the Maritime Freight Rates Act subsidy in 1957 probably had a positive, but essentially limited, effect.

The application of various subsidies to railway rates had the unwelcome side effect of keeping truck rates too low to support a vigorous industry. More important, until very recently Nova Scotia lacked modern highways. Both the mileage and rate of growth of paved highways and rural roads was, it is true, relatively high, comparing favorably with other parts of Canada, including the industrialized Quebec-Ontario region, on both per thousand inhabitants and per square mile bases. The main difference, and the reason for the preponderance of railway transportation, is to be found in their quality; narrow and poorly surfaced, most roads in Nova Scotia have sharp bends, steep gradients, and cross numerous narrow bridges. This is corroborated by the fact that between 1946 and 1962 Quebec and Ontario invested about one and a half times as much per mile of road as Nova Scotia, in the face of approximately identical land and construction costs. Lack of modern roads, a twenty percent higher cost of fuel due to provincial taxes, and a low demand for haulage nowhere approaching the levels attained between the industrial centers in Central Canada, are the main reasons given by George for the present state of the trucking industry in Nova Scotia. As an outcome of this situation, the costs of haulage per ton-mile by truck are significantly higher than in the Quebec-Ontario region. The 1962 per ton-mile revenues of for-hire trucks were 10.5 cents in Nova Scotia as against 7.0 cents in Quebec-Ontario, or fifty per cent higher.[31]

The relative railway freight rates present a different picture. An extensive analysis of the rather complicated railway rates structure yields the following summary results:

Average Railway Freight Rate per Ton-mile of Manufactured Goods in Carload Lots in Maritime and Eastern Zones in 1962

Within Maritime	2.627 cents
Within Eastern	2.610 cents

Table 5-4
Public Sector Expenditure Multipliers, Nova Scotia, 1960

Type of Expenditure	Direct Effects	Model I Indirect Effects	Model II Indirect and Induced Effects	Model III Indirect, Induced, and Local Government Effects	Total Effects	Ratio of Total to Direct Effects
	Household Income per One Thousand Dollars Expenditure					
Federal Government						
Defense	613	185	519	638	1,251	2.04
Civil	719	157	525	655	1,374	1.91
Provincial Government	293	357	630	741	1,034	3.52
Municipal Government	429	205	472	581	1,010	2.35
Education	573	210	538	659	1,232	2.15
Hospitals	492	199	489	597	1,089	2.21
	Employment per One Million Dollars Expenditure					
Federal Government						
Defense	136	45	123	149	285	2.10
Civil	177	39	124	153	330	1.86
Provincial Government	56	87	150	175	231	4.12
Municipal Government	128	47	109	133	261	2.04
Education	131	51	127	154	285	2.18
Hospitals	113	48	115	140	253	2.24

Based on: Levitt, *op. cit.*

The second way of grouping components of final demand (according to sectors supplying the commodities or services) leads to an analysis of multiplier effects with important policy implications. In subsidizing or otherwise support- ing new industries in a depressed region, government may consider such criteria as the longrun growth potential of the particular industry, employment generated per unit of public or total investments, or employment and new income generated per unit of output. The last criterion brings up the question of multiplier effects. Industries with low employment-to-output ratio but substantial backward link- ages can stimulate the local economy and create total employment in excess of those with a higher employment per unit of output.

A study of multipliers on the basis of the 1960 input-output tables for Nova Scotia, revised and consolidated to sixteen industrial sectors in order to avoid nondisclosure rules, has been carried out by G. S. Bhalla. [3] In his calculations of direct, indirect, and induced effects of changes in demand upon earned personal income, the latter was defined more narrowly as distributed factor income, generated by the sixteen sectors included in the structural matrix. This definition falls short of the more common concept of personal income used in income and product accounts, because it excludes income originating in various governments and interest and dividends accruing to residents of the province from their invest- ments outside the region. Table 5–5 summarizes the sectoral effects. The deriva- tion of the various coefficients is straightforward. The direct income per dollar of output figures (column 2) were read off the table of technical input-output co- efficients. The direct and indirect income per dollar of final demand figures (column 3) were obtained with the help of the inverse matrix. The direct and indirect income per dollar of output figures (column 4) were obtained by dividing those of column 3 by the output levels indicated on the main diagonal of the inverse matrix, which refer to direct and indirect effects upon each sector asso- ciated with unit level demand for its products.

The direct, indirect, and induced incomes generated per dollar of final demand (column 5) were derived with the help of the inverse of the augmented matrix, including the household sector. The direct, indirect, and induced incomes generated per dollar of output (column 6) were derived by dividing those in column 5 by the appropriate element of main diagonal of the same matrix, which again indicates the level of operation required in order to satisfy the direct, indirect, and induced demand following a unit increase in consumption.

The numbers in columns 7, 8, and 9 show the indirect income effects, the induced income effects, and the indirect and induced income effects together, per unit of output, respectively. The last two columns, 10 and 11, indicate the ratio of direct and indirect income to direct income, and of direct, indirect, and induced income to direct income.

In addition to income multipliers, employment multipliers have also been calculated. The various employment effects were calculated by premultiplying the Leontief inverse, modified to include competitive imports and, where neces-

Table 5-5
Income Multipliers, Nova Scotia

Sector (1)	Direct Income per Unit of Output (2)	Direct and Indirect Income per Unit of Final Demand (3)	Direct and Indirect Income per Unit of Output (4)	Direct, Indirect and Induced Income per Unit of Final Demand (5)	Direct, Indirect and Induced Income per Unit of Output (6)	Indirect Income per Unit of Output (4) − (2) (7)	Induced Income per Unit of Output (6) − (4) (8)	Indirect and Induced Income per Unit of Output (6) − (2) (9)	Ratio of Direct and Indirect Income to Direct Income (4) ÷ (2) (10)	Ratio of Direct, Indirect and Induced Income to Direct Income (6) ÷ (2) (11)
Agriculture	.3549	.4472	.5128	.6615	.7311	.1579	.2183	.3762	1.4449	2.0600
Forestry	.7877	.7413	.9555	1.0965	1.4068	.1678	.4513	.6191	1.2130	1.7859
Fishing	.5611	.5596	.7329	.8278	1.0806	.1718	.3477	.5195	1.3061	1.9258
Mining	.5445	.6719	.6655	.9939	.9756	.1210	.3101	.4311	1.2222	1.7917
Manufacturing										
Food	.2515	.2448	.4473	.3621	.6317	.1958	.1844	.3802	1.7785	2.5117
Capital Goods	.3460	.2641	.5268	.3906	.7753	.1808	.2485	.4293	1.5225	2.2407
Fish Products	.2065	.5730	.5966	.8474	.8770	.3901	.2804	.6705	2.8891	4.2469
Sawmills	.3036	.5670	.6407	.8386	.9439	.3371	.3032	.6403	2.1103	3.1090
Pulp and paper	.2579	.5147	.5740	.7613	.8473	.3161	.2733	.5894	2.2256	3.2853
Boat- and Shipbuilding	.5372	.6231	.6862	.9216	1.0149	.1490	.3287	.4777	1.2773	1.8892
Other	.2196	.2017	.3207	.2983	.4609	.1011	.1402	.2413	1.4603	2.0988
Construction										
Residential	.4006	.6325	.6292	.9354	.9175	.2286	.2883	.5169	1.5706	2.2903
Other	.4222	.6316	.6260	.9343	.9178	.2038	.2918	.4956	1.4827	2.1738
Transportation	.4463	.6034	.5790	.8924	.8109	.1327	.2319	.3646	1.2973	1.8169
Utilities	.4508	.5849	.5728	.8653	.8201	.1220	.2473	.3693	1.2706	2.8192
Service	.4675	.5859	.5280	.8667	.5833	.0605	.0553	.1158	1.1294	1.2477

Based on: Bhalla, G. S., op. cit.

sary, households, by the vector of coefficients representing sectoral direct labor requirements per unit of output. The results of these calculations are shown in Table 5-6.

The generally very low interindustry effects are again noticeable, except for such industries as manufactured fish products and paper and pulp. Somewhat stronger multiplier effects are recorded only when household consumption is included in the structural matrix, so that induced effects are accounted for.

These results differ little from the more recent and extensive investigation based on the full matrix. The total effects of a $1,000 increase in final sales upon household income are strongest in personal services, coal mining, forestry, wholesale and retail, hotels and restaurants, and primary fishing. These sectors and the few ranking immediately below share a relative independence of imported inputs, either because as services they use few, if any, or because they belong to extractive industries based on local resources. The same sectors top the list of industries with high direct impact upon household incomes. Hence, the ratio of total to direct effects in these sectors is invariably among the lowest of all industries, averaging around 2.0.

The pattern of impacts of various sectors upon employment is more confused, as it depends strongly upon at least two unrelated factors — namely labor intensity and strength of backward linkages. The electrical equipment industry, for example, generates a direct employment of 104 persons per million dollar sales and creates a total employment of 187, while pulp and paper mills employ only 61 persons per million dollar sales but generate a total of 201 jobs. Petroleum refining, with a very high multiplier effect, generates only 32 jobs per million dollar sales, undoubtedly because it is extremely capital intensive with only 6 directly employed for this volume of output. The industries generating the highest total employment per million dollars of sales are (1) primary fishing, (2) personal service, (3) coal mining, (4) hotels and restaurants, (5) sawmills, (6) wholesale and retail, (7) fish processing, and (8) forestry.

Finally, of some interest are the average income multipliers generated by the existing patterns of final demand expenditures.

The average multiplier in 1960, calculated with the help of the consolidated input-output matrix, stood at 1.476, differing only slightly from the one calculated for the same year, on the basis of the full matrix, as equal to 1.419.

Of far greater significance is the fact that the average demand multiplier for 1965, calculated on the basis of income and product accounts (see page 000), amounted to 1.37. This multiplier has been calculated according to the formula

$$\frac{1}{1-c+m}(I+G+E);$$

where

Table 5-6
Employment Multipliers, Nova Scotia

Sector (1)	Direct Employment Generated per 1000 Units of Output (2)	Direct and Indirect Employment Generated per 1000 Units of Final Demand (3)	Direct and Indirect Employment Generated per 1000 Units of Output (4)	Direct, Indirect and Induced Employment Generated per 1000 Units of Final Demand (5)	Direct, Indirect and Induced Employment Generated per 1000 Units of Output (6)	Indirect Employment per 1000 Units of Output (4) − (2) (7)	Induced Employment per 1000 Units of Output (6) − (4) (8)	Indirect and Induced Employment per 1000 Units of Output (6) − (2) (9)	Ratio of Direct and Indirect Employment to Direct Employment (4) ÷ (2) (10)	Ratio of Direct, Indirect and Induced Employment to Direct Employment (6) ÷ (2) (11)
Agriculture	.2302	.2362	.2708	.3017	.3334	.0406	.0626	.1032	1.1763	1.4483
Forestry	.1522	.1752	.2258	.2837	.3639	.0736	.1381	.2117	1.4835	2.3909
Fishery	.1963	.1835	.2403	.2654	.3464	.0440	.1061	.1501	1.2241	1.7646
Mining	.1360	.1665	.1649	.2648	.2599	.0289	.0950	.1239	1.2125	1.9110
Manufacturing										
Food	.0444	.0648	.1184	.1006	.1755	.0740	.0571	.1311	2.6666	3.9527
Capital Goods	.0620	.0540	.1077	.0927	.1840	.0457	.0763	.1220	1.7370	2.9677
Fish Products	.0616	.1773	.1846	.2611	.2702	.1230	.0856	.2086	2.9967	4.3863
Sawmills	.1097	.1690	.1909	.2520	.2836	.0812	.0927	.1739	1.7402	2.5852
Pulp and Paper	.0417	.1088	.1213	.1842	.2050	.0796	.0837	.1633	2.9088	4.9160
Boat- and Shipbuilding	.1020	.1247	.1373	.2159	.2377	.0353	.1004	.1357	1.3466	2.3303
Other	.0484	.0461	.0733	.0756	.1168	.0249	.0435	.0684	1.5144	2.4132
Construction										
Residential	.0828	.1472	.1464	.2398	.2352	.0636	.0888	.1524	1.7681	2.8405
Other	.0828	.1393	.1380	.2318	.2277	.0552	.0897	.1449	1.6666	2.7500
Transportation	.1065	.1489	.1428	.2372	.2155	.0363	.0727	.1090	1.3408	2.0234
Utilities	.0611	.0944	.0924	.1800	.1706	.0313	.0782	.1095	1.5122	2.7921
Service	.1527	.1836	.1654	.2693	.1812	.0127	.0158	.0285	1.0831	1.1866

Based on: Bhalla, *op. cit.*

c = average propensity to consume,

m = average propensity to import,

I = investments,

G = government expenditures,

E = exports.

The two multipliers are not directly comparable, because the one derived on the basis of income and product accounts indicates simply total additional output associated with a unit increase in final demand, and the one obtained from the input-output study indicates that each unit increase in final demand that is coming from sectors other than household consumption generates an additional 0.419 units of income in industries directly and indirectly supplying consumer goods and services. Thus, while the first disregards interindustry effects, the second is limited to impact upon household incomes. Yet their closeness is undoubtedly due to the extreme openness of the Nova Scotia economy and relative insignificance of interindustry effects. [4]

4 Foreign Trade and Leakages

More than any other system of social accounting, input-output provides reliable data on foreign trade of subnational economies without recourse to detailed and, as a rule, unavailable statistics on movements of goods and services over regional boundaries. An analysis of Nova Scotia exports proved their relative unimportance in the provincial economy, as revealed by the fact that they generated only 18.6 percent of household incomes and 20.2 percent of employment; yet the volume of imports of goods and services is almost double that of exports, and their very size is one of the fundamental features of the structure of the economy of Nova Scotia.

The low multiplier effects characteristic of the Nova Scotia economy result from high import components in most sectors of the local economy.

While the small size of the economy and lack of manufacturing resources provide a ready explanation of the phenomenon, the fact has important and far-reaching repercussions for government development policy. The absence of significant multiplier effects severely limits the effectiveness of investments and of government outlays, and forms an obstacle to growth known as the "North-South problem." Described by Williamson, [5] Chenery, [6] and others, it is encountered both in developed and under developed countries, although in geographically larger countries it seems to assume more extreme forms. Such otherwise diverse nations as Italy, Yugoslavia, and Brazil (where, however, the South is more developed) display striking similarities in this respect. The phenomenon seems to exist also in the Maritime Provinces of Canada.

Chenery [7] has shown that investments in Southern Italy, located in order to stimulate local development, tended to generate higher multiplier effects in the industrialized North. In a recently completed doctoral dissertation Lyall, [8] by applying a model proposed by Casetti, [9] has speculated that the policy of the Yugoslav government of forcing economic development in the southern regions of the country by channeling there new productive investments has seriously affected the total national output. Moreover, while this policy was responsible for the GNP falling short of otherwise achievable levels, the location of productive investments in the South failed to raise the Southern standards of living in line with the sacrifices that it entailed.

Nova Scotia's dependence on imports was well illustrated by Hooker, [10] who expressed the 1960 consumption of various products in Nova Scotia as percentage of local production. His results showed that consumption substantially exceeded output even in some relatively well-established industries, as shown in the accompanying list.

	Consumption as Percentage of Provincial Output
Meat production	453.8
Poultry products	154.4
Dairy products	139.0
Fruit and vegetable products	353.9
Animal feed stuffs	136.7
Distilleries	461.4
Breweries	117.0
Canvas and cordage	626.7
Knitwear	275.4
Sawmilling	104.6
Furniture	339.0
Paper conversion	153.8
Foundries, metal rolling	630.7
Boiler plates, etc.	134.1
Communications equipment	142.6
Calbes and electrical goods	1,274.2
Clay and concrete	250.2
Chemicals	133.7

An examination of backward linkages and of direct, indirect, and induced multipliers characteristic of the economy leads to somewhat similar conclusions. A pertinent question related to interregional linkages is whether the impact of new investments or expanded production in Nova Scotia is felt mainly in the province itself, in the other Atlantic Provinces, in Central Canada, or abroad, but cannot, in the absence of a study dealing specifically with this problem, be answered unambiguously.

Table 5-7 shows that in the "open" model total leakages due to competitive and noncompetitive imports, estimated remittances of dividends and interest, and retained earnings of nonresident corporations amounted in 1960 to $599.0 million or 44.8 percent of total primary inputs, which stood at $1,338.4 million.

While the import components of final demand expenditures were very high, amounting on the average to 44.8 percent, their range between various categories was considerable. The share of total direct and indirect imports in personal consumption was 40.0 percent, reflecting the weakness of the local economy in the production and processing of foodstuffs, but was limited to only 10.1 percent in federal government civil expenditures. Capital formation had the highest share of imports, reaching 54.0 percent, obviously as a direct result of the lack of a manufacturing base. In view of the smallness of the economy, it is not surprising to find that most of the machinery and equipment and even some building materials involved in investments had to be imported. Thus, more than half of investment outlays in Nova Scotia generates incomes elsewhere, mainly in Central Canada and abroad, a fact which dampens much of the overoptimistic hopes attached to recent relatively high investments in the province. Even the import components of Nova Scotia exports are high, despite the fact that they consist mainly of primary products only slightly processed.

The second model developed by Levitt, "closed" with respect to households, shows much higher ratios of imports to expenditures in all sectors, as illustrated in Table 5-8. Especially noteworthy is the sharp rise in the import components of federal government expenditures and exports. The implied conclusion is that the respective multipliers associated with these types of final demand are low, which has some ominous implications for the effectiveness of policies aimed at stimulating the local economy by boosting direct government expenditures and, to a lesser extent, exports of primary products. Model II also raises, albeit insignificantly, the average level of total direct and indirect imports required for a given level of final demand.

The import components and leakages are further raised, although only slightly, by closing the model with respect to local government expenditures. This is illustrated in Table 5-9.

It is interesting to speculate about the share in total leakages due to transfers of profits of local subsidiaries of nondomiciled corporations, but the published tables do not provide any clues. On other evidence, however, financial transfers from the province, because of their relatively modest volume, do not seem to present a major problem deserving an in-depth study.

5 A Multivariate Analysis of Industrial Groupings

A careful analysis of the interindustry relations revealed the extreme "openness" of the provincial economy, a significant lack of strong multiplier effects,

Table 5-7
Import Content of Final Demand, 1960 (Model I)

Category	Noncompetitive Imports, Including Remittances of Profits, etc.	Competitive Imports	"Open" Model Total Imports, Direct and Indirect	Percentage Distribution of Imports	Percentage Share of Total Direct and Indirect Imports in Total Final Expenditures
	(in millions of dollars)				
Personal Consumption	165.6	153.3	318.9	53.2	40.0
Capital Formation	18.4	80.4	98.8	16.5	54.0
Federal Government	8.5	15.2	23.7	4.0	14.2
Defense	4.8	10.9	15.7	2.6	17.8
Civil	3.7	4.3	8.0	1.4	10.1
Local Public Sector	29.8	15.2	45.0	7.5	23.5
Provincial	12.7	7.4	20.1	3.4	28.4
Municipal	4.3	1.1	5.4	0.9	23.0
Education	6.3	3.3	9.6	1.6	16.7
Hospital	6.5	3.4	9.9	1.6	24.8
Exports	80.5	24.5	112.6	18.8	36.7
To Atlantic Provinces	29.6	7.6	37.2	6.2	52.0
To Rest of Canada	34.1	6.7	40.8	6.8	32.0
To Foreign Countries	16.8	17.8	34.6	5.8	32.2
Total	302.8	296.2	599.0	100.0	44.8

Adapted from: Levitt, *op. cit.*

Table 5-8
Import Content of Final Demand, 1960 (Model II)

Category	Noncompetitive Imports, Including Remittances of Profits, etc.	Competitive Imports (in millions of dollars)	Model "Closed" with Respect to Households		
			Total Imports, Direct and Indirect	Percentage Distribution of Imports	Percentage Share of Total Direct and Indirect Imports in Total Final Expenditures
Exogenous Personal	38.6	34.8	73.4	12.0	57.7
Capital Formation	39.1	98.0	137.1	22.4	74.9
Federal Government	46.6	49.6	94.2	15.4	56.4
Defense	24.0	27.2	51.2	8.4	58.1
Civil	22.6	20.4	43.0	7.0	54.5
Local Public Sectors	66.1	46.2	112.3	18.4	58.7
Provincial	25.2	18.1	43.3	7.1	61.1
Municipal	8.3	4.6	12.9	2.1	55.0
Education	18.6	13.7	32.3	5.3	56.4
Hospital	14.0	9.8	23.8	3.9	59.6
Exports	124.6	69.7	194.3	31.8	63.3
To Atlantic Provinces	37.0	14.1	51.1	8.4	71.4
To Rest of Canada	54.4	23.9	78.3	12.8	61.4
To Foreign Countries	33.2	31.7	64.9	10.6	60.3
Total	315.0	296.3	611.3	100.0	45.7

Adapted from: Levitt, *op. cit.*

Table 5-9
Import Content of Final Demand, 1960 (Model III)

Category	Model "Closed" with Respect to Households and Local Governments				
	Noncompetitive Imports, Including Remittances of Profits, etc.	Competitive Imports (in millions of dollars)	Total Imports, Direct and Indirect	Percentage Distribution of Imports	Percentage Share of Total Direct and Indirect Imports in Total Final Expenditures
Exogenous Personal	41.7	36.4	78.1	12.6	66.9
Capital Formation	43.8	101.2	145.0	23.4	79.3
Federal Government	53.6	52.5	106.1	17.1	63.6
Defense	27.5	29.7	57.2	9.2	64.9
Civil	26.1	22.8	48.9	7.9	62.0
Local Government	48.6	28.4	77.0	12.4	
Federal Transfers	37.1	20.3	57.4	9.2	68.4
Borrowing	11.5	8.1	19.6	3.2	64.5
Exports	136.2	78.0	213.9	34.5	69.7
To Atlantic Provinces	39.1	15.7	54.5	8.8	76.1
To Rest of Canada	59.8	27.7	87.5	14.1	68.6
To Foreign Countries	37.3	34.6	71.9	11.6	66.8
Total	323.9	296.2	620.1	100.0	46.3

Adapted from: Levitt, *op. cit.*

and absence of clusters of related industries, which according to both location
and development theory are important determinants of regional attractiveness
and of the pull that it exercises upon industries looking for suitable locations.
Among the various types of spatial groupings acting as growth poles, an important category is formed by industrial complexes. According to some hypotheses, a
group of industries complementary to one another, characteristic of an industrial
complex, constitutes the most propitious background for initiating self-support-
ing growth processes. Under modern conditions, the strength and variety of
forward and backward interindustry links generate economies of scale and
agglomeration that are the basis of regional growth and development.

Since the introduction of scattered plants into Nova Scotia failed to increase
perceptibly the multiplier effects and a major breakthrough in this respect seems
to be far off, a conviction has been growing among planners and some decision
makers that a more efficient alternative to encouraging numerous unrelated
industries might consist in introducing a self-contained industrial complex. In
view of the small size of the Province such a complex would have to be small,
yet above its typical threshold size and adapted to local conditions. The analytic
problem consisted here in first identifying, from among all the sectors of which
the economy is comprised, those forming an industrial cluster with internal and
relatively weak external flows. [11] It was hypothesized that in some regions such
subsystems might account for a substantial part of total multiplier effects capable
of being generated.

Other implications for investment policy of the existence in a region of
identifiable clusters of interlinked industries are obvious, since by fostering the
establishment of new complementary plants the emergence of a full industrial
complex may be advanced. Investments rejected when examined in isolation in
favor of alternatives offering greater immediate payoffs might prove more efficient because of long-run considerations brought to the fore by the comprehensive approach suggested.

The second objective of the study was to try to verify the hypothesis that
in an urban agglomeration the various ancillary links with suppliers of technical,
commercial, or financial services take precedence over links based on flows of
raw materials, basic production ingredients, or outputs. If the hypothesis were
vindicated, it would mean that in a metropolitan agglomeration industrial
complexes based on technical affinity among plants are relatively rare and that
economies of urbanization are more important than those due to localization.[b]

In order to be useful for Nova Scotia, the model had to be applied to several
other regions, especially to highly industrialized ones possessing well-developed
complexes. This part of the study made it also possible to ascertain the minimum

---

[b]External economies, as opposed to economies of scale, are customarily classified into
economies of agglomeration resulting from spatial concentration of like plants and into
economies of urbanization resulting from agglomeration of unlike activities. Together they
are referred to as economies of spatial juxtaposition.

size of input-output tables usable for sophisticated regional analysis. Since the research was based on an examination of regional interindustry flow tables using different industrial classifications, a degree of homogeneity was achieved by a progressive grouping of industries into a decreasing number of sectors. In the process the unwelcome effects of declining size of the tables become apparent and were studied. Unfortunately, with results confined so far to four regions no great reliance can yet be placed on observed regularities.

An industrial complex is usually defined as a set of activities with total output above a certain minimum size, occurring at a given location, and belonging to a subsystem subject to important production, marketing, or other interrelations. The extent of relative "closeness" of a local economy, or conversely its dependence upon exports and imports, can be simply measured with the help of the following index:

$$S = \Sigma_i \Sigma_j w_{ij} / \Sigma_i V_i;$$

where

S = index of relative "closeness" of the regional economy,

w_{ij} = flow of goods and services in dollars from industry i to industry j, both located in the study region,

V_i = total output of industry i.

Alternatively, one could use value added rather than flows, although the results are slightly different.

$$U = \Sigma_j q_j / \Sigma_i V_i;$$

where

q_j = value added (primary inputs) in industry j.

Other indexes could measure the dependence of the regional economy upon particular types of imports or take into account differences in price levels. Such synthetic measures fail, however, to account explicitly for the important indirect and induced effects that are at the heart of a growing agglomeration. This failure and their generality make them devoid of analytic and policy applications.

The alternative approach suggested here starts by identifying industries belonging to a subgroup with closer links among themselves than with the rest of the local economy. Two industries, k and l, may be operationally defined as "forming" an industrial complex if they are connected by strong flows of goods or services. Four coefficients may describe this type of relationship:

$$a_{kl} = \frac{v_{kl}}{V_l} \; ; \quad a_{lk} = \frac{v_{lk}}{V_k} \; ; \quad b_{kl} = \frac{v_{kl}}{V_k} \; ; \quad b_{lk} = \frac{v_{lk}}{V_l} \; ;$$

An a coefficient exceeding a certain arbitrary cut-off point ($a_l \geqslant a^*$) indicates a dependent industry, while a large b coefficient ($b_l \geqslant b^*$) indicates a complementary industry. An example of a dependent industry may be a plant producing glue out of waste products of a fish-processing plant, while an example of a complementary industry may be a plant producing, say, windshields for a car factory, with the relationship being important in terms of the supplying unit.

Far more significant analytically are indirect links. Two industries, k and l, may be members of an industrial complex in the absence of direct links. For example, an oil refinery and a pharmaceutical plant may both belong to a petrochemical complex even though they may not trade with one another. The link in this more typical and important case is established through other activities of the complex. More generally, two industries, k and l, may be considered to be members of a complex if their trading patterns with suppliers or purchasers involve the same group of industries. This type of link is revealed by correlation analysis.

Specifically, four coefficients of correlation describe the similarity between the input-output structures of two industries:

$$r(a_{ik} \cdot a_{il}), \quad r(b_{ki} \cdot b_{li}), \quad r(a_{ik} \cdot b_{li}), \quad r(b_{ki} \cdot a_{il}).$$

A high $r(a_{ik} \cdot a_{il})$ coefficient indicates that the two industries, k and l, have similar input structures or draw their supplies from the same producers. A high $r(b_{ki} \cdot b_{li})$ coefficient signifies that the two industries, k and l, supply their products to a similar set of users. A high $r(a_{ik} \cdot b_{li})$ coefficient implies that the suppliers of k industry are users of the products of l. Finally, a high $r(b_{ki} \cdot a_{il})$ coefficient points toward a reverse relationship between k and l, namely the users of the products of k are suppliers of l. Provision has to be made to eliminate similarities based on high import and export content of the two industries, undifferentiated by region and sector of origin or destination.

The formal model for studying the interindustry linkages was developed in the following major steps:

1. A set of four zero order correlation coefficients of the form

$$r(a_{ik} \cdot a_{il}), \quad r(b_{ki} \cdot b_{li}), \quad r(a_{ik} \cdot b_{li}), \quad r(b_{ki} \cdot a_{il});$$

$$(i = 1, \ldots n)$$

was derived for all possible pairs of industries included in the interindustry flow table examined.

2. A symmetric intercorrelation matrix R was set up by selecting the highest of the four coefficients,[c] or

$$r_{lk} = r_{kl} = \max \left[r(a_{ik} \cdot a_{il}), r(b_{ki} \cdot b_{li}), r(a_{ik} \cdot b_{li}), r(b_{ki} \cdot a_{il}) \right] ;$$

The study reported below was based on an examination of intercorrelation matrices R set up by selecting the highest of the four zero order correlation coefficients. The entries in the R matrix helped to identify affinities between pairs of industries based on their links with a subgroup forming a hypothetical complex.

More formally, the first two steps can be summarized as follows: Given an $n \times n$ matrix of input-output flows expressed in dollars,

$$V = \begin{bmatrix} v_{11} & v_{12} & \cdots & & & & v_{1n} \\ v_{21} & v_{22} & \cdots & & & & v_{2n} \\ \cdot & & & & & & \\ \cdot & & & & & & \\ \cdot & & & & & & \\ v_{n1} & v_{n2} & \cdots & & & & v_{nn} \end{bmatrix} ;$$

an $n \times 4n$ matrix of zero order correlation coefficients was derived:

$$r = \left[r(a_{ik} \cdot a_{il}) \mid r(b_{ki} \cdot b_{li}) \mid r(a_{ik} \cdot b_{li}) \mid r(b_{ki} \cdot a_{il}) \right] .$$

---

[c]Two additional approaches were considered and tested. The weaker involved the use of pooled coefficients of correlation in the construction of the matrix, whose entries become:

$$\rho_{ij} = \frac{(n_1 - 3)z'_1 + (n_2 - 3)z'_2 + (n_3 - 3)z'_3 + (n_4 - 3)z'_4}{\sqrt{n_1 - 3) + (n_2 - 3) + (n_3 - 3) + (n_4 - 3)}} ;$$

where

$$z' = \tfrac{1}{2} \log_e \frac{1 + r}{1 - r} ;$$

A somewhat stronger alternative involved constructing an R matrix in which in addition each coefficient was set equal to zero, or

$$r_{lk} = r_{kl} = 0 \quad \text{whenever } t \leqslant t_{.05} ;$$

and where

$$t = \frac{r}{s_r}, \text{ and } s_r = \sqrt{\frac{1 - r^2}{n - 2}} ;$$

Furthermore, one could also examine four separate matrices of coefficients of correlation, or construct an R matrix by selecting the smallest of the four coefficients describing the relation between any pair of industries.

Each entry in the first submatrix is a measure of the degree of affinity between any two industries k and l on the basis of similarity in their buying patterns. Each entry in the second submatrix is a measure of the degree of affinity between any two industries k and l on the basis of similarity in their selling patterns. The entries in the third and fourth submatrices measure the degree of affinity between pairs of industries by correlating the suppliers of the one with customers of the other. Each complete row of the matrix is interpretable as a description of an industry in terms of $4n$ characteristics, each of which measures its affinity to other industries in terms of various relations to the remaining sectors in the system.

Next an $n \times n$ covariance matrix was formed:

$$K = E[(r - \bar{r})(r - \bar{r})^T] \; ;$$

Notice that the matrix of deviations was postmultiplied by its transpose, since the purpose of this step was to compare pairwise industries on the basis of their characteristics, with the final objective of reducing the number of industries while maximizing total variance.

The covariance matrix was transformed into an $n \times n$ correlation matrix

$$R = D\left(\frac{1}{\sigma_i}\right) K D\left(\frac{1}{\sigma_i}\right) ;$$

where

$\quad D$ = diagonal matrix of standard deviations of the variates (r's).

3. In order to identify, from the set of all industries, the subgroup belonging to a complex, an iterative process was applied. For this purpose all industries having either a null column or a null row vector [or all k industries for which either r_{ik}, $r_{ki} = 0$ $(i = 1, \ldots . . n)$ were removed from the R matrix, and the whole process repeated until no more null vectors were left.

4. The relative strength of the links binding the remaining industries together was assessed with the help of eigenvalues of the R matrix, computed as:

$$(Ra - Ia\lambda) = \underline{0};$$

$$(R - I\lambda)a = \underline{0};$$

$$|R - I\lambda| = \underline{0};$$

where

$\quad a$ = eigenvector, or characteristic vector,

$\quad \lambda$ = eigenvalue, or characteristic root.

Electricity	140.0	0.8
Capital	100.0	8.0
Local taxes	100.0	2.0
All inputs	104.3	96.4

The difference thus appears to be relatively minor and is mainly due to the significantly higher transportation costs. The differences in costs of materials and fuel and of electricity can be disregarded, the former as being probably due to differences in product mix and the latter as amounting to barely 0.8 percent of total production outlays. The main weakness of the above analysis seems to reside in the assessment of labor cost differentials, and an insufficient data basis for an in-depth treatment of external economies.

It appears thus that the main reason for the failure of Nova Scotia to attract new industries is not so much its meagre natural endowment and unsophisticated technology employed but its relative remoteness and the more elusive effects of lack of significant agglomerations. The analysis presented in the next chapter reinforces the often expressed opinion that lack of a viable manufacturing complex with strong multiplier effects and of a substantial market for final and intermediate products, combined with the distance from other centers is the main cause of the economic plight of the province.

5

Sector and Linkages: Contribution of Input-Output Studies

1 The Disaggregated Approach

The various analytic tools so far brought to bear on the problem of economic growth of Nova Scotia failed to attack the sectoral structure and existing interrelations in a consistent, systematic way. The various aggregate models, while providing some illuminating insights into numerous aspects of the working of a provincial economy, are generally incapable of generating guidelines for regional development policies, which as a rule have to address themselves to specific sectors or industries. The few analyses of individual industries were not only admittedly crude but failed, moreover, to probe deeply into the existing linkages and interrelations, and consequently the resulting multiplier effects, often considered to be the main elements of major economic advances. [1]

The problem can also be viewed in a slightly different way. In a small open economy a major breakthrough can result only from the introduction of new productive activities, the importance of which resides not only in the volume of new employment and income that it generates but very often primarily in its indirect impact, the strength of which can be effectively measured with the help of input-output analysis. A common feature of depressed regions is the general weakness of multiplier effects generated in their economies, due mainly to the size of leakages present. The absence of substantial indirect effects ordinarily accompanying new investments constitutes one of the greatest obstacles to efforts aimed at invigorating the economies of depressed regions, and makes the process at best a slow and expensive one. Yet, the introduction of new industries progressively reduces leakages and reinforces the indirect impact of new activities until a point is reached when, in a group of related industries linked by flows of goods and services, the multiplier effects become significantly stronger, signaling a qualitative as well as a quantitative change. Such a breakthrough can hardly be recognized by examining one industry after another in isolation, since an analysis on a sector by sector basis will fail to reveal effects characteristic of, and advantages accruing to, groups of industries only.

The 1960 input-output tables of Nova Scotia were developed by Levitt of McGill University [2] and her associates during 1961–1967 as part of a broader study covering all four Atlantic Provinces and sponsored by the Atlantic Provinces Economic Council, the Canada Council, and the Atlantic Development Board. Updated tables will be available shortly, but preliminary tests performed on the more recent tables show that the main analytical results are not materially

changed. The 58 x 58 input-output table is integrated into and forms part of a larger set of tables encompassing the four Atlantic Provinces: Nova Scotia, New Brunswick, Prince Edward Island, and Newfoundland. The interprovincial flows have been estimated, at considerable research cost, because of the interregional nature of the accounts, but from the point of view of Nova Scotia alone, the geographic destination of its exports and the spatial origin of its imports are less relevant.

The final demand was disaggregated, showing the commodity composition of exports separately for each of five geographic destinations; the three other Atlantic Provinces, the rest of Canada, and foreign countries. Competitive imports were estimated separately for each of the three other Atlantic Provinces, leaving a residual covering the rest of Canada and foreign countries. In the face of total absence of direct data, competitive imports, by commodity and by sector, had to be obtained as a residual or difference between total purchases by all users and local output. Noncompetitive imports were presented as a separate row among the primary inputs. Aside from statistical necessity, a good case can be made for distinguishing between imports that are of a type similar to commodities produced locally and those that are not, although the distinction is obviously a function of the degree of aggregation of the tables: the higher the level of aggregation the larger the share of competitive imports appears to be. In the context of the interregional study considered here, a commodity was treated as local if it was produced in at least one Atlantic Province.

The bill of goods is composed of eighteen vectors, covering personal consumption, capital formation, inventory changes, five vectors dealing with exports, four dealing with imports, and six dealing with government expenditures disaggregated by level of government and, in some cases, by function.

The primary inputs were disaggregated into seven vectors, covering taxes, subsidies, noncompetitive imports, wages and salaries, unincorporated business income, profits-rents-interest, and depreciation. An interesting feature of the study is that the usual groupings of primary inputs were transformed into sectors corresponding to national income accounting categories.

Three models have been developed by Levitt in order to analyze the structures of the provincial economies. The first is best summarized by the relationship

$$g = (I + \hat{\beta} - A)^{-1} [D_{ik}i + (I + \hat{\beta})X_{ih}i];$$ (1)

where

g = (58 X 1) column vector of output levels,

I = (58 X 58) identity matrix,

$\hat{\beta}$ = (58 X 58) diagonal matrix of competitive import coefficients,

A = (58 × 58) matrix of technical coefficients,

D_{ik} = (58 × 9) matrix of domestic final demand by producing sector and type of demand,

X_{ih} = (58 × 6) matrix of exports by producing sector and destination,

m = (58 × 1) column vector of competitive imports,

x = (58 × 2) column vector of exports summed over all destinations,

V = (58 × 58) matrix of interindustry flows,[a]

i = unit vector of appropriate size,

$$\hat{\beta} = \hat{m}(\hat{g} - \hat{x})^{-1}; \tag{2}$$

$$A = V\hat{g}^{-1}; \tag{3}$$

$(I + \hat{\beta} - A)^{-1}$ is obviously a (58 × 58) matrix of direct and indirect interindustry requirements per unit of final demand.

In this system, all direct export demand is supplied from provincial output, while all other direct and indirect requirements are supplied from both provincial output and competitive imports according to a fixed ratio derived for the base year and assumed constant over time. The assumption that export production does not use competitive imports is not plausible in the extremely open economies of the Atlantic Provinces and proves unnecessarily restrictive. Actually, a good case could be made for the claim that in the face of capacity limits sharp increases in export production would boost competitive imports rather more than local output of intermediate products.

The second model is closed with respect to households; that is, the two vectors describing incomes and consumption of households are transferred to the structural matrix. Households are thus treated as a new "industry," purchasing consumer goods and selling primary inputs. This new and strong assumption asserts in effect that personal consumption of every commodity is a fixed proportion of total earned incomes accruing to households. Excluded are unearned incomes, such as transfers, and income from property located outside the province, as well as unilateral transfers to nonresidents. Furthermore, the model assumes that personal income taxes and household savings are paid from incomes earned in the province, and that incomes deriving from transfer payments are fully consumed.

The basic equation of the model can be written as

$$\bar{g} = (I + \hat{\beta} - \bar{A})^{-1} [\bar{D}_{ik}i + (I + \hat{\beta})X_{ih}i]; \tag{4}$$

---

[a]Capital letters refer to matrices, lower case letters to column vectors, capped letters to diagonal matrices obtained from vectors, and the superscript $^{-1}$ refers to an inverse.

where

$\bar{g}$ = (59 X 1) vector of industry output levels, augmented by one additional sector, households (Eh),

$\bar{A}$ = (59 X 59) matrix of technical coefficients with one column vector of personal consumption and one row vector of primary inputs added,

$\bar{D}_{ih}$ = matrix of domestic final demand modified by replacing the first vector d_1 by $\bar{d}_1$,

h = vector of personal consumption adjusted for unearned incomes

$$h = \alpha d_1 - a; \tag{5}$$

α = scalar, adjustment factor

$$\alpha = \frac{Z_1 - t}{Z_1}; \tag{6}$$

Z_1 = aggregate personal expenditures,

t = aggregate transfers,

d_1 = vector of personal expenditures in base year,

a = null vector except for three entries: personal income taxes, personal savings, expenses on out of province tourism,

$\bar{d}$ = adjusted vector of exogenously determined personal expenditures:

$$\bar{d}_1 = d_1(1 - \alpha); \tag{7}$$

This model obviously yields much higher multipliers, but the additional heroic assumption upon which it is predicated, although often used in analytically desperate situations, does not appear plausible.

The third model developed by Levitt closes the system with respect to provincial and local governments' operations as well, thus restricting "leakages" still further. The basic equation of the model now becomes

$$\bar{\bar{g}} = (I + \hat{\beta} - \bar{\bar{A}})^{-1} [\bar{\bar{D}}_{ik} i + (I + \hat{\beta}) X_{ih} i]; \tag{8}$$

where

$\bar{\bar{g}}$ = (62 X 1) vector of industry output levels including, besides house-

Nova Scotia represented 57.0 percent of the value of factory shipments, as
against 53.9 percent in Quebec-Ontario. By itself the comparison is meaningless,
as the disparity is probably attributable mainly to a different mix of products
and to a lesser extent to a different degree of vertical integration. Whether the
more relevant but difficult to establish differences due to transportation costs
or markups by intermediaries were also involved can at best only be conjectured.

The costs of fuel as a percentage of the value of shipments amounted in
1962 to 1.6 and 1.1 percent in Nova Scotia and Quebec-Ontario respectively.
The analytical relevance of this information is subject to the same limitations
as in the case of materials. It could be enhanced by a study of prices of various
types of fuels available, which was, however, not attempted. At any rate, it
might not have been easy to estimate changes in production functions due to
replacement of locally more expensive inputs.

The situation with respect to electricity is straightforward. The average
cost per kwh charged to manufacturing industries in 1962 was 8.00 mills in Nova
Scotia as against 5.72 mills in Quebec-Ontario. Thus Nova Scotia producers
had to bear a 40.0 percent higher price than that paid by competitors. The
availability of off-peak contracts and other forms of reduced rates requires far
more elaborate computations, but does not seem to be able to affect the basic
conclusion significantly. The smallness of manufacturing demand in Nova
Scotia both in absolute and relative terms (compared to value of shipments)
makes it appear of relatively little consequence.

Such problems as costs of investments and burden of local taxation can be
disposed of in a few words. Sufficient evidence exists that both the costs of
raising investment capital and of purchasing machinery and equipment are
virtually the same in Nova Scotia as in any other part of Canada, including the
Quebec-Ontario region. Significant differences seem to exist in costs of construction, but these are difficult to quantify at the macro level. Finally, local taxes
in Nova Scotia are deemed to be at essentially the same level as in Quebec-
Ontario.

The following overall picture of the costs of supplying the Quebec-Ontario
market with manufactured goods from plants producing in Nova Scotia and
in Quebec-Ontario in 1962 emerged from the study of George:

	Nova Scotia as a Percentage of Quebec-Ontario	Percentage of Total Costs
Labor	100.1	21.8
Transportation	149.0	5.2
Materials and fuel	102.0	58.6

Maritime to Eastern	1.464 cents
Eastern to Maritime	2.429 cents

The Maritime manufacturers appear to have a net advantage, but this disappears rapidly when distance to markets is considered. By multiplying the freight rates by the average distance of haulage the following more relevant picture emerges:

Average Cost of Consigning One Ton of Manufactured Freight in Maritime and Eastern Zones in 1962

(1) Maritime–Maritime	5.258 cents
(2) Eastern–Eastern	7.188 cents
(3) Maritime–Eastern	10.711 cents
(4) Eastern–Maritime	18.256 cents

In view of the very limited market existing in Nova Scotia, the potential destination of major new export products is likely to be the Quebec-Ontario region. A comparison between transportation costs of producers located in Nova Scotia and in Quebec-Ontario, both supplying the latter market, is obtained from items (2) and (3) which show that the approximate transportation costs borne by a producer in Nova Scotia would be forty-nine percent greater than those borne by a producer located further west. An attempt by the latter to ship to the Maritimes, however, would encounter a substantial transport cost disadvantage, of the order of 247.2 percent.

To obtain a more relevant picture of the disadvantage of Nova Scotia producers, one would have to cast the transport cost differential against the market potential. This problem, formulated earlier by Harris, Dunn, Isard and others, [32] was only partly taken account of. A correction was introduced by standardizing the shipments to account for the fact that Quebec-Ontario manufacturers were buying more rail transportation services for goods that were relatively cheap to transport, the bulky products evidently being sold to customers or bought from suppliers located nearer to the producing plant. The standardization resulted in increasing the cost difference from 49.0 percent to 52.4 percent to the disadvantage of the Nova Scotia producer; however, this adjustment was not used in the final analysis.

Having tackled the problems of labor and transportation, one has to come to grips with the relatively less important but elusive elements of production costs represented by costs of materials, fuel, electricity, capital equipment, financial charges, and local taxation.

In 1962 the cost of materials purchased by manufacturing industries in

expenditures, provincial government, municipal governments, education, and hospitals); five represent various types of exports grouped according to destination (foreign, rest of Canada other than Atlantic Provinces, New Brunswick, Prince Edward Island, and Newfoundland); and four group the negative entries corresponding to competitive imports (New Brunswick, Prince Edward Island, Newfoundland, and residual imports).

The classification based on types of commodities or services required can comprise up to fifty-eight industrial sectors and fourteen types of primary inputs – namely, wages and salaries; unincorporated business income; profits, subdivided into those remaining in Nova Scotia, those transferred out of the province, and federal corporation taxes; rents and interests, subdivided into those remaining in Nova Scotia, and those transferred to the rest of the world; indirect taxes, subdivided into federal, provincial, municipal, and education and hospitals; subsidies, subdivided into federal and provincial; and depreciation.

The first set of results is summarized in Table 5-3, showing the dependence of household income and employment upon various exogenously determined categories of final demand. It shows the relative importance of direct, indirect, and induced effects of various types of expenditures upon both household income and employment. Any increase in demand affects the economy in several different ways: First, there is a direct effect of increased output on the sectors concerned. Second, there is the indirect effect due to increased production in sectors supplying their output directly or indirectly to the one which had to step up its production to cope with increased demand. Its sum can be calculated with the help of the Leontief inverse. Third, there is the induced effect due to increased consumption by households enjoying incomes generated by the new productive activity. This is the well-known Keynesian consumption effect. It can be calculated with the help of the inverse of the augmented structural matrix to which the household sector has been added. The underlying assumption that consumer purchases of each commodity are a direct proportion of income has been discussed before. Fourth, there is the effect due to increased revenues and expenditures of local government having to serve a larger economy. Fifth, there are increases in income due to a change in demand for investment equipment. This results in the acceleration effect, which, however, has not been considered.

The direct and indirect income effects generated by a unit increase in final demand can be calculated as

$$q(I + \hat{\beta} - A)^{-1} \; ;$$

where

q = vector of distributed primary incomes associated with unit outputs.

The inverse matrix can be written in full

Table 5-3
Household Income and Employment by Category of Final Demand, 1960

	Model I "Open" Model				Model II "Closed" with Respect to Households				Model III "Closed" with Respect to Households and Local Governments			
	Income		Employment		Income		Employment		Income		Employment	
Final Demand	($ millions)	(%)	('000)	(%)	($ millions)	(%)	('000)	(%)	($ millions)	(%)	('000)	(%)
Private consumption	243.7	31.0	56.8	30.0	16.6[d]	2.1	3.8	2.0	21.9	2.8	5.0	2.6
Private capital formation[a]	75.8	9.6	18.7	9.9	107.5	13.6	26.0	13.8	121.1	15.2	29.1	15.4
"Export base" sectors[b]	12.5	1.6	3.1	1.6	4.9	0.6	1.2	0.6	5.5	0.7	1.3	0.7
Utilities[c]	13.6	1.7	3.4	1.8	15.0	1.9	3.6	1.9	17.0	2.1	4.1	2.2
Housing and other private investment	49.7	6.3	12.2	6.4	87.6	11.1	21.2	11.3	98.6	12.4	23.7	12.5
Federal government	168.4	21.4	39.8	21.0	239.0	30.5	56.3	29.8	273.0	34.2	63.9	33.8
Defense	70.3	8.9	16.0	8.4	99.7	12.7	22.9	12.1	110.2	13.8	25.2	13.3
Civil	69.1	8.8	17.0	9.0	98.1	12.5	23.8	12.6	108.4	13.6	26.1	13.8
Transfers	29.0	3.7	6.8	3.6	41.2	5.3	9.6	5.1	54.4	6.8	12.6	6.7
Local government	136.9	17.5	31.9	16.9	194.1	24.7	45.3	23.9	117.7[e]	14.8	25.9	13.7
Provincial	46.0	5.9	10.2	5.4	65.3	8.3	14.6	7.7				
Municipal	14.9	1.9	4.1	2.2	21.1	2.7	5.6	3.0				
Education and hospitals	72.4	9.2	16.8	8.9	102.7	13.1	23.9	12.6				
Transfers	3.6	0.5	0.8	0.4	5.0	0.6	1.2	0.6				
Exports	161.2	20.5	42.0	22.2	228.8	29.1	57.8	30.5	262.5	33.0	65.3	34.5
To other Atlantic provinces	27.2	3.5	6.7	3.6	38.6	4.9	9.5	5.0	44.2	5.6	10.6	5.6
To the rest of Canada	74.1	9.4	18.9	10.0	105.2	13.4	26.1	13.8	121.1	15.2	29.7	15.7
To foreign countries	59.9	7.6	16.4	8.6	85.0	10.8	22.2	11.7	97.2	12.2	25.0	13.2
Total	786.0	100.0	189.2	100.0	786.0	100.0	189.0	100.0	796.2	100.0	189.2	100.0

[a]Including inventory change.
[b]Defined to include agriculture, fishing, forestry, mining, paper products, and primary iron and steel.
[c]Transportation, electricity, and all other utilities.
[d]Limited to tourism and external services.
[e]Limited to expenditures directly imputable to federal transfers and borrowing.
Based, with slight modifications, on: Levitt, Karl, *A Macro Economic Analysis of the Structure of the Economy of the Atlantic Provinces 1960*, Paper presented at a meeting of the Canadian Economics Association, June 1969, Mimeographed, pp. 46–61.

$$(I + \hat{\beta} - A)^{-1} = \begin{bmatrix} r_{11} \, r_{12} & \cdots & r_{1n} \\ \cdot & & \\ \cdot & & \\ \cdot & & \\ r_{n1} & \cdots & r_{nn} \end{bmatrix} ;$$

where

r_{ij} = level of operation of sector i associated with unit demand for outputs of sector j, and

$\dfrac{1}{r_{ii}}$ = level of final demand for products i per unit operation of sector i.

Hence, total direct and indirect distributed primary incomes generated by a unit output in sector i are

$$\frac{1}{r_{ii}} \, (q_1 r_{1i} + q_2 r_{2i} + \ldots q_n r_{ni});$$

similarly, the induced effects can be read off the inverse of the augmented matrix, where households form the 59th sector. The first model is confined to direct and indirect interindustry effects, the second model comprises in addition the induced effects of changes in household incomes, while the third treats also changes in local government revenues as endogenous and estimates the resulting repercussions. Thus, each model classifies differently the factors affecting the regional economy (the units responsible for various types of expenditures) into exogenous and endogenous. These differences in classification not only affect the size of the multiplier effects generated but also result in shifts in the emphasis placed on various components of final demand.

A perusal of results obtained with the help of the first, "open" input-output model reveals once more what has already transpired from the Income and Product Accounts; namely, that the Nova Scotia economy is highly dependent on public sector expenditures. The direct and indirect (or interindustry) effects of local spending of the federal and local governments generated 38.9 percent of the incomes of households and 37.9 percent of total employment. Exports to all destinations, on the other hand, exercised a far lesser influence, being responsible for barely 22.1 percent of total household incomes and 23.8 percent of employment. Of particular interest is the fact that foreign exports generated only 7.6 percent of household incomes and 8.6 percent of employment, which underscores the links between the Nova Scotia economy and the rest of Canada. The interregional input-output study also clearly illustrates the relatively low cohesion

among the four Atlantic Provinces, which do not in any sense seem to form a single nodal region.

The role of private consumption and capital formation in generating household incomes and employment is, on the other hand, conspicuously low. Private capital formation was responsible for barely 10 percent of total employment, but the method of disaggregation of this item presented in Table 5-3 and the implied connection between the so-called "export base" sectors and actual export demand for Nova Scotia products is rather tenuous. The crude breakdown into exporting and nonexporting sectors that has been applied is not valid, and hence no analytic significance can be attached to this figure. In percentage terms the differences between household income and employment figures are insignificant, a fact deserving perhaps some further study.

The second model, closed with respect to households and hence showing much stronger multiplier effects, marks a change in the relative importance of various sectors in generating household income. Private consumption is shown to account for only 2.1 percent of household income, and even this figure, referring to expenditures by nonresident tourists and to income derived from external services, or invisible exports, does not really form part of private consumption in the first place. This model brings even more to the fore the role of federal government spending in the regional economy. By redefining and restricting the factors considered exogenous, the impact of public, especially federal, spending has been underlined. The secondary importance of exports, despite the small size of the Nova Scotia economy, again stresses its one-sided structure, with a weak resource base and undeveloped manufacturing.

The more controversial third model treats most local government expenditures as endogenous except for those directly imputable to federal transfers and borrowing. The further restriction of exogenously determined demand reveals even more starkly the role of federal government in generating household incomes and employment. The reason for the total income of households being slightly higher is not immediately obvious.

Government expenditures being one of the most powerful tools for influencing regional development, the assessment of the repercussions of, and multiplier effects associated with, various types of public sector expenditures is of considerable analytic interest. Of importance to the regional economy is not so much the direct employment and income effect of an increase in public spending as the total direct, indirect, and induced impact. Table 5-4 summarizes the employment and income effects associated with one million dollars of government expenditure.

In terms of employment, federal defense expenditures and education outlays produce the greatest total effects, even though the direct employment resulting from civil federal expenditures is substantially greater. On the other hand, the differences between those three sectors as sources of household income are less pronounced, due undoubtedly to the lower wage rates paid to defense personnel and teachers.

holds, four vectors representing provincial government, municipal governments, hospitals, and education institutions,

$\bar{\bar{A}}$ = (62 × 62) augmented matrix of technical coefficients,

$\bar{\bar{D}}_{ik}$ = modified matrix of domestic final demand

$$D_{ik} = \bar{\bar{d}}_1 \, d_2 \, d_3 \, d_4 \, d_5 \, d_x \, d_y \; ; \tag{9}$$

$$\bar{\bar{d}}_1 = d_1(1 - \bar{\alpha}) \; ; \tag{10}$$

$$\bar{\alpha} = \frac{Z_1 - \bar{t}}{Z_1} \; ; \tag{11}$$

$\bar{t}$ = t without transfer payments from provincial and municipal governments,

d_2 = vector of capital formation,

d_3 = vector of inventory changes,

d_4 = vector of federal government defense spending,

d_5 = vector of civil federal government spending,

d_x = null vector except for entries showing federal transfers to provincial government, municipal governments, education, and hospitals, and among primary inputs "import leakage,"

d_y = null vector except for entries showing savings of the provincial government, municipal governments, education, and hospitals.

This somewhat unusual, though analytically interesting formulation yields still larger multipliers. It is, nonetheless, questionable whether local government expenditures respond quickly to changes in the level of operation of the regional economy, especially in the short run.

2 Input-output and Other Types of Accounts

The Nova Scotia interindustry study sheds new light on the estimates embodied in the income and product accounts by providing some valuable comparisons with aggregates partly obtained by different methods and partly derived from direct field surveys. In principle, the transition from an input-output system to income and product accounts and the derivation of the major aggregates is straightforward. Table 5-1 represents the Nova Scotia income and product accounts in the less usual matrix form, bringing to the fore the similarity and

Table 5-1
Income and Product Accounts, Nova Scotia, 1960 (in millions of current dollars)

	Business		Households		
			Goods and services		722.4
Business					
Households	Wages	374.6	Wages		22.7
	Farm income	13.0			
	Profits	86.0			
	Interests, dividends	72.0			
	Transfers	.5	546.1		
Governments	Corporate taxes	16.8	Social security	23.8	
	Indirect taxes	160.9	Direct taxes	55.0	78.8
	Profits of government enterprises	25.6	203.3		
Capital	Depreciation Undistributed profits	113.6 5.5	Personal savings		31.2
	Residual error	30.4	149.5		
Rest of the World	Imports	435.2	Expenditures abroad		16.7
	Interests, dividends	16.2	451.4		
			1,350.3		871.8

differences between estimates derived with the help of the various approaches underlying the income and product and interindustry accounts.

In this form the entries in the first column correspond to the row totals of the primary inputs, and the first row, to column totals of the bill of goods. Adjusted for differences in definitions of sectors, the input-output table yields totals as shown in Table 5-2.

Two entries, representing the government deficit and the unfavorable balance of trade resulting in a growing indebtedness toward the rest of the world, are missing in the input-output accounts, which do not deal with changes in financial holdings. They have been added in the summary table in order to facilitate

Governments			Capital		Rest of the World		
Military pay	30.3		Investments	176.2	Exports	219.1	
					Interests	5.4	224.5
Goods and services	134.6						1,350.3
Interests and sub-sidies	62.2	227.2					
Wages	129.7				Wages	1.0	
Military pay	30.3				Transfers	16.0	17.0
Transfers	126.0	286.0					871.8
			Surplus or deficit	228.0	Taxes		3.1
							513.2
					Surplus or deficit		223.5
							404.2
							468.1
		513.2		404.2			468.1

comparisons. More important, indirect taxes have been charged to households instead of business, which, however, justified for interindustry accounts, makes for more laborious comparisons.

The differences between the two sets of accounts are substantial, reflecting to a large extent deviations between the input-output study and the statistics published by the Dominion Bureau of Statistics and assumed to be correct for purposes of constructing the Nova Scotia income and product accounts. The major differences occur in the estimates of exports and imports. Both are sub-stantially (by some $70–80 million) higher in the input-output study, although the estimates of the resulting unfavorable balance of trade are very close. Because

Table 5–2
Input-Output, Nova Scotia, 1960

	Business	House-holds	Govern-ments	Capital	Rest of the World	
Business	–	615.0	140.7	182.9	315.7	1,254.3
Households	592.2	–	287.7		21.3	901.2
Governments	58.1	147.1	–	255.1*	–	460.9
Capital	92.7	59.9	5.5	–	279.9*	438.0
Rest of the World	511.3	78.6	27.0	–	–	616.9

of the nature of the accounts and of the underlying data basis, greater credence is often given to the input-output study. Fairly substantial difference occurs also in the case of wage income, while among the other comparable estimates, net income of unincorporated business enterprises and consumption of households come surprising close – in the latter case being practically identical.

The only major aggregate derived in the input-output study (gross regional product) is not directly comparable with the income and product accounts estimate. The amount indicated in the study itself as Gross Domestic Product ($980.0 million) refers actually to gross domestic product at factor costs. Adjusting it for indirect taxes raises it to $1,068.5 million but still refers to volume of output within the geographic boundaries of Nova Scotia. The Gross Regional Product derived from income and product accounts refers to goods and services produced with the help of factors of production owned by residents of the province and amounted in 1960 to $1,035.8 million. The two amounts seem quite close, but an actual adjustment would be very dubious because transfers of earnings between provinces are among the most uncertain estimates.

3 Income and Employment Multipliers

The inverse matrix $(I + \hat{\beta} - A)^{-1}$, which connects final demand sectors with primary inputs, makes possible a study of the dependence of various sources of income upon fluctuations in final demand. For purposes of analysis the components of final demand can be grouped (1) according to the unit in which the expenditure originates, or (2) according to the sector supplying the goods and services, roughly corresponding to commodity or service required.

In the Nova Scotia input-output study the first classification can comprise at most eighteen categories, each of which is represented by a vector in the bill of goods. Of the eighteen categories, three correspond to ultimate private users (personal consumption, capital formation, and inventory changes); six represent governments (federal government defense expenditures, federal government civil

The ratios of the characteristic roots to the trace of the R matrix define an Index of Association

$$C_n = \frac{\lambda_n}{\text{tr } R} \times 100;$$

This provides an aggregate measure of the strength of the ties connecting the industries remaining in the R matrix — a large C_1 indicating the existence of an industrial complex, and a fairly large C_1 and C_2 pointing toward the existence of two identifiable complexes.

The eigenvalues, λ_i, are interpretable as variances along a particular dimension and determine the degree of affinity of industries forming a subsystem because the elements of the eigenvectors were standardized by setting

$$a_i' a_i = 1;$$

5. Finally, in order to eliminate similarities based on high import and export contents, all industries were removed from the matrix for which both

$$\frac{m_i}{V_i} \geqslant \alpha^* ; \quad \text{and} \quad \frac{e_i}{V_i} \geqslant \beta^*;$$

where

m_i = total imports of industry i,

e_i = total exports of industry i,

α^*, β^* = arbitrary constants determined by an iterative process and finally set at $\alpha^* = \beta^* = .30$.

The removed industries were those with relatively weak links with the regional economy. Any similarities in trading patterns of such industries revealed by correlation analysis were thus deemed to be spurious, based solely on ancillary inputs or outputs.

The above model has been applied to the input-output table of Nova Scotia and, in order to gain some insight into the nature of clustering of industries in the presence and absence of spatial juxtaposition, to the input-output tables of the United States, Philadelphia SMSA, Washington State, and West Virginia. Two of the regions examined, namely Philadelphia and Washington State, were selected because they represent highly industrialized economies comprised of groups of industries expected to meet the criteria of industrial complexes, while West Virginia was selected because, like Nova Scotia, it is an extremely "open" economy with scant manufacturing activity.

The five tables used in the study differed greatly in size, methods of classification of sectors, criteria used for routing and valuation, and date of construction. The United States economy was studied with the help of the 1958 (77 X 77) input-output table, [12] enlarged to 89 X 89 on the basis of additional information [13] by expanding three sectors: (1) Food and kindred products to nine separate industries; (2) Primary nonferrous metals manufacturing to three industries; and (3) Electric, gas, and sanitary services also to three industries. The 1963 (85 X 85) input-output table for the United States [14] became available recently, but preliminary tests showed that as far as the model reported here is concerned no significantly different results were forthcoming.

The 1959 Philadelphia SMSA table (89 X 89) was derived by aggregating the original 496 X 496 matrix, [15] the 89 sectors being identical with those appearing in the United States table.

The 1963 Washington State table [16] (54 X 54) differs in several respects from the United States and reduced Philadelphia tables, [17] but was made comparable by aggregation to size 43 X 43, 36 X 36, and 31 X 31.

The West Virginia table [18] (48 X 48) is highly disaggregated with respect to primary industries. Attempts to reduce its size in order to make it comparable to the other regional tables yielded a 23 X 23 matrix.

More important from the point of view of the study, the 1960 Nova Scotia table [19] (58 X 58) is based on a different industrial classification. Only 28 sectors proved roughly comparable to those used in the United States and Philadelphia studies.

In order to make the five tables comparable with one another in terms of sectoring, the number of sectors in each was successively reduced to 43 X 43, 36 X 36, and 31 X 31. The aggregation was carried out with the help of grouping and weight matrices:

$$A^* = G A G'_w \; ;$$

where

A^* = reduced matrix,

A = original matrix,

G = grouping matrix,

G'_w = transpose of weight matrix with entries $g_w = 0, 1, w_{ij}$,

$$0 \leqslant g_{w \cdot ij} \leqslant 1; \text{and} \sum_{i=1}^{n} g_{w \cdot ij} = 1;$$

The relative importance of each sector in terms of output was used as weight.

The large differences in classification precluded a direct comparison of the

eigenvalues and Indexes of Association derived with the help of the original
tables, while aggregation resulted in tables too small for a meaningful analysis.
The sectors in the aggregated tables frequently comprised such heterogeneous
activities that flows between them reflected the accidents of presence or absence
of certain plants rather than technical affinity. On the basis of a careful perusal
of the results, it appears that valid conclusions cannot be based on tables comprised of less than fifty to sixty sectors. While methods of sectoring or grouping
of plants affect interregional comparisons, the treatment of vertical integration,
either physical or institutional, is likely to assume even greater importance. The
lack of evidence of flows internal to a plant might lead to surprising conclusions.
For example, the important aerospace complex in Washington State does not
stand out as a cluster of interlinked activities, because the bulk of the flows of
inputs and outputs either takes place within the complex itself or between it and
the rest of the world.

The Indexes of Association derived with the help of the model for the five
regions analyzed are summarized in Table 5-10.

Several aspects of the results deserve attention. First, the values of the
Indexes increase consistently and significantly with increasing aggregation (and
decreasing size of the tables). This was to be expected, but the strength of the
effect makes interregional comparisons based on tables of different dimensions
impossible. Notice that in the Philadelphia SMSA table a reduction from 89×89
to 43×43 increased C_1 by more than one half, while a reduction of the West
Virginia table from 48×48 to 23×23 almost tripled the value of C_1.

Second, interregional comparisons may have to encompass more than the
first three eigenvectors. The relatively low values of C_1 in the case of Philadelphia,
and even more so in the case of the United States, result from substantial clustering along other dimensions as well, whereas in the case of Washington State and
West Virginia the first three eigenvalues are the only substantial ones. While this
is precisely the phenomenon the Index of Association is designed to measure, a
consideration of a profile based on all eigenvalues may be more relevant for other
purposes.

In spite of these limitations certain tentative conclusions can be drawn on
the basis of the Indexes of Association. Within the roughly comparable size range
of 89×89 to 48×48, the United States, Philadelphia SMSA, and Washington
State tables show a distinctly higher degree of association than Nova Scotia and
West Virginia.[d] The contrast would be even sharper were it not for the fact that
in the latter two cases the service sectors have been far more disaggregated than
in the former.

While the Indexes of Association provide a crude measure of the degree of

---

[d]This becomes even more evident when the absolute values of the first eigenvalues are
considered, namely 21.21, 23.02, and 21.68 for the United States, Philadelphia SMSA, and
Washington State respectively, as against 17.95 and 13.79 for Nova Scotia and West Virginia.

Table 5-10
Values of the Indexes of Association $C_n = \dfrac{\lambda_n}{\operatorname{tr} R} \times 100$;

Region		Size of the R matrix								
		89 X 89	58 X 58	54 X 54	48 X 48	43 X 43	36 X 36	31 X 31	28 X 28	23 X 23
Nova Scotia	C_1		31.51						52.38	
	C_2		14.36						16.00	
	C_3		10.75						12.02	
United States	C_1	23.86				35.88	44.64	43.49		
	C_2	11.99				11.57	12.72	13.36		
	C_3	7.27				8.23	8.11	8.45		
Philadelphia SMSA	C_1	25.85				38.94	44.36	43.74		
	C_2	12.84				13.10	14.29	14.57		
	C_3	9.61				11.79	10.86	10.37		
Washington State	C_1			40.25		43.49	46.12	47.83		
	C_2			10.36		11.60	11.32	12.59		
	C_3			8.98		10.00	9.13	9.74		
West Virginia	C_1				28.75					74.20
	C_2				12.22					13.43
	C_3				8.90					6.71

clustering along some dimensions and an indication of the formation, in the regional economy, of industrial groupings based on direct and indirect inter-sectoral flows, interesting insights can be gained by studying the composition of eigenvectors. The sectors associated with the highest values in the first three eigenvectors are listed in Table 5-11. The cutoff points were chosen so as to exclude sectors contributing little to total variance along each particular dimension.

The relatively large United States table displays some features clearly related to the size and complexity of the economy. It is the only table from which the effects of spatial juxtaposition are absent. The first two eigenvectors are headed, in terms of associated values, by industries belonging to a metal complex, with the second showing a more pronounced orientation toward machinery- and equipment-producing industries. The third vector has few large entries, but those most prominent seem associated with chemicals, drugs, and photographic equipment.

The Philadelphia SMSA and Washington State tables are most interesting. The first eigenvector of the Philadelphia table is characterized by strong ties among the industries it encompasses. It contains mostly metal fabricating and machinery- and equipment-producing industries. Rather surprisingly, it also contains the wholesale and retail trade sector, which, at variance with the national economy, forms part of the first eigenvector of every regional table examined. The second eigenvector seems to combine elements of two complexes: an urban-oriented, mainly food-processing, group of industries, and some services. Despite the fact that some of the sectors represented are often found in harbor-based industrial complexes, the group as a whole seems clearly to be oriented toward the agglomeration of consumers and the large market of Philadelphia and its hinterland. The third eigenvector is composed entirely of services, many of which are typically found in large metropolitan areas.

The Washington State table presents a different, but not less intriguing, pattern. The sectors associated with the first eigenvector do not fall clearly into any one category, although typically urban services are very prominent. The second and third eigenvectors, on the other hand, are composed of industries with obvious technical links. Thus, the second subsystem clearly revolves around wood products, while the third has at its core food products and packaging materials. Both might properly be termed industrial complexes. The strong links between the components of the latter two groups are noticeable. The pattern displayed in the Washington State table may point toward the conclusion that in a regional economy the links due to spatial juxtaposition take precedence over those due to technical affinity. The latter make their appearance only after the former have been accounted for and their effects removed.

The regional economies of both West Virginia and Nova Scotia are characterized by a rather weak manufacturing base. The 48 X 48 West Virginia table groups primarily services in all three first eigenvectors. The links displayed are anyway

Table 5–11
Industries Associated with Largest Values in Eigenvectors

First Eigenvector No. Industry	Value	Second Eigenvector No. Industry	Value	Third Eigenvector No. Industry	Value
		United States 89 X 89 Matrix			
C_1 = 23.86		C_2 = 11.99		C_1 = 7.27	
54 Farm machinery & equipment	.1748	51 Stampings, screw machine products and bolts	.1843	73 Optical, opthal-mic & photographic equipment	.1802
5 Iron & ferro-alloy ores mining	.1690	52 Other fabricated metal products	.1784	36 Plastics and synthetic materials	.1703
52 Other fabricated metal products	.1681	55 Construction, mining & oil field machinery	.1744	37 Drugs, cleaning, & toilet prepara-tions	.1578
50 Heating, plumb-ing & structural metal products	.1651	45 Primary iron & steel manufac-turing	.1683	38 Paints & allied products	.1567
51 Stampings, screw machine products and bolts	.1643	59 General indus-trial machinery & equipment	.1643		
65 Electric lighting & wiring equip-ment	.1637	57 Metal working machinery & equipment	.1550		
71 Other transpor-tation equipment	.1546	50 Heating, plumb-ing & structural metal products	.1537		
58 Special industrial machinery & equipment	.1534	56 Materials handling machinery & equipment	.1520		
49 Metal containers	.1527				
		Philadelphia SMSA 89 X 89 Matrix			
C_1 = 25.85		C_2 = 12.84		C_3 = 9.61	
81 Wholesale & retail trade	.2109	19 Sugar	.2058	76 Other communi-cations	.1967
54 Farm machinery & equipment	.2086	17 Grain mill products	.2016	82 Finance & insurance	.1947
62 Service industries machines	.2072	33 Paperboard con-tainers & boxes	.1932	78 Electric utilities	.1893
52 Other fabricated metal products	.2043	76 Other communi-cations	.1848	85 Business services	.1865
50 Heating, plumb-ing & structural metal products	.2032	3 Forestry & fishery products	.1828	83 Real estate & rental	.1592
57 Metal working machinery & equipment	.1951	21 Beverage industries	.1816	87 Automobile repair services	.1575
58 Special industry machinery & equipment	.1940	2 Other agricultural products	.1756	79 Gas utilities	.1554

First Eigenvector No. Industry	Value	Second Eigenvector No. Industry	Value	Third Eigenvector No. Industry	Value

Philadelphia SMSA 89 × 89 Matrix

$C_1 = 25.85$		$C_2 = 12.84$		$C_3 = 9.61$	
49 Metal containers	.1938	34 Printing & publishing	.1734	84 Hotels, personal & repair services	.1534
31 Other furniture & fixtures	.1927	22 Miscellaneous food & kindred products	.1695		
45 Primary iron & steel manufacturing	.1899	82 Finance & insurance	.1692		
51 Stampings, screw machine products, and bolts	.1883	4 Agriculture, forestry & fishing products	.1588		
53 Engines & turbines	.1858	1 Livestock & livestock products	.1570		
64 Household appliances	.1813	14 Meat products	.1570		
56 Materials handling machinery & equipment	.1747	37 Drugs, cleaning & toilet preparations	.1562		
59 General industry, machinery & equipment	.1740	84 Hotels, personal & repair services	.1558		
60 Machine shop products	.1687	20 Confectionary & related products	.1535		
69 Motor vehicles & equipment	.1644	78 Electric utilities	.1532		
30 Household furniture	.1637	85 Business services	.1521		
55 Construction, mining & oil machinery	.1511	18 Bakery products	.1501		

Washington State 54 × 54 Matrix

$C_1 = 40.25$		$C_2 = 10.36$		$C_3 = 8.98$	
47 Communications	.2295	17 Sawmills	.3418	11 Other foods	.3334
52 Real estate	.2033	15 Forestry	.3392	2 Vegetables	.3294
30 Iron & steel	.1994	18 Plywood	.3335	8 Caning & preserving	.3009
53 Business services	.1968	21 Pulpmills	.3146	5 Fishing	.2501
49 Wholesale & retail	.1966	19 Other wood products	.2965	28 Glass & stone	.2441
19 Other wood products	.1874	22 Paper mills	.2474	34 "Light" metal products	.2417
54 Personal services	.1863	16 Logging	.2175	23 Paper board mills	.2343

Table 5-11 (continued)

First Eigenvector No. Industry	Value	Second Eigenvector No. Industry	Value	Third Eigenvector No. Industry	Value
		Washington State 54 × 54 Matrix			
$C_1 = 40.25$		$C_2 = 10.36$		$C_3 = 8.98$	
24 Printing & publishing	.1807			9 Grain mill products	.2079
33 "Heavy" metal products	.1788			21 Pulpmills	.2028
37 Nonelectric industrial equipment	.1780				
45 Gas companies	.1769				
20 Furniture & fixtures	.1745				
48 Construction	.1729				
50 Finance	.1706				
43 All transportation	.1694				
14 Mining	.1693				
51 Insurance	.1677				
46 Water services	.1658				
17 Sawmills	.1650				
		West Virginia 48 × 48 Matrix			
$C_1 = 28.75$		$C_2 = 12.22$		$C_3 = 8.90$	
31 Retail gasoline service stations	.2666	30 Retail food stores	.2698	35 Insurance agents & brokers	.2440
41 All other services services	.2467	10 Food & kindred products (dairies)	.2662	38 Hotels & other lodging places	.1791
38 Hotels & other lodging places	.2387	9 Food & kindred products (meats g.n.e.c.)	.2598	31 Retail gasoline service stations	.1727
43 Trucking & warehousing	.2292	32 All other retail	.1981	45 Communications	.1634
8 Special trades contractors	.2267	12 Food & kindred products (beverages)	.1910	33 Banking	.1577
32 All other retail	.2118	39 Medical & legal services	.1870	39 Medical & legal services	.1519
33 Banking	.2044	33 Banking	.1510	32 All other retail	.1494
34 Other finance	.2019	1 Agriculture	.1381	46 Electric companies & systems	.1369
45 Communications	.1979	37 All other finance, insurance & real estate	.1368	41 All other services	.1302

First Eigenvector No. Industry	Value	Second Eigenvector No. Industry	Value	Third Eigenvector No. Industry	Value
West Virginia 48 × 48 Matrix					
C_1 = 28.75		C_2 = 12.22		C_3 = 8.90	
35 Insurance agents & brokers	.1925	13 Apparel & accessories	.1015	24 Electrical machinery & apparatus	.1291
29 Wholesale trade	.1894			34 Other finance	.1053
48 Water & sanitary services	.1852				
28 Eating & drinking establishments	.1705				
Nova Scotia 58 × 58 Matrix					
C_1 = 31.51		C_2 = 14.35		C_3 = 10.75	
51 Wholesale & retail trade	.2475	9 Poultry processors	.3742	24 Sawmills & other wood products	.3135
31 Iron foundries, metal rolling stock	.2349	10 Dairy factories	.3609	25 Miscellaneous wood industries	.2253
7 Quarries & sandpits	.2163	14 Feed manufac- turers	.3485	30 Iron & steel mills	.2041
50 Gas & water systems	.2073	8 Meat products	.3211	39 Clay & concrete	.2030
38 Electric wire, cable & batteries	.2046	22 Cordage, canvas, cloth mills, etc.	.2944		
54 Finance, insur- ance & real estate	.2012	2 Forestry	.2571		
39 Clay & concrete	.1998	1 Agriculture	.2196		
47 Transportation	.1981				
25 Miscellaneous wood industries	.1979				
22 Cordage, canvas, cloth mills, etc.	.1964				
48 Radio broad- casting, telephone & telegraph	.1960				
52 Automobile operation	.1920				
30 Iron & steel mills	.1872				
46 Nonresidential construction	.1855				
12 Secondary fishery (all other) – i.e., not shellfish	.1833				

weak, and their appearance may be due to the fact that these sectors have been disaggregated to a much greater extent than in the other tables.

Examined against this background, the Nova Scotia economy reveals some interesting properties. The ratio of the first eigenvalue to total variance is relatively high and by itself explains 31.51 percent of total dispersion. Since the next two eigenvalues combined reach only 25.11 percent, it might be concluded that strong interindustry linkages occur primarily along one dimension. This is clearly different from the situation prevailing in the United States and Philadelphia SMSA economies.

An examination of industries associated with the highest values in the first eigenvector reveals a grouping of technically heterogeneous activities. The composition of this relatively tight cluster of activities seems to vindicate the hypothesis that in a spatial agglomeration the exchange of goods and services between unrelated industries exceeds in volume that between technically related ones. Indirectly this supports the thesis that for plants attracted to urban agglomerations the very existence, rather than the nature of the numerous and manifold links, is a prime consideration. [20] Industries associated with the highest elements in the second eigenvector, on the other hand, seem to be technically related to one another and, with one exception, related to food processing. The links among industries entering the third eigenvector are less obvious, although the few on top of the list are all based on local extractive activities.

Thus, similar features are revealed in all regional economies examined. Strong interindustry links based apparently on technical requirements become dominant in industries associated with high values in the second and sometimes third eigenvectors, while the first is dominated by tertiary activites or by a mixture of manufacturing and service industries. Significantly, these characteristics are absent in the United States economy and are less prominent in the vast manufacturing center of the Philadelphia SMSA.

Recapitulating the main methodological findings, it seems that multivariate analysis may be a useful tool for analyzing linkages existing in regional economies. The sample of input-output tables examined was far too small for any regularities to emerge. Nonetheless, the pervasiveness of links based on spatial proximity rather than technical affinity in the first subsystems falls in line with theoretical considerations and deserves careful attention. [21] Other considerations limiting the validity of the conclusions tentatively formulated, inherent in the use of a fixed coefficients production function underlying input-output tables and the dependence of the results upon accidents of an industrial classification developed for other purposes, especially in the treatment of services, have already been mentioned.

The study shows also that the rather frequent use of small, highly aggregated input-output tables for regional studies limits their usefulness in several ways. As far as multivariate analysis is concerned, the highest possible degree of detail would be required.

6

Invested Capital and Infrastructure: Contribution of Wealth Accounts

1 Classification and Methods of Measurement

The concern of classical economists with wealth, both as a measure of economic progress and of differences in factor endowment responsible for specialization, division of labor, and trade, faded during a period of severe business recessions of the inter-war years and with advances in the theories of value and capital that forced the recognition of the tenuous assumptions and concepts underlying wealth estimation. With its theoretical bases in dispute, its methodologies relatively crude and few in number, its optimum formats and alternative uses unexplored, wealth accounting remains the least developed area of social accounting despite the substantial amount of work devoted to it recently.

The lack of interest of economists in stock variables creates a significant imbalance in regional studies since the sectoral and spatial distribution of regional wealth reflects characteristics resisting rapid change and has long formed the basis of policies dealing with space. Not surprisingly some regional, as opposed to national, growth theories tend to stress the importance of such stock phenomena as the quantity of machinery, equipment, and structures used in production; the pool of laborers and entrepreneurs; various natural resources; the transportation system; or social overhead capital. The preoccupation of location theory with existing factors and facilities and of planners with land uses predates the current efforts at a systematic exploration of stock variables.

With modern technological progress, an overwhelming role is assumed by the part of wealth consisting of man-made capital. There are several criteria according to which items of invested or man-made capital can be classified. The first, and often used, division groups assets according to type or some inherent characteristics, yielding the following major categories: (1) reproducible assets, (2) nonreproducible assets, (3) intangible assets, and (4) financial capital.

A second criterion for classifying assets is their main use, sometimes combined with some secondary characteristics inherent in the assets themselves. This classification is composed of the following categories:

(1) Producer capital – subdivided into (a) machinery and equipment, (b) non-residential construction, (c) livestock and inventories;
(2) Consumer capital – subdivided into (a) housing and residential structures, (b) consumer durables;

243

(3) Defense installations;[a] and
(4) Infrastructure — subdivided into (a) transportation and communications,
     (b) water, sewerage, engineering constructions, (c) urban facilities meeting
     cultural, communal, sports, or entertainment requirements, (d) educational
     facilities, (e) health and welfare installations, (f) investments related to
     administration and protection (police, fire, etc.), and (g) extensive, largely
     suburban, recreational facilities.

The size and value of the physical infrastructure have long been recognized
as significant elements influencing regional development. Yet the placing of
money values on assets forming part of infrastructure is beset with many complex problems. The marginal contribution of such investments to the production
of goods and services cannot ordinarily provide the basis for valuation because
their outputs often have some or all characteristics of public goods. Such services
are either given away free of charge or priced at rates independent of costs and
neither affected by nor affecting demand. In many cases their contributions to
regional production or to satisfaction are indirect and difficult to trace.

The third criterion for classifying regional assets is the sectoral structure of
industries using these assets as capital goods, while the fourth, related criterion is
the sectoral structure of industries producing the assets. The two approaches are
obviously different, but both are of practical importance and often applied in
regional studies.

The fifth classification uses control as the main criterion. Two other criteria,
namely degree of mobility and location within the region, are self-explanatory.
They are sometimes used in conjunction with some of the other systems of classification.

The methods of valuation of man-made capital demand to a large extent
upon the purpose of the study and traditionally the most common use of estimates of invested capital was in studies of production functions and in various
direct and indirect methods of assessing the technology of the regional economy.
The significant potential applications, such as estimates of the extent to which
economies of agglomeration are generated or the closely related issue of absolute
and relative attractiveness of the region for new investments, have hardly affected
the methodology of regional wealth estimates.

For purposes of implementing production functions, capital must be
measured in a way correlative with production, since at bottom the measurement
of product and of capital are identical problems. Yet the technical difficulties
involved in measurement of income flows and of stocks are very different in

---

[a]The importance of a defense establishment for regional development appears obvious,
but whether only immobile assets should be counted or some part of the mobile military
hardware as well depends upon the objectives of the study. It is sometimes contended that
only those assets with alternative or subsidiary civilian uses or capable of being converted to
such uses should be considered.

nature. Since they have been discussed elsewhere, it is sufficient to recall here that while items composing income flows are for the most part goods and services currently valued upon the market, the volume of capital goods changing hands is small compared to the total existing, and few are traded at dates near to measurement. Hence, market prices as bases for valuation are the exception rather than the rule. In a perfect market, prices are proportional to marginal utilities and reflect marginal costs. Any deviations between the two are signals to stop or to step up production, thus ensuring an efficient allocation of goods and resources. If the market for a good is not perfect its marginal utility may be unequal to its marginal cost although both may exist, with the price diverging from either or from both; but in the complete absence of a market there is no price. In the face of imperfect markets or in their absence, valuation in terms of utility or in terms of costs may still be possible, but there is no reason why the two should be equal.

Since for most capital items markets are imperfect and transactions few, actual prices are at best poor indicators of value. Two possible principles of valuation for capital assets are often involved, a utility principle and a cost principle, answering two basically different questions. The utility principle corresponds to a comparison of two bundles of consumption goods from the point of view of their capacity to satisfy wants. The cost principle, on the other hand, corresponds to a comparison of two bundles of consumption (or production) goods generating identical utility in terms of resources and factors of production used in their manufacture. The former approach has received more attention, but for measuring capital goods the cost aspect may well be more important.

Practically, seven different methods of valuation of capital assets are possible:

(1) Book value, used mainly for corporate assets,
(2) Original cost to owner,
(3) National original cost, or cost to first owner in the nation or region,
(4) Face value, used in case of financial assets,
(5) Replacement value,
(6) Market value, and
(7) Capitalized net income.

The selection of methodology, or of the combination of methods to be used, depends upon the objectives of the study and data available, but the basic choice to be made is between uniformity of valuation of the assets covered and adherence to the motives of authors of the original data. The difficulties arising are due to differences between the principles upon which are based business accounts, forming the main source of data, and social accounts. The methods used in reported attempts at constructing wealth accounts can be classified into the following four categories: [1]

(1) Sample survey of statistical data, which involves discovering economically

meaningful questions that can be answered by data obtained from business records of a sample of firms.

(2) Sample survey of engineering data, obtained from plans or projects of new establishments submitted in support of applications for government or other financial assistance.

(3) Estimates derived from book values of business firms, adjusted for changing levels of prices and for revaluations, although without attempting to correct unrealistic depreciation policies.

(4) Perpetual inventory methods, based on adjusted income and product accounts. [2] In many ways this seems to be the most promising approach, and since it has been followed in estimating the wealth of Nova Scotia it deserves a closer examination.

The perpetual inventory method is based on, and provides a welcome link to, income and product accounts. Capital stock invested in an industry or sector of the economy at any particular time is derived by adding up purchases of capital goods, as recorded in income and product accounts, over a period of years. In order to determine net additions capital consumption, encompassing depreciation due to physical wear and tear, obsolescence, and accidental damage to fixed assets, has to be deducted. Two methods can be used for estimating yearly capital consumption: (1) historical time series data on capital consumption allowances, which form part of income and product accounts, or (2) independent estimates on capital withdrawals, based on average economic life of capital goods – that is, the length of time that, on average, similar capital goods remain in useful economic production before discarding or scrapping occurs.

The first method has the advantage of consistency, since both investments and capital withdrawals form part of the same set of balanced income and product accounts. Its main drawback, besides the difficulties involved in adjustments, is that the use of two time series does not permit the estimation of the value of the initial stock. In order to minimize the size of the error it is necessary to go very far back in time, when the total reproducible capital of the economy was small. Some estimates, in fact, reach back for over 100 years, which considerably reduces the discrepancy without completely eliminating it. [3] The use of such long time series, partly reconstructed from imperfect records, involves, however, a number of other difficulties that are mainly statistical.

The second method, followed for estimating Canadian capital in manufacturing [4] and in Nova Scotia, is conceptually simpler and provides a consistent estimate but rests on a number of rather strong assumptions concerning the average economic life of various assets. In following this last method three sources of data are needed for deriving the estimates:

(a) Historical time series of gross fixed capital formation by every industry, in current dollars;

(b) Price indexes pertaining to the types of capital goods being estimated, to be used as deflators; and

(c) Data on average economic life by broad categories of assets.

The derivation of the estimates followed by the Dominion Bureau of Statistics can be succinctly explained with the help of the usual mathematical symbolism.

$$GK_{hT} = \sum_{t=1}^{T} (GI_{hT} - R_{hR}) ; \qquad (1)$$

where

GK = constant dollar end-year gross stock of capital,

GI = gross fixed capital formation or gross capital formation in constant dollars,

R = withdrawals from capital stock in constant dollars;

and where the subscripts

t = time in yearly intervals: $1, 2, \ldots T$,

h = industrial sector: $1, 2, \ldots H$,

L = average expected economic life of capital goods in years,

$$R_{ht} = GI_{h(t-L_h)} ; \qquad (2)$$

Substituting and simplifying

$$GK_{hT} = \sum_{t=1}^{T} GI_{ht} - \sum_{t=1}^{T-L_h} GI_{ht} ; \text{ or} \qquad (3)$$

$$GK_{hT} = \sum_{t=T-(L_h-1)}^{T} GI_{ht} ; \qquad (4)$$

In order to arrive at net capital formation the estimated depreciation was deducted by applying the straight line method.

$$NI_{ht} = GI_{ht} - D_{ht} ; \qquad (5)$$

where

NI = net fixed capital formation in constant dollars,

D = estimated capital consumption allowance in constant dollars,

$$D_{ht} = \frac{1}{2L_h} \, [GK_{ht} + GK_{h(t-1)}] \; ; \tag{6}$$

Net capital formation and net capital stock are simply found by substituting

$$NI_{ht} \;\; = \;\; GI_{ht} - \frac{1}{2L_h} \, [GI_{ht} + GI_{h(t-1)}] \; ; \tag{7}$$

$$NK_{ht} \;\; = \;\; \sum_{t=t(L_h-1)}^{T} NI_{ht} = \sum_{t=1}^{T} GI_{ht} - \sum_{h=1}^{T} D_{ht}$$

$$= \;\; \sum_{t=1}^{T-L_h} GI_{ht} + \sum_{t=T-(L_h-1)}^{T} GI_{ht} - \sum_{t=1}^{T} D_{ht}$$

$$= \;\; GK_{hT} - \frac{1}{2L_h} \sum_{t=t(L_h-1)}^{T} [GI_{ht} + GI_{h(t-1)}] \; ; \tag{8}$$

where

NK = constant dollars end-year net stock of capital.

For all industries

$$NK_T = \sum_{h=1}^{H} NK_{nT} \; ; \tag{9}$$

The last step to be carried out is the conversion of gross fixed capital formation data from current to constant dollars with the help of price indexes of capital goods.

2 Producer Capital

Producer capital represents those regional investments whose prime object is production of goods and services to be sold or supplied to other units for consumption or further processing. The bulk of producer capital is owned and operated by business enterprises, although a substantial part is held by nonprofit organizations and various governments.

The assessment of the volume of producer capital invested in the region involves placing money values on its components and is beset with a number of statistical difficulties in addition to the more fundamental conceptual problems already alluded to. In Nova Scotia a number of heroic assumptions had to be made to overcome gaps in the data basis. Very reliable data on provincial gross capital expenditures by twelve sectors are published, [5] but they cover only fourteen years, 1948 to 1961. The time series thus derived is obviously too short, since the economic life of machinery and equipment is usually longer. Moreover, the sectoring is not detailed enough to prevent grouping within one sector of industries with short- and long-lived machinery and equipment. For five of the twelve sectors capital data were also published for 1945-1947, [6] and for the total private capital expenditures in Nova Scotia older, less reliable estimates were available for 1925, 1929, 1933, 1937, and 1941. [7] The sectoral capital expenditures in those years were estimated by using their respective shares during 1945-1961 as allocators. For public and institutional sectors estimates prior to 1948 were based on extrapolation of capital investments in these sectors during 1948-1961, using national trends as a proxy variable.

The new capital expenditures on machinery and equipment were converted from original costs to constant 1949 dollars by using several different price indexes supplied by the Dominion Bureau of Statistics. These were, however, based on Canadian rather than Nova Scotia price levels; moreover, the weights assigned to factor costs and raw material were in accordance with those prevailing in the national economy as a whole.

The next, and final, type of information required for estimating the value of producer capital is average economic life of the various assets. Assuming that capital goods purchased in any year survived for a number of years equal to their mean economic life, at which time they were retired, the perpetual inventory method can be applied with the help of one time series only. Using both United States and Canadian estimates reported either by type of asset or by industrial sector, a set of average economic life statistics were derived ranging from a low of ten years to a high of twenty-nine years. The relatively short expected economic life of some types of assets is explained by the fact that in the rapidly growing Canadian economy the rate of economic obsolescence is high.

Far more tentative were the final estimates of the value of nonresidential structures and engineering constructions, comprising such heterogeneous items as

nonresidential building, dams, sewers, highways, bridges, railway lines, transmission lines, and mines. Published time series data of new capital expenditures
were in this case too short for the application of the perpetual inventory method.
The only way available was to assume that the ratio of value of nonresidential
structures and engineering construction to the value of machinery and equipment
in each sector in 1961 was the same as the corresponding ratio of capital outlays
during 1950–1964, the period for which disaggregated data were available. Only
for agricultural assets were estimates based on direct published data.

Finally, a rather strong assumption was required in order to estimate the
value of business inventories for which only Canadian data were available. An
allocator was computed for each manufacturing industry by assuming that in
each industry the ratio of business inventories in Nova Scotia to the Canadian
total was the same as the province's share in the national value of shipments.

The value of agricultural livestock, on the other hand, was based on very complete and detailed agricultural statistics reported for mid-year 1961. From the
analytic point of view, agricultural livestock stands halfway between producer
capital and business inventories. While it is comparable to machinery, since it is
generating output in biological production processes, it is also a temporarily
stored commodity and, as such, similar to business inventories. The estimated
net value of capital stocks in Nova Scotia is summarized in Table 6-1.

While the size of the error involved in the different items and in the totals is
difficult to assess, and may be considerable, some interesting insights can be
gained from an examination of the table. The per capita value of net capital
stock stands at almost $1,800, which appears rather low. Comparisons with
United States figures are dangerous, not only because of the basic dissimilarity
between the two economies but mainly because of differences in methodology
and coverage of the estimates. Yet the Nova Scotia per capita figure represents
roughly forty percent of the American one, which comes rather close to the ratio
of per capita output of the two economies as measured in terms of their GRP and
GNP respectively. In terms of manufacturing industries only, the Nova Scotia
per capita stock of barely $346 is little over fifty percent of the Canadian figure
and does not reach even that percentage when compared to the United States.

Another interesting comparison emerges from examination of the sectoral
distribution of accumulated investments. A relevant line of analysis can be
followed by dividing total investments into "productive" and infrastructure. The
use of these terms here has to be qualified in view of the meaning attached to
them in classical economics. The dichotomy is based solely on the way in which
the objects or services produced are made available to consumers. Sectors selling
their products or services for prices determined by the market mechanism are
considered as "productive" and thus guided in their production or investment
decisions by existing or anticipated supply and demand conditions. Sectors classified as infrastructure, on the other hand, are those either producing public
goods or goods and services subject to such important externalities that they are

Table 6-1

Net Capital Stock Estimates by Sector, Nova Scotia, 1961 (in millions of 1961 dollars)

Sector	Machinery and Equipment	Nonresidential Structures and Engineering Constructions	Business Inventories and Agricultural Livestock	Total
Agriculture	22.3	22.1	26.1	70.5
Fishing	22.8	4.2		27.0
Forestry	3.2	6.4		9.6
Mining	27.7	16.4		44.1
Construction Industry	22.2	1.7		23.9
Manufacturing	103.0	77.6	72.3	252.9
Trade and Finance	54.7	80.4		135.1
Commercial Services	13.3	8.3		21.6
Subtotal	269.2	217.1	98.4	584.7
Utilities	177.4	147.5		324.9
Schools, Hospitals, and Other Institutions	14.4	110.8		125.2
Provincial and Local Governments	7.1	120.3		127.4
Federal Government in Nova Scotia	22.7	117.0		139.7
Total	490.8	712.7	98.4	1,301.9

either given away or charged at prices that stand in no relation to either costs or characteristics of demand. The levels of output and investments in such sectors usually follow the general growth trend of the regional economy, but may depend largely upon population size, desired level of welfare, or degree of urbanization. More usually, they are to a very large extent subject to sociopolitical considerations and cannot be treated as endogenous variables in models confined to economic factors.

In Nova Scotia capital invested in sectors falling into the latter category amounted in 1961 to $717.2 million, forming 55.1 percent of the total estimated net capital stock. While no directly comparable data for Canada or the United States are available, the share of this type of investments appears excessive. The explanation of this phenomenon may often be found either in the desire, discernible in some regions, to promote growth and attract new industries by providing facilities forming part of infrastructure, or more often in the niggardly state of the "productive" sectors.

In assessing the economic future of the region one should also consider the existing capital stocks of the defense establishment. These do not form part of either producer or consumer capital, yet their presence generates important effects in the regional economy. The fixed assets, once they reach a certain size,

tend to perpetuate themselves through constant additions. The capital stock
of the defense establishment in Nova Scotia, especially in the Halifax Metropolitan area, appears to be considerable and undoubtedly affects the local economy.
Yet no numerical estimates were available because, even aside from nondisclosure, valuation presents a number of conceptual difficulties. Most of the assets
involved do not have market prices and their cost is, partly at least, derived from
nonexhaustive public expenditures.

3 Consumer Capital

Residential structures and consumer durables are often collectively referred
to as consumer capital. The former are by far more significant. For purposes of
analysis residential assets can be classified in a number of ways. Taking location
as the relevant criterion, one could distinguish urban and rural housing, while
according to tenure one might divide residential housing into owner occupied and
renter occupied. From the point of view of structural type, one could list
separately: single detached houses, duplexes, attached houses, walk-up apartment
houses, and high-rise apartments. Still other relevant classifications are based on
characteristics of construction (such as concrete, brick, or wooden frame), on
size of housing units, on the extent to which structures are equipped with
utilities, or on average value and age.

Consumer durables, despite the fact that their total value is usually smaller,
comprise an even wider group of assets of which the most important are automobiles and electric household appliances. Other items, such as furniture, carpets,
pictures, antiques, jewelry, or clothing, may occasionally reach considerable value
but are rarely recorded in published statistics. The common characteristic of all
consumer durables is that they are already owned by their ultimate users In fact,
consumer durables are often defined as those consumption expenditures that
release their utility over a period of time, the generally accepted, although
arbitrary, cut-off point being one year.

The two components of consumer capital are thus possessed of different
characteristics. Not only is the expected lifetime of housing of a different order
of magnitude, but a significant part of its total value is represented by rental
housing, which is not owned by ultimate users. For regional studies the main,
important difference between consumer durables and residential structures is the
fact that while the former are mobile, the latter are not.

The interest of regional scientists in consumer capital in general, and in
housing in particular, is centered on three distinct though related aspects:

(1) Welfare implications of endowment in consumer capital,
(2) Economic implications of housing, which represents a huge, spatially
     immobile investment, and

(3) Sociopolitical consequences of the distribution of housing within metropolitan areas.

Only in the crudest sense are the welfare aspects of housing easily measurable. Such indices as number of rooms per capita or average age of structures, while lending themselves to interregional and intertemporal comparisons, bring to the fore only one aspect of an essentially multidimensional phenomenon. Nor is total, average, or per capita value of the housing stock a suitable measuring rod, since it is strongly influenced by local demand conditions, precluding its use for comparative studies. The development of suitable indicators encompassing the manifold characteristics of housing is badly needed. No attempt is being made here to make use of the abundant numerical material available for drawing conclusions concerning the welfare aspects of consumer capital in the province, since these are bound to be partial at best, and biased by the selection of characteristics used.

The assessment of the economic implications of existing consumer capital, on the other hand, presents few conceptual issues, but is beset with difficult measurement problems, some of which have already been alluded to. In economically developed countries the housing stock represents an accumulation of investments exceeding social overhead capital in value. The capital outlays on housing per urban household do not lag far behind investments required to provide a place of work for its head. This statement has obviously to be qualified somewhat, since investments per place of work depend upon industry, with capital-labor ratios varying over a tremendous range.

The size of invested capital and the immobility and longevity of the housing stock make it an important locational factor, while the changing spatial pattern of industrial developments engenders obsolescence of the housing stock, often outpacing its physical wear and tear. Since the range of commuting is severely circumscribed, the existence of a large housing stock often leads to efforts to induce new industries to locate in labor market areas no longer attractive under changed conditions. Housing may thus contribute to perpetuating inefficient spatial patterns of production. The locational obsolescence of housing is mainly evident at the regional, not at the urban, level of inquiry, and this partly explains the fact that it has attracted rather scant attention. Despite its imperfections, the measurement of capital invested in social services, utilities, and housing is all the more important since the market prices of inputs and of the stream of services produced do not reflect their capital content.

The total housing stock in Nova Scotia, excluding farms, comprised 162,665 units in 1961. Table 6-2 indicates their distribution by tenure, location, and type.

The value of housing was estimated by four different methods. The basic approach was the perpetual inventory method, but here a specific difficulty was encountered due to the fact that residential structures are long-lived assets, with

Table 6–2
Non-Farm Housing Stock, Nova Scotia, 1961

	Owner Occupied	Renter Occupied	Total
Rural Non-farm	58,229	10,129	68,358
Single detatched	54,999	8,089	63,088
Attached	3,230	441	3,671
Apartments or flats	–	1,589	1,589
Urban	60,873	33,434	94,307
Single detatched	50,984	9,523	60,507
Attached	9,889	334	10,223
Apartments or flats (14,880 in Halifax Metropolitan Area)	–	23,577	23,577
Total Non-farm Dwelling Units			162,665

Based on: D.B.S., *1961 Census of Canada: Housing: Dwelling Characteristics by Type and Tenure*, Catalogue No. 93–529.

an average life estimated at sixty years. Published time series on new capital expenditures in housing in Nova Scotia, however, were available only for the years 1948–1961, although for Canada as a whole the data reached as far back as 1900. [8] The Nova Scotia time series could thus be extended backwards by using the share of Nova Scotia in national investments during 1948–1961 as an allocator.

The major defect of this method is the fact that the bulk of Nova Scotia housing was constructed before 1948, with 47.6 percent built before 1920. Hence the main part of the estimated value of total stock was based on extrapolated and not actual data. Moreover, the share of Nova Scotia in housing construction was almost certainly higher before 1948, especially during the war years, than thereafter, so that the figures derived by the perpetual inventory method most likely are an underestimate. Price indexes, on the other hand, were available and presented no problem. The end-year 1961 value of gross housing stock was found to be $1,094 million, and the net value, after making allowances for capital consumption, $706.3 million.

The second method combined the depreciated replacement cost approach for non-farm housing with direct Census estimates for farm structures. Replacement costs of all 162,655 non-farm residences reported in the 1961 Census were assumed to be equal to average costs of construction in Metropolitan Halifax, or $12,390 per unit. This yielded a total undepreciated replacement cost of non-farm housing of $2,015.2 million.

The age of housing was reported according to four age groups, and the following depreciation rates were applied:

Built before 1920	85.0 percent
" 1920–1945	51.7 percent
" 1946–1959	15.0 percent
" 1960–61	2.0 percent

This yielded a total depreciated replacement cost of non-farm housing of $916.6 million.

The 1961 Census reported the total market value of farmland, farm operator's house, and other farm buildings at $89.3 million. By subtracting the value of farmland and other farm buildings, computed elsewhere, the value of the 12,685 residential farm dwelling units was estimated at $35.9 million. The total for all housing was thus $952.5 million, or substantially higher than the one obtained by the perpetual inventory method.

The third approach made use of the reported median value of single detached owner-occupied housing which stood at $5,873 per unit. [9] Applying this number to all types of dwellings and assuming the value of land to be fifteen percent of the total, a crude estimate of $812.0 million for all housing units was obtained.

The fourth approach represents a refinement of the above, making use of reported values of single detached owner-occupied non-farm housing units by location. Nine value intervals were considered.[b] The mean interval values were computed on the basis of a continuous function fitted to the data, yielding total value of 105,983 single detached owner-occupied non-farm dwellings.

In order to calculate the value of the remaining 56,672 non-farm units, it was first assumed that the 17,612 renter-occupied detached units had the same value distribution as the owner-occupied units. Second, it was assumed that the 13,894 owner- and renter-occupied attached units would be fifteen percent lower in value than the detached units, both because of their greater age, on the average, and because of economies in their construction. Third, the value of the 25,166 flats and apartment units was assumed to be on the average twenty percent lower. This last assumption is rather strong since the distribution of values in this category is bimodal, being composed of both older flats (frequently in slum areas) and modern, often luxury, high-rise apartment buildings. The total value of the housing stock computed by this method amounted to $1,230.6 million, and after subtracting the value of land the estimate for non-farm residences stood at $1,045.9 million.

Of these four estimates the second, using the depreciated replacement cost approach for non-farm housing, was considered to be more reliable than the other three.

---

[b]Under $3,000; $3,000–$7,499; $7,500–12,499; $12,500–17,499; $17,500–22,499; $22,500–27,499; $27,500–32,499; $32,500–37,499; and $37,500+.

The *1961·Census of Canada* contains a fairly extensive inventory of a wide range of consumer durables, but without estimates of value. All of these are highly mobile and have rather short economic lives. Value estimates are generally difficult to obtain and very unreliable, except for automobiles. Passenger vehicles are also by far the most significant for regional analysis, since they not only enhance the well-being of the inhabitants but, as the primary mode of transportation to employment modes, are more directly related to the productivity of the labor force.

Data on number of vehicles were obtained from records of household ownership of vehicles, vehicle registration and, for vehicles operated by farmers, from farm surveys that also provided value estimates. The total of non-farm vehicles was then multiplied by their average depreciated cost (based on estimates of car dealers), yielding total value of $177.5 million. Adding to this $7.9 million as the value of the 6,725 vehicles operated by farmers, the total value arrived at of the 107,369 passenger vehicles registered in Nova Scotia in mid-year 1961 was $185.4 million.

Thus the best estimates of consumer capital are limited to two (although the most important) items only, namely

Residential housing	$ 952.5 million
Passenger vehicles	185.4 million
Total	$1,037.9 million

Even in the absence of comparative figures for other regions, the concentration of wealth in consumer capital as revealed by the above partial estimates seems excessive. Total producer capital in Nova Scotia, including utilities and infrastructure was estimated at only $1,301.9 million. Hence consumer capital, even without most consumer durables and nonreproducible assets, represented 73.2 percent of producer capital.

In total reproducible assets, which stood at $2,439.8 million, the share of consumer capital was 39.0 percent. On a per capita basis, no doubt, the accumulation of consumer capital is not excessive in prosperous Canada, but the stock of producer capital is even more deficient in comparison. The distribution of assets seems merely to confirm the tentative findings, derived from an analysis of the income and product accounts, suggesting a relatively high level of consumption in excess of local productive capacity.

A perusal of the basic characteristics of housing in Nova Scotia brings into sharp focus another major problem related to all fixed assets, namely their inefficient spatial distribution, which might be termed locational obsolescence. A cartographic analysis of the age and degree of utilization of existing housing resources clearly shows their uneven division and utilization in various parts of the province. The older agglomerations, especially the cluster of towns around Sydney, possess ample housing resources (although a high proportion is relatively old and often lacking modern facilities) and a low ratio of inhabitants to number of rooms. This is perhaps not surprising in view of the almost nonexistent or problem-ridden economic base of these parts of the province, combined with persistent substantial outmigration.

It nonetheless places the policy makers in the dilemma of either encouraging new industries to move into otherwise unattractive or inefficient locations or facilitating the removal of population and creating the phenomenon of "ghost towns." The problem has much broader aspects than housing and, because of its social and political implications, largely transcends purely economic considerations. Yet before examining some of the issues involved and the curious and, potentially at least, disastrous solutions taking shape in Nova Scotia, it might be worthwhile to consider in more detail the existing infrastructure, the volume of fixed assets invested in its operation, and the associated flow phenomena.

4 Service Activities

In advanced modern economies there is a perceptible shift from resource oriented and manufacturing activities toward services. The trend is due primarily to three causes: (1) technological progress, which increases the amount of processing applied to each unit of basic raw materials, (2) growing complexity of organization required for production, finding its expression in the changing structure of employment within particular industries and enterprises, and (3) growing affluence of Western societies, with the attendant increase in the demand for services.

The trend, according to Baumol, [10] contains the seeds of its own undoing. This reasoning can be succinctly summarized as follows: If in a two sector economy productivity per man-hour rises cumulatively in one of the two sectors while wages move together, then wages and costs in the nonprogressive sector will rise cumulatively and without limit. In the progressive sector increases in costs will be offset by increases in productivity, but in the traditional sector costs and prices will rise. Thus, according to this model, the very progress of the technology is the cause of rising costs in many sectors, with their products being either driven from the market or constituting a drag on the economy, often beyond the control of government. The model explains correctly some observable phenomena. It is evident that in the developed countries retail, for example, absorbs an increasing proportion of the national labor force, and marketing costs are rising despite technological changes such as self-service supermarkets and pre-wrapping. Obviously not all services face inelastic demand, and those that do not either are completely driven from the market or become luxury goods. Examples include fine pottery and glassware, fine restaurants, theaters, construction of stately homes, handworked furniture, and made-to-measure tailoring.

The shift from extractive and manufacturing to service activities in

developed Western countries is not to be confused with the growth of employment in services characteristic of many cities in the undeveloped world. The
rapid expansion of population of those cities is often generated by massive waves
of inmigration of the "push" type. The prime cause of those displacements seems
to be the inability of agriculture to sustain an overpopulated rural countryside.
With marginal productivity of redundant farm population near zero, the moves
into the cities in quest of food are made irrespective of employment opportunities. The undeveloped urban manufacturing base and the low level of skills of the
migrants result in an increase in low-paid service employment of a type characterized by low capital intensity. To differentiate between the two types of
service activities requires an in-depth analysis of their structure, in terms of a fine
sectoral breakdown, and their relative size and capital intensity.

The important question with respect to the sizable Nova Scotia service
sector is whether its development is due to a genuine demand or results simply
from inertia coupled with a lack of alternative employment opportunities of
factors of production. Available studies do not furnish an unambiguous answer
to this question. Table 6–3 indicates that in 1961 total service sector labor force
stood at 149,146, or 20.24 percent of total population and 37.24 percent of
urban population.

The corresponding ratios for Ontario indicated a share of labor force in
service sectors amounting to 21.05 percent of total population, or slightly more
than in Nova Scotia, but only 27.21 percent of urban population. The difference
in the latter ratio is considerable and has deep causes.

Comparisons with nonservice labor force are equally impressive and seem to
indicate an excessive concentration in the service sector of the Nova Scotia
economy. A closer scrutiny reveals, however, that the effect is largely due to the
relatively large employment in defense. If defense is disregarded, the following
picture emerges:

	Nova Scotia	*Ontario*
Ratio of service sector labor force to total population	16.51%	20.11%
Ratio of service sector labor force to total urban population	30.38%	26.00%

Nova Scotia still seems to have an overdeveloped service sector in relation to
its urban, although not to its total, population, but even that may be spurious
since some services are undoubtedly oriented toward the military establishment
in and around Halifax — a fact not revealed by the usual classification.

The suspicion that the service sector in Nova Scotia is too large and represents a misallocation of resources is based on comparisons with gross regional
product. While in 1961 the Nova Scotia ratio of GRP to service sector labor was

Service Sector Labor Force, Nova Scotia and Ontario, 1961

Industry	Nova Scotia				Ontario			
	Labor Force	Labor Force as Percentage of Total Population	Labor Force as Percentage of Urban Population	Labor Force in Service Sectors as Percentage of Total Nonservice Labor Force	Labor Force	Labor Force as Percentage of Total Population	Labor Force as Percentage of Urban Population	Labor Force in Service Sectors as Percentage of Total Nonservice Labor Force
Transportation, Storage, Communications, and Other Utilities	24,962	3.39	6.23	28.47	195,223	3.13	4.05	18.07
Transportation	16,863	2.29	4.21	19.23	116,330	1.87	2.41	10.77
Storage	216	.03	.05	.25	3,649	.06	.08	.34
Communications	5,456	.74	1.36	6.22	46,132	.74	.96	4.27
Electric power, gas and water utilities	2,427	.33	.61	2.77	29,112	.47	.60	2.69
Trade	36,763	4.99	9.18	41.93	370,540	5.94	7.68	34.30
Wholesale trade	9,603	1.30	2.40	10.95	102,733	1.65	2.13	9.51
Retail trade	27,160	3.69	6.78	30.98	267,807	4.29	5.55	24.79
Finance, Insurance, and Real Estate	5,652	.77	1.41	6.45	98,454	1.58	2.04	9.11
Financial institutions	3,224	.44	.80	3.68	45,770	.73	.95	4.24
Insurance and real estate	2,428	.33	.61	2.77	52,684	.84	1.09	4.88
Community, Business and Personal Services	44,953	6.10	11.22	51.27	467,127	7.49	9.68	43.74
Education and related	10,421	1.41	2.60	11.89	88,731	1.42	1.84	8.21
Health and welfare	11,725	1.59	2.93	13.37	114,200	1.83	2.37	10.57
Religious organizations	2,079	.28	.52	2.37	14,523	.23	.30	1.34
Motion picture and recreational	1,067	.14	.27	1.22	16,895	.27	.35	1.56
Services to business management	1,856	.25	.46	2.12	44,655	.72	.93	4.13
Personal services	16,114	2.19	4.02	18.38	164,053	2.63	3.40	15.18
Miscellaneous services	1,691	.23	.42	1.93	24,070	.39	.50	2.23
Public Administration and Defense	36,816	5.00	9.19	41.99	181,263	2.91	3.76	16.78
Federal administration	31,907	4.33	7.97	36.39	111,553	1.79	2.31	10.33
Defense	27,474	3.73	6.86	31.34	58,686	.94	1.22	5.43
Other	4,433	.60	1.11	5.06	52,867	.85	1.10	4.89
Provincial administration	1,975	.27	.49	2.25	20,402	.33	.42	1.89
Local administration	2,902	.39	.72	3.31	48,569	.78	1.01	4.50
Other government	32	–	.01	.04	739	.01	.02	.07
Total	149,146	20.24	37.24	170.12	1,312,607	21.05	27.21	121.49

Note: In 1961 Nova Scotia had a population of 737,007 and an urban population of 400,512; the corresponding figures for Ontario were 6,236,092 and 4,823,529. In 1961 the nonservice sector labor force consisted of 57,673 persons in Nova Scotia and 1,080,408 persons in Ontario.

Based on: D.B.S., *1961 Census of Canada, Labor Force*, Catalogue No. 94-518.

The employment figures differ slightly from those in Table 5-2, because 2,132 government employees in Nova Scotia have been reclassified as transportation and other utilities workers in accordance with their functional characteristics.

$8,987, in Ontario it amounted to $12,810, despite the fact that the more developed Ontario economy requires more specialized services.

An examination of the structure of the service sector in terms of industries does not reveal any major differences between Nova Scotia and Ontario. The relatively more modest share of (1) Finance, Insurance, and Real Estate, and (2) Services to Business Management in Nova Scotia is more than compensated by a heavy concentration in defense.

Comparisons over time reveal that the growth of employment in commercial services[c] between 1961 and 1967 has been substantial — from around 104,000 to 122,000. Taking the wage bill as an index of value added, the yearly increments have been, on the average, 6.17 percent, or remarkably close to the average rate of increase of GRP.[d] An examination of changes in the sectoral composition over time does not reveal any clear trend during the past ten years, although sectors characteristic of modern, developed economies seemingly failed to grow in Nova Scotia at above average rates.

Growth has been almost equally distributed among the various sectors, with a slightly higher than average increase in personal services and a net decline in transportation. The only clearly discernible positive factor emerging was the substantial increase in communications and in finance, insurance, and real estate. A more rigorous shift analysis in relation to developments in Canada, discussed in Chapter 4, Section 4, confirmed the relatively high rate of growth in such "traditional" service industries as other personal services and in some types of wholesaling and retailing but on the whole failed to reveal any spectacular deviations from the national pattern.

The important (from the point of view of allocation of resources) question of the relative productivity of services can be only partly explored with the data available. Total investments in trade, finance, and commercial services amounted in 1961 to $156.7 million, or to $3,927 per employee, but as no comparative data for other provinces exist this ratio is not very meaningful. For a similar reason, internal comparisons among groups of sectors do not lead to any unambiguous conclusions.

Table 6-4 presents some comparative data on investments in trade, finance, and commercial services in Nova Scotia and Ontario during the relatively brief period 1961–1968 and relates them to employment.

The relatively higher capital expenditures in the service sector in Nova

---

[c]Commercial services are confined to activities sold at market prices and operated largely by private business enterprises for profit. They are distinguished from public services, which lack one or both of these characteristics. There is some difficulty in classifying border cases, like water utilities, that have been included among commercial services in what follows mainly because of statistical necessity.

[d]During 1961–1965 the total growth in percentage terms has been:

Employment in services	9.00 percent
Total wages in services	20.87 percent
GRP	20.66 percent

Table 6-4
Capital Expenditures and Employees, Selected Services,[a] Nova Scotia and Ontario, 1961-1968

Year	Capital Expenditures (I) ($ million)		Number of Employees (E) ('000)		Change in Number of Employees $(E_t - E_{t-1})$ ('000)		$I/(E_t - E_{t-1})$ ($'000)	
	Nova Scotia	Ontario	Nova Scotia	Ontario	Nova Scotia	Ontario	Nova Scotia	Ontario
1968	36.4	593.4	52.3	753.7	2.1	42.5	17.3	14.0
1967	41.7	616.6	50.2	711.2	1.8	29.9	23.2	20.6
1966	29.0	550.8	48.4	681.3	2.2	39.1	13.2	14.1
1965	31.6	460.2	46.2	642.2	1.9	33.8	16.6	13.6
1964	40.3	399.2	44.3	608.4	2.0	29.0	20.2	13.8
1963	28.8	330.7	42.3	579.4	1.7	22.4	16.9	14.8
1962	26.0	327.8	40.6	557.0	1.0	25.4	26.0	12.9
1961	22.7	313.2	39.6	531.6				
1961–1968	256.5	3,591.9			12.7	222.1	20.2	16.2

[a]Commercial Services, except Transportation, Storage, Communications, and Other Utilities.

Source: D.B.S., Estimates of Employees by Province and Industry, 1961–1968, Catalogue No. 72–508; and D.B.S., Private and Public Investment in Canada, Outlook and Regional Estimates, annual, 1963–1970, Catalogue No. 61–205.

Scotia than in Ontario are noticeable. As a consequence, total investments per new employee were of the order of $20,200 in Nova Scotia as against $16,200 in Ontario. These results may imply a slight shift in Nova Scotia toward the more capital intensive type of services, but in view of the inadequacy of data such a conclusion may not be entirely warranted. Obviously, in the absence of production functions only limited and uncertain conclusions can be drawn.

5 Control over Wealth

The notion of control differs from that of ownership, which is commonly used in national wealth accounting. In view of the progressive scattering in modern law of the bundle of rights to assets forming property, control seems to be a more significant characteristic for purposes of regional economic analysis. Ownership increasingly becomes limited to the right to income produced and to inheritance, while real control of regionally important assets is often exercised by individuals or bodies without any property rights in them. The conceptual difficulty inherent in this classification derives from the implied abandonment of the profit maximizing principle on which much of economic theory is based. It is unfortunate that both notions have so far found only scant application in regional models, although the character of the physical or legal persons exercising control over wealth may obviously be crucial for understanding or projecting its disposition. The main reason seems to be that economics has progressed little beyond the assumption of utility or profit maximizing motivation of ultimate decision-making units, applying it indiscriminately to all wealth holders. This assumption, widely criticized and recognized as unrealistic even with respect to households, is clearly untenable as a basic premise explaining decisions of non-profit organizations or government units. Yet in the absence of any generally accepted alternative hypotheses concerning the motivation and behavior of the increasingly important collective decision makers, endowed with a legal personality, the analytic effect of attempts to disaggregate wealth by control might well be to further limit the scope of assets and phenomena governed by units whose decisions are, however imperfectably, predictable. [11]

The growing volume of assets under the control of various public bodies is obviously not tantamount to the spread of the public sector in the sense of leading to a socialist society. It is important in this connection to distinguish two concepts of the public sector. [12] The first hinges on the organization of production and is based on the distinction between private and public enterprises; it is thus closely related to ownership or control over wealth. The second focuses on the use of resources and is based on the distinction between private and public wants. In general, only private wants can be efficiently satisfied through the operation of the market, because they alone involve goods that are rivals in consumption. In the case of public wants, the allocation of resources with the help of the pricing mechanism is often impossible, and as a rule inefficient, because nonrival goods are involved. Public wants are further subdivided into social wants, which are subject to the individual scale of preference, and merit wants, which reflect the preference scale of the ruling elite and are imposed on the individuals.

This last distinction is less important for purposes of the present discussion. To be noted, however, is the fact that while an increase in the relative volume and importance of public wants is accompanied by an expansion of governmental budgets, it need not necessarily be followed by an increase in the share of public enterprises.

The notion of control over wealth focuses on an important aspect of analysis of the regional economy. Using it as a criterion the institutions exercising control over wealth might be divided into eight categories — namely, non-farm households, unincorporated farms and farm households, business corporations, unincorporated businesses, nonprofit organizations, local and provincial governments, federal government, and non-Canadian foreign units. This division overcomes a number of conceptual problems and numerous, and far more serious, shortcomings of the data basis.

The conceptual difficulties have mainly to do with the nebulous status of certain assets belonging to the Crown, such as game and wildlife or water resources, since the Crown is both federal and provincial governments. Similarly, ocean resources that are government property involve the unsettled, political rather than legal, question of whether they belong to the federal or the provincial government. With respect to subsoil resources that are owned by the Crown and are under the control of the provincial government, numerous exceptions have to be made for such assets as gypsum, limestone, and structural materials, which belong to the landowners.

The inadequacy of the data basis is largely the outcome of the general dearth of information concerning assets. Numerous, some of them strong, assumptions had to be made, supplemented by heavy reliance on unpublished data and on expert opinion, in order to derive a breakdown of regional wealth by control. The final results are summarized in Table 6-5, while a more detailed total regional wealth estimate by type of assets is given in Appendix H.

The distribution of assets among the eight sectors is strongly influenced by the high value assigned to human resources. The two sectors among which this nontransferable resource has been apportioned acquire here very great importance. If human resources, in the last resort perhaps not quite commensurable with man-made capital and natural resources, are left out of consideration, most assets seem to be concentrated in the hands of non-farm households, local and provincial government, and business corporations. Significantly, 43.0 percent of man-made capital was controlled by non-farm households (bearing witness again to the importance of housing in the provincial economy), 23.9 percent was in the hands of business corporations, and 14.3 percent was operated by local and provincial governments. With respect to natural resources, however, the situation

Table 6-5
Regional Wealth by Type and Control, Nova Scotia, 1961 (in millions of dollars)

Control over Wealth	Natural Resources	Manmade Capital	Human Resources	Total
Non-Farm Households	302.2	1,001.0	16,198.0	17,501.2
Unincorporated Farms and Farm Households	78.1	111.8	557.8	747.7
Business Corporations	105.5	581.9		687.4
Unincorporated Businesses	29.5	128.7		158.2
Nonprofit Organizations	4.0	125.2		129.2
Local and Provincial Governments	749.1	154.1		903.2
Federal Government	19.6	195.0		214.6
Non-Canadian Foreign Units	69.8	142.0		211.8
Total	1,357.8	2,439.7	16,755.8	20,553.3

was reversed, with local and provincial governments controlling 56.6 percent, non-farm households 22.3 percent, and business corporations only 7.8 percent of the total. It is perhaps unfortunate that no breakdown between Nova Scotia domiciled business corporations and households and those based in the rest of Canada was obtainable.

The foreign ownership of regional assets is a sensitive political issue but the accounts provide scant support to the contention of excessive foreign penetration. Admittedly, however, an integration of these considerations into a rigorous analytic framework is so far not achievable. Here is clearly an area in which data availability and practical planning is well ahead of applied regional theory.

6 Urban Spaces

The spatial distribution of wealth within the province is an economically, socially, and politically significant factor that can be studied from several different points of view. Two aspects are examined here. First, as an outcome of concentration of wealth at certain nodal points, values are generated that cannot be explained by reference to opportunity costs of resources used up in the construction of fixed assets. Second, the spatial polarization of wealth is at the core of the phenomenon of growth poles, which according to some theories are alone capable of inducing economic progress in the surrounding countryside under modern conditions.

The first aspect is part of the phenomenon of land rent, which has long occupied the attention of economists. The economic importance of location rent is obviously not confined to the redistribution of social product, but may be used as an index of economies due to spatial agglomeration and juxtaposition that often defy direct measurement. Unfortunately, prices paid for urban real property recently traded are a poor guide to the value of the bulk of urban assets because, even when known, they are often established in a very imperfect market.

A model currently being implemented by the author [13] attempts to quantify the various factors affecting the spatial distribution of investments and activities within a metropolitan area in order to analyze the mechanism generating location rents. It is predicated on the idea that a city or metropolitan area may be viewed as a place fulfilling a great number of complex economic, social, and political functions, most of which require space. These requirements are very unequal, depending partly upon intensity of land use. The notion of land use intensity has two different meanings attached to it:

(1)   Investment intensity, which measures the volume of investments per unit area, and
(2)   Trip intensity, which measures the volume of trips generated by or terminating in an area per unit of time.

The two criteria are far from synonymous but, despite some spectacular exceptions, the agreement between them is very large.

The imperfections of the real estate market notwithstanding, the more intensive land use categories are able to outbid other uses that may not be less vital to the operation of the urban organism. Three broad land use categories stand out, because of their extent, as being largely responsible for shaping the spatial structure of an urban area and, under modern conditions, for much of the land absorption into urban uses at the fringes:

(1)   Manufacturing, with ancillary storage, warehousing, wholesaling, and so on,
(2)   Housing, and
(3)   Commercial services, mainly retailing, traditionally largely concentrated in the Central Business District but now increasingly found in outlying shopping centers.

The study now under way analyzes, with the help of quantitative techniques, the factors affecting and the forces shaping the spatial distribution of the first two, with less attention paid to the location of service and retail facilities and to forecasting their future development. [14]

The proposed, and now being implemented, model is fully reproducible by another researcher. It is composed of several submodels, is time-recursive, and incremental. While the submodels are analytic, the model itself is a planning model comprised of controllable policy variables as major outputs. The basic hypotheses concerning the behavior of various decision-making units such as households, manufacturers, and government agencies are part of the model and of respective submodels in a form enabling their rigorous testing. The model is being calibrated and simulated primarily on the basis of data pertaining to the Halifax-Dartmouth metropolitan area, except for the manufacturing submodel, which also makes use of data for individual industries from other metropolitan areas. The part of the model immediately relevant to the present discussion, allocating space to various uses and generating a land use balance sheet and land values, is based on two submodels.

a. Manufacturing submodel

The following hypotheses are explicitly recognized:

(1) The location factors that affect the distribution of industries within a metropolitan area, or among sub-areas of an industrial region, are on the whole different from those that affect the choice of location among cities.
(2) Since the available supply of urban land is limited, industrial users compete for land among themselves and with other users, some of whom develop land more intensively and hence are able to outbid industry.
(3) The locational preferences of industries are diverse and generally do not permit grouping of industries in the usual S.I.C. categories; consequently, industries have to be reclassified and regrouped by location characteristics.

This leads to the consideration of the following categories of major land users:

(1) Large industrial corporations. These do not respond in a consistent manner to the usual urban environmental forces. When possessed of unused land reserves they tend to maintain their existing locations, while when they seek new locations the existence of large blocks of inexpensive land or some other special circumstances are often decisive.
(2) Quarrying and building materials producers.
(3) Other manufacturers, comprising both intensive and extensive land users.

The manufacturing submodel begins with a study of locational preferences of industries. Among the many factors affecting location decision are:

(a) Those related to distance and general accessibility to other industries, to central metropolitan functions, and to labor force residential areas, and
(b) Those dealing with the site itself, such as slope conditions, soil resistance, availability of sewerage, waterfront, zoning, or value of existing structures.

The study of locational preferences of industries is preceded by a number of accessibility studies. The basic assumption underlying the accessibility studies is that within an urbanized area any facility is always available, but the time-distance involved in reaching it varies greatly from one site to another. From the point of view of intrametropolitan location, of importance is accessibility to other manufacturing plants, to central urban functions, and to residential areas (labor).

Accessibility indices to manufacturing should measure the well-known tendency of industries to cluster within several rather well-defined areas. These clusters often contain establishments belonging to certain groups of industries or, sometimes, complementary to one another. For each site this index can be defined as:

$$A_{lt} = \sum_{j=1}^{n} w_j \frac{m_j}{d_{tj}^{\alpha}} \, ;$$

where

A_{lt} = accessibility index to manufacturing from site t,

m_j = manufacturing employment at site j,

d_{tj} = time-distance between manufacturing sites t and j,

w_j, α = parameters.

Accessibility to central urban functions refers to access to land use areas associated with:

(1) Government offices (federal, provincial and local),
(2) Private offices (commercial, financial, real estate, professional services, and so forth),
(3) Research facilities, universities, university hospitals, and institutes,
(4) Transportation terminals, in particular rail and bus stations and in-city air terminals,
(5) Hotels and motels, and
(6) Cultural facilities and amusements.

These functions are usually highly concentrated in one or several small zones. [15] The index can be defined as:

$$A_{2t} = \sum_{j=1}^{n} w_j \frac{I_j}{d_{tj}^{\beta}} \ ;$$

where

A_{2t} = accessibility index to central urban functions from site t,

I_j = measure of central urban functions at zone j defined as number of persons entering the zone per unit of time for purposes connected with the six functions listed above,

d_{tj} = time-distance between t and j,

w_j, β = parameters.

Accessibility to residential areas can be defined as:

$$A_{3t} = \sum_{j=1}^{n} w_j \frac{R_j}{d_{tj}^{\gamma}} \ ;$$

where

A_{3t} = accessibility index to residential areas from site t,

R_j = number of inhabitants in sub-area j,

d_{tj} = time-distance between site t and centroid of sub-area j,

w_j, γ = parameters.

Other variables that have to be considered refer to characteristics of the site itself, such as value of existing structures per square foot of area (F_1), zoning (F_2), and percentage of area without slope (F_3). Finally, one would have to divide all sites into those having or lacking the following facilities: sewerage, waterfront, and easy access to railroads (for purposes of constructing sidings) or highways.

The next stage consists of an analysis of existing plants and yields the value per square foot placed by specific industries on sites possessing certain characteristics. This is being done with the help of regression analysis of the following form:

$$_k V_t = {}_k a + {}_k b_1 A_{1t} + {}_k b_2 A_{2t} + {}_k b_3 A_{3t} + {}_k c_1 F_{1t} + {}_k c_2 F_{2t} + {}_k c_3 F_{3t} + R;$$

where

$_k V_t$ = value per square foot of land used by plant t of industry k,

$_k a$ = regression constant,

R = residual,

$_k b_1$, $_k b_2$, $_k b_3$, $_k c_1$, $_k c_2$, $_k c_3$ = regression coefficients; each of these indicates the contribution of a characteristic to the value put on the land by a particular industry.

There will be k such regression equations, one for each industry.

Next, sites (preferably contiguous) are aggregated into sub-areas. The criterion for aggregation is similarity of characteristics, so that within any sub-area i the variance of the values A_1, A_2, A_3, F_1, F_2, and F_3 around their mean values should be small.

Once a sub-area is characterized by some specific values of A_1, A_2, A_3, F_1, F_2, and F_3, estimates of land values in this area can be obtained for each of the k industries via regression equations of the form given above. Where actual plants of industry k exist in a sub-area i, the average of the adjusted assessed value of land for these plants in this industry can be used, and in any case will not differ too much from the estimated $_k V_i$. Where no plants in an industry k exist in sub-area i, as is frequently the case, one has to rely exclusively on estimates derived via regression. In the following table the term $_k V_i$ represents value of land in sub-area i, for industry k, where at times it represents an average of adjusted

			Sub-Areas			Total area required by industry
			1	2	3	
i						
K						
I	1		$_1 V_{\text{--}1}$	$_1 V_{\text{--}2}$	$_1 V_{\text{--}3}$ $\cdots$	$_1 V_{\text{--}i}$
N						
D	2		$_2 V_{\text{--}1}$	$_2 V_{\text{--}2}$	$_2 V_{\text{--}3}$ $\cdots$	$_2 V_{\text{--}i}$
U						
S			.			
T						
R			.			
I						
E			.			
S	k		$_k V_{\text{--}1}$	$_k V_{\text{--}2}$	$_k V_{\text{--}3}$ $\cdots$	$_k V_{\text{--}i}$
Total area available by sub-area						

assessed value of land for existing plants, and at other times, the estimated value $_k V_i$.

Obviously each plot of land (or each area homogeneous with respect to its characteristics) has a different value for each industry. One could thus construct the accompanying table.

For a period of time, say θ years, it may be assumed that the values of A_1, $A_2, \ldots, F_3$ do not change. For that time period one may allocate land in several different ways. One way is to assume that the market mechanism operates with no friction so that conditions of pure competition may be said to be approximated. Under this assumption a simple allocation model designed to maximize the total value of land over all sub-areas may be employed. It resembles, in many ways, a transportation linear programming model.

With the help of this model one can thus obtain a probability distribution of industries by sub-areas for any anticipated land requirements for year θ. Assuming that the actual distribution will approximate this pattern, for the next period one will have to reckon with changed values of several of the variables, especially A_1, A_2, and A_3. Hence a new probability distribution by sub-areas will result, starting an iterative process.

One major shortcoming is the fact that spatial patterns display considerable stickiness due largely to high relocation costs, which often overshadow all other considerations. Another somewhat related difficulty is due to the fact that the observed pattern on which the probabilities are based is the result of long developments, during which the relative importance of locational factors might have undergone considerable change.

b. Housing submodel

The main hypotheses on which this submodel is based are:

(1) Households try to maximize their utility subject to a budget constraint. In terms of location, utility is mainly a function of the immediate physical and social neighborhood and of the disutility of travel to places of work, major retail and service areas (primarily shopping goods), and recreation. Operationally this hypothesis can also be expressed as minimization of cost of land subject to a minimum utility level depending upon the socioeconomic group to which the household belongs.

(2) There is no basic analytical difference between owner-occupied and rental housing.

(3) Supply and demand equations for housing are easily identifiable; hence, for purposes of quantifying the strength of locational preferences of various types of households, demand only needs to be considered.

In order to study locational preferences as revealed by demand, all housing has to be classified by the number of bedrooms (j = 1, 2, 3, 4, 5), into one-family units, duplex and row houses, walk-up apartments, and high-rise apartments (K = 1, 2, 3, 4), and according to locational characteristics.

One could divide present and potential users of housing into a number of meaningful cohorts with different housing preferences. All households could be divided into four groups: husband-wife households, other male head, other female head, one-person households (T = 1, 2, 3, 4).

The position of the household in the life cycle may influence its housing preferences. It could be measured by the age of head of household; for example, head under 44 years old, 45–64 years, over 65 (A = 1, 2, 3).

The presence or absence of children and their age may also be important. From this point of view, one could classify households into those without children, with children below school age, with children of school age, and with both younger and older children (F = 1, 2, 3, 4).

Occupation of the head of household may be another important variable. Three categories only are being used: white-collar workers, blue-collar workers, and self-employed workers (W = 1, 2, 3).

Next, income should be considered. For this purpose all households are divided into five income classes (Y = 1, 2, 3, 4, 5), with income ranges defined so as to follow the income group classification used in the Census. This kind of cross-classification can yield a great number of cohorts, but the results of some preliminary research indicate that not all these categories and subdivisions are meaningful.

Finally, the various types of housing are combined with the various house-

		Sub-Areas				Total area required by households
		1	2	3		
i						
k						
H	1	$V_{1\text{-}1}$	$V_{1\text{-}2}$	$V_{1\text{-}3}$	$\cdots$ $V_{1\text{-}i}$	
O						
U	2	$V_{2\text{-}1}$	$V_{2\text{-}2}$	$V_{2\text{-}3}$	$\cdots$ $V_{2\text{-}i}$	
S						
E		$\cdot$				
H						
O		$\cdot$				
L						
D		$\cdot$				
S	k	$V_{k\text{-}1}$	$V_{k\text{-}2}$	$V_{k\text{-}3}$	$\cdots$ $V_{k\text{-}i}$	
Total area available by sub-area						

hold categories in one matrix. The rows of the matrix correspond to the various housing types, the columns to the household categories.

The marginal row totals indicate the number of acres of land in each category, while the column totals show the resulting demand. In the cells of the matrix is recorded the value of each square foot of residential land having some specific characteristics for a particular type of household.

The values placed on various locations by households are derived by regressing prices paid per lot (net of structures) $(_k V_i)$ on three sets of variables:

(1) General factors, such as quantity available of type desired at that time (expressed by number of vacancies), and business climate,
(2) Characteristics of site and immediate neighborhood, such as cost of improvements, physical and social environment, or local school,
(3) Accessibility index to places of work, central urban functions, and recreation.

c. Optimizing model

The results obtained with the help of the manufacturing, housing, and retail[e] submodels, together with studies dealing with other land use categories, are combined in a programming model of the following form:

For each sub-area or census tract

Maximize $\quad z = p_1 E_1 + p_2 E_2 + \ldots + p_n E_n;$

subject to $\quad a_{11} E_1 + a_{12} E_2 + \ldots + a_{1n} E_n \leqslant L_1;$

$$a_{21} E_1 + a_{22} E_2 + \ldots + a_{2n} E_n \leqslant L_2;$$

.
.
.

$$a_{m1} E_1 + a_{m2} E_2 + \ldots + a_{mn} E_n \leqslant L_m;$$

and to

$$0 \leqslant E_1 \leqslant e_1;$$

---

[e] The retail submodel is exactly similar to the two discussed in detail above and is omitted here.

$$0 \leqslant E_2 \leqslant e_2;$$

$$0 \leqslant E_3 \leqslant e_3;$$

.
.
.

$$0 \leqslant \qquad \qquad E_n \leqslant e_n;$$

The dual takes the form

Minimize $\quad S = r_1 L_1 + r_2 L_2 + \ldots + r_m L_m;$

subject to $\quad a_{11} r_1 + a_{21} r_2 + \ldots + a_{m1} r_m \geqslant p_1;$

$$a_{12} r_1 + a_{22} r_2 + \ldots + a_{m2} r_m \geqslant p_2;$$

.
.
.

$$a_{1n} r_1 + a_{2n} r_2 + \ldots + a_{mn} r_m \geqslant p_n;$$

and to

$$r_1 \qquad \qquad \geqslant 0;$$

$$r_2 \qquad \qquad \geqslant 0;$$

.
.
.

$$r_m \geqslant 0;$$

In the usual matrix notation the problem may be stated as

Primal

Objective function $\quad Z = pE;$

Constraints $\qquad aE \leqslant L; \qquad 0 \leqslant E \leqslant e;$

Dual

Objective function $S = rL$;

Constraints $ar \geqslant p$; $r \geqslant 0$;

where

E_i = total quantity of housing units of a particular type,

p_i = price of a unit of housing of a particular type,

a_{ij} = area of land of a specific type required per unit of housing or unit of manufacturing output, storage, and so on,

L_n = total supply of land of type n,

e_i = total demand for this particular type of housing or activity. This constraint may in some cases prove redundant.

The primals of the linear programs yield an allocation of land in each sub-area to the various uses. The duals yield a distribution of average land rents achievable for each type of land in each sub-area, or the so-called shadow prices.

The peculiarity of mathematical programming models may result, however, in the models assigning a maximum of land in each sub-area up to the e_n constraint to the most intensive use, namely to high-rise apartments. In order to overcome this difficulty two solutions are explored. The first, and probably the more efficient, amounts to a decomposition analysis. A very simple computer program is being developed that selects from all sub-areas those acreages assigned to the most intensive use. Next, out of these, those yielding the highest rent (r) are selected, noted, and deducted from the total land supply (L_n). The set can then be rerun and the process repeated for the next most intensive land use activity. An alternative approach consists in running all the linear programs simultaneously as an interregional program.

By running the model over yearly time intervals, both the directions of land absorption and the emerging spatial structure can be studied. Backward projections and sensitivity tests will be applied in order to assess the reliability of the estimates.

7 Polarization Processes

The spatial concentration of investments is a matter of deep concern both from the point of view of its growth generating effects and as an expression of the extent of organization of the geographic environment.

Unfortunately, the evidence which might help to assess the extent and growth potential of existing agglomerations in Nova Scotia is scant. The wealth

Table 6–6
Regional Wealth by Location, 1961 (in millions of dollars)

Location	Natural Resources[a]	Forest Reserves	Farm-Land and Capital	Other Land and Capital	Human Resources	Total
Halifax County	90.7	18.6	8.1	1,140.7	6,954.3	8,212.4
Cape Breton County	26.9	9.6	5.1	338.0	3,032.4	3,412.0
Rest of Nova Scotia	781.5	146.0	130.4	1,102.0	6,769.1	8,929.0
Total	899.1	174.2	143.6	2,580.7	16,755.8	20,553.4

[a]Except forest reserves and land.

accounts do not provide any conclusive evidence on this point; because of severe limitations imposed by the inadequate data basis, the tentative estimates single out only Halifax County, Cape Breton County, and Rest of Nova Scotia. The potential growth points of Halifax-Dartmouth and Sydney are thus embedded in the rest of their respective counties, which (especially in the case of Halifax) comprise substantial portions of agricultural countryside where the economic dominance of the center is at best uncertain. The results are presented in Table 6–6.

With about fifty percent of the population outside the two urban centers, it is hardly surprising that the share of the Rest of Nova Scotia was overwhelming in natural resources, forest reserves, and farmland and capital and substantial even in human resources and other land and capital. The very small share of both Halifax County and Cape Breton County in farmland and capital is more unexpected, as both comprise substantial agricultural areas.

While the extent of concentration in absolute terms is the prime interest for assessing potential growth processes, interesting conclusions can be drawn from an analysis of distribution of wealth on a per capita basis. Table 6–7 illustrates the situation.

In terms of non-farm land and capital the share of Halifax was fourteen percent higher than its share of total population, which amounted to 30.6 percent. Similarly, Halifax County, with 41.5 percent, ranked highest in the value of its human resources, while Cape Breton County contained only 18.1 percent, or scarcely more than its share of total population. The estimates of accumulated wealth reflect the fact that relative to Nova Scotia, Halifax is a growing region, while Cape Breton is declining rather rapidly, but even in the case of Halifax the absolute magnitude of concentrated resources seems far from sufficient to engender self-sustaining growth. In terms of man-made capital the urban agglomeration of Halifax-Dartmouth seems to have accumulated less than one billion

Table 6-7
Regional Wealth Per Capita, 1961 (in dollars)

Location	Natural Resources[a]	Forest Reserves	Farm Land and Capital	Other Land and Capital	Human Resources	Total
Halifax County	401.8	82.4	35.9	5,053.5	30,809.0	36,382.6
Cape Breton County	204.6	73.0	38.8	2,570.2	23,058.8	25,945.4
Rest of Nova Scotia	2,057.8	384.4	343.4	2,901.7	17,823.9	23,511.2
Nova Scotia	1,219.9	236.4	194.8	3,501.6	22,735.1	27,887.9

[a]Except forest reserves and land.

dollars of immobile resources – a volume probably far short of a critical mass, despite the somewhat more favorable picture conveyed by the per capita figures.[f] By contrast the decline in Cape Breton finds its expression in extremely low per capita values of land and man-made capital combined with per capita value for human resources near the Nova Scotia average. This seems to suggest that adjustment to change was more rapid in capital and land markets than in labor markets and that psychic and other reasons retarded adjustment to decline.

Interpretation of the results of the study of regional wealth cannot be pushed too far both because of the limited scope and uncertain reliability of the estimates, and because of lack of a firm theoretical framework for incorporating stock phenomena into regional economic studies. The present inquiry, without a claim to a major contribution, underscores existing limitations in this important area of major divergence between practical, largely intuitive, decision processes and formal approaches of regional scientists.

The emerging picture of Nova Scotia is one of severe underinvestment, particularly in the manufacturing sectors. Its endowment in consumer capital and the level of investments in services is incomparably higher, raising the question of possible hypertrophy in the traditional, labor intensive types. This finding adds a new dimension to the important policy issue of sectors to be promoted and of allocation of resources to manufacturing as opposed to infrastructure. At the very least, wealth accounts indicate the magnitude of investments involved.

Findings of an entirely different character are related to the spatial distribution of existing facilities. The lack of agglomerations capable of acting as growth poles and the dispersion of assets, especially housing, in areas without growth prospects or potential are manifestations of locational obsolescence hardly

---

[f]Parenthetically, it should be noted that new investments, by bidding up land values and wages, might improve the indexes in the future.

revealed by an examination of flow phenomena. The magnitude of the problem involved in any substantial relocations, aside from the more obvious socio-political consequences, is underscored by the value of resources that would have to be abandoned. The issue is of immediate practical relevance because in view of the poor endowment of the province in agricultural and mineral resources relative to the rest of Canada, the only way toward economic development appears to be through the rise of a strong urban-industrial agglomeration in one of the two existing centers. Halifax with its greater concentration of assets is probably in a better position for generating important external economies, at any rate in the near future.

Methodologically, the important issue is integration of results of wealth accounting into a rigorous analytic framework. A major obstacle is due to an almost total lack of comparative data since nothing even approaching the pioneering effort made in Nova Scotia has been achieved in other regions and few estimates exist as time series of any length. Nonetheless, in the econometric model of Nova Scotia, presented in the following chapter, the confrontation of hypotheses relating regional growth to the presence of both man-made and natural resources was accomplished with the help of variables derived from wealth accounts.

7

A Simple Econometric Formulation

1 Simultaneous Analysis

An analysis in depth of the natural, human, and man-made resources of the province and of the working of its economy as revealed by a set of social accounts and by an input-output study still fails to uncover the interrelations existing between the various phenomena examined. The multipliers derived by a judicious analysis of income and product accounts leave unexplored the possible repercussions that might result from the introduction of new industries with the attendant reduction in leakages; a study of input-output relations, while capable of discovering clusters of industries forming potential nuclei of future growth poles and industrial complexes, neglects such effects as may result from increased urbanization. Some of these factors can be brought to the fore through the formulation of a general econometric model bringing together in one set of equations the various elements so far examined. The process of calibrating such a model and confronting it with data leads, moreover, to new, sometimes previously unsuspected, insights into existing relations.

Like any other model, an econometric formulation is essentially a description of the real world devoid of those elements that are considered irrelevant or unimportant. Thus defined, a model does not differ significantly from a theory, except that in a theory the focus is on the derivation of observable propositions capable of being tested from parsimonious assumptions, while a model is bound by data availability and often has to be specific where a theory may be more vague.

Regional analysis can be conceived as the study of the relationships among sets of observable and essentially measurable variables such as prices, outputs, savings, or employment. These relationships, derived from the complex behavior and interactions of a multitude of households, firms, and government units producing and exchanging numerous commodities and services, can be represented by a system of mathematical equations. Unfortunately a theoretically complete representation is not possible, as millions of equations would be needed to describe a single household or firm in all its actions and motivations. Moreover, these equations would be as complex as human behavior and involve the elaborate interactions of numberless variables, many of which might be unmeasurable.

Neither the time nor the resources to deal with such a vast system of equations are available; to proceed at all, it is necessary to simplify and condense.

279

Millions of individual households become a single "household sector," millions of products become a single item of expenditure (for example, "durable goods"), and complex mathematical relationships among thousands of variables become simple linear approximations involving two or three aggregates. An econometric model of the economy is obtained by confronting these highly simplified equations with data arising from the historical operation of the economic system and deriving, by appropriate statistical techniques, numerical estimates for their parameters.

The minimum number of equations necessary for an adequate representation of the economic system depends on a number of considerations, but clearly the fewer the equations, the greater must be the level of aggregation and the less accurate and useful the results. On the other hand, the larger the number of equations and the greater the detail shown in the variables, the more complicated it is to derive the individual equations and to see the implications of the model, even though with modern computing facilities the mere size of the model is no longer a serious barrier for manipulating the resulting system.

There are several ways of classifying models and variables. The most common classification of variables is the dichotomy into jointly determined or endogenous variables and predetermined variables. However, a slightly more elaborate system may yield useful insights into the structure of a model. [1] According to this system the following categories can be identified:

(1) *Target Variables* are those in whose behavior we are interested (for example, per capita income, outmigration, etc.). As a rule, each of these variables has some welfare significance.

(2) *Intermediate Variables* are involved in the description and operation of the model but are of no immediate interest by themselves (for example, total population of Nova Scotia, total wage income, personal net savings, etc.).

(3) *Instrument Variables* can be influenced by policy makers (for example, direct investments by government, defense spending in Nova Scotia, etc.). Which variables are to be considered as policy instruments depends upon who is going to use the model. For purposes of the model described here, instrument variables have been defined as either those controlled directly by the Government of Nova Scotia or those controlled by the Government of Canada, but subject to the influence of the Government of Nova Scotia.

(4) *Data Variables* are determined outside the model (for example, average yearly wage income per worker in Canada, rate of interest on loans, Canadian Gross National Product, etc.). Some of the data variables are used with various time lags.

(5) *Lagged Endogenous Variables*   Some of the intermediate and target variables also enter the model with time lags and hence have to be considered as endogenous. Instrument variables, both unlagged and lagged data variables, and lagged endogenous variables are preated as predetermined variables. In addition,

the model contains eight predetermined parameters. Thus one hundred four variables and eight predetermined parameters have been identified.[a]

2 Structure of Model

Every variable involved in a model can be treated as its input or as its output. Depending upon which variables are treated as inputs and which as outputs, several types of models can be distinguished:

(1) *Analytical or Descriptive Models*   Their purpose is to reduce the complexity of the regional economy by presenting the relevant features in a more aggregate way. They may also provide a shortcut to field work by generating reliable values for variables which are hard to measure. Such models, however, do not provide any information about the future and do not indicate how to choose among alternatives.

(2) *Forecasting Models*   In contrast with analytical models, the casual relationships existing in the regional economy have to be spelled out. In a forecasting model, the data and instrument variables are used as inputs into the model while the intermediate and target variables are the output, as shown in Figure 7-1.

They are an important aid in planning. In order to use this type of model the planner has to specify the most likely level of all instrument variables involved on the basis of additional partial studies or by assuming future behavior. The important and widespread use in regional planning of such models with varying degrees of sophistication stems from the fact that population, employment, and land-use forecasts play a key role and provide the meeting point between socioeconomic and purely physical regional planning. The work of physical planners in the initial stages is based on these forecasts, and their reaction to the requirements of socioeconomic planning leads in turn to alternative projections by socioeconomic planners.

(3) *Conditional Models*   These are a variation of forecasting models. They are used in those cases in which no definite future values can be assigned to some of the input variables.[b]

---

[a]Strictly speaking the number of variables and of equations is slightly greater because some variables and some equations are given in matrix notation. Each variable in vector notation actually denotes several variables and similarly equations in matrix notation comprise several equations.

[b]For example the future growth of a small town may depend upon the building of a new factory. Assuming that this event cannot be foreseen with certainty several alternative growth forecasts may be developed, either by making conditional estimates or by assigning probabilities to various outcomes.

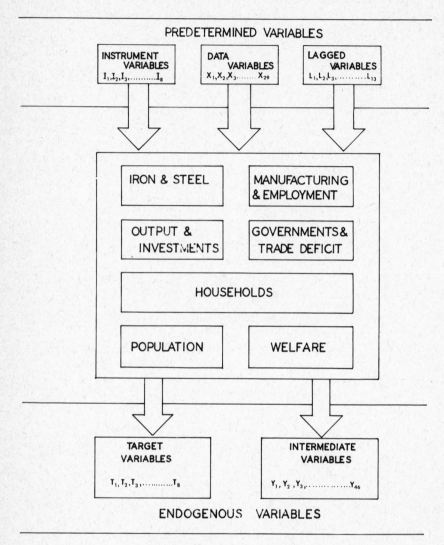

Figure 7-1. Regional Model.

(4) *Planning Models*   These are in a sense the inverse of forecasting models. The data and target variables become inputs into the model while the instrument variables are the outputs. The difference between forecasting and planning models can be illustrated by examining the type of problems to which they address themselves or the questions they try to answer.

A forecasting model may, for example, answer the question: "What will be the rate of growth of GRP given that the government intends to invest one billion dollars in the development of the regional economy, over the next five years?" A planning model, on the other hand, will attack the problem in the following way: "How much has the government to invest in the development of the regional economy over the next ten years in order to achieve a five percent yearly growth rate of GRP?" The rate of increase of GRP (target variable) is here stipulated on the basis of political considerations.

Planning models help to explore efficiently a very wide range of alternatives in order to select the one that maximizes the objective function while staying within the constraints of the real world. They are especially suitable for regional studies.

The difference between forecasting and planning models is mainly in the way in which they are operated. In practical application they do not differ much.

The procedure for changing a model from a forecasting to a planning device involves treating the target variables as inputs and the instrument variables as outputs. This can easily be achieved in linear models by inverting the matrix of endogenous variables. [2]

The model of Nova Scotia is not only nonlinear but it comprises the population and migrations submodel which is composed of a system of matrices. [3] Hence, in order to transform it from a forecasting to a planning model an iterative process would have to be programmed. For present purposes, the treatment of instrument variables as inputs will greatly enhance the practical applications of the model to regional planning.

The full system of equations and variables involved is as follows:

Structural Equations

$$X_{IS(t)} = 7.827 + .6497K_{IS(t)}; \qquad\qquad R^2 = .7922$$
$$\phantom{X_{IS(t)} =} (4.7040)\ \ (6.5531) \qquad\qquad\qquad d = 1.6505 \qquad (1)$$

$$Q_{IS(t)} = 2.49X_{IS(t)}; \qquad\qquad\qquad\qquad R^2 = .9176$$
$$\phantom{Q_{IS(t)} =} (12.5) \qquad\qquad\qquad\qquad\qquad\qquad\qquad\qquad (2)$$

$$e_{IS(t)} = .9848Q_{IS(t)}; \qquad\qquad\qquad\quad R^2 = .9994$$
$$\phantom{e_{IS(t)} =} (752.2053) \qquad\qquad\qquad\qquad\quad d = 1.8549 \qquad (3)$$

$$E_{1(t)} = 2.643 + 1.1029FZ_{(t)}; \qquad\qquad R^2 = .1338$$
$$\phantom{E_{1(t)} = }(.1790) \quad (1.9040) \qquad\qquad\qquad d = .2597 \qquad (4)$$

$$E_{4(t)} = -80.696 + .4708P_{u(t)}; \qquad\qquad R^2 = .8333$$
$$\phantom{E_{4(t)} = }(-3.6023) \quad (8.4261) \qquad\qquad\qquad d = .3193 \qquad (5)$$

$$E_{5(t)} = 24.061 + .6741DF_{s(t)} - 2.0454t; \qquad R^2 = .8207$$
$$\phantom{E_{5(t)} = }(11.9162) \quad (7.7784) \qquad (-7.7027) \qquad d = 1.7141 \qquad (6)$$

$$I_{m(t)} = 1.1488\,[GI_G + GS_m]_{(t-4)} + .0186Z_{1(t-4)}; \quad R^2 = .6404$$
$$\phantom{I_{m(t)} = }(2.6590) \qquad\qquad\qquad (1.1821) \qquad\quad d = 1.7254 \qquad (7)$$

$$Z_1 = .5483U_Y + .5767U_{E3} + .6056H_H$$

$$e_{m(t)} = 26.185 + 1.2436GNP_{(t)} + .6672(\bar{p}_m^C - \bar{p}_m^{NS})_{(t)};$$
$$\phantom{e_{m(t)} = }(2.9136) \quad (3.1628) \qquad\quad (2.3635)$$

$$R^2 = .3932$$
$$d = 1.9141 \qquad (8)$$

$$X_{m(t)} = -239.599 + 1.2005K_{m(t)}; \qquad\qquad R^2 = .9727$$
$$\phantom{X_{m(t)} = }(-10.7214)(19.8214) \qquad\qquad\qquad d = 1.5105 \qquad (9)$$

$$E_{3(t)} = .0304X_{m(t)} + .3795SZ_{(t)}; \qquad\qquad R^2 = .6261$$
$$\phantom{E_{3(t)} = }(2.8514) \qquad (17.7193) \qquad\qquad\qquad d = 1.3214 \qquad (10)$$

$$X_{CS(t)} = -629.923 + 9.2050E_{4(t)}; \qquad\qquad R^2 = .9448$$
$$\phantom{X_{CS(t)} = }(-8.0764) \quad (12.2848) \qquad\qquad\qquad d = 1.9770$$
$$\rho = .1221 \qquad (11)$$

$$I_{CS(t)} = .1079X_{CS(t)} + 6.2032i_{(t)}; \qquad\qquad R^2 = .8024$$
$$\phantom{I_{CS(t)} = }(2.7744) \qquad (2.4635) \qquad\qquad\qquad d = 1.6936 \qquad (12)$$

$$I_{H(t)} = 14.714 + .1450\Delta GRP + 1.6289GS_{H(t)}; \quad R^2 = .6099$$
$$\phantom{I_{H(t)} = }(2.5542) \quad (1.8159) \qquad (4.2178) \qquad\quad d = 1.7120 \qquad (13)$$

$$\log W_{(t)} = -2.1494 + .7742\log GRP_{(t)} + .6382\log \bar{p}_{(t)}^{NS};$$
$$\phantom{\log W_{(t)} = }(-1.8830) \quad (8.4429) \qquad\qquad (1.8587)$$

$$R^2 = .9916$$
$$d = 1.0947$$
$$\rho = .4583 \qquad (14)$$

$$F_{a(t)} = -22.245 + .0428A_{L(t)} + .5177FZ_{(t)}; \quad R^2 = .9430$$
$$\phantom{F_{a(t)} = }(-9.1337) \quad (8.2933) \qquad (4.5502) \qquad d = 2.0261 \qquad (15)$$

$$F_{m(t)} = 1.869 + .0156X_{m(t)}; \qquad R^2 = .4022 \qquad (16)$$
$$(3.0689)$$

$$F_{s(t)} = .0835X_{CS(t)} + .3509\bar{p}_{(t)}^{NS};$$
$$(3.7470) \qquad (5.4255)$$
$$R^2 = .9285$$
$$d = 1.7623$$
$$\rho = .5307 \qquad (17)$$

$$i_{p(t)} = -66.060 + 1.5133NH_{(t)}; \qquad R^2 = .9801$$
$$(27.9972) \qquad\qquad\qquad (18)$$

$$SIP_{(t)} = -4.022 + .0525W_{(t)}; \qquad R^2 = .9125$$
$$(-1.9578) \quad (12.5468) \qquad\qquad d = 1.3600 \qquad (19)$$

$$T_{(t)} = -31.933 + .0494Y_{p(t)} + 293.944t_{r(t)}; \qquad R^2 = .9669$$
$$(-3.5966) \quad (6.7526) \qquad (1.7762) \qquad d = 1.8360 \qquad (20)$$

$$C_{1(t)} = -225.407 + 2.1035H_{(t-1)} + .4197Y_{DP}; \qquad R^2 = .9966$$
$$(-2.3577) \quad (2.6386) \qquad (8.3267) \qquad d = 2.0583 \qquad (21)$$

$$C_{4(t)} = -45.236 + .1682Y_{DP(t)} + .2461P_u; \qquad R^2 = .9970$$
$$(17.4463) \qquad (3.5707) \qquad\qquad (22)$$

$$C_{5(t)} = -66.924 + .7370NH_{(t)} + .1291Y_{DP}; \qquad R^2 = .9982$$
$$(-7.5404) \quad (2.4088) \qquad (5.3614) \qquad d = 2.1316 \qquad (23)$$

$$T_{c(t)} = 12.624 + .0126GRP_{(t)}; \qquad R^2 = .5022$$
$$(4.6854) \quad (4.0166) \qquad\qquad d = 1.4026 \qquad (24)$$

$$T_{IN(t)} = -35.363 + .2469Y_{E(t)}; \qquad R^2 = .9837$$
$$(-5.5414) \quad (29.0736) \qquad\qquad d = 2.1291 \qquad (25)$$

$$e_{L(t)} = 25.989 + .2184GNP_{(t)}; \qquad R^2 = .4853$$
$$(13.7460) \quad (3.8913) \qquad\qquad d = .9704 \qquad (26)$$

$$\log e_{A(t)} = 1.5110 \log F_{B(t)} + .3954 \log \sum_{t=1}^{-4} GS_{A(t)}; \quad R^2 = .8114$$
$$(22.5825) \qquad\qquad (4.5464) \qquad\qquad d = 1.4292 \qquad (27)$$

$$m_{(t)} = .3969Y_{E(t)} + .2860[X_{L(t)} + X_{IS(t)} + X_{m(t)}]$$
$$(12.0557) \qquad (4.8400)$$
$$+ .3377I_{(t)} + .9173DS_{s(t)}; \qquad R^2 = .9977$$
$$(2.8554) \quad (4.7760) \qquad\qquad d = 2.8846 \qquad (28)$$

$$M_{(t)} = -3.007 + .3718D^L_{(t-1)}; \qquad\qquad R^2 = .3687$$
$$(2.5349) \tag{29}$$

$$q_{e(t)} = 24.920 + .2603GI_{ED(t)}; \qquad R^2 = .6208$$
$$(50.4639)(4.1680) \qquad\qquad d = 2.3583 \tag{30}$$

$$q_{v(t)} = 220.858 + 17.8200GI_{V(t)}; \qquad R^2 = .3947$$
$$(14.2888) \quad (3.5096) \qquad\qquad d = .4443$$
$$\rho = -.0925 \tag{31}$$

Definitional Equations

$$K_{IS(t)} = K_{IS(t-1)} + I_{IS(t)} \tag{1}$$

$$K_{m(t)} = K_{m(t-1)} + I_{m(t)} \tag{2}$$

$$X_{G(t)} = \bar{w}^{NS}_{G(t)} E_{5(t)} \tag{3}$$

$$GRP_{(t)} = X_{A(t)} + X_{L(t)} + X_{IS(t)} + X_{m(t)} + X_{CS(t)} + X_{G(t)} \tag{4}$$

$$I_{(t)} = I_{L(t)} + I_{IS(t)} + I_{m(t)} + I_{CS(t)} + I_{H(t)} \tag{5}$$

$$MPA_{(t)} = .5 \, DF_{s(t)} \tag{6}$$

$$Y_{p(t)} = W_{(t)} + F_{a(t)} + F_{m(t)} + F_{s(t)} + i_{p(t)} + F^G_{(t)} + F^{nr}_{(t)}$$
$$- SIP_{(t)} + MPA_{(t)} \tag{7}$$

$$tr_{(t)} = \frac{T^c_{(t)}}{Y^c_{p(t)}} \tag{8}$$

$$Y_{DP(t)} = Y_{p(t)} - (T_{(t)} + T_{s(t)}) \tag{9}$$

$$Y_{E(t)} = C_{1(t)} + C_{4(t)} + C_{5(t)} + S_{(t)} \tag{10}$$

$$\bar{n} = \Gamma \bar{P}_{(t-1)} \tag{11}$$

$$L = \bar{R}' \bar{n}_{(t)} \tag{12}$$

$$D^L_{(t)} = E_{(t)} - (1-h) L_{(t)} \tag{13}$$

$$\bar{\mu}_{(t)} \quad = \quad \bar{\pi}\mu_{(t)} \tag{14}$$

$$P_{(t)} \quad = \quad \bar{\delta}' \bar{P}_{(t)} \tag{15}$$

$$q_{H(t)} \quad = \quad \frac{NH_{(t)}}{P_{(t)}} \tag{16}$$

$$\bar{y}_{DP(t)} \quad = \quad \frac{Y_{DP(t)}}{P_{(t)}} \tag{17}$$

$$\bar{y}_{A(t)} \quad = \quad \frac{\eta W_{(t)} + F_{a(t)} + \alpha F_{(t)}^{G} + \beta F_{(t)}^{nr}}{(P - P_u)_{(t)}} \tag{18}$$

Balance Equations

$$E_{(t)} \quad = \quad E_{1(t)} + E_{2(t)} + E_{3(t)} + E_{4(t)} + E_{5(t)} + E_{6(t)} \tag{1}$$

$$Y_{DP(t)} = Y_{E(t)} \tag{2}$$

$$T_{(t)} + T_{c(t)} + T_{s(t)} + T_{IN(t)} + SIP_{(t)} + GD_{(t)}$$

$$= DF_{s(t)} + [GI_{G(t)} + GI_{ED(t)} + GI_{V(t)} + GS_{A(t)} + GS_{L(t)}$$

$$+ GS_{m(t)} + GS_{H(t)}] + GS_{c(t)} + F_{(t)}^{G} \tag{3}$$

$$W_{(t)} + F_{a(t)} + F_{m(t)} + F_{s(t)} + i_{p(t)} + C_{rp(t)} + D_{p(t)} + T_{IN(t)} + MPA_{(t)} + REA_{(t)}$$

$$= C_{1(t)} + C_{4(t)} + C_{5(t)} + [DF_{s(t)} + (GI_{G(t)} + GI_{ED(t)} + GI_{V(t)}$$

$$+ GS_{A(t)} + GS_{L(t)} + GS_{m(t)} + GS_{H(t)} + GS_{c(t)} + F_{(t)}^{G}] + [I_{L(t)}$$

$$+ I_{IS(t)} + I_{m(t)} + I_{CS(t)} + I_{H(t)}] + [e_{A(t)} + e_{L(t)} + e_{IS(t)}$$

$$+ e_{m(t)} + e_{s(t)}] - m_{(t)} + F_{(t)}^{nr} - BRW_{(t)} - GD \tag{4}$$

$$\bar{P}_{(t)} \quad = \quad \bar{n}_{(t)} + \bar{\mu}_{(t-1)} \tag{5}$$

Target Variables [4]

$$E \quad = \quad \text{total employment (thousands)} \tag{1}$$

| GRP | = Gross Regional Product | (2) |

μ_t = balance of migrations during (t) (thousands) (3)

q_e = index of educational standards (4)

q_v = index of health standards (5)

q_H = index of housing standards (6)

$\bar{y}_{DP}$ = per capita disposable income (dollars) (7)

$\bar{y}_A$ = per capita disposable income in agriculture (dollars) (8)

Intermediate Variables

K_{IS} = total capital invested in iron and steel industry (millions of dollars) (1)

X_{IS} = value added in iron and steel industry (millions of dollars) (2)

Q_{IS} = value of shipments in iron and steel industry (millions of dollars) (3)

e_{IS} = exports of iron and steel industry (millions of dollars) (4)

E_1 = employment in agriculture, forestry, and fisheries (thousands) (5)

E_4 = employment in commercial services (thousands) (6)

E_5 = government employment (including military) (thousands) (7)

I_m = investments in manufacturing (millions of dollars) (8)

K_m = total capital invested in manufacturing (millions of dollars) (9)

e_m = exports of manufactured products (millions of dollars) (10)

X_m = value added by manufacturing (millions of dollars) (11)

E_3 = employment in manufacturing (thousands) (12)

X_{CS} = value added in commercial services (millions of dollars) (13)

X_G = value added in government services (millions of dollars) (14)

I_{CS} = investments in commercial services (millions of dollars) (15)

I_H = investments in housing (millions of dollars) (16)

I = total investments (millions of dollars) (17)

W = total wage income (millions of dollars) (18)

F_a = net income of farm operators (millions of dollars) (19)

F_m = net income of unincorporated manufacturing (millions of dollars) (20)

F_s = net income of unincorporated service enterprises (millions of dollars) (21)

i_p = interest, dividends, and rental income of persons (millions of dollars) (22)

SIP = employers' and employees' contributions to social insurance (millions of dollars) (23)

MPA = payments to military personnel resident in Nova Scotia (millions of dollars) (24)

Y_p = total personal income (millions of dollars) (25)

t_r = average rate of direct personal taxes (26)

T = total personal income taxes (millions of dollars) (27)

Y_{DP} = total personal disposable income (millions of dollars) (28)

Y_E = total personal expenditures (millions of dollars) (29)

C_1 = consumption of goods by households (millions of dollars) (30)

C_4 = consumption of services and travel expenditures by households (millions of dollars) (31)

C_5 = rents and interest payments by households (millions of dollars) (32)

S = personal net savings (millions of dollars) (33)

T_c = corporate profit taxes (millions of dollars) (34)

T_{IN} = total indirect taxes (millions of dollars) (35)

GS_c = current government expenditures (millions of dollars) (36)

e_L = exports of mining products (millions of dollars) (37)

e_A = exports of agricultural, forestry and fishing products (millions of dollars) (38)

m = total imports (millions of dollars) (39)

BRW = surplus or deficit on current account with the rest of the world (millions of dollars) (40)

$\bar{n}$ = column vector, the elements of which are various age-sex population cohorts (excluding migrations) (thousands) (41)

L = potential labor force (thousands) (42)

D^L = unsatisfied demand for labor (or labor surplus) (thousands) (43)

$\bar{\mu}$ = column vector, the elements of which are net migrations in each age-sex cohort (thousands) (44)

$\bar{P}$ = column vector, the elements of which are various age-sex population cohorts (thousands) (45)

P = total population (thousands) (46)

Instrument Variables

DF_s = payments to military personnel (millions of dollars) (1)

GS_H = government subsidies and investments in housing and commercial services (millions of dollars) (2)

GI_G = direct general government investments (transportation, communication, power and technical facilities, etc.) (millions of dollars)   (3)

GI_{ED} = direct government investments in education and training (millions of dollars)   (4)

GI_V = direct government investments in health, welfare, and administration (millions of dollars)   (5)

GS_A = government subsidies and investments in agriculture, forestry, and fisheries (millions of dollars)   (6)

GS_m = government subsidies and investments in manufacturing (millions of dollars)   (7)

GD = aggregate surplus or deficit of all governments relating to Nova Scotia income and product transactions (millions of dollars)   (8)

Data Variables

I_{IS} = investments in iron and steel (millions of dollars)   (1)

FZ = number of commercial farms as a proportion of all farms   (2)

P_u = total urban population (thousands)   (3)

t = time   (4)

GNP = Canadian Gross National Product (billions of dollars)   (5)

$\bar{p}_m^C$ = price index of manufactured goods in Canada (1949 = 100)   (6)

$\bar{p}_m^{NS}$ = price index of manufactured goods in Nova Scotia (1949 = 100)   (7)

SZ = index of average size of plant   (8)

E_2 = employment in mining (thousands)   (9)

E_6 = employment in iron and steel (thousands)   (10)

$\bar{w}_G^{NS}$ = average yearly wage-income of government employees (dollars)   (11)

X_A = value added in agriculture, forestry, and fisheries (millions of dollars)   (12)

X_L = value added by mining (millions of dollars)   (13)

i = rate of interest on loans   (14)

I_L = investments in mining (millions of dollars)   (15)

$\bar{p}^{NS}$ = consumer price index for Nova Scotia (1949 = 100)   (16)

A_L = amount of cultivated land (thousands of acres)   (17)

NH = number of housing units constructed after 1920   (18)

F^G = federal and provincial government transfer payments to households (millions of dollars)   (19)

F^{nr} = transfer payments from nonresidents to households (millions of dollars)   (20)

T^C = total direct personal taxes in Canada (billions of dollars)   (21)

Y_p^C = total personal income in Canada (billions of dollars)   (22)

T_s = estate and miscellaneous personal taxes (millions of dollars)   (23)

GS_L = government subsidies and investments in mining (millions of dollars)   (24)

F_B = number of fishing boats   (25)

C_{rp} = retained corporate earnings (millions of dollars)   (26)

D_p = capital consumption allowances (millions of dollars)   (27)

REA = unpaid corporate profits other than C_{rp}, Federal government investment income, subsidies not accounted for elsewhere, and residual statistical discrepancy (millions of dollars)   (28)

e_s = exports of services (millions of dollars)   (29)

$GI_{G(t-4)}$ = direct government investments in general facilities with a lag of four years (millions of dollars)   (30)

$GS_{m(t-4)}$ = government subsidies and investments in manufacturing with a lag of four years (millions of dollars)   (31)

$U_{E3(t-4)}$ = index of relative accessibility with respect to manufacturing with a lag of four years   (32)

This index gives the relative location of industrial centers in relation to Nova Scotia as a function of employment and distance:

$$U_{E3} = \frac{\displaystyle\sum_{i=1}^{34} E_{3 \cdot i} D_{h \cdot i}}{\displaystyle\sum_{i=1}^{34} E_{3 \cdot i}} \; ;$$

where

$E_{3 \cdot i}$ = manufacturing employment in city i, and

$D_{h \cdot i}$ = distance between Halifax and city i (rail and road average)

$U_{Y(t-4)}$ = index of relative accessibility with respect to total personal income with a lag of four years   (33)

This index gives the relative accessibility of Nova Scotia to markets in Canada as a function of income and distance:

$$U_Y = \frac{\displaystyle\sum_{i=1}^{34} Y_i D_{h \cdot i}}{\displaystyle\sum_{i=1}^{34} Y_i} \; ;$$

where

Y_i = total personal income of urban center i, and

$D_{h \cdot i}$ = distance between Halifax and city i (rail and road average)

$H_{H(t-4)}$ = tonnage handled in Halifax harbor with a lag of four years (thousands)   (34)

$H_{(t-1)}$ = number of households in the previous period (thousands)   (35)

$\displaystyle\sum_{t=1}^{-4} GS_{A(t)}$ = government subsidies and investments in agriculture, forestry, and fisheries, cumulated over four years (millions of dollars)   (36)

Lagged Endogenous Variables

$K_{IS(t-1)}$ = total capital invested in iron and steel in the previous period (millions of dollars)   (1)

$K_{m(t-1)}$ = total capital invested in manufacturing in the previous period (millions of dollars)   (2)

$GRP_{(t-1)}$ = Gross Regional Product in the previous period (millions of dollars)   (3)

$P_{(t-1)}$ = column vector whole elements are population in the previous period in different age-sex cohorts (thousands)   (4)

$D_{(t-1)}^{L}$ = unsatisfied demand for labor or real unemployment in the previous period   (5)

$M_{(t-1)}$ = column vector whose elements give net migrations in each age-sex cohort in the previous period (thousands)   (6)

Predetermined Parameters

Γ = square matrix of order equal to the number of age-sex cohorts. The elements of the matrix are probabilities of survival of individuals from different age-sex cohorts, and age specific birthrates. The form of the matrix is

$$
\begin{bmatrix}
0 & 0 & . & . & . & 0 & b_1^M & 0 & b_2^M & . & . & 0 \\
0 & 0 & & & & & b_1^F & 0 & b_2^F & & & \\
d_1^M & 0 & 0 & . & . & . & . & . & . & . & . & 0 \\
0 & d_1^F & 0 & 0 & . & . & . & . & . & . & . & 0 \\
0 & 0 & d_2^M & 0 & 0 & & & & & & & \\
0 & 0 & 0 & d_2^F & 0 & 0 & . & . & . & . & . & 0 \\
. & . & . & . & . & . & . & . & . & . & . & . \\
. & . & . & . & . & . & . & . & . & . & . & . \\
. & . & . & . & . & . & . & . & . & . & . & . \\
0 & . & . & . & . & . & . & . & . & . & . & .
\end{bmatrix}
$$

d_i = the probability that an individual selected at random from the ith age-sex group will survive another unit of time

b_i = the age specific fertility rate in the ith childbearing age group

$\bar{R}'$ = a row vector, the elements of which are the labor force participation rates of different age-sex cohorts in Canada   (2)

h = structural unemployment rate   (3)

$\bar{\pi}$ = a column vector whose elements are the percent of total migrations in each age-sex cohort   (4)

$\bar{\delta}'$ = unit row vector   (5)

η = share of agricultural employees in total wage bill   (6)

α = share of government transfers going to agricultural population   (7)

β = share of transfers from nonresidents going to agricultural population   (8)

Table 7-1
Variables and Equations

(1)	Target Variables	8	Structural Equations	31
(2)	Intermediate Variables	46	Balance Equations	5
	Total Endogenous Variables	54	Definitional Equations	18
			Total	54
(3)	Instrument Variables	8		
(4)	Data Variables			
	Unlagged	29		
	Lagged	7	36	
(5)	Lagged Endogenous Variables	6		
	Total Predetermined Variables	50		
	Predetermined Parameters[a]	8		

[a]Actually in the final version of the model four of the predetermined parameters, namely h, α, β, and η, etc. change slightly from year to year. As they do not appear in any structural equation their classification has been left unchanged.

3 Properties of the Model

The model of Nova Scotia presented here is comprised of an equal number of equations and endogenous variables. This is illustrated in Table 7-1

The eight target variables are included among the endogenous variables. The number of target variables equals the number of instrument variables; otherwise some of the instrument variables would be redundant and left at zero level.

The model may be described as relatively open. The number of exogenous variables is substantially smaller than the number of endogenous variables; yet, the ratio of unlagged predetermined variables to endogenous variables is not so small as to make the model unstable. This is shown in the results of simulation experiments and is discussed in more detail in this connection.[c] This relative stability of the model is bought, however, at a price because it makes more difficult the use of the models for the purposes of forecasting or exploring the implications of alternative courses of action. Each time one wants to use the model, all future values of all exogenous variables have to be estimated outside the model.

Another feature of the model is that it contains relatively few lagged variables. This is often the case in one-year models. There are not many economic relationships which occur with a lag of one year's duration. More important, lagged relationships lead to a loss of additional degrees of freedom, which had to be avoided in view of the limited number of observations available.

[c]It is intuitively obvious that a model with a high number of endogenous relative to the number of exogenous variables will generally be more sensitive to changes in values of exogenous variables. The term stability as used here is not to be confused with its use in connection with economic equilibrium.

Among the twenty-nine data variables, five relate to the national economy. They are Gross National Product (GNP); index of prices in Canada ($\bar{p}^C$); interest rates (i); total direct taxes in Canada (T^C); and total personal income in Canada ($Y_p^{C'}$). While this list is not as extensive as might be possible, it definitely ties the model to developments in the national economy. Of the twenty-nine data variables, four appear only in balance equations and hence could really be eliminated or replaced by a single variable. These are: undistributed corporate profits (C_{rp}), capital consumption allowance (D_p), residual error of estimates (REA), export of services (e_s), and balance with the rest of the world on transactions pertaining to income and product accounts (BRW). The reason they were retained, despite the fact that they do not affect any of the structural equations, lies simply in accounting convenience.

Among the eight instrument variables treated as predetermined, one, namely government deficit on income and product transactions (GD), does not affect any structural relation. Together, therefore, six exogenous variables appear only in balance equations. Hence, in fact, we are dealing not with thirty-seven but rather with thirty-one unlagged exogenous variables.

The model represents a consistent structure in the sense that each equation in the model has at least one variable which appears in at least one other equation of the model. The thirty-one structural equations of which the model is composed are linear in parameters. Two of them describe exponential relationships and are introduced in logarithmic form. In five of the eighteen definitional equations the explanatory variables appear in multiplicative form or as quotients.

In its final version the model can be decomposed neatly into seven submodels:

(1) Iron and Steel Industry,
(2) Manufacturing and Employment,
(3) Output and Investments,
(4) Households,
(5) Governments and Trade Deficit,
(6) Population and Migrations, and
(7) Welfare.

With only seven sectors the structure of the regional economy is presented in aggregate form. A fair amount of disaggregation will probably be required in order to make the results obtainable from the model more sharply focused and hence more useful for policy purposes.

The model is balanced at the level of the whole economy only. Balance equations for individual sectors could not be derived, mainly because profits accruing to business could not be apportioned by sector. The significant exceptions are households, for which personal disposable income balances personal expenditures, and governments. The balance of receipts and expenditures has been established, however, for all levels of government combined. The total performance of the regional economy or GRP has been calculated in three ways: as the sum of value added in all sectors of the economy; as the sum of income or claims against the product accruing to factors of production; and as the sum of components of product by type of use made of them.

The model of Nova Scotia presented here may be characterized as recursive. This refers to the fact that during each time period the causal arrows are running in one direction only. The notion of recursiveness can be illustrated with the help of the following simplified example in which the problem of identification is disregarded. [5] The example describes an interdependent economy in which the total output is divided between consumption and investments, with no government or foreign trade. By lagging one of the relations one can transform it from an interdependent to a recursive system.

Interdependent $(t-1)$ (t) $(t+1)$ *Endogenous Variables*

$$C_{(t)} = f(Y_{(t)}) \quad ; \quad Y$$

$$I_{(t)} = f(Y_{(t-1)}) \quad ; \quad C$$

$$Y_{(t)} = C_{(t)} + I_{(t)} \quad ; \quad I$$

	C	0	Y
	0	I	0
	C	I	Y

Recursive $(t-1)$ (t) $(t+1)$ *Endogenous Variables*

$$C_{(t)} = f(Y_{(t-1)}) \quad ; \quad Y$$

$$I_{(t)} = f(Y_{(t-1)}) \quad ; \quad C$$

$$Y_{(t)} = C_{(t)} + I_{(t)} \quad ; \quad I$$

	C	0	0
	0	I	0
	C	I	Y

Notice that in the recursive case the endogenous variables form a triangular matrix with zero entries above the main diagonal, while in the interdependent case, there is no ordering of equations and endogenous variables such that a triangular matrix would result. This last property is the basis for defining a recursive system in a more rigorous way from the estimator's point of view. A model is described as "recursive if there exists an ordering of the endogenous variables and an ordering of the equations such that the ith equation can be considered to describe the determination of the value of the ith endogenous variable during period t as a function of the predetermined variables and of the endogenous variables of index less than i. A model is said to be interdependent if it is not recursive." [6]

In a strictly recursive system the following two conditions hold: [7]

(1)   The matrix of endogenous variables is triangular or

$$Y_{ij} = 0; \text{ for all } j > i, \text{ and}$$

(2)   The covariance matrix of residuals is diagonal or, in other words,

$$E\left(\epsilon_{it}\,\epsilon_{jt}\right) = 0; \text{ for all } j \neq i.$$

With these two constraints satisfied, each structural equation can be considered as representing the causal determination of the ith endogenous variable.
Consequently, a multiple regression of the dependent variable on all other
variables occurring in the same structural equation provides a consistent estimator of this equation.[d] In each equation all endogenous variables except one
have been previously determined and hence can be treated in exactly the same
way as predetermined variables.

Some econometricians, especially H. Wold, claim that a good model should
describe causal chains and therefore be recursive, since in reality one quantity
cannot be at the same time cause and effect of another. Others, however, particularly those of the Klein school, claim that a description of real world phenomena would ordinarily result in interdependent systems.

However that may be, the model of Nova Scotia had to be developed as
recursive and not interdependent, even at the risk of oversimplifying some of the
relationships or violating some preconceived notions as to the behavior of the
economy. The model has been estimated on the basis of time series data covering
the period of fiteen to sixteen years. Hence estimating the model, even on an
equation by equation basis, leaves very few degrees of freedom and introduces
some awkward problems associated with small samples. With an interdependent
system, however, one would have to resort to some simultaneous estimating
procedures, such as two-stage least squares or limited information maximum
likelihood methods. The number of variables involved, even in a small interdependent subsystem, would easily exhaust the available degrees of freedom.
There could never be any question, of course, of estimating the whole system
simultaneously as it contains many more variables than observations.

The model of Nova Scotia may be described as diagonally recursive. [8] The
matrix of endogenous variables is triangular with all dependent variables on the
main diagonal; hence, single equation estimating procedures are fully justified.
Furthermore, each of the balance equations also has one variable on the main
diagonal. In effect, they are definitions establishing the value of one of their
variables without imposing additional constraints upon the system.

A less obvious condition that the model satisfies is that of identification.
The idea of identifiability refers to the issue whether or not the model is suf-

---

[d]This has been abundantly proven by Malinvaud, *op. cit.,* while Fox has shown that in
a fully identified system under certain rather stringent restrictions ordinary least squares
applied to the reduced equations yield virtually identical results with those obtained by
indirect least squares, Fox, Karl A., *Econometric Analysis for Public Policy,* Iowa State College Press, 1958.

ficiently restrictive so that when confronted with data just one hypothesis is consistent with both model and data. Putting it differently, in a fully identified system there should be a one to one correspondence between the structural and reduced form coefficients. This is an important problem and in a very real sense has to be examined prior to attacking statistical estimation. [9] Thus an equation is considered to be identified if it is impossible to obtain by means of a linear combination of two equations in the system a new equation of a form identical, up to the scale factor, to the one considered.

In order to test whether each equation is identified, two conditions have to be satisfied; namely, the order and the rank conditions. The order condition states that an equation in a model of n linear equations must exclude at least $(n - 1)$ of the variables that appear in the model. Supposing that a system has g endogenous variables, k predetermined variables, and $n = g$ equations. Then the order condition states that in each equation there must be at most $g + k - (n - 1)$ $= (k + 1)$ variables. [10] This condition is usually easily satisfied in open systems — that is, systems having a relatively large number of exogenous variables compared to the number of endogenous variables. This is the case with respect to the model of Nova Scotia.

The second condition, namely the rank condition, requires that it should be possible to define a nonvanishing determinant of order $(n - 1)$ from the full array of coefficients from which the row pertaining to this particular equation and all the columns in which the equation in question has nonzero coefficients have been excluded. The rank condition imposes a more stringent restriction, and if it is satisfied, the order condition will be fulfilled automatically. The model of Nova Scotia has been subjected both to a priori identification and to checks of this type.[e] The general finding is that the system is fully identified.

4 Sectoral Analysis

An examination of the seven sectors into which the regional economy has been disaggregated and of their economic underpinnings is extremely fruitful in revealing their internal structure and the problems they are facing. It also brings into sharper focus the analytic properties of the model.

Three of the seven sectors (iron and steel industry, manufacturing and employment, and output and investments) deal in a broad sense with productivity and efficiency in the Nova Scotia economy. Three others (households, governments and trade deficit, and welfare) are concerned mainly with consumption and welfare, and the means of satisfying their demands. Finally, the submodel dealing with population and migrations summarizes, in a way, the outcome of the operation of the other sectors in terms of migrations and population

---

[e]Strictly speaking, the order and rank conditions of identifiability do not apply to nonlinear models; hence, for purposes of testing, the few equations appearing in logarithmic form have been eliminated from the system.

changes. A more detailed breakdown into numerous productive sectors was not feasible at this stage of the work, mainly because of data limitations.

The seven subsectors differ from each other in degree of simplicity, in the number of equations, and in the ratio between statistical and accounting equations. Some of the submodels, like the welfare submodel, are internally simple and straightforward. Others, like the manufacturing and employment submodel, are quite involved, in that they are made of two subsystems, one embedded in the other. Still others, like population and migrations, are computationally very complex. The submodels differ also in terms of their stochastic descriptiveness. Some, like iron and steel and population and migrations, contain but a few structural equations and develop a good deal of information through the use of definitional and balance equations. On the other hand, the households submodel is designed so as to have a high ratio of estimated coefficients to the total number of equations.

The way in which the submodels have been presented below also varies. Some follow the causal chain developing the structural equations one after another and concluding with a balance statement. The argument of output and investments submodel, on the other hand, is centered about the statistical explanation of one concept, GRP.

The economic structure of the model, like its mathematical form, is simple; and so is the economic rationale behind most of the structural equations. The economic agrument becomes more meaningful when the submodels are taken as a whole. Some of the simplicity was imposed by the shortness of the time series data on which the estimating procedure was based. Its associated problem of degrees of freedom imposed the necessity of remaining within the bounds of a recursive model.

a. Iron and steel industry

This submodel comprises three equations and one identity, (D.1), (S.1), (S.2), and (S.3). Together they describe total capital invested in the industry as the sum of capital invested up to the previous period plus new investments, value added as a function of capital stock, value of shipments as a function of value added, and exports as a function of value of shipments.

Several features of this submodel are worth noticing. The production function is extremely simple and describes value added as a function of capital invested only. This is due to the fact that the size of employment in the iron and steel plant at Sydney is largely the outcome of political considerations and of government policy and does not necessarily follow fluctuations in output. Several variants of the production equation (S.1), were tested but no significant relationship was found to exist over time between output and employment.

The submodel concentrates on the supply side without trying to establish separately the sector's supply and demand schedules and the resulting balance. This follows from the fact that Nova Scotia production forms only a small part of total Canadian output and does not influence appreciably price formation at

Table 7-2
Iron and Steel Sub-Model

Equation Number	Endogenous Variables			Predetermined Variables	
(D.1)	K_{IS}			$K_{IS(t-1)}, I_{IS}$	Capital formation
(S.1)	K_{IS}	X_{IS}			Production
(S.2)		X_{IS}	Q_{IS}		Output
(S.3)			Q_{IS} e_{IS}		Exports

the national level, which is clearly outside the system. On the other hand, only a relatively small proportion of the total output of the Sydney plant is consumed within the province. A corollary of this approach is that exports are treated as a function of output only. Table 7-2 illustrates the resulting system.

There are four endogenous variables and four equations. The submodel is fully determined and recursive, a feature allowing estimates to be made by nothing more sophisticated than ordinary least squares. The causal chain of this submodel, in its final version, is illustrated in the accompanying chart.

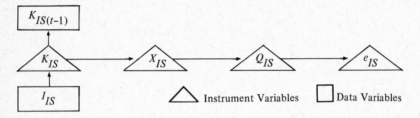

Actually a demand equation of the following form was also tried:

$$Q^D_{IS(t)} = 13.316 + 1.186\, GNP_{(t)}; \quad R^2 = .7507$$
$$\qquad\quad (2.4471)\ (6.336) \qquad\qquad d = 1.8026$$

$$Q^D_{IS(t)} = Q^S_{IS(t)};$$

The system including these two equations, however, would clearly be over-determined, as is illustrated in Table 7-3.

In this alternative version, the submodel would comprise five endogenous variables and six equations. The reason the more conventional approach fails in this case is that, at variance with national models, it is impossible to treat prices as endogenous variables.

b. Manufacturing and employment

This submodel, as it stands, is composed of seven equations and two identities (S.4), (S.5), (S.6), (S.7), (D.2), (S.8), (S.9), (S.10), and (B.1). It deals with two closely related problems: total employment in the regional economy

Table 7-3
Iron and Steel Submodel (Alternative Version)

Equation Number	Endogenous Variables			Predetermined Variables	
(D.1)	K_{IS}			$K_{IS(t-1)}, I_{IS}$	Capital Formation
(S.1)	K_{IS}	X_{IS}			Production
(S.2)		X_{IS}	Q^S_{IS}	GNP	Output
			Q^D_{IS}	e_{IS}	Demand
(S.3)		Q^S_{IS}	Q^D_{IS}		Exports
			Q^D_{IS}		Balance

and developments in the manufacturing sector. In what follows, manufacturing excludes primary iron and steel production, which has been dealt with elsewhere.

Total employment is defined in equation (B.1) as the sum of employment in agriculture, forestry, and fisheries; mining; manufacturing; commercial services; governments; and iron and steel industry. Of the six basic components of employment in the regional economy, two, namely employment in mining (mainly coal mining), and employment in the primary iron and steel industry, are largely determined by political and not by economic considerations. Consequently their determination lies outside the system, and they have been treated throughout as data variables. Employment in agriculture, forestry, and fisheries, in commercial services, and in governments, including military personnel, depends to a certain extent at least upon developments in the Nova Scotia economy, and has been dealt with in equations (S.4), (S.5), and (S.6). Yet these sectors have only been partially treated in the model as their full development was beyond the scope of the present study.

Employment in agriculture, forestry, and fishing has been explained as a function of commercial farming. In view of the heterogeneous nature of this sector, the explanatory and predictive power of this relation is open to doubt. Employment in commercial services has been explained as a function of the degree of urbanization. This seems plausible as urban populations usually require a higher degree and greater concentration of commercial services than dispersed rural ones. Employment in governments has been explained as a function of military expenditures. Military employment is, of course, the most flexible component of total employment in this sector, and so it proved to be statistically the most significant one. The equation also contains time as a shift parameter. The coefficient associated with time has a negative sign but is not very large.

With respect to manufacturing, the general paucity and low quality of data precluded the successful estimation of a production function of a conventional type. Equations (S.9) and (S.10) explain value added as a function of capital stock and of average size of plant. The determination of capital invested in manufacturing hinged upon a successful estimation of an investment function. Investment in manufacturing has been explained in equation (S.7) as a function of government investments in elements of infrastructure, such as power plants, transportation facilities, and industrial estates, and of an accessibility index defined with the help of principal components. [11] This last variable refers to changes in accessibility to centers of manufacturing activity in Canada (of importance to producers of intermediate goods), in accessibility to population centers (represented by aggregate personal income), and to the tonnage handled in Halifax harbor). Both explanatory variables were taken with a four-years' lag, the length of which appears reasonable. This is undoubtedly an interesting relationship but, unfortunately, owing to the short time series available, the number of degrees of freedom left is too small for one to feel quite comfortable about the explanatory or predictive power of this equation. Attempts to explain the share of Nova Scotia in total investments in manufacturing in Canada by means of a more elaborate investment function proved unsuccessful.[f]

Finally, exports of manufacturing products have been explained in terms of demand in the rest of the country, measured by GRP, and of the competitive ability of the Nova Scotia manufacturing production, represented by the difference in price levels for manufactured products in Canada and Nova Scotia. This relationship is statistically significant. Attempts to determine this relationship from the supply side did not yield satisfactory results. The main reason appears to be the relatively short time series on which the equation was estimated.[g]

The system as finally adopted is illustrated in Table 7-4. Notice that there are here nine endogenous variables and nine equations. The system is diagonally recursive, a feature which enables it to be estimated by ordinary least squares. The causal chain of this submodel is illustrated in Figure 7-2.

---

[f]The variable

$$I^S_{m(t)} = \frac{I^{NS}_{m(t)}}{I^C_{m(t)}};$$

where

$I^{NS}_{m(t)}$ = level of investment in manufacturing in Nova Scotia, and

$I^C_{m(t)}$ = *level of investment in manufacturing in Canada,*

could not be meaningfully related to explanatory variables. The investment function has been of the form

$$I^S_{m(t)} = a + b_1 Z_{1(t)} + b_2 Z_{2(t)} + b_3 \sum_{t=1}^{-4} [GI_G + GS_m]_{(t)} + b_4 t;$$

where

$Z_{1(t)} = PC(U_{Y(t)}, U_{E3(t)}), H_{H(t)}$;

$Z_{2(t)} = PC(\Delta\, GRP, PRM_{(t-1)})$; defined as principal components.

[g]The system covering both the supply and the demand side and balanced at the level of exports is interdependent. It includes the following relationships:

$e_{m(t)}$ = 26.185 + 1.2436 $GNP_{(t)}$ + 6.6720 $(p^C_m - p^{-NS}_m)$; R^2 = .3932
          (2.9136) (3.1268)   (2.3635) d = 1.9141

X_m = -232.805 + 5.6234 $E_{3(t)}$ + .4338 $K_{m(t)}$; R^2 = .9456
                  (2.4572)   (10.0724)

E_3 = .0783 X_m - .0384 K_m + .4441 SZ; R^2 = .3745
        (2.5331)   (-2.5018)   (19.7267) d = 1.9939

Table 7–4
Manufacturing and Employment Sub-Model

Equation Number	Endogenous Variables								Predetermined Variables
(S.4)	E_1								Employment in agriculture
(S.5)		E_4							Employment in services
(S.6)			E_5						Government employment
(S.7)				I^m					Investments
(D.2)				I_m	K_m				Capital
(S.8)					K_m	e_m			Exports
(S.9)							X_m		Value added
(S.10)							X_m	E_3	Employment in manufacturing
(B.1)	E_1	E_4	E_5					E_3	Total employment E

15 Variables

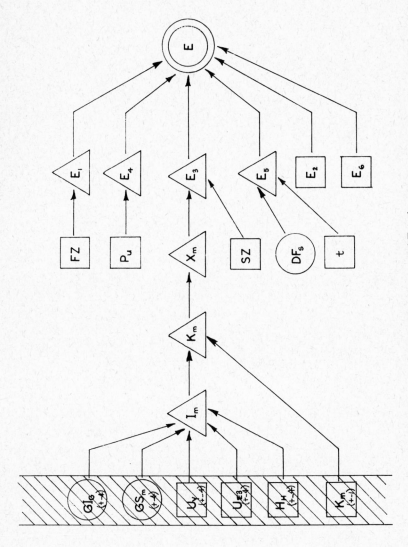

Figure 7-2. Manufacturing and Employment.

c. Output and investments

This submodel comprises three equations and three identities (D.4), (S.11), (D.3), (D.5), (S.12), and (S.13). The first part defines Gross Regional Product as the sum of value added in the six sectors with which the model is dealing, namely agriculture, forestry, and fisheries; mining; iron and steel; manufacturing; commercial services; and governments. Value added in agriculture, forestry, and fisheries and in mining are treated throughout the model as data variables. Because of the complex nature of these primary sectors no attempt has been made in the model to develop a comprehensive predictive system of their behavior. Value added in the iron and steel industry and in other manufacturing have been explained in submodels dealing specifically with those industries; hence, these variables are treated in the submodel discussed here as predetermined. Value added in commercial services is explained as a function of employment in this sector. Value added in government is defined as the product of employment in the government sector (explained in the submodel dealing with manufacturing and employment) and of average wages of government employees in Nova Scotia.[h]

The second part of the model defines total investments as the sum of investments in mining, iron and steel, manufacturing, commercial services, and housing. Investments in mining and in the iron and steel industries are treated as data variables because they are largely determined by political rather than economic considerations, thus falling outside the system. Investments in manufacturing have already been explained in the submodel dealing with manufacturing and employment. The remaining two components, namely investments in

---

$$X_m = \underset{(126.4873)}{.4126} Q_{m(t)}; \qquad\qquad\qquad \begin{aligned} R^2 &= .9729 \\ d &= 1.4042 \end{aligned}$$

$$e_{m(t)} = \underset{(20.1460)}{.1319} Q_{m(t)}; \qquad\qquad\qquad \begin{aligned} R^2 &= .2604 \\ d &= .8015 \quad (S.8) \end{aligned}$$

Notice that there are here five equations and five endogenous variables. However, it is impossible to obtain a triangular matrix of endogenous variables. Hence, ordinary least squares are actually not applicable.

[h]A different form of this relationship using an index of urbanization of Nova Scotia has also been tried. The regression of the form

$$X_{CS} = \underset{(4.3868)}{11.0347} E_4 - \underset{(-3.1414)}{2.0638} P_u; \qquad\qquad\qquad \begin{aligned} R^2 &= .7596 \\ d &= 1.0584 \end{aligned}$$

is statistically significant despite the low value of the Durbin-Watson statistic. Notice, however, that the coefficient of the last variable, P_u, has a negative sign. This is hardly acceptable because ordinarily urban populations require more services than rural. Moreover, the way in which these variables were defined makes the two universes not directly comparable, quite aside from the quality of the data. Hence, the simpler version has been preferrred, despite the high value of the constant term.

commercial services and in housing, are dealt with in equations (S.12) and (S.13). An interesting feature of the latter equation is the heavy dependence of investments in housing upon government investments and upon subsidies to housing construction.

The system is fully determined and recursive as may be seen in Table 7-5.

The submodel introduces six endogenous variables and six equations that did not appear previously. The necessity of avoiding simultaneous estimation methods resulted in some of the equations being less sophisticated than their corresponding reality. This is particularly true of equation (S.12) and, to a certain extent, equation (S.13)[i] The causal chain in this subsystem, as illustrated in Figure 7-3, clearly shows the links with the iron and steel and the manufacturing and employment submodels discussed above.

d. Households

This submodel comprises ten equations and six identities (D.7), (S.14), (S.15), (S.16), (S.17), (S.18), (S.10), (D.6), (S.20), (D.8), (D.9), (B.2), (D.10), (S.21), (S.22), and (S.23).

The households submodel really consists of three parts. The first part, comprising a definition of total personal income, explains the components of income as a function of other variables. The second part defines direct personal taxes as a function of other variables and derives total disposable personal income as the difference between total personal income and total personal direct taxes. The third part starts with an identity between total personal disposable income and total personal expenditures and explains, by means of structural equations, various components of personal consumption in terms of exogenous variables. From this part, personal savings are derived as the difference between total personal expenditures and consumption in (D.10).

---

[i]Actually, equation (S.12) has also been regressed on increments in Gross Regional Product, on government subsidies to housing, and on interest rate, as is shown below:

$$I_{CS(t)} = 4.6234 \, \Delta \, GRP + 4.1785 \, GS_{H(t)}; \qquad\qquad R^2 = .7232$$
$$\qquad\quad (1.9149) \qquad\quad (4.2044) \qquad\qquad\qquad\qquad d = 1.4316 \quad (1)$$

$$I_{CS(t)} = 1.4362 \, GS_{H(t)} + 10.8649 \, i_{(t)}; \qquad\qquad R^2 = .7625$$
$$\qquad\quad (2.8695) \qquad\quad (9.4436) \qquad\qquad\qquad\qquad d = 1.3858 \quad (2)$$

The regression on $\Delta \, GRP$ and GS_H has been rejected because the same variables appear in the equation explaining investments in housing, which would cause identification difficulties. Regression on GS_H and i has not been adopted because it was felt that value added in commercial services (or $X_{CS(t)}$) is a theoretically more significant variable than government subsidies and interest rates. Regressions using lagged relationships and some forms of the acceleration principle failed to produce statistically significant results.

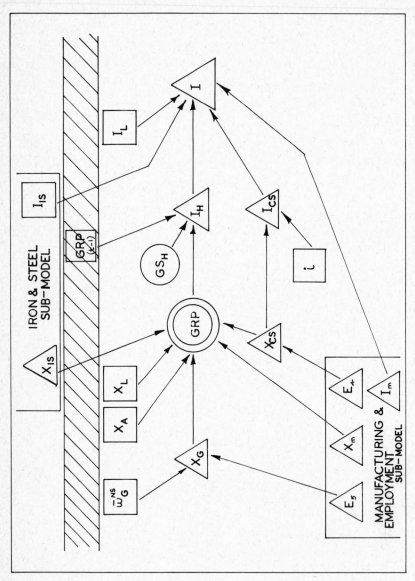

Figure 7-3. Output and Investments.

Table 7-5
Output and Investments Submodel

Equation Number	Endogenous Variables						Endogenous Variables explained in other sub-models	
(S.11)	X_{CS}					E_4		
(D.3)		X_G				E_5		
(D.4)	X_{CS}	X_G	GRP				X_{IS}	X_m
(S.12)	X_{CS}			I_{CS}				
(S.13)			GRP		I_H			
(D.5)				I_{CS}	I_H	I		I_m

Predetermined Variables						
$\bar{w}_G^{NS}$						Value added in commercial services
	X_A	X_L				Value added in governments
			i			GRP defined
						Investments in commercial services
			$GRP_{(t-1)}$	GS_H		Investments in housing
				I_L	I_S	Total investments defined

Total wage income is explained as a function of the level of operation of the local economy and of the price level. This appears reasonable because the price level is obviously an element in establishing the wage rate.

Net income of farm operators replaces a fully developed agricultural sector. This sector is, in fact, quite involved but is reduced to three equations that explain (1) net income of farm operators, (2) employment in agriculture, and (3) agricultural exports. Employment in agriculture has already been discussed within the framework of the submodel dealing with manufacturing and employment in equation (S.4), while exports of agricultural products are treated as part of governments and trade deficit submodel in equation (S.27). The net income of farm operators is explained in terms of the amount of cultivated land and the number of commercial farms. In view of the fact that subsistence farming is extensive in Nova Scotia, this last variable was expected to affect the operation of the sector. It is indeed gratifying to find that the coefficient associated with it is statistically significant.[j]

---

[j]Another version was attempted, bringing the role of government to the fore. Income of unincorporated farm enterprises minus government subsidies to agriculture was treated as the dependent variable, and number of commercial farms as a proportion of all farms was taken to be the independent variable. The resulting equation took the form:

$$[F_{a(t)} - GS_{A(t)}] = -5.192 + \underset{(3.5553)}{.9948\, FZ_{(t)}}; \qquad R^2 = .4930$$

Table 7–6
Households Submodel

Equation Number	Endogenous Variables	Endogenous Variables Explained in Other Submodels	Predetermined Variables
(S.14)	W	GRP	A_L, FZ
(S.15)	F_a		DF_a
(S.16)	F_m	X_m	
(S.17)	F_s	X_{CS}	
(S.18)	i_p, SIP		$\bar{p}^{NS}$
(S.19)	W, F_s, i_p, SIP, MPA		F^G, NH
(D.6)	W, F_a, F_m, F_s, i_p, SIP, MPA, Y_p		$\bar{p}^{NS}$, F^{nr}
(D.7)	Y_p		
(D.8)	Y_p, t_r, T		T^C
(D.9)	t_r, T, Y_{DP}		Y^C_p, T_a
(B.2)	Y_{DP}		
(S.21)	Y_{DP}, C_1		
(S.22)	Y_{DP}, Y_X, C_1, C_4		
(S.23)	Y_X, C_4, C_5		NH
(D.10)	C_5, S		$E_{(t-1)}$, P_m

W — Wages
F_a — Farm income
F_m — Unincorporated manufacturing
F_s — Unincorporated services
i_p — Interest, dividends and rent
SIP — Social security payments
MPA — Military pay
Y_p — Personal income
t_r — Tax rate
T — Direct personal taxes
Y_{DP} — Personal disposable income
Y_X — Balance of households
C_1 — Consumption of goods
C_4 — Consumption of services
C_5 — Rents paid by households
S — Personal savings

The net incomes of both unincorporated manufacturing enterprises and of unincorporated service enterprises were a function of value added generated in those sectors. Moreover, the price index was found to affect not only the wage level but also the net income of small unincorporated service enterprises. Again, this seems to be quite reasonable under Nova Scotia conditions. In the case of unincorporated manufacturing enterprises the relationship is trivial but proved to be statistically significant. The regression coefficient associated with value added is actually quite small, but this is perhaps understandable, because most current development has taken place in new and more efficient corporate organizations.

Interest, dividends, and rental income of persons is explained as a function of the existing number of relatively new housing units. This appears intuitively reasonable because in Nova Scotia rental income dominates other components of this variable almost to the point of exclusion. In order to arrive at net wage income accruing to households, employers' and employees' social insurance and government pension plans contributions have to be deducted. That their level is a function of total wages is shown in equation (S.19). Payments to resident military personnel are a proportion of total payments to military personnel.[k]

In order to arrive at personal disposable income it is necessary to consider direct personal taxes. Their main component is personal income taxes. Other direct personal taxes, like succession duties, are less important and are treated as a data variable. The equation explaining total personal income taxes is treated as a behavioral and not a technical relationship. The tax rate has been derived as a ratio of Canadian direct personal taxes to personal income and has been treated as a separate variable. In this equation the tax rate and total personal income are the two explanatory variables.

Turning next to the expenditure side, one has to consider the three main components of household consumption — namely, consumption of goods, consumption of services, and rents and interest payments. The explanation of all three is straightforward:*Consumption of goods* is explained as a function of total personal disposable income and of the number of households. There is surprisingly little multicollinearity between the two independent variables appearing in this equation. *Consumption of services* has been derived as a function of total personal income and of the degree of urbanization of Nova Scotia. This seems quite reasonable because urban households usually spend a higher proportion of their income on services than rural ones do. Finally, *rents and interest payments by households* have been related to personal disposable income and to the number of relatively new housing units. Table 7-6 illustrates the whole system.

---

[k]The remainder — that is, payments to military personnel who declared themselves as residents of other provinces — is not treated as accruing to factors of production in Nova Scotia.

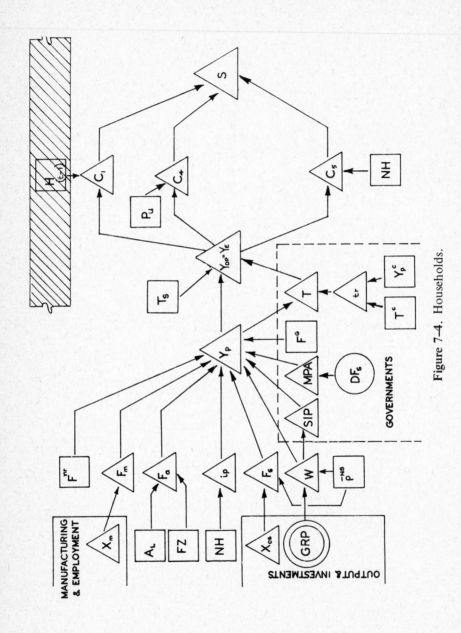

Figure 7-4. Households.

There are sixteen endogenous variables, other than those that have already appeared in other submodels, and sixteen equations. The endogenous variables introduced for the first time form a triangular matrix with all the dependent variables on the main diagonal. Thus this submodel is also recursive. The causal chain of this submodel in its final version is illustrated in Figure 7–4. Despite the large number of variables involved, it shows a single uninterrupted flow.

e. Governments and trade deficit

This submodel comprises five equations and two identities, (S.24), (S.25), (B.3), (S.26), (S.27), (S.28), and (B.4). It really consists of two interconnected parts, the first dealing with total government receipts and expenditures, and the second defining the external balance of the region with the rest of the world on transactions pertaining to income and product, embedded in an overall balance of the regional economy. The connecting link between the two parts of the model lies in the fact that a large share of the substantial foreign trade deficit is covered by local expenditure of, and unilateral transers from the federal government.

An examination of the first part of the submodel covering identity (B.3) and equations (S.24) and (S.25) reveals that the overall government deficit (GD) is treated in the model as an instrument variable, whereas the current government spending (GS_c) is introduced as endogenous to the system and defined as an intermediate variable.[1] The two are clearly interdependent, but it appears that in Nova Scotia the important components of current government expenditures cannot be changed at will by the federal or provincial governments. So far, no real attempt has been made at explaining statistically the behavior of this variable.

Turning to the structural equations, corporate profit taxes are explained by reference to the level of operation of the regional economy as represented by Gross Regional Product. Indirect taxes are satisfactorily explained as a function of total personal expenditures. This is what one would expect, in view of the fact that sales taxes are the most important component of total indirect taxes and this relationship is statistically highly significant. Other components of government receipts have been dealt with in submodels covering output and investments, and households. The causal chain in this part of the submodel is

---

[1]Total government income consists of personal income tax, other personal direct taxes, corporate profit taxes, social insurance contributions, indirect taxes, and surplus (or deficit) on income and product transaction.

Total government spending consists of military pay and allowances; government investments in: power, water, transportation and other elements of technical infrastructure; education and training; health, welfare, and administration; investments and subsidies to agriculture, forestry, and fisheries; mining; manufacturing; housing and commercial services; current government expenditures; and government transfers.

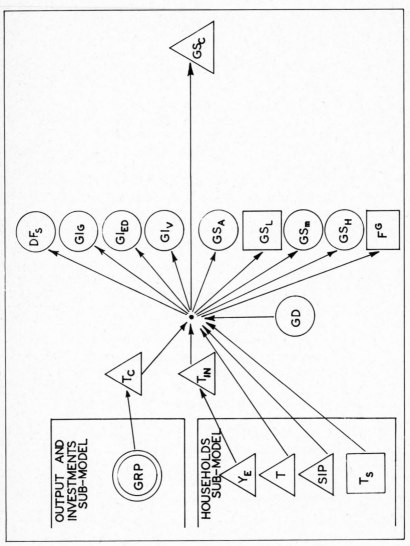

Figure 7-5. Governments.

shown in Figure 7–5. The second part of the submodel describes an overall balance of the economy, equating total regional income and total regional expenditure.[m]

Several features of this identity may be noted. The left-hand side corresponds to Gross Regional Product by shares of factors of production, although the balance has been brought about by introducing the variable REA. It comprises several adjustments that make equation (B.4) balance at the level of the Gross Regional Product. The adjustments incorporated in the variable REA are:

(1) Interest payments on debts of nonlocal governments received by local residents,

(2) Undistributed corporate profits other than retained earnings that have not been introduced explicitly as C_{rp}, such as charitable contributions and corporate profits taxes,

(3) Profits of federal, provincial, and local government business enterprises,

(4) Government subsidies, appearing as instrument variables on the right-hand side of the equation (in income and product accounts they are deducted from indirect taxes, which thus are net of subsidies), and

(5) Residual error, balancing income and product accounts.

The right-hand side of equation (B.4) contains several balancing items that do not properly belong to the concept of Gross Regional Product, such as unilateral transfers from nonresidents (F^{nr}), part of defense spending (DF_s), and government deficit on items pertaining to income and product accounts (GD). Defense spending in the model is represented by an index, (FD_s), which covers only payments to military personnel stationed in Nova Scotia. Part of the personnel are treated as residents of Nova Scotia and payments made to them properly belong in Gross Regional Product and are included in the variable (MPA) on the left-hand side of equation (B.4), but an adjustment has to be made for the remainder. This overall balance equation defines the deficit (BRW) of the

---

[m]Total regional income consists of wage income; net income of farm operators; net income of unincorporated manufacturing and service enterprises; interest, dividends, and rental income; corporate retained earnings; capital consumption allowances; indirect taxes; payments to resident military personnel; and adjustments for corporate profits not paid to stockholders other than retained earnings, residual error on income and product accounts, and federal government investment income and subsidies not accounted for elsewhere.

Total regional expenditures consist of *consumption* of agricultural and manufactured goods and services, and rents and interest payments by households; *government spending* for defense, general facilities, education, health, welfare and administration, agriculture, forestry and fisheries, mining, manufacturing, housing and commercial services, current government operating expenses, and unilateral transfers; *investments* in mining, iron and steel, manufacturing, commercial services, and housing and *foreign trade* including exports of agricultural, mining, iron and steel, and manufactured products and services adjusted for imports. The balancing items include unilateral transfers from nonresidents, balance with the rest of the world, and budgetary surplus (or deficit) on transactions related to income and product.

province toward the rest of the world on transactions pertaining to income and product accounts.

While this balance recapitulates and ties together most of the endogenous variables that have appeared and been discussed so far, it also introduces three more pertaining to foreign trade of the province: exports of mining products (e_L), exports of agricultural products (e_A), and imports (m). Other components of total exports — namely, exports of iron and steel products (e_{IS}) and of other manufactured products (e_m) — have been introduced earlier as part of the discussion of the respective sectors.

Exports of services (e_s) do not behave consistently and are treated as an exogenous variable. The necessity to remain within the constraints of a diagonally recursive system requires that these variables be introduced before concluding the discussion of the regional economy with an overall balance (B.4). Exports of mining products (e_L) consist mainly of coal and are the only endogenous variable left of the mining submodel, which at an earlier stage comprised four equations. Investments in mining, employment, and value added are treated in the final version as exogenous variables to be determined outisde the model. The export equation is of the demand type, relating exports (e_L) to GNP. Statistically it may be considered satisfactory, yet not too much faith can be placed in it in view of the fact that it has been derived on the basis of a small sample. Violent shifts might be expected in this sector of the Nova Scotia economy, which is both contracting and changing in character.

The operation of coal mining, although now by far the most significant component of the mining sector in Nova Scotia, is only partly based on consideration of profitability. By and large, mining in Nova Scotia is a declining industry, and the outputs and employment therein are governed by governmental subsidies rather than by the more familiar economic laws that can be incorporated into the traditional production functions. Yet attempts to explore the impact of governmental regulations in the mining sector proved futile. As a result, time series on employment and value of output are not significantly correlated. Similarly, changes in capital invested in this sector bear no relation to output because the sector has been notoriously underinvested for a very long period of time.[n]

Exports of agricultural products (e_A) have been explained as a function of

---

[n]The following equations were tried. They have been found to be statistically acceptable yet have been rejected in the final analysis:

$$X_{L(t)} = 48.619 + .5634 V_{(t)} ; \qquad\qquad R^2 = .3958$$
$$\quad\;\;\;(30.7512)\;\;(2.8641) \qquad\qquad\qquad\qquad d = 1.3233$$

Value added in mining is a function of the value of resources, a rather trivial result.

$$S_{L(t)} = 3.647 + .3711 K_{L(t)} ; \qquad\qquad R^2 = .9435$$
$$\quad\;\;\;(1.2940)\;\;(14.7680) \qquad\qquad\qquad\qquad d = 2.7608$$

the number of fishing boats and the sum of government subsidies to and investment in agriculture, cumulated over a period of four years. This equation is
statistically satisfactory but it is based on a small sample. More fundamental
doubts as to its validity are raised by the fact that it is essentially of a "mongrel"
type. It can be argued, of course, that fish and fish products are the main
export item in this sector and thus increase the explanatory power of the
variable relating to number of fishing boats; but this reasoning is not entirely
convincing. The sector covers several very heterogeneous activities; namely, subsistence agriculture, commercial farming, and fishing and forestry. Are we then
to believe that the number of fishing boats is the main variable affecting its
exports? The second variable refers to government subsidies to and investments
in agriculture, but these do not have the fostering of exports as their main
objective. Besides, they were cumulated over a period of four years, a fact which
reduced dangerously the number of degrees of freedom.[o]

Imports have been explained quite satisfactorily in equation (S.28). Their
level was found to be a function of four types of demand:

(1) Consumption of final goods by private households (Y_E),
(2) Consumption of intermediate products by regional industries, itself a
     function of the level of operation of the main sectors of the provincial

---

Value added in mining is a function of capital in mining.

$$Q_L = -50.579 + 2.1914\, X_L ;$$

$$R^2 = .9736$$
$$d = 1.9431$$

Value of shipments is a function of value added.

$$[Q^S_{L(t)} - GS_{L(t)}] = \underset{(3.29)}{1.035}\, X_{L(t)} ;$$

$$R^2 = .477$$

The difference between value of shipments in mining and government subsidies and investments in mining is a function of value added in mining, bringing somewhat to the fore the
role of government, but statistically unsatisfactory.

$$e_L = \underset{(18.0092)}{.5090}\, Q_L ;$$

$$R^2 = .5694$$
$$d = 1.2457$$

Exports of mining products are a proportion of output.

[o]Ideally this sector should really be split up into three or four separate ones. In each,
the main factors affecting supply and demand should be introduced explicitly. The existing
data basis would allow one to engage in more detailed research, but it was felt that this
would prove to be a major study in itself and would be outside the scope of the model
described here. As it is, the sector is represented by three equations only.

Besides exports, employment has been explained in the submodel dealing with manufacturing and employment (S.4), and income of farm operators has been dealt with among
the relationships governing the components of personal income and consumption (S.15).

economy − namely, mining, iron and steel, and other manufacturing
$(X_L + X_{IS} + X_m)$,

(3) Consumption of investment goods fluctuating with the level of investments
(I), and

(4) Requirements of the military establishment, represented by an index based
on military pay and allowances in Nova Scotia (DF_s).

The system is diagonally recursive. The seven endogenous variables that
appear for the first time correspond to seven new equations. This is illustrated in
Table 7-7. The matrix is triangular, with all dependent variables on the main
diagonal. Other endogenous variables covered have been introduced earlier.
Hence, the submodel describes a self-contained, recursive system.

f. Population and migrations

The submodel consists of one equation and six identities (D.11), (D.12),
(D.13), (S.29), (D.14), (B.5), and (D.15). At variance with the other submodels,
however, most of the relationships are expressed in compact matrix notation,
hence each of them represents really a system of equations. The submodel can
be succinctly explained by starting with population existing in the previous
period which is aged by the application of the survivorship matrix to yield a
population that would be generated by natural increase. The survivorship matrix
Γ is a square matrix of order equal to the number of age-sex cohorts, with nonzero elements on the sub-sub-diagonal and in the first, second, and last two rows.
The elements on the sub-sub-diagonal and in the last two rows refer to the probabilities of survival for another year of an individual picked at random from the
ith age-sex group. The entries in the first two rows represent age specific fertility
rates in the ith child-bearing age group.

Labor force at time t is described as the product of a row vector whose
elements represent the potential labor force participation rates in each age-sex
cohort, and a column vector whose elements represent the size of each age-sex
cohort obtained by natural increase. This leads to unsatisfied demand for labor
(or labor surplus) which equals the difference between total employment and
potential labor force, taking into consideration the structural unemployment
rate (h).

Next, migrations are explained as a function of unsatisfied demand for labor
or of labor surplus (unemployment) in the previous period. The age-sex structure
of migrants is obtained as a product of a column vector whose elements are
typical relative shares of each age-sex cohort in migrating populations and of a
scalar representing the total balance of migrations at time t. Thus population of
each age-sex cohort equals the sum of population resulting from natural increase
in each age-sex cohort and the net balance of migrations (in each cohort) in the

Table 7-7

Governments and Foreign Trade Sub-Model

Equation Number	Endogenous Variables						Endogenous Variables Explained in Other Sub-Models	Predetermined Variables	
(S.24)	T_C								Corporate income taxes
(S.25)	T_{IN}								Indirect taxes
(B.3)	T_{IN}	GS_c	e_L	e_A	m		21 variables	21 variables	Balance of governments finance
(S.26)									Exports of mining products
(S.27)				e_A					Exports of agricultural products
(S.28)					m				Imports
(B.4)	T_{IN}	GS_c	e_L	e_A	m	BRW			Balance of the economy

previous period. A simple application of a unit vector yields total population
at each period.

Several features of this model are worth discussing. The elements of $\bar{R}$ in
equation (D.12) are defined as typical labor force participation rates of each
age-sex cohort. Average Canadian rather than Nova Scotia labor force participation rates were used because, in a declining region, labor force participation
rates typically tend to be low. This is at least partly due to social customs prevailing in the more traditional rural areas where women, as a rule, tend to stay
at home. More important, in areas with high unemployment, people do not
register with labor exchanges and hence are not counted as members of the labor

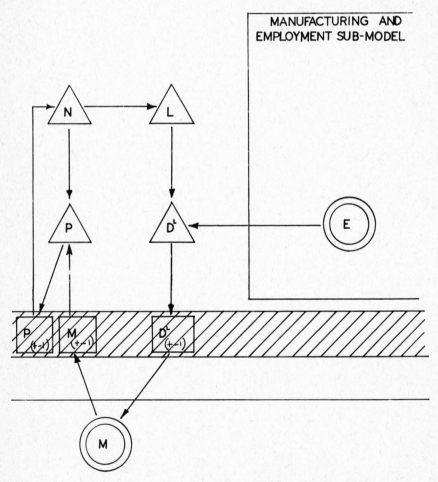

Figure 7-6. Population and Migrations.

force. This lack of interest in registration is a direct outcome of the low probability of obtaining a job through the labor exchange.

In this submodel total employment is taken to be equal by definition to total demand for labor. This transpires from identity (S.13) where unsatisfied demand for labor is derived as the difference between total employment and total potential labor force.

The vector $\bar{\pi}$ which defines the typical age-sex structure of migrating populations is based on net migrations, with the result that some of its entries are negative. This may cause some difficulties in the application of the model in case of a drastic change in the direction of migrations. Because of data limitations, however, it could hardly be avoided. Gross migration data for Nova Scotia are simply not available.

Equation (S.29) explains migrations (or, strictly speaking, outmigration) as a function of surplus labor in the previous period. This is in line with theoretical considerations, although it has hardly ever been derived statistically. The reason appears to be that most studies dealing with "pull" type migrations concentrate on characteristics of regions receiving immigrants, whereas in Nova Scotia one is dealing essentially with outmigrations. The model is illustrated in Figure 7-6. Notice that there are two loops involving migrations.

From a theoretical point of view, in addition to employment opportunities, relative wage levels or the relative level of earnings in the region should be a significant variable. Both propositions were explored as a ratio of average wages in Nova Scotia to average wages in Central Canada, as a difference between these two wage levels, and as differences between per capita disposable incomes, but did not yield any statistically significant results.[p]

The other variable to be tried was the industrial image of the province, defined as the relative rate of growth of manufacturing employment. Several variants were tried, but no positive results were forthcoming.[q]

The major input into the model is total employment, which is derived from the manufacturing and employment submodel. The two major outputs of the model are migrations and total population. Migrations is one of the target variables because the desire to regulate migrations, or rather check outmigrations, is a

---

[p]The following variables were tried directly and with a year's time lag, yielding negative results:

$$\left(\frac{\bar{w}^{NS}}{\bar{w}^{c}} \right), \left(\bar{w}^{NS} - \bar{w}^{c} \right), \left(\frac{Y_{DP}}{P} \bigg/ \frac{Y_{DP}^{C}}{P^{C}} \right), \left(\frac{Y_{DP}}{P} - \frac{Y_{DP}^{C}}{P^{c}} \right).$$

[q]The explanatory variable tried out was defined as:

$$\left(\frac{\Delta E_{3}}{\Delta E_{3}^{C}} \cdot \frac{E_{3}^{C}}{E_{3}} \right), \left(\frac{E_{3(t)}}{E_{3(t-1)}} \bigg/ \frac{E_{3(t)}^{C}}{E_{3(t-1)}^{C}} \right).$$

major policy objective of the provincial government. This is understandable because of welfare considerations and because of the hardships involved in out-migrations of unskilled labor. Equally important are the detrimental effects of outmigration upon the composition of the remaining population and labor force, owing to the highly selective nature of this process. During the period covered by the data, especially during the last few years, migrations have been growing steadily, in line with the growing discrepancy between the potentially available labor force and actual demand for labor.

The population and migrations submodel has two aspects. On the one hand it is embedded in the planning model, but on the other it may stand and be operated by itself. While this characteristic is of no immediate interest in the context of the model of Nova Scotia as a whole, it confers upon it some other-wise useful properties.

g. Welfare

This submodel consists of two equations and three identities (S.30), (S.31), (D.16), (D.17), and (D.18).

Index of per capita educational standards is described as a function of government investments in education and training; index of health standards is a function of government investments in health, welfare, and administration; and index of housing standards is defined as the ratio of total number of housing units built after 1920 to total population. The structure of this submodel is extremely simple. It admittedly oversimplifies a complex problem, but owing to the paucity of data it was impossible to probe deeper into the underlying phenomena.

While all three indexes are rather poorly defined and determined by the model in a way hardly justifying their use for forecasting purposes, per capita disposable income is by itself an insufficient indicator of the province's progress and hence is an inadequate target variable. Actually, "living standards" are in-creasingly measured not only by the size of the per capita disposable income but also by the volume of intangible goods supplied to the inhabitants; hence this submodel represents an admittedly crude attempt at measuring some of these values. Far greater importance has to be attached to the traditional variables — namely, per capita income and per capita income in agriculture, which are both highly sensitive to developments taking place in the regional economy and are powerful indications of its progress. They are introduced as ratios because of the aggregate structure of the model. Table 7–8 illustrates the resulting system.

The system consists of five endogenous variables that are defined for the first time, six predetermined variables, and four previously explained endogenous variables which can, consequently, be treated here as predetermined. It is diagonally recursive and strongly related to several other submodels — namely,

Table 7-8
Welfare Submodel

Equation Number	Endogenous Variables					Endogenous Variables Explained in Other Submodels			
(S.30)	q_e								
(S.31)		q_v							
(D.16)			q_H			P			
(D.17)				$\bar{y}_{DP}$		P	Y_{DP}		
(D.18)					$\bar{y}_A$	P		W	F_a

Predetermined Variables				
GI_{ED}				Education
	GI_v			Health
		NH		Housing
				Per capita income
		F^G	F^{nr} P_u	Per capita income in agriculture

households, population and migrations, and governments and trade deficit. The causal chain of this submodel in its final version is illustrated in Figure 7-7.

5 Quality of Data and Estimating Procedures

One of the more important aspects of constructing a model is the confrontation of the various hypotheses embodied in the model with actual data. In a very real sense, a model, no matter how careful the construction of the various structural relationships and how elaborate and sophisticated the estimating techniques, cannot be better than the data basis upon which it is built.

In this respect, considerable difficulties exist at the regional level that are not encountered or no longer exist with national models. Many types of data, particularly those relating to interregional flows, are not collected at the subnational level. In some cases the conceptual basis for many flows is lacking or controversial. Furthermore, not only are published data for provinces far less abundant but they do not go back beyond 1951-1952, and for many series, end in 1963. With very few exceptions, the Dominion Bureau of Statistics has so far released only preliminary data for later years. Another source of considerable difficulties is the use of nondisclosure rules. For obvious reasons, these operate in a much more stringent manner in a small region than in the nation.

In view of the general paucity and lack of reliability of data collected at the

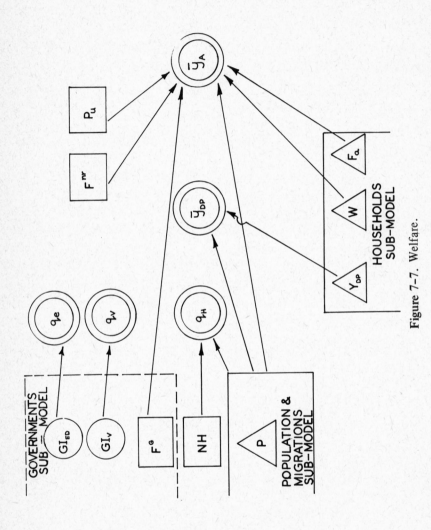

Figure 7-7. Welfare.

regional level, regional social accounts assume great importance. The discipline imposed by the double-entry system of social accounting goes a long way toward removing some of the inherent weaknesses of regional data, while helping in other places to fill in some remaining gaps. Unfortunately, regional income and product accounts would have to be constructed according to a format designed to meet regional needs, and more particularly, the needs of an econometric model. In Nova Scotia, such studies were initiated at the Institute of Public Affairs, but at the time of writing, an essentially unsuitable format, closely following the DBS format for National Income and Expenditure Accounts, had to be used. The problem has been discussed already in Chapter 3 but, moreover, the numerical results of the study referred to above were not available at the time of calibrating the model and rather crude estimates had to be used.

There is another aspect of the data problem that may be worth mentioning here. Regional economic studies and regional models are concerned almost exclusively with long-run growth and consequently with breaks and shifts in regional structure. These structural breaks can hardly be derived and estimated on the basis of a study of past developments in the region considered. There is, for example, no way in which the future impact of a new industry can be estimated from the study of past developments in a region from which this particular industry was absent. Hence, interregional data or, generally speaking, cross-sectional data assume great importance. Such data are ordinarily not available. They could be derived only from a fairly uniform system of regional social accounting operating throughout the nation.

The above view stands in marked contrast with practices followed in the construction of national econometric models where time series data are considered to be more relevant for analytic and forecasting purposes. However, national models dealing with business cycles are often based on quarterly or monthly data and consequently on fairly long series. Yearly time series data are often claimed to have a smaller variance than cross-section data, but this advantage is ordinarily more than compensated for by the larger sample size of the latter.

Finally, at the regional level one is very often concerned with stock rather than with flow phenomena; hence wealth accounting and the quantitative evaluation of both tangible and intangible regional resources would be of fundamental importance for the construction of meaningful regional growth models. Again, such data do not exist, while the whole problem of wealth accounting, even at the national level, is still beset with many conceptual difficulties. In Nova Scotia this difficulty may be relieved, to a certain extent, by a pioneering effort which resulted in a system of regional wealth accounts discussed in Chapter 6.

The lack of cross-section data and the shortness of time series available have imposed the use of simple estimating techniques and of simple equation forms. In the majority of cases the time series used have been limited to fifteen years, which has often been the length of the shortest series among several variables involved in each equation.

The data basis upon which the model described here has been estimated can be divided into several major categories:

(1) Data taken directly from published sources,
(2) Data derived indirectly by means of relatively simple techniques,
(3) Indexes constructed by means of several techniques, and
(4) Data obtained from field surveys.

Data taken directly from published sources supplemented by data derived by interpolation in order to maintain temporal consistency represent approximately forty percent of all data used. The major part of these data have been obtained from several Dominion Bureau of Statistics publications, such as *National Accounts, Income and Expenditures, Private and Public Investments in Canada, Vital Statistics,* and *Statistics on Employment and Unemployment.*

The second category, data derived indirectly, covers variables estimated as a ratio to a national total. In some cases fixed ratios were used while in others the ratio was extrapolated; in still other cases proxy allocators were used.

Data covering survival rates, fertility rates, age and sex structure of local and migrating populations derived from a study of vital statistics, and population studies also fall into this category. Data on foreign trade were obtained with the help of the technique based upon the modified location quotients approach. [12]

This third category comprises indexes computed from original data by using the technique of principal components described in some detail in Appendix J. This category includes such variables as index of health standards (q_v) and index of regional attractiveness (Z_1). Other techniques applied in order to derive indexes were accessibility studies, closely related to gravity and potential models.

The fourth and last category, data specially collected by means of field surveys, covers very few items. It is essentially limited to data pertaining to various components of government expenditures and investments in the province.

The inability to use simultaneous equations estimating procedures because of data limitations has imposed a severe constraint upon the system developed. The model of Nova Scotia is a diagonally recursive one, and hence nothing more sophisticated than ordinary least squares applied to structural equations yields consistent and unbiased estimates of the parameters. With all dependent variables on the main diagonal of a triangular matrix of endogenous variables, ordinary least squares applied to the structural equation should yield very similar results to those obtained by the use of indirect least squares.[r]

The multiple regression program yielded the usual statistics of which the following were used:

---

[r]The regressions were run on the Dalhousie University computer, IBM 360/65.

$$R^2 = \frac{b_1 \Sigma(X_1 Y) + b_2 \Sigma(X_2 Y) + \ldots \ldots b_i \Sigma(X_i Y)}{\Sigma_Y^2} ;$$

t, or Student's t, which may be defined as

$$t = \frac{r}{s_r} ,$$

where

r = coefficient of partial correlation, and

s_r = standard error of r, or

$$s_r = \frac{1 - r^2}{n - 2} ;$$

The t values are given in parentheses under each regression coefficient. Typically, most of the regressions had 10-12 degrees of freedom. Hence, at 5 percent level of significance the regression coefficients for which the t values exceeded 2.228, 2.201, and 2.179 (for 10, 11, and 12 degrees of freedom respectively) may be considered significant.

$$d = \frac{\displaystyle\sum_{t-2}^{n} (u_t - u_{t-1})^2}{\displaystyle\sum_{t=1}^{n} u_t^2} ;$$

This statistic defines the degree of autocorrelation existing in the residuals. A value of the statistic above 2.0 corresponds to a random distribution of residuals; a lower value indicates autocorrelation, which may be caused by the existence of an implied variable affecting the relationship. In most cases in which the bias introduced by autocorrelation of residuals has been detected, it could be removed by the use of the autoregressive model developed by Cochrane-Orcutt. This procedure involves an iterative process which operates as follows: [13]

First the equation in question, say of the form

$$Y_t = a + bX_t + u_t ;$$

is estimated using row data — that is, as if the disturbances were serially independent. Next, the residuals are computed, presumably yielding

$\rho(y_t, u_{t-1}) \neq 0;$

which corresponds to

$d \leqslant 2.0;$

After computing the autoregression coefficient of the series u_t according to

$u_t = \alpha u_{t-1} + \epsilon_t \; ;$

the computed value of α is used to transform each variable to a new series whose current value is the current value of the original data minus α times the lagged value.

$$(Y_t - \alpha Y_{t-1}) = (1 - \alpha)a + b(X_t - \alpha X_{t-1}) \; ;$$

This is the end of the first iteration. The residuals are again computed and a test carried out on these residuals to establish whether they are autocorrelated. If they are, the process is repeated. Ordinarily the process converges rather rapidly until the coefficient of autocorrelation ρ vanishes. Otherwise, in the program used, the process was stopped after twenty iterations. The value of the last ρ, or coefficient of serial correlation of residuals, is given in all those cases in which the model has been used.

6 Simulation Experiments

The purpose of simulation experiments is to test the behavior of the model, its stability and forecasting ability.[s] The tests allow conclusions to be drawn concerning specific parts of the model and thus point out the areas that may require further analysis.

The model of Nova Scotia has been tested with the help of a program developed at the University of Pennsylvania, which uses the structural rather than the reduced form of the model. Consequently, no inversions of matrices of co-efficients are required and it can be used to solve systems of equations that may or may not be linear. Three types of simulation tests were performed on the model of Nova Scotia:

(1) Sensitivity analysis,

---

[s]The term stability as used here is defined to mean that no stimulus can produce an unbounded response. More technically, stability refers to a stable state of solution of differential and, in the present case, difference equations involved in the model.

(2) Yearly solutions, and
(3) Forecasts.

The sensitivity analysis consisted of repeatedly solving the model for 1961, increasing one of the exogenous variables by one hundred percent in each run. After each run the effects on all endogenous variables were noted and analyzed. In order to evaluate the voluminous results of these tests, they were grouped according to certain key problems.

The first to be explored has been the study of relationships between the target variables and instrument variables. They are grouped in Table 7-9, which includes some other closely related variables. An examination of this table leads to some interesting conclusions. The target variables are scarcely affected by the main instrument variables representing various types of government spending. Of the eight instrument variables only defense spending seems to affect significantly several of the target variables.

This negative and rather surprising result may be due to defects of the model. Yet another explanation offers itself: the values of the instrument variables during the period under study have been insignificantly small. This would mean that the tools currently at the disposal of the government of Nova Scotia are altogether insufficient for influencing the target variables and bringing about a major change.

Target variables, especially GRP and the related variables defining per capita disposable income, per capita disposable income in agriculture, and total employment, are significantly affected by a number of other variables, of which the degree of urbanization (P_u) is by far the most important. The performance of the latter variable revealed by the tests points to an interesting and quite unexpected feature of the model. A one hundred percent change in the degree of urbanization influences almost every aspect of the regional economy. Besides the more obvious, although surprising strong changes generated in the level of commercial services, in investments in housing, and in other investments, such diverse elements as consumption level (both of goods and services), imports, balance of payments with the rest of the world, savings, various tax revenues, current government spending, and the wage bill are affected. This otherwise plausible result is the more surprising because the model was not designed to test the effects of economics of urbanization.

The effects upon the economy of a second group of variables, those connected with agriculture, are revealed by the sensitivity tests. This group comprises variables defining the number of commercial farms as a proportion of all farms and changes in the amount of cultivated land. As might be expected, the variables relating directly to agriculture, such as employment in agriculture, net income of unincorporated farm enterprises, and per capita disposable income of agricultural population, are those most strongly affected.

An interesting role is played by the variable describing the price level in

Table 7-9
Sensitivity Tests: Targets and Instruments

Instruments				Targets							
	GRP	$\bar{y}_{DP}$	$\bar{y}_A$	E	M	q_E	q_v	q_H	X_{CS}	I_{CS}	F_s
DF_3	21.9	13.3	10.5	16.9	20.2						16.6
GS_H											
GI_G											
GI_{ED}						10.3					
GI_v							10.8				
GS_A											
GS_m											
GD											
Date											
X_A	6.2	2.8	3.0								
A_L		2.3	39.9								
FZ		1.5	26.4	11.7							
F^G		14.8	7.3								
F^{nr}		2.4	4.4								
X_L	4.9	2.2	2.4						416.8	239.2	181.5
P_u	166.4	84.1	72.0	77.2							
$\bar{w}NS$	18.5	8.4	9.0								
$\bar{p}NS$		38.1	35.4								54.2
NH	15.8						100.8				

Intermediate

w	E_1	F_a	I_H	I	i_p	S	GS_c	T_c	T	T_{IN}	m
			56.0	18.8		69.3	-7.7	11.4	15.3	16.0	
			55.8	18.8			-7.8				2.0
							-11.1				
							-4.0				
							-.5				
							-.4				
							-1.0				
							100.6				
4.7			15.8	5.3		14.7	3.5	3.2	3.2	3.4	2.3
		164.1				12.0	2.2		2.7	2.8	1.4
	92.0	108.3				7.9	1.5		1.8	1.8	.9
						76.7	-35.7		17.0	17.7	8.9
3.7			12.4	4.2		12.2	2.3		2.7	2.8	1.4
113.5			425.2	250.0		11.5	2.8	2.5	2.6	2.7	4.4
14.1			47.3	15.9		219.6	101.6	86.6	96.7	100.8	77.3
55.6						43.4	10.5	9.6	9.6	10.0	6.7
						197.4	42.6		43.8	45.6	22.8
					184.4	66.5	15.1		18.2	18.9	9.5

Nova Scotia. This variable affects such diverse components of the regional economy as per capita disposable income in money terms, total wage bill, income of unincorporated enterprises, consumption, savings, tax revenues, and current government spending.

As expected, interesting results are produced upon housing standards and rental income of persons (an important component of i_p) by new housing construction. Less obvious results, although reasonable, are revealed by a drop in savings and increases in indirect taxes, current government expenditures, and several other variables.

The second problem examined has been the degree of interaction between the national and the regional economy as revealed by the model. This interaction is illustrated in Table 7-10.

More specifically, the table explores the effects upon Nova Scotia of the five variables pertaining to the national economy. Their influence is on the whole almost negligible. Gross National Product (GNP) affects only exports of mining and manufacturing products and the balance of the regional economy with the rest of the world. Changes in the rate of interest affect several variables, but the direction of those changes seems to imply that the correlations are spurious.

Changes in the level of prices of manufacturing products in Canada affect both exports of Nova Scotia manufactured products and the balance of the region with the rest of the world. The remaining two variables (namely, personal income in Canada and total direct taxes in Canada) affect several variables to a rather significant and expected extent while their relatively large effect on direct taxes and the tax rates is of lesser interest. Exports of services including the tourist industry did not seem to affect significantly the economy during the study period. It is difficult to establish without further analysis whether this result is due primarily to the construction of the model and to the insufficient weight given to the export sector or whether it simply reflects the fact that a relatively unproductive regional economy depending upon government spending and unilateral transfers does not respond strongly to changes in the national economy. Partial evidence from correlation analysis seems to validate the second argument.

On the whole, sensitivity tests reveal that the regional economy is sensitive to quite a number of variables, among which the following are worth mentioning: I_{IS}, $\bar{w}^{NS}$, X_A, X_L, $\bar{p}^{NS}$, F^G, F^{nr}, T_s. The model appears perhaps oversensitive to such variables as A_I and FZ. These results may be due on the one hand to the fact that the model is relatively open, with many exogenous variables. This characteristic would ordinarily dampen sensitivity. Similarly, the recursiveness of the system and the almost complete lack of lagged relationships should produce a similar outcome, limiting the effects of changes in many exogenous variables beyond the equations in which they are directly involved. [14]

The second type of test consisted in finding yearly solutions from the 1954 base for all years between 1954 and 1961. The solutions have been found over

Table 7-10
Sensitivity Tests: External Forces

External Forces	Affected Variables									Variables Affected to a Limited Extent
	e_L	e_m	m	BRW	I_{CS}	I	$\bar{y}_{DP}$	T	tr	
GNP	23.6	87.4		-51.3						
i			2.0	-22.0	42.6	19.0				
$\bar{p}_m^C$		150.1		-75.0						
Y_β^C			.9	8.4			1.5	33.0	-50.0	$C_1, C_4, C_5, T_{IN}, GS_c, S$
T^C			1.8	-16.8			-3.0	66.0	100.0	$C_1, C_4, C_5, T_{IN}, GS_c, S$

the estimation period and compared with actual values from the data listing. For each run, the actual values of all exogenous variables and of lagged endogenous variables are used.

Figure 7-8 illustrates the results for 1961. [15] It clearly shows that the vast majority of endogenous variables are estimated with an error under ten percent and most of them with an error less than five percent. Occasionally, however, one or two variables show very large deviations from actual values.

The third type of test explores the forecast values of endogenous variables. Forecasts differ from the yearly solutions in that beyond the first year the input values of lagged endogenous variables are generated by the model itself. This test therefore is a projection of the model from 1954 to 1961 using only the series for the exogenous variables. The time path of the key variables has been compared to that of actual values. This test gives some idea of the validity of results generated by the model for forecasting and policy purposes. If the series of endogenous variables generated by the model diverge from their actual values, or if errors tend to cumulate, the validity of the forecast will decrease with time. The forecast might also give an idea of admissible forecasting horizons – that is, of the time period during which the actual and forecasted values of endogenous variables do not diverge significantly.

On the whole, the tests carried out show satisfactory results. Figure 7-9 illustrates the distribution of percentage deviations between the actual and forecast values for 1961. [16]

Again, wide deviation from actual values is relatively rare; yet it should not be overlooked that both types of results have been obtained strictly within the sampling range.

Next, the results of both yearly solutions and forecasts have been plotted. The values for some of the more significant variables are shown in Figure 7-10.

The calculated values of Gross Regional Product, personal disposable income, total investments, investments in housing, and investments in manufacturing follow the actual values rather closely. As might be expected with the passage of time, forecasting values deviate more and more from the actual ones, but after seven years the accumulated errors are still within reasonable limits. Generally speaking, the first three variables perform better than investments in housing and in manufacturing.

Analysis of employment, migrations, wages, and total population seems to indicate that the model tends to overestimate total employment, although by a very small percentage. Nonetheless, the effects of employment changes are very strong on equation (S.29), which is highly sensitive to even small changes in the volume of surplus labor. As a consequence, migrations are rather poorly predicted. Moreover, the actual values are unreliable and show sudden changes in the direction of migrations throughout the study period. Population is nonetheless predicted quite well because migrations are small compared to total population. Total wages are persistently overestimated but only by a small percentage.

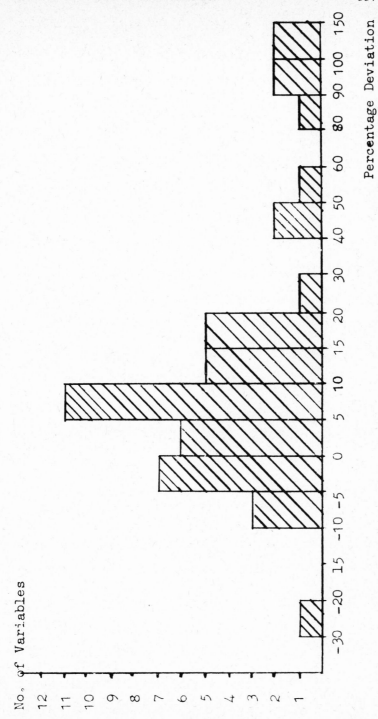

Figure 7-8. Distribution of Deviations between Yearly and Actual Values, 1961.

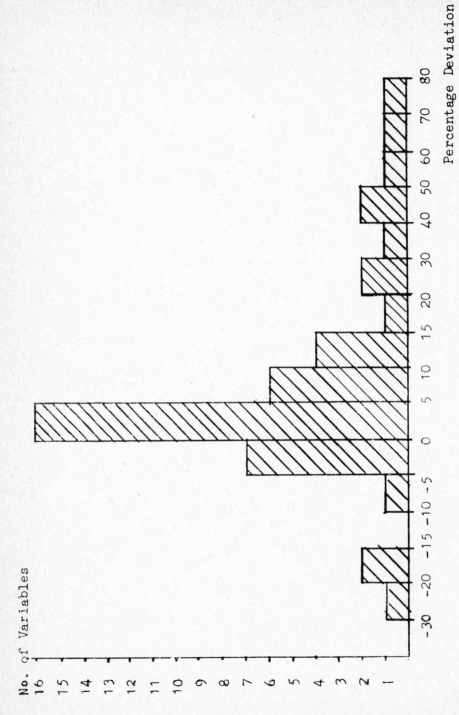

Figure 7-9. Distribution of Deviations between Forecast and Actual Values, 1961.

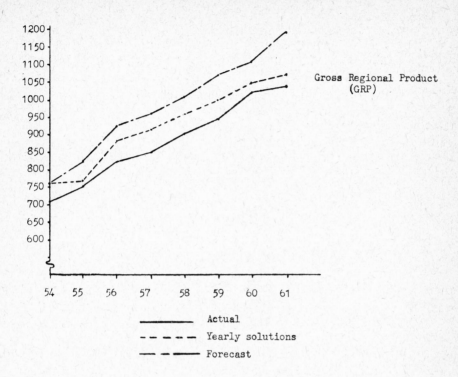

Gross Regional Product
(GRP)

———— Actual

– – – – – Yearly solutions

—– —– Forecast

Total personal disposable income (Y_{DP})

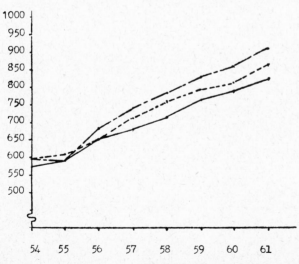

Figure 7-10. Simulation Results.

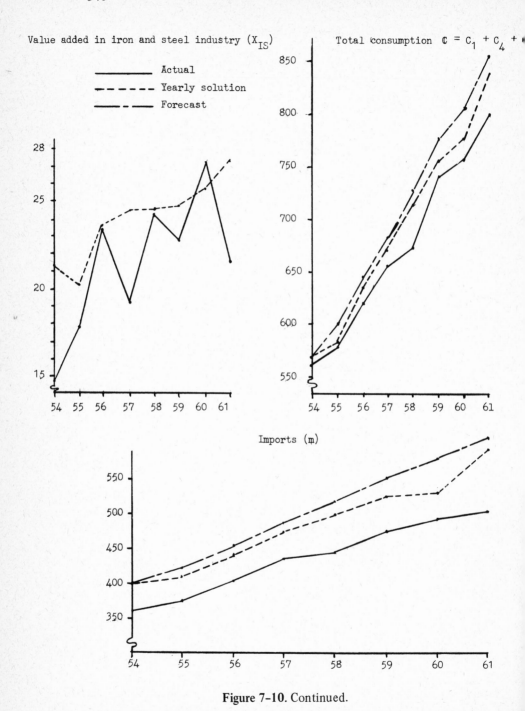

Figure 7–10. Continued.

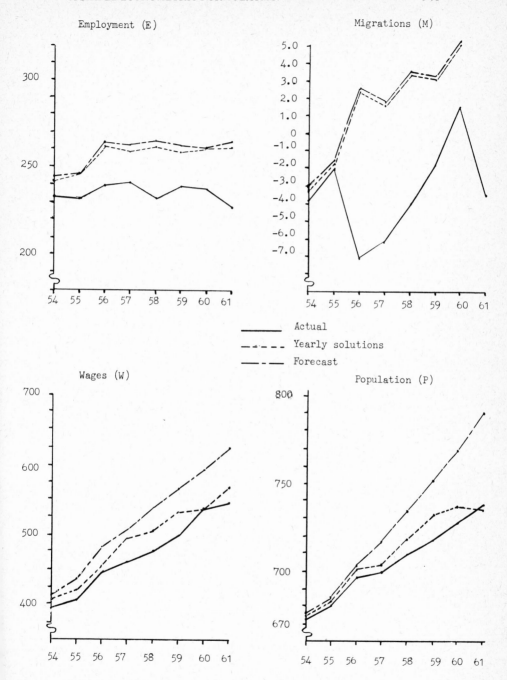

Figure 7–10. Continued.

Investment (I)

Investment in Housing (I_H)

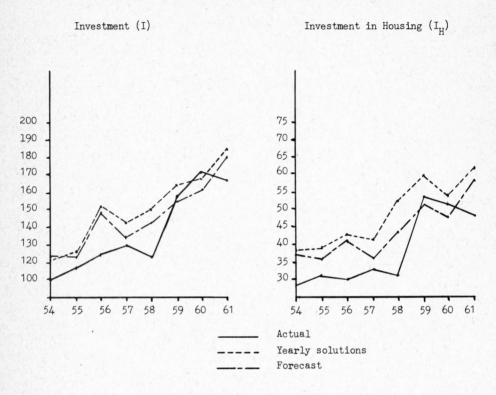

Actual

Yearly solutions

Forecast

Investment in Manufacturing (I_m)

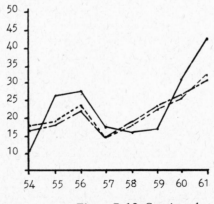

Figure 7–10. Continued.

A few variables can hardly be expected to yield reasonable forecasts by means of a model based on time series data. The reason is clearly due to the inconsistent behavior of the actual data. For example, the sudden changes in value added in iron and steel product (X_{IS}) are hardly due to economic forces and cannot be forecast with the help of the model. As a whole, the simulation tests were favorable. They seem to indicate that within the data limitations the model produces reasonable results.

7 Applications

During the latter part of 1968 and early 1969, the model was intensively used by the Nova Scotia Voluntary Planning Board [17] in connection with work then underway on a long-run development plan for the province. Unfortunately, the planning operation was soon thereafter transferred to other agencies and the plan itself was never completed. Moreover, under the pressure of circumstances, some of the experiments performed with the help of the model were carried beyond the scope of phenomena for which it was designed and as a result proved inconclusive. Nonetheless, the experience is of interest as a case study exploring the methodology of regional planning and probing into the applicability and potential uses for this purpose of aggregate econometric models.

The planning horizon for the long-run development plan was set for 1986, and for the first stage, for 1974. The first stage was to be worked out in much greater detail, including a study of financial resources available, and used as a check on the feasibility of the long-run plan. The scope of the regional development plan for Nova Scotia can be succinctly indicated by enumerating the planning elements, the coordination of which formed the essence of the operation, conveniently grouped as follows:

(1) Basic indicators, among which the Gross Regional Product, rate of growth of the Gross Regional Product, net regional product, regional income, personal income, personal disposable income, personal disposable income in agriculture, consumption of commodities, consumption of services, and personal savings were the most important.
(2) Output and employment measured by value of shipments, value added, employment, productivity, total and average wages, and investments, all disaggregated by some twelve to fifteen industries. Total output, value added, employment, and wages were also to be projected by major sub-areas, especially for the Halifax-Dartmouth Metro area, in order to test the compatibility of the general plan with the development of growth points and to ensure some measure of spatial coordination.
(3) Population and labor force, comprised of projections of population by five-

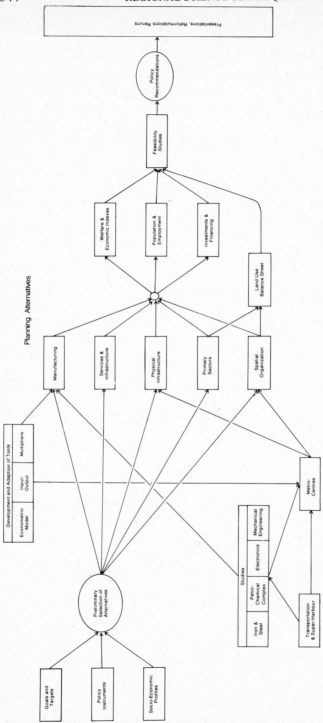

Figure 7-11. Elements of Long-Run Development Plan.

year age-sex cohorts, migrations, labor force, value of human resources, and employment cross-classified by industries and by trades.

(4) Physical infrastructure, involving the consideration of such elements as water supply balance sheets, power needs, and recreation areas, broken down by sub-areas, with estimates of investment outlays required for their develop. ment.

(5) Socioeconomic infrastructure, including housing, retail facilities and centers, education facilities by type and level (students, teachers, classrooms, expenditures, investments), and health and welfare (doctors, clinics, hospital beds, pharmacies, expenditures, investments).

(6) Spatial organization, based on land use balance sheet and covering agriculture and forestry, distribution of population and of productive facilities, transport flows, and investments.

(7) Summary of required investments and outlays by type and sub-area, sources of funds, and elements of government finances.

The planning process itself is best described with the help of the summary diagram presented in Figure 7-11. It covers some basic studies, planning and coordination of the main elements, feasibility studies, development of policy recommendations, and presentation of planning alternatives. Very few of the studies were in fact carried out, and no planning alternatives were developed. The role of the model was conceived to serve as a focal point for studies, data collecting, and planning operations. In the later stages it was to be used not only in order to uncover and quantify meaningful relationships but also, and perhaps primarily, to test the implications of various alternatives, revealing bottlenecks and inconsistencies.

Of the numerous experiments performed on the model, three sets of tests are of general interest because of the light they shed on the applicability and limitations inherent in aggregate econometric models, when used for regional planning.

The first set of experiments had analytic objectives, involving testing the ability of governments to affect regional development by increasing the volume and changing the distribution of public expenditures. In form, the experiments did not differ from sensitivity tests of the model, but instead of increasing the value of all input variables, one after another, by 100 percent, only the values of selected instrument variables were changed, some of them simultaneously, and by amounts considered realistic or interesting and not necessarily by 100 percent. These runs of the model were limited to the time period 1960–1964, for which actual data were available.

First, the effects of changes in total payments to military personnel (DF_s), which in 1964 amounted to $67.0 million, or 53.4 percent of all government expenditures, were explored. For this purpose the value of the variable was assumed to be successively increased by 10 percent or decreased by 10, 20, 30,

Table 7-11
Assumed Shifts in Selected Government Expenditures, 1964

Variable		Actual Value	Assumed Value	Percentage Change
DF_s	Defense spending	67.10	73.81	+10
GS_H	Government investments and subsidies to housing and commercial services	8.20	12.30	+50
GI_{ED}	Government investments in education	9.04	9.94	+10
GI_v	Government investments in health, welfare, and administration	6.10	18.30	+200
GS_A	Government subsidies and investments in agriculture, forestry, and fisheries	2.50	1.25	−50
Other government expenditures		32.75	32.75	−
Total		125.69	148.35	

40, 50, or 100 percent, with other instrument variables unchanged, and using actual data for all the remaining input variables. The results showed a noticeable impact of changes in military spending on several variables. For example, an assumed 10 percent cutback in payments to military personnel caused a decline in Gross Regional Product of 2.6 percent, in total employment of 1.9 percent, in investments in housing of 13.6 percent, in total investments of 2.4 percent, in total wage income of 2.0 percent, and in savings of 9.3 percent.

Next, total government expenditures in 1964 were assumed to have been increased from $125.69 to $148.35 million, with a shift in emphasis from rural programs to those strengthening the urban infrastructure. The specific changes assumed are indicated in Table 7-11. Furthermore, since some of the instrument variables affected other phenomena with lags, similar and compensating changes were assumed in government expenditures beginning in 1960. Especially, government subsidies to agriculture were assumed halved beginning 1960.

The net effect of these assumed changes on output variables measuring the performance of the regional economy was only slight, but the impact on welfare standards was pronounced. Table 7-12 indicates some of the more interesting results.

The final experiment in the first set purported to test the consequences of an assumed 30 percent cut in direct government investments, with partly compensating increases in direct subsidies to manufacturing, housing, and education. The results indicated, after a lag of up to four years, a 1 percent decline in GRP,

Table 7-12
Effects of Assumed Changes in Some Instrument Variables on Selected Output Variables, 1964

		Unit	Actual	Assuming Changes in Some Instrument Variables	
				Level	Percentage Change
GRP	Gross Regional Product	$ millions	1,154.604	1,172.877	+1.6
E	Total employment	thousands	237.4	241.6	+1.8
q_v	Index of health standards	$ millions	334.3	544.3	+62.9
I_m	Investments in manufacturing	$ millions	48.487	38.652	−20.3
X_m	Value added in manufacturing	$ millions	302.171	290.364	−3.9
I_H	Investment in housing	$ millions	32.059	41.387	+29.1
E_5	Government employment	thousands	32.5	37.0	+13.9
e_A	Exports of agricultural products	$ millions	81.9	62.2	−24.0
S	Total savings	$ millions	44.2	47.0	+6.3

3.8 percent decline in value added in manufacturing, 2.7 percent decline in net income of unincorporated manufacturing, 4.8 percent decline in investments, and 3.1 percent increase in investments in housing.

The second set of experiments attempted to explore the consequences of cutbacks in mining and iron and steel industries, which at that time appeared likely. More specifically, the four tests of which the set was comprised assumed a reduction in employment in mining from 7,200 to 2,000, a reduction in investments in mining from $11.1 million to zero, a reduction in employment in the iron and steel industry from 3,900 to zero, and a reduction in investments in the iron and steel industry from $1.4 million to zero. Since the tests were aimed at interrelations partly beyond the scope of those for which the model was originally designed, the impacts of the assumed changes were noticeable mainly in the sectors immediately affected. The spread of the effects to the economy as a whole was weak. These results bring to the fore some of the limitations of aggregate econometric models. Not only are they less efficient than input-output for impact studies, but with all their flexibility they cannot be used for testing phenomena for which they have not been designed. In the case of the mining and

Table 7-13
1974 Values of Selected Endogenous Variables

Variable		Using Simple Extrapolation of Exogenous Variables	Using Expert Advice and Improved Data for Some Exogenous Variables	Percentage Difference
K_{IS}	total capital invested in iron and steel industry	40.399	90.600	+124.3
X_{IS}	value added in iron and steel industry	34.074	66.689	+95.7
Q_{IS}	value of shipments of iron and steel	84.845	166.056	+95.7
e_{IS}	export of iron and steel	83.555	163.532	+95.7
E_1	employment in agriculture, forestry and fisheries	26.506	39.590	+49.4
E	total employment	296.884	308.968	+4.1
GRP	gross regional product	2,257.618	2,304.632	+2.1
W	total wage income	1,163.946	1,182.663	+1.6
F_a	net income of farm operators	2.883	11.734	+307.0
$\bar{y}_p$	per capita personal income	1,714.041	1,740.626	+1.6
S	personal net savings	145.745	152.897	+4.9
m	total imports	1,129.147	1,150.141	+1.9

iron and steel industries, moreover, employment was in the past determined to a large extent by political considerations and was not related to levels of output or investments.

The third set of experiments consisted of forecasting with the help of the model future levels of output variables. By manipulating the values of input variables the planners estimated the future consequences of various government policy measures. The 1974 time horizon of the first stage of the development plan was applied. As a preliminary step the future values of exogenous variables other than government expenditures had to be obtained. Most were derived by a straight line extrapolation of past values, except for a few key variables, the future levels of which were based on expert advice. For the more significant input variables, the future values shown in the accompanying table were used. Moreover, on the basis of more up-to-date information, new extrapolations were made of such variables as commercial farms as a proportion of all frams (FZ), value added in agriculture, forestry, and fisheries (X_Z), and amount of cultivated land (A_L). As a consequence, the results of this set of tests were not directly comparable

| Year | Investments in Iron and Steel | | Employment in Iron and Steel | | Employment in Mining | |
| | Extrapolation | Expert Advice | Extrapolation | Expert Advice | Extrapolation | Expert Advice |
	($ millions)		('000)		('000)	
1966	–	–	3.5	3.6	6.7	6.4
1967	–	–	3.5	3.4	6.3	5.7
1968	1.2	1.5	3.4	3.3	5.9	5.0
1969	1.1	5.0	3.3	3.1	5.5	4.3
1970	1.0	15.0	3.3	3.0	5.1	3.6
1971	0.9	10.0	3.2	3.0	4.7	2.9
1972	0.8	10.0	3.1	3.0	4.3	2.6
1973	0.7	10.0	3.1	3.0	3.8	2.4
1974	0.6	5.0	3.0	3.0	3.4	2.4

with the previous ones, but only rarely did noticeable (in a few cases large) differences result. Table 7-13 lists output variables showing significant changes.

Marked improvements resulted only in variables pertaining to sectors directly related to variables whose future values were assumed on the basis of expert advice. These were again mostly sectors for which estimates of parameters based on past trends were few and whose links with the rest of the economy proved to be surprisingly weak. The total level of government investments implicit in the results of this run of the model was as follows:

1965	$150.61 million
1966	$158.13 million
1967	$165.82 million
1968	$173.42 million
1969	$181.21 million
1970	$188.78 million
1971	$196.48 million
1972	$204.27 million
1973	$211.86 million
1974	$219.55 million

Next, several tests were performed, with the level of total government investments manipulated by increasing it uniformly in each year following 1965 to $200 million, $250 million, $300 million, and $400 million. The distribution of total government expenditures was the same in each case and provided for the following percentage share of various outlays:

| Payments to military personnel | 48% |
| Direct general government investments | 16% |

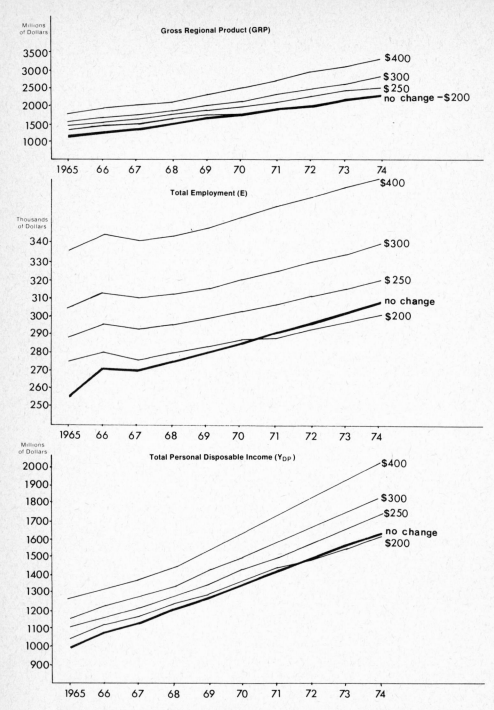

Figure 7-12. Impact of Assumed Levels of Government Investments upon Selected Economic Indicators.

350

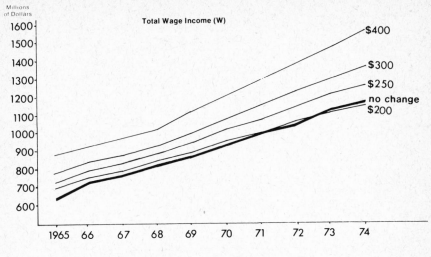

Figure 7-12. Continued

Government subsidies to housing and commercial services	12%
Government investments in education and training	10%
Government subsidies to manufacturing	10%
Government investments in health, welfare, and administration	3%
Government subsidies to agriculture, forestry, and fisheries	1%
	100%

The results of these tests and their impact on key variables measuring the progress of the regional economy are graphically represented in Figures 7-12 and 7-13.

The results of assumed increases in the level of government expenditures but not in their distribution affected most directly and almost uniformly such key indicators as GRP, total employment, total wages, and total personal disposable income. Their impact upon total investments, investments in housing, and manufacturing was far more dramatic. The sharp upward breaks and discontinuities were bound to affect the regional economy profoundly, but because of the time lags involved, the impact would have been most noticeable after 1974, the last year of these tests.

The model, as well as its use in the planning process, raises a number of questions, mainly of a methodological nature. Their discussion, however, forms part of the general evaluation of the effectiveness of the various tools of regional analysis and is best deferred to the following chapter.

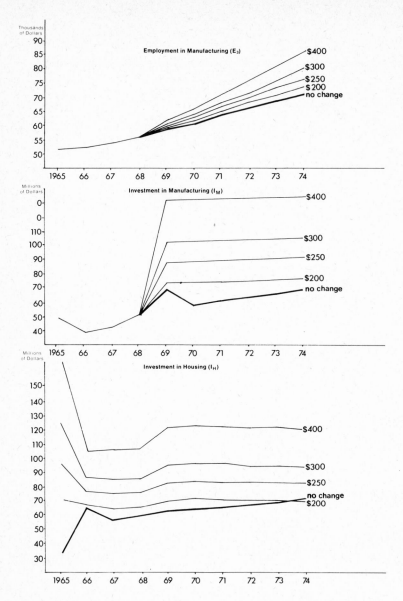

Figure 7-13. Impact of Assumed Levels of Government Investments upon Selected Variables.

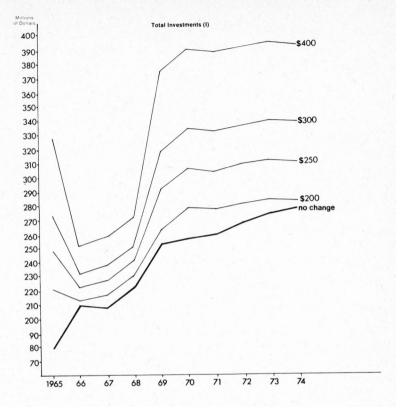

Figure 7-13. Continued.

8 Conclusions

In the analyses presented in the preceding chapters the economy of Nova Scotia, viewed as a system providing livelihood to 750,000 inhabitants of the province, has been examined from several complementary points of view. The conclusions that may be drawn from the study clearly fall into several distinct categories. There are, to begin with, new insights concerning the present state of the local economy with substantial changes in emphasis and in the assessment of the relative importance of various issues and problems confronting it. Next, the various studies shed light upon and enabled a systematic evaluation of past and present regional policies followed in Nova Scotia, indicating areas where the findings might have warranted different decisions from those actually reached. Finally, and perhaps most important, the work carried out in Nova Scotia provided an opportunity to assess the validity and relative efficiency of the various methods of analysis used by regional scientists. It brought to the fore their strengths and weaknesses, areas of inquiry where their judicious use yields interesting results and others where it is more problematic.

Nova Scotia is the product of a more distant historical past than other, more prosperous, parts of Canada. Technological changes, shifting locational preferences of industries and, above all, the opening up of the rich interior of the North American continent have deprived the Atlantic seaboard of much of its former vitality. Failure to adjust to the new realities left the province in its present depressed state. Its location does not confer it many of the once important advantages as a port of entry of the country while its endowment in natural resources is niggardly in comparison with the rest of the country. The human resources of Nova Scotia, depleted by continued outmigration, do not compare favorably in terms of quality with the industrialized parts of Canada. As a corollary of relative unattractiveness to investors, the volume of capital invested in Nova Scotia per capita or even per employee is comparatively small, especially in manufacturing, while the figures of per capita output and income are significantly below the national averages. Another disquieting fact clearly emerging from the analysis of income and product accounts is the heavy reliance of the province on federal spending, which seems indispensable in order to maintain even the present comparatively low living standards. Among other, less significant and not so obvious, facets of the local economy revealed by the various studies is its relative immunity from business cycles, probably also due to the role that federal welfare and transfer payments play in the provincial economy and to their

355

strong anticyclical effects. Wartime conditions, on the other hand, stimulate the Nova Scotia economy far more than other parts of the country, no doubt because of the sheer size of its defense establishment and of its strategic location. Yet, despite the role that defense plays in its economy and the importance of government spending, a highly significant finding was that the number and scale of the instrument variables used so far by both federal and provincial governments has been far too small to have an appreciable impact, let alone to bring about major changes. Recent efforts on the part of the federal government and especially projects now being contemplated, forming part of a national policy of eliminating interregional inequalities, which in Canada loom larger than in most advanced countries, [1] are of an altogether different order of magnitude.

A careful examination with the help of rigorous tools of the historical record and of more recent measures taken to stimulate the Nova Scotian economy leads to a number of interesting conclusions. The studies provide ample additional support for the decision already taken to phase out the coal mining operations on Cape Breton Island. They seem, however, also to indicate that much less reliance should be placed on most other extractive industries, perhaps even on all. Aside from sociopolitical considerations, agriculture, fishing, and forestry, along with mining, do not hold out any hope of ever again becoming important factors in Nova Scotian progress. While fishing and fish processing, forest-based industries, and some specialty types of agriculture may provide welcome additions to the regional economy, the amount of effort and attention that they command appears out of proportion to their real importance. The intrinsic value of the natural base of almost all extractive industries is severely limited, compared to the wealth of other parts of the country.

Considerably more doubtful, in the light of the studies reported, are persistent, relatively substantial investments in infrastructure, both technical and institutional, combined with indirect support to scattered manufacturing plants. The policy seems to be predicated on two different but complementary ideas. It is considered that a small, relatively remote economy may be capable of attracting investments if possessed of comprehensive ancillary facilities. Their provision, supplemented by direct, in several instances heavy, assistance to any industries willing to start operations in the province appears as the main and proper role for government action. The attitude, losing apparently some ground recently, is politically attractive since it avoids frictions with the local business community and obviates the need to engage in elaborate studies of industrial structure and regional planning.

At the national level, investments in infrastructure in depressed regions or small urban centers are often viewed not only as means of promoting regional development but as measures designed, partly at least, to correct for misallocations caused by the presence of important externalities in most public utilities. According to this argument the average cost curve of providing urban services is convex downwards. (See accompanying graph.) There is general agreement as to

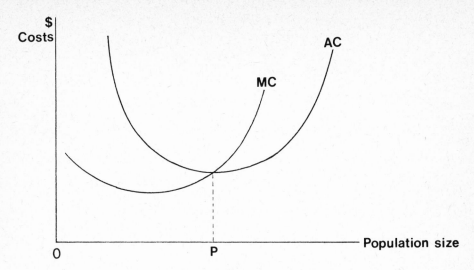

the shape of the curve, although its position has hardly been explored empirically. [2] Hence, the least costs would be incurred if population resided in cities of size P. In both larger and smaller cities the per capita costs are higher, since with increasing size average costs tend to decline up to a point and then advance again. Yet in most nations the population tends to be progressively more and more concentrated in large urban centers, because of economies of production realized in industrial agglomerations and because user charges rarely reflect the costs of providing services. Hence, government investments in, and subsidies to, public facilities in smaller centers partly eliminate social costs since they are financed largely by progressive taxation, with heavier incidence on the wealthier inhabitants of large metropolitan areas. That this falls far short of user charges proportional to costs, which alone could prevent misallocation of resources, goes without saying.

The apparent fallacy of the first argument is more significant. While the studies reported confirm the positive effects of improved facilities albeit with a lag of several years, their impact appears to be relatively weak, easily overshadowed by other considerations brought to the fore by industrial and inter-industry analyses. Not only do the existence, size, and character of previous industrial agglomerations constitute the major locational factor for many, especially small and medium sized plants, but one of the main obstacles to economic progress is the weakness of multiplier effects engendered by the small volume of interindustry flows within the province. Both considerations make it imperative to select carefully the type, size, and mix of industrial activities to be promoted with the help of limited public resources.[a]

---

[a]The selection of specific industries most suitable for Nova Scotia is complicated by a lack of generally agreed goals and objectives of regional development. For although to some the obvious manifestations of backwardness (abundantly illustrated by such standard indicators as per capita output, income, or consumption) loom large, others seem to value the quiet, relaxed way of life characteristic of the Maritime Provinces above the material

The choice of activities has to meet two often incompatible requirements: the short-run need for providing employment opportunities, and the long-run goal of developing an industrial base that will be self-sustaining and income producing. Both objectives have to be analyzed in terms of a number of criteria. The capital intensity and labor productivity have to be contrasted with inherent growth characteristics of various industries, allowing some preliminary screening of activities deserving promotion. The diagrams of Figure 8-1 illustrate the wide divergencies among industries. Diagrams (a) and (b) show value added/labor (V/L) and gross capital/labor (K/L) respectively, plotted against growth in employment $(\%\Delta L)$. Diagrams (c) and (d) show the same ratios plotted against growth in value added $(\%\Delta V)$. All variables refer to United States data, [3] thus presenting a wide diversity of technologically advanced industries.

The important feature of Figure 8-2 is the relative distribution of points compared to the average for all industries. Points to the right of the average have higher than average growth rates and points above it have higher than average K/L or V/L ratios. From a perusal of the figure it immediately becomes apparent why electrical products firms, for example, are highly sought after by depressed regions. The industry has a tremendous growth rate and a relatively low capital/labor ratio. Since in a growing industry one would expect many new plants to be established, such industry might be attracted with relative ease, while capital investments for such plants are not prohibitive. Moreover, since the industry is also growing rapidly in terms of value added, it tends to maintain high productivity. At the other extreme is the petroleum industry, which requires a capital investment of about $114,000 per employee as compared, for example, with $8,240 per employee in the food and beverage industry. In the light of these observations the deuterium oxide plant at Glace Bay with investments, mainly public, around $400,000 per employee appears as a wasteful luxury. These observations obviously provide only a starting point for in-depth studies of specific industries.

Other considerations relevant for the selection of industries are total employment, required training facilities and outlays, estimated wage levels, and distribution of income, especially the share of Nova Scotia residents. Next, the burden of investments required in the public sector, in infrastructure and services, and in direct subsidies or concessions to be granted to the industry have to be determined. Together the various indexes provide a basis for pursuing coordinated policies of attracting industries, although the problem of weights to be placed on various characteristics is far from solved. More importantly, many conclusions derived from existing studies have to be qualified and

---

affluence of other parts of the country. Unfortunately, the political processes at work do not produce any guidelines as to objectives toward which policy recommendations should be directed. What is indisputable is a set of general constraints, including institutional constraints, within which the selection will have to be made, and the matching of locational requirements of industries with the attributes of the region.

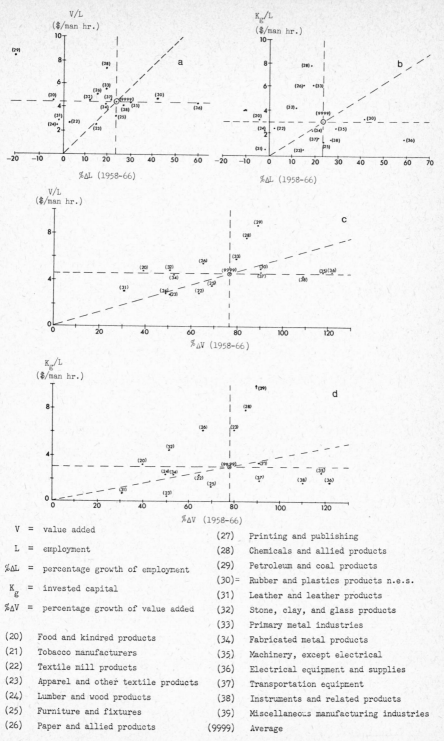

V = value added

L = employment

%ΔL = percentage growth of employment

K_g = invested capital

%ΔV = percentage growth of value added

(20) Food and kindred products
(21) Tobacco manufacturers
(22) Textile mill products
(23) Apparel and other textile products
(24) Lumber and wood products
(25) Furniture and fixtures
(26) Paper and allied products

(27) Printing and publishing
(28) Chemicals and allied products
(29) Petroleum and coal products
(30)= Rubber and plastics products n.e.s.
(31) Leather and leather products
(32) Stone, clay, and glass products
(33) Primary metal industries
(34) Fabricated metal products
(35) Machinery, except electrical
(36) Electrical equipment and supplies
(37) Transportation equipment
(38) Instruments and related products
(39) Miscellaneous manufacturing industries
(9999) Average

Figure 8-1. Growth Characteristics, Selected Industries.

await the results of more broadly based locational analyses that would escape the limitations imposed by our current inability to quantify the relative locational importance of many attributes and characteristics of regions.

But even promotion of a set of industries, carefully selected because of their advanced technology, growth prospects, or low capital/labor ratio, cannot be regarded as constituting a successful development effort. Several studies already alluded to suggest that the real difficulty in generating self-sustained growth in a depressed region is due to the feeble multiplier effects accompanying the introduction of new industries. Hence, a criterion of great, perhaps overriding, importance in selecting new industries to be accorded government subsidies should be the extent of their linkages with other activities. Unfortunately, in Nova Scotia a careful study of input-output accounts and the models and analyses based on them, reveals at best some very modest beginnings of a small-size food processing complex. [4] It appears, therefore, that the introduction of whole new complexes, unrelated to existing industries, might be more promising. At the very least, a self-contained complex would generate those economies of spatial juxtaposition and multiplier effects the lack of which is such an obstacle to progress. Fortunately, this view seems at last to be gaining some belated official recognition. [5] While the technique developed as part of the present set of studies for selecting a set of interrelated activities to be promoted appears valid, final conclusions have to await the results of a substantially expanded inquiry, explicitly including the effects of friction of space and exploring the inability of spatially split, or partial, industrial complexes. Such a model, now being designed and implemented, is broadly based on experiences of other economically more successful regions.

Considerations related to industrial complexes highlight the issue of the container harbor in Halifax. For despite the generally gloomy assessment of the regional resources and growth potential, some recent developments have brought to the fore the admittedly modest, yet tangible advantages and assets that Nova Scotia might put to good use in the future. The deep water endowment could become increasingly valuable in the age of superships. Although comparative experience is lacking, investments in container harbor facilities and the perspective of becoming the terminus of a land bridge might in the future generate effects similar to those once associated with break of bulk, and give rise to a host of related industrial activities. Whether the hopes attached to it are not excessive and what weight ought to be assigned to these new developments in promoting industrial activities is clearly a matter to be carefully explored in further studies.

The reliance to be placed on unbalanced growth and on manufacturing industries is related to the problem of growth poles and more generally of the organization of space. The simulation experiments performed on the econometric model of Nova Scotia vindicate, at least partly, the view that in order to achieve their maximum effects investments have to be spatially highly concentrated. The very strong, in some cases drastic, effects that hypothetical increases in urbanization exercise on most relevant indicators, along with some evidence that the minimum size of a viable growth pole in a relatively remote location cannot fall far short of half a million inhabitants, seem to preclude the possibility of having more than one such focal point in the province. The recent decision of federal authorities to encourage the growth both of Halifax and of the Canso area has to be seen in this light although it is clearly superior to the previously followed policy of encouraging growth in many nodes. The case of Canso, for reasons discussed already at length, appears dubious but, here again, some further studies are badly needed, not only because of the disastrous situation of the huge government-financed projects in the area but even more important because of the apparent locational mistakes committed.

Even aside from the now abandoned strategy of multiple growth poles the spatial policies advocated in the province foresee, besides the two major growth poles, a network of lesser centers judiciously distributed through the province, so as to facilitate the provision of a variety of services to the agricultural population and some other dispersed activities. The towns and urban-type concentrations associated with services might have to be supplemented by a number of resource centers formed by agglomerations of processing industries closely associated with extractive activities, but in most cases these two types of functions will merge in a single town fulfilling a dual role. Thus, in view of the feeble development of the nonurban part of Nova Scotia there is little reason to concur that two separate networks of centers are required.

The tools employed to reach the above conclusions can be classified in a number of ways, depending upon the criteria adopted. In terms of complexity they range from simple methods of organizing data to sophisticated models aimed at extracting useful insights from parsimonious information. The logical starting point of any intensive regional study is a set of social accounts. Income and product accounts, the most often applied of the five systems in use, represent little more than a systematic way of organizing and displaying basic flow statistics cast in a form general enough to enable testing of a number of hypotheses. To be useful, they must be capable of being compared with other numbers. Of the three types of comparisons generally relevant (over time, among various characteristics of the region under study and among parts of the region, and with other regions), the last one depends upon the existence in other provinces and regions of similar accounts. The various comparisons yield a set of direct ratios, indices, and multipliers revealing the leading problems faced by decision makers and planners.

Unfortunately, income and product accounts are not powerful tools for uncovering existing externalities, and generally say little about social benefits or costs. The whole area of social indicators requires further intensive study. The work in Nova Scotia seems also to indicate that the usual format of regional income and product accounts drawing heavily upon national practices is in many ways inadequate. Especially apparent is the need for further subdivision and regrouping of government accounts, so as to separate revenues and expenditures which can be manipulated as instrument variables from those depending for change upon considerations transcending the concern for a single region or altogether incapable of being manipulated by policy makers. Similarly, a sub-division of the households sector would be of great and immediate interest. Not only ought transactions pertaining to nonprofit organizations be separated, but households should be divided by such important characteristics as income level, or type of household.

Several other simple techniques were used in order either to define the leading issues or to provide some preliminary assessment of the regional econo-my. These include accessibility indexes, concentration curves, ratios, and coefficients, and an extensive cartographic analysis. Based on unprocessed, mainly published data, these preliminary analyses form, nonetheless, an indispensable foundation for further work. The logical next step involves a comparative cost-locational analysis study focusing on interregional comparisons and a shift-share analysis examining changes over time. Mathematically, both use a slightly modified analysis of variance approach.

A necessary complement of locational analysis, although hardly ever applied, is a set of wealth accounts. The pioneering effort carried out in Nova Scotia enabled a better assessment of the available natural, human, and man-made resources, and the hard choices facing the region of either abandoning intact but locationally obsolete assets or perpetuating an inefficient settlement pattern. Alas, it also brought into sharper focus a number of conceptual problems still besetting this form of social accounting and its limitations due to lack of compar-ative studies in other regions.

The need to analyze the relevant phenomena and to develop policy recom-mendations in disaggregated form requires the use of interindustry accounts, revealing a wealth of otherwise hardly quantifiable phenomena. Input-output data strongly suggest the weakness of intraprovincial flows and as a direct corol-lary the absence of strong multiplier effects. This in turn leads to the industrial complex approach to further development policy. The somewhat novel multi-variate technique developed for purposes of identifying the most promising regional groupings of industries proved to be fruitful, although requiring for its successful application a number of detailed regional input-output tables.

Finally, an econometric model of the regional economy has been formulated, estimated, and tested. The relative advantages and disadvantages of input-output and econometric stochastic models as used in regional studies are not easily weighed. The real choice is between a highly disaggregated but extremely simple model based on a set of rigid assumptions, and a sophisticated analytical tool. The great weakness of input-output and other simple multipliers is that there is almost nothing in these models to indicate a basic divergence between the par-ticular hypotheses upon which they are predicated and empirical facts. Input-output is really an especially simple version of linear programming and hence, like most programming models, is basically normative and fits better into the regional planning context, in addition to being operated at a highly disaggregated level. Econometric stochastic models, on the other hand, are especially suitable for revealing causal or functional relationships and confronting them with data.

Despite some obvious drawbacks, mainly related to the aggregate level at which such models operate, the lack of time series and, even more important, of cross-section data for many relevant variables, adapting the econometric technique developed for the study of national economies to the needs and realities of an open system such as Nova Scotia proved a promising approach. It involved reformulating some of the previously advanced hypotheses in more precise terms mandatory for a consistent econometric model. Potentially at least, such models should be capable of greater disaggregation. Their usefulness proved to be limited by the fact that without considerable reformulation they could not be used for testing new hypotheses for which they were not designed.

Another potentially powerful technique, linear programming, has been used in Nova Scotia, unfortunately only in the somewhat limited context of land uses and land values. This scarcely does justice to an analytic tool highly significant for planning purposes. But in Nova Scotia the planning goals and objectives have hardly ever been spelled out by the various government agencies involved. In fact, the numerous studies carried out over the past five years have been sponsored by a number of federal and provincial government departments, research foundations, and universities, with the investigating team and principal investigator as the main coordinating elements. This not uncommon dispersion of research and planning efforts underlines the fact that the judicious choice of the most appropriate tools of inquiry is a function not only of the scope and objectives of the study and of the availability of data and research resources, but also of the type of sponsoring agency and the degree to which its activities are coordinated over a sufficiently long span of time.

Appendix A: Estimation of Value of Nonresidential Land

Assessed values of nonresidential urban properties in Nova Scotia were derived from: Nova Scotia Department of Municipal Affairs, *Annual Report of Municipal Statistics for the Year 1961;* Hugh S. MacGlashen, "1961 Report of the Revaluation Commission for the Province of Nova Scotia," December 15, 1961 (mimeographed); and City of Halifax, Office of City Assessor, *Annual Report of the Assessment Department, 1961.*

Estimates for nonresidential urban land were generated by assuming that land values form a constant fraction of the value of structures. The value of some types of developed land was estimated with the help of the opportunity cost approach, although very often the alternative highest use approach yields an underestimate. In the case of park land, for example, it was assumed that the next best use for this acreage would be forested land, the value of which was used as the approximate acre-value of park land. Some nonproductive areas and most of North Cape Breton were assumed to have approximately half of the value per acre of forested land since these are basically wooded areas in poorly accessible locations. Waste land was assumed to be valueless.

The value of agricultural land was obtained from D.B.S., *1961 Census of Canada: Agriculture: Nova Scotia,* Catalogue No. 96–533, which gave value of land and buildings on farms in Nova Scotia for 1961, supplemented by a special farm survey taken three years earlier, which separated the value of land from other farm property. The latter was reported in D.B.S., *1958 Farm Survey Report No. 1: Expenditures, Receipts and Farm Capital,* Catalogue No. 21–506, Table 4, p. 22; and D.B.S., *1958 Farm Survey Report No. 2: Farm and Farm Family Income, Farm Expenditures and Resources in Canadian Agriculture,* Catalogue No. 21–509. The ratio of land value to total property value in 1958 was assumed to hold for 1961. The estimated 1961 land value of farmland was $31.3 million. From this total the value of farm woodlots, which were valued at $1.50 per acre, was subtracted, to get $29.3 million worth of agricultural land. This estimate was checked against the results of sample surveys and records of the Agricultural and Rural Development Administration and the Nova Scotia Farm Loan Board in Truro, N. S. Although the distribution of sample values was platykurtic, the mean at over $31 per acre provided an approximate check on the reported figure.

Appendix B

Estimated Quantity of Marine Life in Northwest Atlantic

	Estimate Early 1950's (Million lbs.)	Projection 1980 (Million lbs.)
Seafish		
Groundfish		
Cod	6,800	6,500
Cusk	30	30
Dogfish	–	–
Flatfish	500	400
Haddock	480	340
Hakes	300	260
Halibut	60	60
Pollock	200	160
Redfish	2,200	1,350
Skates	70	70
Pelagic and Estuarial		
Alewives	100	80
Eels	–	–
Herring	3,800	3,500
Mackerel	–	–
Salmon	10	20
Shad	8	7
Smelts	40	35
Swordfish	50	50
Tuna	–	–
Mollusca and Crustaceans		
Clams	30	28
Lobsters	73	67
Oysters	10	50
Scallops	225	180
Squid	–	–
Seaweeds		
Irish Moss	100	100
Marine Mammals		
Seals	3,000,000[a]	4,000,000[a]
Whales	–	–

[a]Number.

Compiled from data in *The Commercial Fisheries of Canada*, Royal Commission on Canada's Economic Prospects, Queen's Printer, 1957, pp. 18 and 23–25; D.B.S., *Fisheries Statistics – Nova Scotia*, 1964, Cat. No. 24–205, Table 1, pp. 7–8; and D.B.S., *Fisheries Statistics – Canada*, 1961, Cat. No. 24–201, Table 2, pp. 10–11.

Appendix C: Selected Population Characteristics

	Crude Birthrate		Death Rate		Rate of Natural Increase	
Year	*Nova Scotia*	*Canada*	*Nova Scotia*	*Canada*	*Nova Scotia*	*Canada*
1936	21.7	20.3	10.9	9.9	10.8	10.4
1937	21.1	20.1	11.1	10.4	10.0	9.7
1938	22.1	20.7	11.0	9.7	11.1	11.0
1939	21.1	20.6	11.3	9.7	9.8	10.9
1940	22.6	21.6	11.0	9.8	11.6	11.8
1941	24.1	22.4	12.0	10.1	12.1	12.3
1942	25.9	23.5	10.8	9.8	15.1	13.7
1943	25.4	24.2	10.7	10.1	14.7	14.1
1944	25.5	24.0	10.2	9.8	15.3	14.2
1945	25.1	24.3	9.1	9.5	16.0	14.8
1946	29.5	27.2	9.9	9.4	19.6	17.8
1947	31.3	28.9	9.8	9.4	21.5	19.5
1948	28.5	27.3	9.8	9.3	18.7	18.0
1949	28.2	27.3	9.5	9.3	18.7	18.0
1950	27.1	27.1	9.5	9.1	17.6	18.0
1951	26.6	27.2	9.0	9.0	17.6	18.2
1952	27.5	27.9	8.8	8.7	18.7	19.2
1953	27.6	28.1	8.8	8.6	18.8	19.5
1954	28.1	28.5	8.5	8.2	19.6	20.3
1955	27.8	28.2	8.7	8.2	19.1	20.0
1956	27.5	28.0	8.3	8.2	19.2	19.8
1957	27.6	28.2	8.5	8.2	19.1	20.0
1958	26.7	27.5	8.6	7.9	18.1	19.6
1959	26.5	27.4	8.9	8.0	17.6	19.4
1960	26.3	26.8	8.4	7.8	17.9	19.0
1961	26.3	26.1	8.3	7.7	18.0	18.4
1962	26.0	25.3	8.5	7.7	17.5	17.6
1963	25.3	24.6	8.5	7.8	16.8	16.8
1964	24.3	23.5	8.5	7.6	15.8	15.9
1965	21.9	21.3	8.4	7.6	13.5	13.7
1966	20.1	19.4	8.6	7.5	11.5	11.9
1967	18.9	18.2	8.8	7.4	10.1	10.8

Rate of Population Change, Nova Scotia and Canada, 1935-1967 (per 1,000 inhabitants)

Source: D.B.S., *Vital Statistics*, Cat. No. 84–202, 1966, 1967.

Appendix C cont.

Age-Specific Fertility Rates per 1,000 Women
Nova Scotia, Selected Years, 1941–1967

Year	15–19	20–24	25–29	30–34	35–39	40–44	45–49
1941	49.7	164.3	161.7	127.5	80.6	32.3	3.3
1951	65.4	206.7	193.7	144.4	90.8	32.2	3.2
1956	74.7	238.4	219.6	150.8	97.1	34.5	3.3
1957	77.3	245.4	226.7	150.2	95.6	35.3	3.0
1958	78.9	238.9	221.5	147.9	92.5	32.3	2.7
1959	80.4	239.9	227.8	146.4	89.2	32.8	3.6
1960	77.5	246.1	225.0	147.4	90.8	34.8	2.2
1961	77.6	254.2	229.8	146.8	87.0	33.0	3.3
1962	77.0	259.8	220.9	153.7	81.7	31.1	2.6
1963	73.1	247.4	220.1	149.9	82.3	28.9	1.7
1964	66.0	231.4	217.6	149.1	79.6	30.9	2.8
1965	63.9	207.5	186.6	131.8	75.9	25.6	2.1
1966	64.3	193.6	172.2	109.7	64.3	24.0	1.9
1967	59.4	181.9	163.3	95.1	58.4	19.2	1.5

Appendix C cont.

Age Structure, Nova Scotia and Canada 1951, 1961, and 1966

Age Group	1951			1961			1966		
	Canada (%)	Nova Scotia (%)	Ratio of Nova Scotia to Canada (x 100)	Canada (%)	Nova Scotia (%)	Ratio of Nova Scotia to Canada (x 100)	Canada (%)	Nova Scotia (%)	Ratio of Nova Scotia to Canada (x 100)
0-4	12.29	12.86	104.64	12.37	12.38	100.08	10.98	11.32	103.10
5-9	9.99	10.72	107.31	11.40	11.50	100.88	11.51	11.57	100.52
10-14	8.08	9.05	112.20	10.18	10.90	107.07	10.46	10.79	103.32
15-19	7.55	8.02	106.23	7.86	8.72	110.94	9.18	9.80	106.75
20-24	7.77	7.20	92.66	6.49	6.69	103.08	7.30	6.95	95.21
25-29	8.03	7.28	90.10	6.63	5.96	89.89	6.20	5.68	91.61
30-34	7.44	7.23	97.18	6.97	5.88	84.36	6.10	5.47	88.23
35-39	7.13	6.99	98.04	6.97	6.11	87.66	6.43	5.51	85.69
40-44	6.20	5.91	95.32	6.12	6.05	98.87	6.38	5.62	88.09
45-49	5.32	4.69	88.16	5.57	5.58	100.18	5.44	5.54	101.84
50-54	4.73	4.30	90.91	4.73	4.72	99.79	4.94	5.19	105.06
55-59	4.08	3.89	95.34	3.87	3.71	95.87	4.08	4.28	104.90
60-64	3.60	3.32	92.22	3.20	3.19	99.69	3.32	3.38	101.81
65-69	3.10	3.02	97.42	2.67	2.90	108.61	2.65	2.86	107.92
70-74	2.24	2.41	107.59	2.21	2.36	106.79	2.13	2.47	115.96
75-79	1.33	1.63	122.56	1.51	1.70	112.58	1.50	1.73	115.96
80-84	.69	.91	131.88	.81	.99	122.22	.88	1.09	123.86
85-89	.29	.42	144.83	.33	.48	145.45	.39	.52	133.33
90-94	.07	.12	171.43	.09	.15	166.67	.11	.18	163.64
95+	.02	.03	150.00	.02	.03	150.00	.02	.05	250.00
	100.00	100.00		100.00	100.00		100.00	100.00	

Based on: D.B.S.: *Census of Canada*, 1951, 1961, and 1966.

Appendix C cont.

Labor Force Age-Sex Structure – Nova Scotia, Canada, and Ontario, 1961

Age Group	Nova Scotia			Canada			Ontario			Labor Force, 1961, Nova Scotia as a Percentage of	
	Total (%)	Male (%)	Female (%)	Total (%)	Male (%)	Female (%)	Total (%)	Male (%)	Female (%)	Canada	Ontario
15–19	9.06	5.34	3.72	8.04	4.46	3.58	6.81	3.78	3.03	112.44	132.75
20–24	13.69	9.37	4.32	12.39	7.85	4.54	11.32	7.08	4.24	110.49	120.94
25–34	21.31	16.98	4.33	23.81	18.24	5.57	24.03	17.90	6.13	89.50	88.68
35–44	21.88	17.16	4.72	23.06	17.32	5.74	23.92	17.37	6.55	94.88	91.47
45–54	19.03	14.71	4.32	18.34	13.60	4.74	18.73	13.45	5.28	103.76	101.60
55–64	0.69	8.83	2.31	10.66	8.27	2.39	11.26	8.43	2.83	108.92	112.79
65+	4.34	3.46	0.88	3.70	2.96	.74	3.93	3.06	.87	117.30	110.43
All Ages	100.00	75.40	24.60	100.00	72.70	27.30	100.00	71.07	28.93		

Based on: D.B.S., 1961 Census of Canada.

Appendix C cont.

Total Labor Force Participation Rates, by Sex Nova Scotia and Canada, 1911–1961

Census Year	Nova Scotia			Canada[a]			Nova Scotia as a Percentage of Canada		
	Total	Male	Female	Total	Male	Female	Total	Male	Female
1911	52.7	88.7	15.1	56.0	89.7	16.2	94.46	98.89	93.21
1921	53.2	88.4	16.8	54.6	88.7	17.6	97.44	99.66	95.45
1931	52.2	85.5	16.6	55.2	87.5	19.7	94.57	97.71	84.26
1941[b]	52.4	84.3	18.6	54.2	85.8	20.7	96.68	98.25	89.86
1941[c]	46.6	73.1	18.6	50.4	78.4	20.7	92.46	93.24	89.86
1951	50.9	81.5	19.9	54.2	83.8	24.1	93.91	97.26	82.37
1961	49.3	73.5	24.5	53.7	77.7	29.5	91.81	94.85	83.05

[a]Excludes Yukon and Northwest Territories.
[b]Includes persons on Active Service.
[c]Excludes persons on Active Service.
Source: D.B.S., Census of Canada, 1961: Labour Force, Cat. No. 94–501.

Appendix C cont.

Nova Scotia Participation Rates as a Percentage
of Canadian Participation Rates, 1961

Age Group	Males	Females	Total
15–19	96.43	85.92	91.96
20–24	100.35	87.34	97.01
25–34	97.25	80.33	92.98
35–44	97.00	80.13	92.62
45–54	95.82	84.73	94.08
55–64	94.07	89.34	93.01
65+	95.06	94.16	94.24
Total	94.85	83.05	91.81

Based on: D.B.S., 1961 Census of Canada.

Appendix C cont.

Percentage Distribution of Occupations by Years of School Completed Nova Scotia, Canada, and Ontario, 1961

	Elementary		Secondary			University	
	Less than 5	5 and over	1-2	3	4-5	Some	Degree
Nova Scotia							
All occupations	5.36	31.67	29.50	14.27	11.21	4.32	3.67
Scientists	.14	.82	1.78	2.32	4.10	9.84	81.00
Professionals	.47	4.23	6.77	13.82	24.59	16.54	33.58
Managers	2.25	18.80	29.34	20.10	15.08	8.38	6.05
Technicians	1.34	13.40	18.12	21.02	24.71	10.79	10.62
Skilled workers	8.57	42.48	31.92	9.73	5.00	1.80	.50
Semiskilled workers	3.20	27.11	34.06	17.51	13.08	3.72	1.32
Unskilled workers	10.67	48.86	26.81	7.58	4.38	1.45	.25
Canada							
All occupations	6.16	34.32	22.57	9.88	18.28	4.48	4.31
Scientists	.12	1.37	1.42	1.31	6.06	10.78	78.94
Professionals	.20	2.60	4.23	4.71	28.05	19.50	40.71
Managers	3.00	22.35	20.19	11.96	27.15	7.78	7.57
Technicians	1.60	15.71	15.40	10.11	33.95	11.64	11.59
Skilled workers	9.30	46.45	22.95	7.68	11.01	1.94	.67
Semiskilled workers	4.12	31.75	26.67	12.40	20.74	3.25	1.07
Unskilled workers	11.99	47.81	21.68	7.07	9.06	2.01	.38
Ontario							
All occupations	4.04	34.14	22.69	9.87	20.72	3.87	4.67
Scientists	.12	1.26	1.47	1.28	6.02	8.94	80.91
Professionals	.11	2.23	3.21	2.72	31.83	14.34	45.57
Managers	2.00	21.86	19.04	11.20	30.40	6.90	8.60
Technicians	.86	15.74	15.20	8.95	38.99	9.98	10.28
Skilled workers	4.59	47.49	23.22	8.39	13.65	1.86	.80
Semiskilled workers	3.07	32.15	26.98	12.15	21.83	2.68	1.14
Unskilled workers	9.64	49.32	21.70	7.23	9.82	1.82	.47

Based on: D.B.S.: *1961 Census of Canada.*

Appendix D: Derivation of Coefficient C_e for a Hypothetical Case of Three Industries

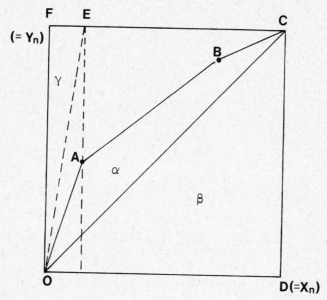

The area of $OABCD$ (α) is equal to

$$\alpha = \sum_{i=1}^{n} \frac{(Y_i + Y_{i-1})}{2} (X_i - X_{i-1}) = \sum_{i=1}^{n} \frac{(Y_i + Y_{i-1})}{2} \frac{1}{n}$$

$$= \frac{1}{n} \left[\sum_{i=1}^{n-1} Y_i + \tfrac{1}{2} Y_n \right] = \frac{1}{n} \sum_{i=1}^{n-1} Y_i + \frac{1}{2n}.$$

The area of OCD (β) is equal to

$$\beta = \frac{X_n Y_n}{2} = \frac{1}{2}.$$

The area of OEF (γ) is equal to

$$\gamma = \frac{X_1 Y_n}{2} = \frac{1}{2n}.$$

Hence, the value of the coefficient (C_e) is

$$C_e = \frac{\alpha - \beta}{\beta - \gamma} = \frac{\dfrac{1}{n} \displaystyle\sum_{i=1}^{n-1} Y_i + \dfrac{1}{2n} - \dfrac{1}{2}}{\dfrac{1}{2} - \dfrac{1}{2n}} = \frac{2\displaystyle\sum_{i=1}^{n-1} Y_i - (n-1)}{(n-1)} \ .$$

Appendix E: Value of Shipments and Indexes of Relative Accessibility to Manufacturing, Nova Scotia and Ontario, 1961

Rank	Place	Value of Shipments ('000)	Index $I_i = \sqrt{\Sigma V_j d_{ij}^2} \, / \, \Sigma V_j$
	Nova Scotia		
1	Truro	13,489	135.19
2	Trenton	10,385	141.14
3	Halifax M.A.	66,607	159.35
4	Hantsport	10,478[a]	160.74
5	Antigonish	1,394	175.70
6	Oxford	811	182.25
7	Berwick	6,147	187.96
8	Lunenburg	4,403	199.59
9	Bridgetown	8,154	208.47
10	Canso	1,753	212.11
11	Amherst	10,648	217.33
12	Sydney Area	64,687[a]	239.00
13	Digby	798	254.21
14	Shelburne	1,835	266.07
15	Clark's Harbour	2,873[a]	291.57
16	Yarmouth	10,890	297.34
	Ontario		
1	Brampton	50,340	162.74
2	Oakville	406,019[a]	163.24
3	Toronto M.A.	4,118,709	163.58
4	Hamilton M.A.	1,168,600	165.12
5	Guelph	110,121	166.93
6	Kitchener M.A.	468,179	171.12
7	Brantford M.A.	162,446	172.32
8	Barrie	44,119	175.99
9	Woodstock	76,608	178.81
10	St. Catherines M.A.	267,229	183.21
11	Stratford	49,704	184.00
12	Port Hope	106,277[a]	185.68
13	Welland	89,661	189.96
14	Dunville	13,268	191.05
15	Cobourg	27,565	191.60
16	Lindsay	21,286	192.16
17	Simcoe	46,008	192.56
18	London M.A.	302,618	193.55
19	Peterborough	114,498	197.44
20	St. Thomas	32,496	199.23
21	Owen Sound	23,286	201.50
22	Trenton	27,480	216.66
23	Belleville	50,306	224.94
24	Sarnia	352,171	234.22
25	Chatham	116,753	237.49
26	Kingston	66,062	262.02

Appendix E cont.

Rank	Place	Value of Shipments ('000)	Index $I_i = \sqrt{\Sigma V_j d_{ij}^2} / \Sigma V_j$
27	Leamington	134,861[a]	265.58
28	Windsor	417,752	277.56
29	Brockville	58,040	295.30
30	Perth	10,704	296.04
31	Sudbury	437,820[a]	303.93
32	Pembroke	17,663	314.12
33	Ottawa M.A.	272,852	324.38
34	Cornwall	89,371	346.47
35	Sault Ste. Marie	214,243[a]	472.04
36	Fort William	67,997	900.88

[a]Estimates

i = any city considered

MA = metropolitan area

Based on: D.B.S., *The Manufacturing Industries of Canada 1961, Section G, Geographical Distribution*, Cat. No. 31–209. Nova Scotia Travel Bureau, *Nova Scotia Highway Map*, 1966–1967. Province of Ontario, *Ontario Highway Map*, 1966.

Appendix F: Methodology of Shift Analysis

The change in employment over the ten-year period may be described with the help of the following matrices and coefficients:

E^t = an $n \times 2$ matrix showing employment in 1951 by sector. The first column refers to Nova Scotia and the second to Canada.

e^t_{ij} = any element of the E^t matrix showing employment in the ith industry in the jth region $(i = 1, 2, \ldots n), j = \begin{bmatrix} \text{Nova Scotia} \\ \text{Canada} \end{bmatrix}$;

E^{t+1} = an $n \times 2$ matrix as above for 1961.

D^{t+1} = an $n \times 2$ growth matrix, showing growth or decline by industry in terms of employment.

$$D^{t+1} = E^{t+1} - E^t;$$

d^{t+1}_{ij} = any element of the D^{t+1} matrix showing the difference in employment in the ith sector in the jth region between 1951 and 1961.

R^{t+1} = an $n \times 2$ net relative change matrix showing in its two columns the relative rates of change in the various industries in Nova Scotia and in Canada.

r^{t+1}_{ij} = any element of the R^{t+1} matrix showing the rate of change of the ith industry in the jth region.

$$R^{t+1} = r^{t+1}_{ij} = d^{t+1}_{ij} / e^t_{ij};$$

g^{t+1}_{ij} = national growth effect on industry i in region j.

k^{t+1}_{ij} = industry mix effect on industry i in region j.

c^{t+1}_{ij} = competitive effect on industry i in region j.

r^{t+1}_{00} = $\Sigma d^{t+1}_{i2} / \Sigma e^t_{i2}$ = average all-industry national rate of change.

d^{t+1}_{i1} = $g^{t+1}_{i1} + k^{t+1}_{i1} + c^{t+1}_{i1} = e^{t+1}_{i1} \cdot r^{t+1}_{00} + (e^t_{i1} \, r^{t+1}_{i2} - e^t_{i1} \, r^{t+1}_{00})$

$$+ (e_{i1}^t \ r_{i1}^{t+1} - e_{i1}^t \ r_{i2}^{t+1}) = e_{i1}^t \ (r_{00}^{t+1} + r_{i2}^{t+1} - r_{00}^{t+1} + r_{i1}^{t+1} - r_{i2}^{t+1})$$

$$= e_{i1}^t \cdot r_{i1}^{t+1} \ ;$$

There is a certain weakness in this formulation, inherent in shift analysis, in that it disregards the consequences of interaction between the national growth effect and the industry mix effect. In other words, the analysis unjustifiably implies that the two factors are independent of one another, whereas in reality part of the national growth is due to the shift from slow-growing to fast-growing industries. Failure to account for this explicitly in the analysis unduly inflates the industry mix effect, which is treated as residual.

In the case of Nova Scotia, the ten-year and five-year periods were selected because of data availability. The technique itself could be adapted to any time period. Nor has the base necessarily to be at the beginning of the period of analysis, 1951 in the present case. In this more general case, a base matrix would be defined as

$$B = aE^t + (1 - a)E^{t+1} \ ;$$

The choice of base year obviously affects all elements except actual change. On the other hand, the analysis is not affected by breaking the region into sub-areas. Finally, changes in the degree of sectoral aggregation do influence both the industry mix and the competitive effects, although they leave the national growth effect and actual change unaffected. The following illustrates the effects upon the various indexes:

Change in	d	g	k	c
(1) Base year		X	X	X
(2) Geographical units				
(3) Industrial classification			X	X

Appendix G
Shift Analysis of Industries in Nova Scotia, 1951–1961

	Canada			
	Employees		Absolute	Percentage
Industry	1951	1961	change	change
Agriculture	827,030	640,786	−186,244	−22.52
Forestry & Logging	129,832	108,580	−21,252	−16.37
Logging	122,051	93,866	−28,185	−23.09
Forestry Services	7,781	14,714	6,933	89.10
Fishing & Trapping	50,579	36,263	−14,316	−28.30
Fishing	44,069	30,191	−13,878	−31.49
Fishery Services	1,884	2,320	436	23.14
Hunting & Trapping	4,626	3,752	−874	−18.89
Mines, Quarries, Oil Wells	103,848	121,702	17,854	17.19
Metal Mines	54,542	68,931	14,389	26.38
Placer Gold Mines	518	651	133	25.68
Gold Quartz Mines	20,289	16,516	−3,773	−18.60
Copper-Gold-Silver Mines	8,709	12,140	3,431	39.40
Nickel-Copper Mines	10,991	17,671	6,680	60.78
Silver-Cobalt Mines	621	601	−20	−03.22
Silver-Lead-Zinc Mines	5,961	4,427	−1,534	−25.73
Iron Mines	4,842	10,026	5,184	107.06
Other Metal Mining	2,611	6,899	4,288	164.23
Fuels	30,951	19,765	−11,186	−36.14
Coal Mines	24,321	12,451	−11,870	−48.81
Petroleum	5,707	6,133	426	07.46
Natural Gas	919	1,172	253	27.53
Oil Shale and Bit. Sand	4	9	5	125.00
Nonmetallic Mines	8,953	11,465	2,512	28.06
Asbestos Mines	5,435	6,850	1,415	26.03
Gypsum Mines	991	673	−318	−32.09
Salt Mines	151	972	821	543.71
Other Non-metal Mines	2,376	2,970	594	25.00
Quarries & Sand Pits	4,909	6,120	1,211	24.67
Stone Quarries	2,528	2,641	113	04.47
Sand Pits or Quarries	2,381	3,479	1,098	46.12
Services Incidental to Mining	4,493	15,421	10,928	243.22
Oil Prospecting	3,309	4,459	1,150	34.75
Other Prospecting	883	1,282	399	45.19
Other Services	301	9,680	9,379	3,115.95
Manufacturing Industries	1,296,878	1,404,865	107,987	08.33
Food & Beverage Industry	150,481	219,185	68,704	45.66
Slaughtering & Meat Processing	22,318	29,441	7,123	31.92
Dairy Products	12,967	39,144	26,177	201.87
Fish Products	17,027	20,464	3,437	20.19
Fruit & Vegetable Canners	10,445	13,881	3,436	32.90
Feed Manufacturers	3,620	7,308	3,688	101.89
Flour Mills	6,508	5,493	−1,015	−15.60
Break. Cereal Manufacturers	2,128	1,985	−143	−06.72
Biscuit Manufacturers	6,028	6,862	834	13.84
Bakeries	25,418	38,561	13,143	51.71

	Nova Scotia				
Employees 1951	1961	Absolute change	Percentage change	Industry growth effect	Competitive effect
23,331	12,038	-11,293	-48.40	-5,254	-6,039
5,913	4,296	-1,617	-27.35	-968	-649
5,752	4,022	-1,730	-30.08	-1,328	-402
161	274	113	70.19	143	-30
9,769	7,493	-2,276	-23.30	-2,765	489
9,441	7,155	-2,286	-24.21	-2,973	687
323	334	11	03.41	75	-64
5	4	-1	-20.00	-1	0
15,570	10,105	-5,465	-35.10	2,676	-8,141
225	76	-149	-66.22	59	-208
1	7	6	600.00	0	6
17	7	-10	-58.82	-3	-7
6	31	25	416.67	2	23
15	8	-7	-46.67	9	-16
4	0	-4	-100.00	0	-4
158	1	-157	-99.37	-41	-116
18	12	-6	-33.33	19	-25
6	10	4	66.67	10	-6
14,147	8,887	-5,260	-37.18	-5,113	-147
14,145	8,883	-5,262	-37.20	-6,904	1,642
2	0	-2	-100.00	0	-2
0	4	4	—	0	4
0	0	0	0	0	0
1,084	952	-132	-12.18	304	-436
0	0	0	0	0	0
806	621	-185	-22.95	-259	74
110	196	86	78.18	598	-512
168	135	-33	-19.64	42	-75
102	144	42	41.18	25	17
35	85	50	142.86	2	48
67	59	-8	-11.94	-31	-39
12	46	34	283.33	29	5
0	0	0	0	0	0
4	14	10	250.00	2	8
8	32	24	300.00	249	-225
34,703	34,081	-622	-1.79	2,891	3,513
7,156	10,626	3,470	48.49	3,267	203
99	305	206	208.08	32	174
513	1,526	1,013	197.47	1,036	-23
3,865	5,275	1,410	36.48	780	630
295	394	99	33.56	97	2
58	140	82	141.38	59	23
11	2	-9	-81.82	-2	-7
3	5	2	66.67	-0	2
92	90	-2	-02.17	13	-15
621	987	366	58.94	321	45

Appendix G cont.

	Canada			
Industry	Employees 1951	1961	Absolute change	Percentage change
Confectionery Manufacturers	8,328	8,298	−30	−00.36
Sugar Refineries	3,226	2,926	−300	−09.30
Soft Drinks	9,590	13,846	4,256	44.38
Distilled Beverages	4,145	4,832	687	16.57
Wineries	480	580	100	20.83
Breweries	10,251	10,474	223	02.18
Misc. Food Industries	8,002	15,090	7,088	88.58
Tobacco Products Industry	8,480	8,833	353	04.16
Rubber Industries	21,695	18,844	−2,851	−13.14
Rubber Footwear	5,644	4,391	−1,253	−22.20
Other Rubber Industries	16,051	14,453	−1,598	−09.96
Leather Industries	32,058	33,166	1,108	03.46
Leather Tanneries	4,829	3,656	−1,173	−24.29
Leather Gloves	2,429	1,830	−599	−24.66
Shoe Factories	19,364	21,239	1,875	09.68
Other Leather Goods	5,436	6,441	1,005	18.49
Textile Industries	81,422	62,252	−19,170	−23.54
Cotton Yarn and Cloth	28,906	20,530	−8,376	−28.98
Woolen Yarn	4,363	2,126	−2,237	−51.27
Woolen Cloth	11,031	6,090	−4,941	−44.79
Synthetic Textiles	17,705	15,021	−2,684	−15.16
Thread Mills	804	710	−94	−11.69
Cordage, Rope and Twine	1,483	1,034	−449	−30.28
Canvas	1,565	1,562	−3	−00.19
Cotton and Jute Bags	1,830	1,073	−757	−41.37
Linoleum and Coated Fabrics	2,015	2,212	197	09.78
Misc. Textiles	9,756	10,126	370	03.79
Carpets, Mats and Rugs	1,964	1,768	−196	−09.98
Clothing Industries	120,545	111,674	−8,871	−07.36
Children's Clothing	3,554	6,542	2,988	84.07
Men's Clothing	33,926	33,693	−233	−00.69
Women's Clothing	28,341	30,800	2,459	08.68
Fur Goods	7,114	5,532	−1,582	−22.24
Hats and Caps	5,407	4,006	−1,401	−25.91
Foundation Garments	2,800	4,044	1,244	44.43
Custom Tailoring	12,446	5,446	−7,000	−56.24
Hosiery	11,220	8,908	−2,312	−20.61
Knit Goods	12,730	10,838	−1,892	−14.86
Other Clothing	3,007	1,865	−1,142	−37.98
Wood Industries	115,867	98,871	−16,996	−14.67
Sawmills	74,464	58,163	−16,301	−21.89
Sash, Door & Planing Mills	19,120	19,026	−94	−00.49
Veneer and plywood mills	5,445	10,455	5,010	92.01
Box Factories	4,391	3,198	−1,193	−27.17
Coffin & Casket Industry	1,296	1,375	79	06.10
Misc. Wood Industries	11,151	6,654	−4,497	−40.33

| | | | | Industry | |
| Employees | | Absolute | Percentage | growth | Competitive |
1951	1961	change	change	effect	effect
818	737	−81	−09.90	−3	−78
52	18	−34	−65.38	−5	−29
387	529	142	36.69	172	−30
1	32	31	3,100.00	0	31
0	7	7		0	7
195	229	34	17.44	4	30
146	350	204	139.73	129	75
10	4	−6	−60.00	0	−6
9	50	41	455.56	−1	42
2	3	1	50.00	0	1
7	47	40	571.43	−1	41
151	99	−52	−34.44	+5	−57
6	2	−4	−66.67	−1	−3
1	0	−1	−100.00	0	−1
51	15	−36	−70.59	5	−41
93	82	−11	−11.83	17	−28
791	616	−175	−22.12	−186	11
516	526	10	01.93	−150	160
0	0	0	0	0	0
131	29	−102	−77.86	−59	−43
4	5	1	25.00	−1	2
0	0	0	0	0	0
77	5	−72	−93.51	−23	−49
20	22	2	10.00	0	2
0	0	0	0	0	0
1	2	1	100.00	0	1
19	22	3	15.79	1	2
23	5	−18	−78.26	−2	−16
1,785	1,370	−415	−23.25	−131	−284
1	1	0	0	1	−1
296	154	−142	−47.97	−2	−140
6	4	−2	−33.33	1	−3
37	3	−34	−91.89	−8	−26
475	102	−373	−78.53	−123	−250
8	12	4	50.00	4	0
364	127	−237	−65.11	−205	−32
4	111	107	2,675.00	−1	108
563	852	289	51.33	−84	373
31	4	−27	−87.10	−12	−15
7,291	4,032	−3,259	−44.70	−1,070	−2,189
5,242	2,529	−2,713	−51.75	−1,147	−1,566
1,268	934	−334	−26.34	−6	−328
1	3	2	200.00	1	1
250	276	26	10.40	−68	94
67	67	0	0	4	−4
463	223	−240	−51.84	−187	−53

Nova Scotia

Appendix G cont.

	Canada			
Industry	Employees 1951	1961	Absolute change	Percentage change
Furniture Industry	29,762	35,696	5,934	19.94
Paper & Allied Industries	89,972	101,640	11,668	12.97
Pulp & Paper Mills	66,826	72,141	5,315	07.95
Paper Boxes and Bags	12,710	17,266	4,556	35.85
Asphalt Roofing	2,960	2,570	−390	−13.18
Other Paper Products	7,476	9,663	2,187	29.25
Printing, Publishing & Allied Industry	62,968	84,265	21,297	33.82
Commercial Printing	21,896	32,697	10,801	49.33
Engraving, Stereotyping and Allied Industries	8,339	7,091	−1,248	−14.97
Printing and Publishing	32,733	44,477	11,744	35.88
Metal Products	250,873	243,193	−7,680	−03.06
Agricultural Implements	18,219	12,797	−5,422	−29.76
Boilers and Plate Work	5,628	7,148	1,520	27.01
Fabricated Structural Steel	7,841	14,054	6,213	79.24
Hardware and Tools	14,482	9,987	−4,495	−31.04
Heating Equipment	10,112	7,202	−2,910	−28.78
House, Office, Store Machinery	11,302	6,381	−4,921	−43.54
Machine Shop Products	10,156	9,521	−635	−06.25
Other Machinery	24,346	28,720	4,374	17.97
Primary Iron and Steel	34,942	38,763	3,821	10.94
Wire and Wire Products	5,036	9,872	4,836	96.03
Aluminum Manufacture	8,610	7,580	−1,030	−11.96
Copper Products	9,008	4,053	−4,955	−55.01
Ornamental Metal Industry	5,814	8,571	2,757	47.42
Other Metal Products	85,377	78,544	−6,833	−08.00
Nonmetallic Mineral Products	35,734	47,019	11,285	31.58
Abrasives	3,120	2,661	−459	−14.71
Asbestos	2,605	3,124	519	19.92
Cement	2,905	4,073	1,168	40.21
Concrete Products	4,139	13,158	9,019	217.90
Clay Products	5,787	6,271	484	08.36
Glass and Glass Products	8,194	11,321	3,127	38.16
Lime and Gypsum	2,392	2,828	436	18.23
Stone Products	2,574	2,005	−569	−22.11
Other Nonmetallic Products	4,018	1,578	−2,440	−60.73
Transportation Equipment	129,447	118,021	−11,426	−08.83
Aircraft and Parts	17,045	29,467	12,422	72.88
Motor Vehicles	36,140	32,564	−3,576	−09.89
Motor Vehicle Parts	16,615	16,420	−195	−01.17
Railway and Rolling Stock	39,806	14,790	−25,016	−62.84

				Industry	
Employees		Absolute	Percentage	growth	Competitive
1951	1961	change	change	effect	effect
298	401	103	34.56	59	44
1,641	1,839	198	12.07	213	-15
1,527	1,549	22	01.44	121	-99
42	133	91	216.67	15	76
9	2	-7	-77.78	-1	-6
63	155	92	146.03	18	74
1,338	1,776	438	32.74	453	-15
388	447	59	15.21	191	-132
59	41	-18	-30.51	-9	-9
891	1,288	397	44.56	320	77
7,741	6,178	-1,563	-20.19	-237	-1,326
5	0	-5	-100.00	-1	-4
167	285	118	70.66	45	73
7	345	338	4,828.57	6	332
54	39	-15	-27.78	-17	2
254	151	-103	-40.55	-73	-30
161	49	-112	-69.57	-70	-42
250	308	58	23.20	-16	74
149	264	115	77.18	27	88
5,929	3,918	-2,011	-33.92	649	-2,660
1	321	320	320.00	1	319
12	11	-1	-08.33	-1	0
4	3	-1	-25.00	-2	1
25	157	132	528.00	12	120
723	327	-396	-54.77	-58	-338
687	804	117	17.03	217	-100
3	2	-1	-33.33	0	-1
50	99	49	98.00	10	39
50	17	-33	-66.00	20	-53
40	223	183	457.50	87	96
266	271	5	01.88	22	-17
2	15	13	650.00	1	12
68	39	-29	-42.65	12	-41
158	85	-73	-46.20	-35	-38
50	53	3	06.00	-30	33
4,421	4,292	-129	02.92	-390	261
460	1,191	+731	158.91	335	39
11	16	+5	45.45	-1	6
19	6	-13	-68.42	0	-13
1,511	399	-1,112	-73.59	-950	-16

Appendix G cont.

	Canada			
	Employees		Absolute	Percentage
Industry	1951	1961	change	change
Shipbuilding and Repair	14,589	16,271	1,682	11.53
Boat Building and Repair	2,975	4,634	1,659	55.76
Misc. Vehicle Manufacture	2,277	3,875	1,598	70.18
Electrical Apparatus	70,514	84,924	14,410	20.44
Batteries	2,023	1,825	−198	−09.79
Heavy Electrical Equipment	8,103	13,427	5,324	65.70
Electrical Appliances	27,085	23,438	−3,647	−13.47
Radios and T. V.'s	10,413	7,781	−2,632	−25.28
Other Electrical Products	22,890	38,453	15,563	67.99
Petroleum and Coal Products	14,004	16,959	2,955	21.10
Petroleum Refineries	12,740	16,036	3,296	25.87
Other Petroleum and Coal Prod.	1,264	936	−341	−26.98
Chemical Products	51,148	69,510	18,362	35.90
Explosives and Ammunition	5,966	4,734	−1,232	−20.65
Fertilizers	1,615	2,280	665	41.18
Medicines, Pharmaceuticals	8,590	11,110	2,520	29.34
Paints and Varnishes	6,517	7,760	1,243	19.07
Soaps and Cleaning Compounds	4,332	5,416	1,084	25.02
Toilet Preparations	2,006	5,649	3,643	181.61
Other Chemical Products	19,791	27,427	7,636	38.58
Plastics	2,331	5,134	2,803	120.25
Miscellaneous Manufacturing Ind.	31,908	50,813	18,905	59.25
Sporting Goods and Toys	3,830	6,410	2,580	67.36
Other Misc. Manufactures	28,078	44,403	16,325	58.14
Construction	305,896	431,093	80,197	22.85
Building and other Construction	298,463	388,873	90,410	30.29
Highways, Bridges & Streets	52,433	42,220	−10,213	−19.48
Transport, Communication, Storage	402,707	490,354	87,647	21.76
Transportation	332,898	385,031	52,133	15.66
Air Transport & Airports	10,469	20,274	9,805	93.66
Water Transportation	23,919	24,072	153	00.64
Bus & Coach Transport	8,055	6,812	−1,243	−15.43
Railway & Express	170,956	139,643	−31,313	−18.32
Truck Transport	60,554	88,795	28,241	46.64
Taxicab	22,010	21,266	−744	−03.38
Urban Transit Systems	21,831	18,653	−3,178	−14.56
Water Transport Services	12,242	14,796	2,554	20.86
Other Transport Services	1,809	43,934	42,125	2,328.63
Other Transportation	1,053	6,786	5,733	544.44
Storage	14,480	17,677	3,197	22.08
Grain Elevators	8,528	10,813	2,285	26.79
Warehousing	5,952	6,864	912	15.32
Communication	55,329	87,646	32,317	58.41
Radio & T.V.	5,778	17,392	11,614	201.00
Telephone	48,966	62,120	13,154	26.86
Other Communications	585	8,134	7,549	1,290.43
Utilities	61,814	70,504	8,690	14.06
Electric Power	43,185	53,041	9,856	22.82

Nova Scotia					
Employees		Absolute	Percentage	Industry growth	Competitive
1951	1961	change	change	effect	effect
2,041	2,228	187	09.16	235	-48
348	423	75	21.55	194	-119
31	29	-2	-06.45	22	-24
251	522	271	107.97	51	220
3	11	8	266.67	0	8
24	42	18	75.00	16	2
47	44	-3	-06.38	-6	3
162	5	-157	-96.91	-41	-116
15	420	405	2,700.00	10	395
623	537	-86	-13.80	131	-217
549	531	-18	-03.28	142	-160
74	6	-68	-91.89	-20	-48
353	634	281	79.60	127	154
1	1	0	0	0	0
61	82	21	34.43	25	-4
77	44	-33	-42.86	23	-56
69	74	5	07.25	13	-8
11	11	0	0	3	-3
4	266	262	6,550.00	7	255
128	154	26	20.31	49	-23
2	2	0	0	2	-2
157	301	144	91.72	93	51
8	14	6	75.00	5	1
149	287	138	96.62	87	51
16,392	15,524	-868	-05.30	3,746	-4,614
12,227	13,698	1,471	12.03	3,704	-2,233
4,165	1,826	-2,339	-56.16	-811	-1,528
18,169	20,403	2,234	12.30	3,954	-1,720
15,524	16,863	1,339	08.63	2,431	-1,092
156	372	216	138.46	146	70
1,947	2,136	189	09.71	12	177
493	303	-190	-38.54	-76	-114
7,011	5,216	-1,795	-25.60	-1,284	-511
2,611	2,700	89	03.41	1,218	-1,129
1,010	933	-77	-07.62	-34	-43
241	259	18	07.47	-35	53
2,003	1,586	-417	-20.82	418	-835
37	3,272	3,235	8,743.24	862	2,373
15	86	71	473.33	82	-11
290	216	-74	-25.52	64	-138
3	2	-1	-33.33	1	-2
287	214	-73	-25.44	44	-117
2,355	3,324	969	41.15	1,376	-407
370	758	388	104.86	744	-356
1,876	2,171	295	15.72	504	-209
109	395	286	262.39	1,407	-1,121
2,569	2,427	-142	-05.53	361	-503
2,113	2,154	41	01.94	482	-411

Appendix G cont.

Industry	Canada			
	Employees		Absolute	Percentage
	1951	1961	change	change
Gas Distribution	4,261	9,578	5,317	124.78
Water Systems	14,013	5,934	−8,079	−57.65
Other Utilities	355	1,951	1,596	449.58
Trade	767,293	991,490	224,197	29.22
Wholesale Trade	195,323	289,884	94,561	48.41
Apparel and Dry Goods	8,400	8,048	−352	−04.19
Drugs and Toilet Preparations	5,183	7,399	2,216	42.76
Electrical Machinery & Supplies	9,771	14,237	4,466	45.71
Farm Machinery & Equipment	4,207	13,455	9,248	219.82
Machinery & Supplies (Other)	14,900	33,505	18,605	124.87
Furniture & House Furnishings	2,905	3,765	860	29.60
Fuel	19,707	26,866	7,159	36.33
Hardware, Plumbing & Heating Equipment	16,438	17,439	1,001	06.09
Paper Products	6,005	5,472	−533	−08.88
Lumber & Building Materials	11,514	36,624	25,110	218.08
Motor Vehicles & Accessories	10,888	18,051	7,163	65.79
Food & Farm Products	45,064	47,746	2,682	05.95
Scrap & Waste	5,765	7,759	1,994	34.59
Other Wholesale Trade	34,576	49,518	14,942	43.21
Retail Trade	571,970	701,606	129,636	22.66
Food Stores	133,655	151,552	17,897	13.39
General Merchandise Stores	133,886	162,314	28,428	21.23
Fuel Dealers	13,583	10,030	−3,553	−26.16
Apparel & Shoe Stores	50,789	62,191	11,402	22.45
Hardware Stores	17,422	20,231	2,809	16.12
Household Furniture & Appliance Stores	24,652	37,165	12,513	50.76
Drug Stores	18,537	26,933	8,396	45.29
Book Stores	4,307	4,986	679	15.77
Florists	3,326	5,226	1,900	57.13
Jewelry	9,283	11,456	2,173	23.41
Liquor, Wine & Beer	6,489	9,664	3,175	48.93
Tobacco Stores	3,374	2,887	−487	−14.43
Automobile Parts, Accessories & Tires	4,116	14,218	10,102	245.43
Service Stations	16,220	46,363	30,143	185.84
Automobile Dealers	35,248	59,828	24,580	69.73
Other Retail Stores	39,558	20,458	−19,100	−48.78
Auto Repair & Garages	57,525	56,104	−1,421	−02.47
Finance, Insurance & Real Estate	143,995	228,905	84,910	58.97
Banking	47,104	95,477	48,373	102.69
Insurance & Real Estate	75,129	117,969	42,840	57.02
Investment	21,762	15,459	−6,303	−28.96
Services	779,450	1,263,362	483,912	62.08
Education	146,639	266,901	120,262	82.01
Health & Welfare	173,948	307,433	133,485	76.74

Nova Scotia					
Employees		Absolute	Percentage	Industry growth	Competitive
1951	1961	change	change	effect	effect
4	13	9	225.00	5	4
450	199	-251	-55.78	-259	8
2	61	59	2,950.00	9	50
32,048	36,763	4,715	14.71	9,364	-4,649
8,239	9,603	1,364	16.56	3,989	-2,625
202	226	24	11.88	-8	32
124	194	70	56.45	53	17
385	534	149	38.70	176	-27
62	140	78	125.81	136	-58
356	868	512	143.82	445	67
94	63	-31	-32.98	28	-59
1,248	1,302	54	04.33	453	-399
570	650	80	14.04	35	45
219	199	-20	-09.13	-19	-1
599	1,087	488	81.47	1,306	-818
253	315	62	24.51	166	-104
3,032	2,548	-484	-15.96	180	-664
203	257	54	26.60	70	-16
892	1,220	328	36.77	385	-57
23,809	27,160	3,351	14.07	5,395	-2,044
7,254	7,384	130	01.79	971	-841
5,516	5,657	141	02.56	1,171	-1,030
402	264	-138	-34.33	-105	-33
1,844	2,179	335	18.17	414	-79
670	474	-196	-29.25	108	-304
813	1,380	567	69.74	413	154
850	892	42	04.94	385	-343
179	183	4	02.23	28	-24
135	170	35	25.93	77	-42
353	461	108	30.59	83	25
297	496	199	67.00	145	54
57	59	2	03.51	-8	10
95	432	337	354.74	233	104
783	1,931	1,148	146.62	1,455	-307
1,705	2,787	1,082	63.46	1,189	-107
877	635	-242	-27.59	-423	18
1,979	1,776	-203	-10.26	-49	-154
3,559	5,652	2,093	58.81	2,099	-6
1,580	3,011	1,431	90.57	1,622	-191
1,448	2,428	980	67.68	826	154
531	213	-318	-59.89	-154	-164
32,250	44,953	12,703	39.39	20,021	-7,318
6,603	10,421	3,818	57.82	5,415	-1,597
7,090	11,725	4,635	65.37	5,441	-806

Appendix G cont.

| Industry | Canada | | | |
| | Employees | | Absolute | Percentage |
	1951	1961	change	change
Religion	38,803	53,130	14,327	36.92
Recreation & Theaters	28,703	39,837	11,134	38.79
Services to Business Management	54,301	98,987	44,686	82.29
Accountancy	10,913	18,586	7,673	70.31
Advertising	5,137	8,657	3,520	68.52
Engineering & Scientific Serv.	11,235	25,103	13,868	123.44
Legal Service	15,675	24,896	9,221	58.83
Other Business Service	11,341	21,745	10,404	91.74
Personal Services	332,479	488,806	156,327	47.02
Barbering & Hairdressing	23,772	41,705	17,933	75.44
Hotels, Lodging Houses,				
Restaurants & Taverns	155,452	238,941	83,489	53.71
Laundries	33,780	39,580	5,800	17.17
Private Households	83,012	98,343	15,331	18.47
Photography	4,669	5,908	1,239	26.54
Shoe Repair	6,259	5,185	-1,074	-17.16
Funeral Services	2,964	3,744	780	26.32
Other Personal Services	22,571	55,400	32,829	145.45
Labor & Trade Organizations	4,577	8,268	3,691	80.64
Government	304,274	525,353	221,079	72.66
Federal Government	208,290	327,381	119,091	57.18
Defense	101,275	173,029	71,754	70.85
Other Federal Admin.	77,329	111,924	34,595	44.74
Post Office	29,686	42,428	12,742	42.92
Local Government	53,347	123,729	70,382	131.93
Other Government Offices	5,559	5,482	-77	-01.39
Provincial Government	37,078	68,761	31,683	85.45
Unspecified Industry	67,557	158,593	91,036	134.75
All Industries	5,286,153	6,471,850	1,185,697	22.43
Total of Detailed Industry				
Breakdown	-	-	-	-

Based on: D.B.S., *1961 Census of Canada, Labour Force*, Cat. No. 94-551, *Occupation and Industry Trends.*

Nova Scotia					
Employees		Absolute	Percentage	Industry growth	Competitive
1951	1961	change	change	effect	effect
1,574	2,079	505	32.08	581	−76
970	1,067	97	10.00	376	−279
1,357	1,856	499	36.77	1,117	−618
278	433	155	55.76	195	−40
28	75	47	167.86	19	28
211	468	257	121.80	260	−3
447	560	113	25.28	263	−150
393	320	−73	−18.58	361	−434
14,589	17,694	3,105	21.28	6,860	−3,755
996	1,428	432	43.37	751	−319
4,759	6,538	1,779	37.38	2,556	−777
1,067	1,160	93	08.72	183	−90
6,526	6,297	−229	−03.51	1,205	−1,434
178	143	−35	−19.66	47	−82
247	167	−80	−32.39	−42	−38
133	190	57	42.86	35	22
683	1,771	1,088	159.30	993	95
67	111	44	65.67	54	−10
22,890	38,948	16,058	70.15	16,632	−574
19,812	34,039	14,227	71.81	11,329	2,898
15,376	27,474	12,098	78.68	10,894	1,204
2,698	4,433	1,735	64.31	1,207	528
1,738	2,132	394	22.67	746	−352
1,791	2,902	1,111	62.03	2,363	−1,252
18	32	14	77.78	0	14
1,269	1,975	706	55.63	1,084	−378
3,643	4,136	493	13.53	4,909	−4,416
220,806	236,819	16,013	07.25	49,527	−33,514
−	−	−	−	45,281	−

Appendix H: Regional Wealth Estimates by Type, Nova Scotia, 1961

Type of Wealth	Value ($ million)
[Immobile Wealth]	
Natural resources	1,357.8
A. Surface resources	460.7
1. Land	284.5
2. Forest reserves	174.2
3. Game and wildlife	2.0
B. Water resources	0.0
C. Subsoil resources	766.5
1. Base metals	84.0
2. Nonmetallics	530.6
3. Coal	0.0
4. Structural materials	151.9
D. Ocean resources	130.6
1. Seaweeds	1.3
2. Shellfish	78.8
3. Pelagic and estuarial fish	50.5
Man-made capital	(2,439.8)
A. Reproducible assets	(2,439.8)
1. Residential structures	952.5
2. Consumer durables	(185.4)
3. Nonresidential structures and engineering construction	712.7
4. Machinery and equipment	490.8
5. Agricultural livestock	26.1
6. Business inventories	(72.3)
7. Defense establishment	n.a.
B. Nonreproducible assets	n.a.
Subtotal	3,797.6
Intangible wealth	n.a.
Human resources	16,755.8
Financial assets and liabilities	n.a.
[Mobile Wealth]	n.a.
Total regional wealth	(20,553.4)
Net worth	n.a.

n.a. = not available

( ) = partial estimate

Appendix I: Hypothetical Derivation of a Planning from a Forecasting Model

Supposing a model has the following variables:

Targets: $Y_1, Y_2,$

Intermediate: $Y_3,$

Instruments: $X_1, X_2,$

Data: $X_3, X_4,$

and the original system is

$$c_{11}Y_1 + c_{12}Y_2 \qquad\qquad = \qquad\qquad\qquad b_{13}X_3 + b_{14}X_4;$$

$$c_{23}Y_3 = b_{21}X_1 + b_{22}X_2 \qquad\qquad + b_{24}X_4;$$

$$c_{31}Y_1 + \qquad\quad c_{33}Y_3 = b_{31}X_1 + \qquad\quad b_{33}X_3 + b_{34}X_4;$$

or in matrix notation

$$\tilde{C}Y = \tilde{B}X;$$

$$Y = (\tilde{C}^{-1}\tilde{B})X;$$

or

$$\tilde{I}Y = \tilde{\pi}\hat{X};$$

This in the reduced form corresponds to a forecasting formulation:

$$Y_1 = \pi_{11}X_1 + \pi_{12}X_2 + \pi_{13}X_3 + \pi_{14}X_4;$$

$$Y_2 = \pi_{21}X_1 + \pi_{22}X_2 + \pi_{23}X_3 + \pi_{24}X_4;$$

$$Y_3 = \pi_{31}X_1 + \pi_{32}X_2 + \pi_{33}X_3 + \pi_{34}X_4;$$

The next step would involve putting instrument variables on the left-hand side and targets on the right-hand.

$$-\pi_{11}X_1 \ - \ \pi_{12}X_2 \qquad = -Y_1 \qquad + \ \pi_{13}X_3 \ + \ \pi_{14}X_4;$$

$$-\pi_{21}X_1 \ - \ \pi_{22}X_2 \qquad = \qquad -Y_2 \ + \ \pi_{23}X_3 \ + \ \pi_{24}X_4;$$

$$-\pi_{31}X_1 \ - \ \pi_{32}X_2 \ + \ Y_3 \ = \qquad \qquad + \ \pi_{33}X_3 \ + \ \pi_{34}X_4;$$

or in matrix notation:

$$\widetilde{F}\,\hat{A} = \widetilde{D}\,\hat{G};$$

where

$\widetilde{F}$ is a 3 × 3 matrix,

$$\widetilde{F} \ = \ \begin{bmatrix} -\pi_{11} & -\pi_{12} & 0 \\ -\pi_{21} & -\pi_{22} & 0 \\ -\pi_{31} & -\pi_{32} & 1 \end{bmatrix} \ ;$$

$\hat{A}$ is a 3 × 1 vector,

$$\hat{A} \ = \ \begin{bmatrix} X_1 \\ X_2 \\ Y_3 \end{bmatrix} \ ;$$

$\widetilde{D}$ is a 3 × 4 matrix,

$$\widetilde{D} \ = \ \begin{bmatrix} -1 & 0 & \pi_{13} & \pi_{14} \\ 0 & -1 & \pi_{23} & \pi_{24} \\ 0 & 0 & \pi_{33} & \pi_{34} \end{bmatrix} \ ;$$

and $\hat{G}$ is a 4 × 1 vector,

$$\hat{G} = \begin{bmatrix} Y_1 \\ Y_2 \\ X_3 \\ X_4 \end{bmatrix};$$

By inverting, one obtains a system in which target variables appear as inputs, while instrument variables are outputs.

$$\hat{A} = (\widetilde{F}^{-1} \widetilde{D}) \hat{G};$$

or
$$\hat{A} = \widetilde{\psi} \hat{G};$$

which corresponds to a Planning Model.

In nonlinear systems, even those involving only logarithmic transformations, this simple method is not applicable because of obvious difficulties in defining the relevant matrix.

Appendix J: The Method of
Principal Components

The method of principal components provides a useful technique for reducing a number of variables to a compact form, thus yielding a more parsimonious description of the dependence structure of an equation. It can also be used in order to derive an index for a phenomenon that would otherwise be difficult to quantify. The methodology is somewhat similar to orthogonal least squares developed by K. Pearson [1] and later extended by H. Hotelling [2] for analyzing correlation structures.

The following is intended only as a brief explanation of the method of principal components. A more complete description can be found in texts dealing with multivariate analysis. [3]

Suppose there is a trivariate distribution — that is, a population, each element of which has three measurable characteristics.

For T observations, one would obtain the following matrix:

$$P = \begin{bmatrix} X_{1.1} & X_{1.2} & X_{1.3} \\ X_{2.1} & X_{2.2} & X_{2.3} \\ X_{3.1} & X_{3.2} & X_{3.3} \\ \cdot & \cdot & \cdot \\ \cdot & \cdot & \cdot \\ \cdot & \cdot & \cdot \\ X_{T.1} & X_{T.2} & X_{T.3} \end{bmatrix} ;$$

Each member of this population can be represented by a vector in a three dimensional space, where each dimension corresponds to one characteristic. Figure A–2 shows the whole distribution as a swarm of points.

On each axis, a unit vector $(\epsilon_1, \epsilon_2, \epsilon_3)$ is marked in appropriate units. The variables (X_1, X_2, X_3) can now be treated as scalars such that each vector (Z_i) can be defined as a linear combination of observations on three variables:

$$Z_i = \epsilon_1 X_{i.1} + \epsilon_2 X_{i.2} + \epsilon_3 X_{i.3} ;$$

For simplicity, the axes are situated so that the point of sample means $(\overline{Z}_i)$ is coterminus with the origin.

401

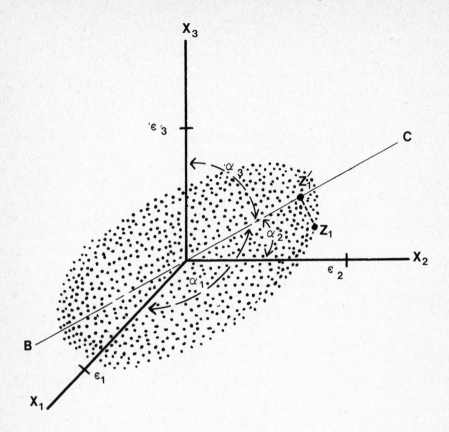

Figure A-2

Assume that there is an arbitrary ray, *BC*, passing through the origin. The ray can be completely defined by the three angles formed with the original axes $(\alpha_1, \alpha_2, \alpha_3)$. A necessary condition for a unique ray to be defined is that

$$\cos^2\alpha_1 + \cos^2\alpha_2 + \cos^2\alpha_3 = 1;$$

Suppose each vector is projected onto the ray *BC* by means of a perpendicular. Each projection onto *BC* can then be defined as a function of the three direction cosines of *BC* $(\alpha_1, \alpha_2, \alpha_3)$ since the length of each vector is

$$\|Z_i\| = \epsilon_1 X_{i\cdot 1} \cos\alpha_1 + \epsilon_2 X_{i\cdot 2} \cos\alpha_2 + \epsilon_3 X_{i\cdot 3} \cos\alpha_3;$$

Suppose the collection of vectors, each representing a member of the population, is not randomly distributed, but forms an ellipsoid, as shown in the diagram. If the ray is to represent this ellipsoid, it is desirable not to have an arbitrary ray, but one which passes as near as possible to the major axis of the ellipsoid.

This can be achieved in two ways:

(1) By minimizing the sums of squared distances for each point to its projection on the ray. This is the method of orthogonal regression.

(2) By maximizing the variance of the projections on the ray; in other words, by maximizing the sum of squared lengths of the projections of vectors.

The next step is to select the angles α in such a way that the variance be maximized subject to the condition that they define a unique ray passing through the origin.

To simplify notation, let:

$$a_1 = \epsilon_1 \cos \alpha_1;$$

$$a_2 = \epsilon_2 \cos \alpha_2;$$

$$a_3 = \epsilon_3 \cos \alpha_3;$$

The total variance is equal to

$$V = \sum_{i=1}^{T} (a_1 X_{i \cdot 1} + a_2 X_{i \cdot 2} + a_3 X_{i \cdot 3})^2 \; ;$$

This expression has to be maximized subject to

$$a_1^{\,2} + a_2^{\,2} + a_3^{\,2} = 1 ;$$

In matrix notation and noting that V is a quadratic form, maximize $a'Sa$ subject to $a'a = 1$, where

$$a = \begin{bmatrix} a_1 \\ a_2 \\ a_3 \end{bmatrix} ; \qquad S = \begin{bmatrix} \sigma_{11} & \sigma_{12} & \sigma_{13} \\ \sigma_{21} & \sigma_{22} & \sigma_{23} \\ \sigma_{31} & \sigma_{32} & \sigma_{33} \end{bmatrix} ;$$

S = variance-covariance matrix, the elements of which are

$$\sigma_{rk} = \sum_{i=1}^{T} X_{i \cdot r} X_{i \cdot k} - \frac{\sum_{i=1}^{T} X_{i \cdot r} \sum_{i=1}^{T} X_{i \cdot k}}{T} = \mathrm{cov}\,(X_r, X_k)\,;$$

In the case of a population in which the characteristics are in different units, the correlation matrix can be used in place of the covariance matrix.

$$R = \begin{bmatrix} 1 & \rho_{12} & \rho_{13} \\ \rho_{21} & 1 & \rho_{23} \\ \rho_{31} & \rho_{32} & 1 \end{bmatrix}\,;$$

where

$$\rho_{rk} = \frac{\sum_{i=1}^{T} X_{i \cdot r} X_{i \cdot k} - \dfrac{\sum_{i=1}^{T} X_{i \cdot r} \sum_{i=1}^{T} X_{i \cdot k}}{T}}{\sqrt{\left[\sum_{i=1}^{T} X_{i \cdot r}^{2} - \dfrac{\left(\sum_{i=1}^{T} X_{i \cdot r}\right)^{2}}{T}\right]\left[\sum_{i=1}^{T} X_{i \cdot k}^{2} - \dfrac{\left(\sum_{i=1}^{T} X_{i \cdot k}\right)^{2}}{T}\right]}}\,;$$

This is equivalent to normalizing each expression of the covariance matrix [cov (X_r, X_k)] by dividing it by $\sqrt{\mathrm{var}\,(X_r)\,\mathrm{var}\,(X_k)}$. The mathematical properties of the principal component analysis in the second case are not the same as when the variance-covariance matrix is used. The model, however, is frequently applied in this form.

To find the major axis (BC) by maximization, the Lagrangian expression is formed:

$$L \;=\; [a' Sa + \lambda\,(1 - a'a)]\,;$$

Setting the partial derivatives with respect to a equal to zero yields the maximizing value:

$$\frac{\partial L}{\partial a} = 2(Sa - \lambda Ia) = 0;$$

$$(S - \lambda I)a = 0;$$

This can be satisfied only if either

$$(S - \lambda I) = 0;$$

or $\qquad a = 0;$

where

0 is the null vector.

In order to have a nontrivial solution as well as to satisfy the constraint that there is a unique ray through the origin, only the first alternative is open, or

$$(S - \lambda I) = 0;$$

The matrix $(S - \lambda I)$ is singular if $|S - \lambda I| = 0$, or

$$\begin{vmatrix} (\sigma_{11} - \lambda) & \sigma_{12} & \sigma_{13} \\ \sigma_{21} & (\sigma_{22} - \lambda) & \sigma_{23} \\ \sigma_{31} & \sigma_{32} & (\sigma_{33} - \lambda) \end{vmatrix} = 0;$$

Solving for λ gives the characteristic roots of the matrix $(\lambda_1, \lambda_2, \lambda_3)$ for a trivariate population.

Selecting the largest or principal root, the corresponding characteristic vector is derived by substituting λ into the equation:

$$(S - \lambda I)a = 0;$$

Thus the values of a (i.e., the principal components of the three variables) are determined.

The values can now be applied to standardize the values of the original tri-variate population and to derive observations on the first principal component.

$$Z_1 = a_1 X_{1 \cdot 1} + a_2 X_{1 \cdot 2} + a_3 X_{1 \cdot 3} ;$$

$$Z_2 = a_1 X_{2 \cdot 1} + a_2 X_{2 \cdot 2} + a_3 X_{2 \cdot 3} ;$$

$$
\begin{array}{cccc}
. & . & . & . \\
. & . & . & . \\
. & . & . & . \\
\end{array}
$$

$$Z_T = a_1 X_{T \cdot 1} + a_2 X_{T \cdot 2} + a_3 X_{T \cdot 3} ;$$

Usually this new variable will explain the major part of the variance of the trivariate distribution. It will characterize the original variables with a minimum loss of information.

References

Airov, Joseph. *The Location of the Synthetic Fiber Industry: A Study in Regional Analysis.* The M.I.T. Press and John Wiley, 1959.

Ashby, Lowell D. "Regional Projections in a National Setting," United States Department of Commerce, Regional Economics Division, no. 66143 (unpublished).

Atlantic Development Board, Planning Division. *A Study of New Manufacturing Establishment and Expansions in Canada and in the Atlantic Region, 1956–1965.* August 1967.

—. *Derivation of Capital Stock and Capital Output Ratios for Industries in the Atlantic Provinces.* Draft report, July 1968.

Atlantic Development Council. *A Strategy for the Economic Development of the Atlantic Region, 1971–1981.* 1971.

Atlantic Provinces Economic Council. *Agriculture in the Atlantic Economy.* Pamphlet No. 10, July 1966.

Bachi, Roberto. *Graphical Rational Methods.* Israel University Press, 1960.

—. "Standard Distance Measures and Related Methods for Spatial Analysis," *Papers, Regional Science Association*, X, 1963, pp. 83–132.

Barna, Tibor. "On Measuring Capital," in F. A. Lutz, Chairman, D. C. Hague (ed.) *The Theory of Capital.* Macmillan, 1963, pp. 75–94.

Barnard, Jerald R. *Design and Use of Social Accounting Systems in State Development Planning.* Bureau of Business and Economic Research, College of Business Administration, University of Iowa. 1967.

Baumol, William J. "Macroeconomics of Unbalanced Growth: The Anatomy of Urban Crisis," *American Economic Review*, LVII, 3, June 1967, pp. 415–426.

Bell, Frederick W. "An Econometric Forecasting Model for a Region," *Journal of Regional Science*, VII, 2, 1967, pp. 109–127.

—. *The Elasticity of Substitution, Regional Wage Differentials and Structural Unemployment in Urban Economies.* Unpublished Ph.D. dissertation, 1964.

Bentzer, R., and B. Hansen. "On Recursiveness and Interdependency in Economic Models," *The Review of Economic Studies*, XXII, 3, 1954–55, pp. 153–168.

Bhalla, G. S. "Sectoral Employment Multipliers in the Atlantic Provinces." Planning Division, Department of Regional Economic Expansion. Unpublished report, May 1969.

—. "Sectoral Income Multipliers in the Atlantic Provinces." Planning Division, Department of Regional Economic Expansion. Unpublished report, July 1968.

Bogue, Donald J. *The Structure of the Metropolitan Community: A Study in Dominance and Subdominance.* University of Michigan Press, 1949.

Bonbright, J. C. "May the Same Property Have Different Values for Different Purposes?" *Proceedings of the National Tax Association*, 1927, pp. 279–295.

Bourque, Phillip J., Edward J. Chambers, J. S. Chin, F. L. Derman, Barney Dowdle, Guy G. Gordon, Morgan Thomas, Charles M. Tiebout, and Eldon E. Weeks. *The Washington Interindustry Study for 1963*. Center for Urban and Regional Studies, University of Washington, Seattle, 1966.

Bowen, W. G., and R. A. Berry. "Unemployment Conditions and Movements of the Money Wage Level," *Review of Economics and Statistics*, XLV, 1963, pp. 162-172.

Brewis, T. N. *Regional Economic Policies in Canada*. Macmillan, 1969.

Canada. Department of Fisheries and Fisheries Research Board of Canada. *The Commercial Fisheries of Canada*. Royal Commission on Canada's Economic Prospects, 1957.

Canada. Department of Forestry, A.R.D.A. *Federal-Provincial Rural Development Agreement, 1965-70*. Queen's Printer, 1965.

Canada. Department of Forestry and Rural Development, A.R.D.A. *The Canada Land Inventory*. Various reports, 1965-1967.

Canada. Department of Labour, Economics and Research Branch, Surveys Division. *Wage Rates, Salaries and Hours of Labour*. Annual Report No. 44, October 1961.

Canada. Department of National Revenue. *Taxation Statistics*. Annual.

Canada. Department of Trade and Commerce. *Private and Public Investment in Canada, 1947*.

——. *Private and Public Investment in Canada: Outlook*. Annual, 1950 to 1960.

——. *Private and Public Investment in Canada: Outlook and Estimates*. Annual, 1961 to 1963.

Canada. Dominion Bureau of Statistics. *Canada Year Book*, 1968 and 1969. Catalogue No. 11-202.

——. *Canadian Forestry Statistics*, 1961. Catalogue No. 25-202.

——. *Canadian Statistical Review*, June 1967 and April 1969. Catalogue No. 11-003.

——. *1921 Census of Canada*.

——. *1951 Census of Canada*.

——. *1956 Census of Canada*.

——. *1961 Census of Canada*.

——. *1961 Census of Canada: Agriculture*. Catalogue No. 96-520.

——. *1961 Census of Canada: Agriculture*. Catalogue No. 96-527.

——. *1961 Census of Canada: Agriculture: Nova Scotia*. Catalogue No. 96-533.

——. *1961 Census of Canada: Canadian Families*. Catalogue No. 99-526.

——. *1961 Census of Canada: Characteristics of Immigrants*. Catalogue No. 92-562.

——. *1961 Census of Canada: Educational Levels and School Attendance*. Catalogue No. 99-520.

——. *1961 Census of Canada: Family Incomes*. Catalogue No. 98-504.

—. *1961 Census of Canada: Housing: Dwelling Characteristics by Type of Household*. Catalogue No. 93–521.

—. *1961 Census of Canada: Housing: Dwelling Characteristics by Type of Tenure*. Catalogue No. 93–529.

—. *1961 Census of Canada: Labour Force*. Catalogue No. 94–501, 94–518 to 94–522, 94–532, 94–547.

—. *1961 Census of Canada: Population*. Catalogue No. 92–517, 92–536, 92–539.

—. *1961 Census of Canada*. Special tabulations.

—. *1966 Census of Canada*, Catalogue No. 92–602.

—. *1966 Census of Canada: Agriculture: Nova Scotia*. Catalogue No. 96–604.

—. *1966 Census of Canada: Population*. Catalogue No. 92–602, 92–603, 92–610.

—. *Electric Power Statistics:* Vol. II, *Annual Statistics, 1967 and 1968*. Catalogue No. 57–202.

—. *Estimates of Employees by Province and Industry, 1961–1968*. Catalogue No. 72–508.

—. *Fisheries Statistics – Canada*, annual, 1961. Catalogue No. 24–201.

—. *Fisheries Statistics – Nova Scotia*, annual, 1964. Catalogue No. 24–205.

—. *Fixed Capital Flows and Stocks, Manufacturing, Canada, 1926–1960: Methodology*. Catalogue No. 13–522.

—. *General Review of the Manufacturing Industries of Canada*, annual, 1966. Catalogue No. 31–201.

—. *Manufacturing Industries of Canada: Atlantic Provinces*, annual, 1957 to 1962. Catalogue No. 31–204.

—. *Manufacturing Industries of Canada: Geographical Distribution*, annual, 1961. Catalogue No. 31–209.

—. *General Review of the Mineral Industries (Mines, Quarries and Oil Wells)*, annual, 1961. Catalogue No. 26–201.

—. *Manufacturing Industries of Canada*, 1962. Special tabulations.

—. *National Accounts, Income and Expenditure*, annual, 1950 to 1966. Catalogue No. 13–201, 13–502.

—. *National Accounts, Income and Expenditure, by Quarters, 1947–1961*. Catalogue No. 13–519.

—. *National Income of Canada, 1919–1938*. Queen's Printer, 1940.

—. *Preliminary Report on Mineral Production*, annual, 1961, 1963, 1965. Catalogue No. 26–203.

—. *Preliminary Statistics of Education*, annual, 1951–52, 1952–53, 1953–54. Catalogue No. 81–201.

—. *Private and Public Investment in Canada, Outlook and Regional Estimates*, annual, 1963–1970, Catalogue No. 61–205.

—. *Survey of Education Finance*, annual, 1954 to 1961. Catalogue No. 81–208.

Balance Sheet of the United States. Princeton University Press for National Bureau of Economic Research, 1963.

Goodman, L. Landon. *Man and Automation.* Penguin Books, 1957.

Graham, John F. *Fiscal Adjustment and Economic Development.* University of Toronto Press, 1963.

Halliday, W. E. D. *A Forest Classification for Canada.* Canada Department of Mines and Resources, Forest Service Bulletin No. 89, 1937.

Harris, Chauncy D. "The Market as a Factor in the Localization of Industry in the United States," *Annals of the Association of American Geographers,* December 1954.

Harvey, Andrew S. *Human Resources in North Eastern Nova Scotia.* Institute of Public Affairs, Dalhousie University, 1968.

Hawbolt, L. S., and R. M. Bulmer. *The Forest Resources of Nova Scotia.* Nova Scotia Department of Lands and Forests, 1958.

Hedlin-Menzies & Associates. *The Report of the Eastern Canada Farm Survey.* 1963.

Hildebrand, G., and T. C. Liu. *Manufacturing Production Functions in the United States, 1957.* New York State School of Industrial and Labor Relations, Ithaca, 1965.

Hirsch, Werner Z. "Design and Use of Regional Accounts," *American Economic Review,* LII (May 1962), pp. 365–373.

——. "The Supply of Urban Public Services," in Harvey S. Perloff and Lowdon Wingo, Jr. (eds.) *Issues in Urban Economics.* John Hopkins Press, 1968, pp. 477–524.

——. (ed.) *Elements of Regional Accounts.* Johns Hopkins Press, 1964.

——. (ed.) *Regional Accounts for Policy Decisions.* Johns Hopkins Press, 1966.

Hirschman, Albert O. *The Strategy of Economic Development.* Yale University Press, 1960.

Hochwald, Werner (ed.). *Design of Regional Accounts.* Johns Hopkins Press, 1961.

Homans, George Caspar. *Social Behavior: Its Elementary Forms.* Harcourt, Brace & World, 1961.

Hood, Wm. C. and Anthony Scott. *Output, Labour and Capital in the Canadian Economy.* Report of the Royal Commission on Canada's Economic Prospects, 1957.

Hooker, Owen T. "Input-Output Analysis in Development Planning for Nova Scotia," manuscript, 1969.

Hoover, Edgar M., Jr. "Integration of Processes in Plant, Concern and Production Center," in National Resources Planning Board. *Industrial Location and National Resources.* U.S. Government Printing Office, 1943.

Hotelling H. "Simplified Calculation of Principal Components," *Psychometrika,* I (1936), pp. 27–35.

Howland, R. D. "Some Regional Aspects of Canada's Economic Development," *Royal Commission on Canada's Economic Prospects,* November 1957.

Hugo-Brunt, Michael. "The Origin of Colonial Settlements in the Maritimes," in L. O. Gertler (ed.), *Planning the Canadian Environment*. Harvest House, 1968.

Isard, Walter. "Interregional and Regional Input-Output Analysis: A Model of a Space-Economy," *Review of Economics and Statistics*, XXXIII, November 1951.

——. *Methods of Regional Analysis: An Introduction to Regional Science*. The M.I.T. Press and John Wiley & Sons, 1960.

Isard, Walter, and Stanislaw Czamanski. "A Model for the Projection of Regional Industrial Structure, Land Use Patterns and Conversion Potentialities," *Papers, Peace Research Society (International)*, V, 1966, pp. 1–13.

——. "Techniques for Estimating Local and Regional Multiplier Effects of Changes in the Level of Major Governmental Programs," *Papers, Peace Research Society (International)*, III, 1965, pp. 19–45.

Isard, Walter, and Robert E. Kuenne. "The Impact of Steel Upon the Greater New York–Philadelphia Industrial Region," *The Review of Economics and Statistics*, XXXV, **4**, November 1953, pp. 289–301.

Isard, Walter, and Thomas W. Langford Jr. *Regional Input-Output Study: Recollections, Reflections and Diverse Notes on the Philadelphia Experience*. The M.I.T. Press, 1971.

Isard, Walter, Thomas W. Langford, Jr., and Eli Romanoff. *Philadelphia Region Input-Output Study*. Department of Regional Science, University of Pennsylvania, and Regional Science Research Institute, 1966.

Isard, Walter, Eugene W. Schooler, and Thomas Vietorisz. *Industrial Complex Analysis and Regional Development*. The M.I.T. Press and John Wiley, 1959.

Isard, Walter *et al.* "On the Linkage of Socio-economic and Ecological Systems," *Papers, Regional Science Association*, XXI, 1968, pp. 79–99.

Isard, Walter, in association with Tony E. Smith and Peter Isard, Tze Hsiung Tung, and Michael Dacey. *General Theory, Social, Political, Economic, and Regional*. The M.I.T. Press, 1969.

Johnston, Jr. *Econometric Methods*. McGraw-Hill, 1963.

Karaska, Gerald J., and David F. Bramhall. *Locational Analysis for Manufacturing: A Selection of Readings*. The M.I.T. Press, 1969.

Klein, L. R. *Textbook of Econometrics*. Row-Peterson & Co., 1953.

Koopmans, T. C. "Measurement Without Theory", *Review of Economic Statistics*, XXIX (1947).

Kuznets, Simon. "On the Measurement of National Wealth," Conference on Research in Income and Wealth, *Studies in Income and Wealth*, II. National Bureau of Economic Research, 1938.

Larsen, H. L. *Demand and Production Analysis of Agricultural Products in Nova Scotia 1950–1972*. Voluntary Economic Planning, Nova Scotia Department of Finance and Economics, 1964.

Leontief, Wassily W. *Input-Output Economics*. Oxford University Press, 1966.

Leven, Charles L. "Regional Income and Product Accounts: Construction and Applications," in Werner Hochwald (ed.), *Design of Regional Accounts*. John Hopkins Press, 1961.

——. *Theory and Method of Income and Product Accounts for Metropolitan Areas, Including the Elgin-Dundee Area as a Case Study*. Ames, Iowa, Iowa State University, 1958 (mimeographed).

Leven, Charles L., John B. Legler, and Perry Shapiro. *An Analytical Framework for Regional Development Policy*. The M.I.T. Press, 1970.

Levitt, Kari. "A Macro Economic Analysis of the Structure of the Economy of the Atlantic Provinces, 1960." Paper presented at a meeting of the Canadian Economics Association, June 1969.

Litton Industries, Development Division. *A Preliminary Analysis for an Economic Development Plan Called the Appalachian Region*. Report to the Appalachian Regional Commission, Contract No. C–181–65 (NEG) United States Department of Commerce, Area Development Administration, November 1965.

Loesch, August. *The Economics of Location*. Translated by William H. Woglom, with the assistance of Wolfgang F. Stolper. Yale University Press, 1954.

Lyall, Kathrine. *Regional Investment Allocation: Equity and Efficiency in Yugoslav Development Planning*. Unpublished Ph.D. dissertation, Cornell University, 1969.

Machlup, Fritz. *The Production and Distribution of Knowledge in the United States*. Princeton University Press, for the National Bureau of Economic Research, 1962.

Malinvaud, E. *Statistical Methods of Econometrics*. Rand McNally, Chicago, 1966.

Malinvaud, E., and M. O. L. Bacharach. *Activity Analysis in the Theory of Growth and Planning*. Macmillan, 1967.

Malizia, Emil E. *Regional Wealth Accounting as a Means of Quantitative Evaluation of Regional Resources*. Ph.D. dissertation, Cornell University, 1969.

Metzler, Lloyd A. "A Multiple-Region Theory of Income and Trade," *Econometrica*, XVIII, 4, 1950, pp. 329–54.

Miernyk, William H. *The Elements of Input-Output Analysis*. Random House (1957), 1965.

Miernyk, William, *et al*. *An Interindustry Analysis of the West Virginia Economy*. West Virginia University Foundation, forthcoming.

Morrison, D. G. *Multivariate Statistical Methods*. McGraw-Hill, 1967.

Morse, Chandler. *Basic Concepts of Private and Social Accounting: An Economic Approach*. Norton Printing Co., 1954.

Musgrave, Richard A. *Fiscal Systems*. Yale University Press, 1969.

Myrdal, Gunnar. *Economic Theory and Underdeveloped Regions*. G. Duckworth, 1957.

Nichols, Vida. *Growth Poles: An Investigation of Their Potential as a Tool for*

Regional Economic Development. Regional Science Research Institute, Discussion Paper No. 30, May 1969. Mimeographed.

Niedercorn, J. H., and B. V. Bechdolt, Jr. "An Economic Derivation of the 'Gravity Law' of Spatial Interaction," *Journal of Regional Science*, XX, 2, 1969, pp. 273-282.

Nova Scotia Department of Education. *Annual Report of the Department of Education for the Year Ending July 31, 1961.*

Nova Scotia Department of Mines. *Annual Report on Mines, 1964.*

——. *Annual Report on Mines, 1967.*

Nova Scotia Department of Mines, Groundwater Section. *Nova Scotia Water Resources Study.* Prepared for the Atlantic Development Board, April 1967.

Nova Scotia Voluntary Planning Board. *First Plan for Economic Development to 1968.* Nova Scotia Department of Finance and Economics, February 1966.

——. *1967 Annual Report and Economic Review.* Nova Scotia Department of Finance and Economics, 1968.

Okun, Bernard, and Richard W. Richardson. "Regional Income Inequality and Internal Population Migrations," in John Friedmann and William Alonso (eds.), *Regional Development and Planning.* The M.I.T. Press, 1964.

Pearson, K. "On Lines and Planes of Closest Fit to Systems of Points in Space," *Philosophical Magazines*, II (1901), pp. 559-572.

Perloff, Harvey S. "A National System of Metropolitan Information and Analysis," *American Economic Review*, LII (May 1962), pp. 356-364.

——. "Relative Regional Economic Growth: An Approach to Regional Accounts," in Werner Hochwald (ed.), *Design of Regional Accounts.* Johns Hopkins Press, 1961.

Perloff, Harvey S., Edgar S. Dunn, Jr., Eric E. Lampard, and Richard F. Muth. *Regions, Resources, and Economic Growth.* Johns Hopkins Press, 1960.

Perroux, François. "Note sur la notion de 'Pole de croissance'," *Économie appliquée*, January-June, 1955, pp. 307-320.

Peterson, Wallace C. *Income, Employment, and Economic Growth.* W. W. Norton, 1962.

Phillips, A. W. "The Relation between Unemployment and the Rate of Change of Money Wage Rates in the United Kingdom, 1861-1957," *Economica*, XXV, 1958, pp. 283-299.

Pred, Allan R. *The Spatial Dynamics of U.S. Urban-Industrial Growth: 1800-1914.* The M.I.T. Press, 1966.

Putman, Donald F. (ed.) *Canadian Regions: A Geography of Canada.* Toronto: J. M. Dent & Sons, 1952.

Redfern, Philip. "Net Investment in Fixed Assets in the United Kingdom, 1938-1953," *Journal of the Royal Statistical Society*, CXVIII, Part VI, 1955, pp. 141-192.

Report of the Royal Commission on Coal. The Honourable I. C. Rand, Q. C., Commissioner. Queen's Printer, 1960.

Revell, Jack. "The National Balance Sheet of the United Kingdom," *Review of Income and Wealth*, Series XII (December 1966), pp. 281–310.

Rogers, Andrei. "Matrix Methods of Population Analysis," *Journal of the American Institute of Planners*, XXXII, January 1966, pp. 40–44.

Rosen, Sam. *National Income, Its Measurement, Determination, and Relation to Public Policy*. Holt, Rinehard and Winston, 1963.

Ross, Philip. "Labor Market Behavior and the Relationship Between Unemployment and Wages," *Industrial Relations Research Association: 14th Annual Proceedings*, 1961, pp. 275–288.

Royal Commission on Canada's Economic Prospects. *Final Report*. Queen's Printer, 1957.

Ruggles, Richard, and Nancy D. Ruggles. *National Income Accounts and Income Analysis*. McGraw-Hill, 1956.

Sanderson, M. E., and D. W. Phillips. *Average Annual Water Surplus in Canada*. Climatological Studies, No. 9. Canada, Department of Transport, Meteorological Branch, 1967.

Schultz, Theodore W. "Capital Formation by Education," *Journal of Political Economy*, LXVIII, **6**, 1960, pp. 571–583.

Schultze, Charles L. *National Income Analysis*. Prentice-Hall, 1964.

Scitowsky, Tibor. "Two Concepts of External Economies," *The Journal of Political Economy*, LXII, **2**, April 1954, pp. 143–151.

Scott, Anthony. *Natural Resources: The Economics of Conservation*. Canadian Studies in Economics, No. 3, University of Toronto Press, 1955.

Stone, Leroy O. *Urban Development in Canada*. Dominion Bureau of Statistics, 1967.

Stone, Richard. *Input-Output and National Accounts*. Organization for Economic Co-operation and Development, 1961.

Streit, M. E. "Spatial Associations and Economic Linkages between Industries," *Journal of Regional Science*, IX, **2**, 1969, pp. 177–188.

Tinbergen, Jan. *Economic Policy: Principles and Design*. North Holland Publishing Co., 1956.

Tintner, G. *Econometrics*. John Wiley & Sons, 1952.

Ullman, Edward L., and Michael F. Dacey. "The Minimum Requirements Approach in the Urban Economic Base," in The Royal University of Lund, Sweden, *Proceedings of the I.G.U. Symposium in Urban Geography, Lund, 1960*. C. W. K. Gleerup, 1962.

United Nations, Department of Economic and Social Affairs. *Problems in Input-Output Tables and Analysis*. New York, 1966.

United States Department of Commerce. Business and Defense Services Administration. *Industry Profiles, 1958–1966*. Washington, D.C., 1968.

——. Office of Business Economics. *Survey of Current Business*, XLV, **9**, September 1965.

——. Office of Business Economics. *Survey of Current Business*, XLVI, **4**, April 1966.

——. Office of Business Economics. *Survey of Current Business,* XLIX, 11, November 1969.

Urquhart, M. C., and K. A. Buckley (eds.). *Historical Statistics of Canada.* Macmillan Company of Canada, 1965.

Walsh, J. R. "Capital Concept Applied to Man," *Quarterly Journal of Economics,* XLIX, 1934–35, pp. 255–285.

Weber, Alfred. *Theory of the Location of Industries.* Translated by Carl J. Friedrich, University of Chicago Press, 1929.

Weisbrod, Burton A. "The Valuation of Human Capital," *Journal of Political Economy,* LXIX, 5, 1961, pp. 425–436.

White, Charles L. *et al. Regional Geography of Anglo-America.* 3rd ed. Prentice-Hall, 1964.

Wiles, P. J. "The Nation's Intellectual Investment," *Bulletin of the Oxford University Institute of Statistics,* XVIII, August 1956, pp. 279–290.

Williamson, J. G. "Regional Inequality and the Process of National Development," *Economic Development and Cultural Change,* XIII, 1965, pp. 3–45.

Wood, K. S. *Income and Product Accounts of Nova Scotia.* Institute of Public Affairs, Dalhousie University, 1970.

Notes

1. For a description of this technique and a review of the voluminous literature see Isard, Walter *et al., Methods of Regional Analysis: An Introduction to Regional Science*, M.I.T. Press and John Wiley & Sons, 1960, pp. 493–568.
2. There have been attempts recently at providing a theoretical justification for the use of the gravity formula. See Niedercorn, J. H. and B. V. Bechdolt, Jr., "An Economic Derivation of the 'Gravity Law' of Spatial Interaction," *Journal of Regional Science*, **IX, 2,** 1969, pp. 273–282.
3. The following discussion of land forms draws heavily from Putnam, Donald F. (ed.), *Canadian Regions: A Geography of Canada*, J. M. Dent & Sons, 1952, pp. 70–76.
4. White, Charles L. *et al., Regional Geography of Anglo-America*, Prentice-Hall, 1964, pp. 73–76.
5. Hugo-Brunt, Michael, "The Origin of Colonial Settlements in the Maritimes," in L. O. Gertler (ed.), *Planning the Canadian Environment*, Harvest House, 1968, pp. 42–83.
6. White, *et al., op. cit.*, pp. 73–74.
7. Hugo-Brunt, *op. cit.*, pp. 46–49.
8. Graham, John F., *Fiscal Adjustment and Economic Development*, University of Toronto Press, 1963, pp. 13–15.

Chapter 2

1. Several of the estimates of quantities of various resources available were compiled by my research assistant K. Scott Wood, while most of the values quoted were calculated by my student and research assistant Emil E. Malizia upon whose doctoral dissertation, *Regional Wealth Accounting as a Means of Quantitative Evaluation of Regional Resources*, this Chapter as well as Chapter 6 draws.
2. Scott, Anthony, *Natural Resources: The Economics of Conservation*, Canadian Studies in Economics, No. 3, University of Toronto Press, 1955, pp. 8 and 66.
3. Isard, Walter, et al., "On the Linkage of Socio-Economic and Ecological Systems," *Papers, Regional Science Association*, XXI, 1968, pp. 79–99.
4. For example, see Weisbrod, Burton A.: "The Valuation of Human Capital," *Journal of Political Economy*, LXIX, 5, 1961, pp. 425–436.
5. Wiles, P. J., "The Nation's Intellectual Investment," *Bulletin of the Oxford University Institute of Statistics*, XVII, August 1956, pp. 284–285; Schultz, Theodore W., "Capital Formation by Education," *Journal of Political Economy*, LXVIII, **6,** 1960, pp. 571–574; and Walsh J. R., "Capital Concept Applied to Man," *Quarterly Journal of Economics*," XLIX, 1934–35, pp. 265–266.
6. See Machlup, Fritz, *The Production and Distribution of Knowledge in the United States*, Princeton University Press, for the National Bureau of Economic Research, 1962, pp. 51–55.

7. Goldsmith, "Measuring National Wealth in a System of Social Accounting," pp. 63–64; and Revell, Jack, "The National Balance Sheet of the United Kingdom," *Review of Income and Wealth*, Series XIII (December 1966), p. 286.

8. See Bonbright, J. C., "May the Same Property Have Different Values for Different Purposes," *Proceedings of the National Tax Association*, 1927, p. 287.

9. Canada, Department of Forestry and Rural Development, A.R.D.A., *The Canada Land Inventory*, various reports, 1965 to 1967.

10. Atlantic Provinces Economic Council, *Agriculture in the Atlantic Economy*. Pamphlet No. 10, July 1966, p. 7.

11. For details see Larsen, H. K., *Demand and Production Analysis of Agricultural Products in Nova Scotia, 1950–1962*, Voluntary Economic Planning, Nova Scotia Department of Finance and Economics, 1964.

12. Canada, Department of Forestry, A.R.D.A., *Federal-Provincial Rural Development Agreement*, 1965–70, Queen's Printer, 1965.

13. Hedlin-Menzies & Associates, *The Report of the Eastern Canada Farm Survey*, 1963, p. 3.

14. The quantity estimates were provided by Dr. James Nowlan, Deputy Minister, Nova Scotia Department of Mines, and his staff, while costs were derived from D.B.S., *Preliminary Report on Mineral Production*, Cat. No. 26-203, 1961, 1963, 1965, Tables 4, 5, 14, 17, 20, 35, 56, and 62. Transportation rates were supplied by the Carload Freight Office, Canadian National Railways. Transportation costs were calculated from railroad freight rate schedules by multiplying average distance from production sites to Halifax by the appropriate freight rates.

15. Malizia, *op. cit.*, pp. 276–284.

16. Donald, J. R., *The Cape Breton Coal Problem*, Queen's Printer, 1966.

17. Cost statistics came from two published sources: D.B.S., *General Review of the Mineral Industries (Mines, Quarries and Oil Wells)* 1961, Cat. No. 26-201, Table 29, p. A-30 and Table 24, p. A-26; and Nova Scotia Department of Mines, *Annual Report on Mines*, 1964, pp. 112–137.

18. Canada, Territorial Sea and Fishing Zones, *Statutes of Canada*, 1964–65, Ch. 22.

19. For details of calculations and sources of data, see Appendix B.

20. Sanderson, M. E., and D. W. Phillips, *Average Annual Water Surplus in Canada*, Climatological Studies, No. 9, Department of Transport, Meteorological Branch, 1967, p. 1 and Table A, p. 72. The authors carefully calculated average runoff figures by drainage basin and plotted isolines of water surplus on contoured base maps. Their results, given in cubic feet per second per year as well as in acre-feet, were supplemented by estimates made by Dr. James Nowlan, Deputy Minister of the Nova Scotia Department of Mines, along with some calculations completed by his staff.

21. A detailed description of water supply by town and village is contained in a publication of the Nova Scotia Department of Mines, Groundwater Section, *Nova Scotia Water Resources Study*, prepared for the Atlantic Development Board, April 1967.

22. The tables and estimates appearing in this Section were compiled by my

assistants Andrew S. Harvey, Tien Jung Huang, and Emil E. Malizia. For further information see: Harvey, Andrew S., *Human Resources in North Eastern Nova Scotia*, Institute for Public Affairs, Dalhousie University, 1968.

23. For details see Appendix C.

24. D.B.S., *Census of Canada, 1961: Characteristics of Immigrants*, Catalogue No. 92-562.

25. Phillips, A. W., "The Relation Between Unemployment and the Rate of Change of Money Wage Rates in the United Kingdom, 1961–1957," *Economica*, XXV, 1958, pp. 283–299.

26. Bowen, W. G. and R. A. Berry, "Unemployment Conditions and Movements of the Money Wage Level," *Review of Economics and Statistics*, XLV, 1963, pp. 162–172.

27. Bell, Frederick W., "An Econometric Forecasting Model for a Regions," *Journal of Regional Science*, VII, 2, 1967, pp. 109–127.

28. Bell, Frederick W., *The Elasticity of Substitution, Regional Wage Differentials and Structural Unemployment in Urban Economies*, unpublished Ph.D. dissertation, 1964.

29. Ross, Philip, "Labor Market Behavior and the Relationship Between Unemployment and Wages," *Industrial Relations Research Association: Fourteenth Annual Proceedings*, 1961, pp. 275–288.

30. See Chapter 7, Subsection f.

31. Okun, Bernard and Richard W. Richardson, "Regional Income Inequality and Internal Population Migrations," in John Friedman and William Alonso (eds.), *Regional Development and Planning*, M.I.T. Press, 1964, p. 306.

32. For methods of aging a given population see, for example, Rogers, Andrei, "Matrix Methods of Population Analysis," *Journal of the American Institute of Planners*, XXXII, January 1966, pp. 40–44.

33. D.B.S., *1961 Census of Canada: Family Incomes* (Catalogue No. 98–504); D.B.S., *1961 Census of Canada: Canadian Families* (Catalogue No. 99–526); Canada, Department of Labour, Economics and Research Branch, Surveys Division, *Wage Rates, Salaries and Hours of Labour*, Annual Report No. 44, October 1961; and D.B.S., *National Accounts, Income and Expenditure*, annual, 1950–1965 (Catalogue No. 13–201). Data on consumption expenditures were available in D.B.S., *National Accounts: Income and Expenditure*, *1926–1956* (Catalogue No. 13–502); D.B.S., *National Income of Canada*, *1919–1938*, 1940; D.B.S., *Urban Family Expenditure*, 1959 (Catalogue No. 62–521); and Urquhart, M. C. and K. A. Buckley (eds.), *Historical Statistics of Canada*, Macmillan Company of Canada, 1965.

34. The data were obtained from D.B.S., *Survey of Education Finance*, 1954–1961 (Catalogue No. 81–208); Nova Scotia Department of Education, *Annual Report of the Department of Education for the Year Ending July 31, 1961*; D.B.S., *Preliminary Statistics of Education*, 1951–52, 1952–53, 1953–54 (Catalogue No. 81–201); D.B.S., *Survey of Higher Education*, 1944–46 and 1952–54 Catalogue No. 81–402); and D.B.S., *1961 Census of Canada: Educational Levels and School Attendance* (Catalogue No. 99–520).

35. For details see Appendix C.

36. For details see Appendix C.
37. For details see Appendix C.

Chapter 3

1. Perloff, Harvey S., "A National System of Metropolitan Information and Analysis," *American Economic Review*, LII (May 1962), pp. 356–364; Hirsch, Werner Z., "Design and Use of Regional Accounts," *American Economic Review*, LII (May 1962), pp. 365–373; Hochwald, Werner (ed.), *Design of Regional Accounts*, Johns Hopkins Press, 1961; Hirsch, Werner Z. (ed.), *Regional Accounts for Policy Decisions*, Johns Hopkins Press, 1966; Hirsch, Werner Z. (ed.), *Elements of Regional Accounts*, Johns Hopkins Press, 1964; Friedmann, John, "Focus on Public Policy," in Iowa State University Center for Agricultural and Economic Development, *Research and Education for Regional and Area Development*, Iowa State University Press, 1966, pp. 215–233; Barnard, Jerald R., *Design and Use of Social Accounting Systems in State Development Planning*, Bureau of Business and Economic Research, College of Business Administration, University of Iowa, 1967; and Leven, Charles L., John B. Legler, and Perry Shapiro, *An Analytical Framework for Regional Development Policy*, the M.I.T. Press, 1970.
2. Morse, Chandler, *Basic Concepts of Private and Social Accounting: An Economic Approach*, Norton Printing Co., 1954.
3. Perloff, Harvey S., "Relative Regional Economic Growth: An Approach to Regional Accounts," in Werner Hochwald (ed.), *Design of Regional Accounts*, Johns Hopkins Press, 1961, p. 60.
4. Koopman, T. C., "Measurement Without Theory," *Review of Economic Statistics*, XXIX (1947), pp. 161ff.
5. For details see Czamanski, S., "Regional Science and Regional Planning," *Plan: Journal of the Town Planning Institute of Canada*, IX, 2, 1968, p. 63.
6. The methodology of the Nova Scotia Income and Product Accounts has been developed by the author and published in Czamanski, *Regional Income and Product Accounts of North-Eastern Nova Scotia*. The accounts, which covered all of Nova Scotia in addition to the nine northeastern counties for the years 1961–1964, were later extended by K. S. Wood for the years 1950–1954 under my direction but without changing the methodology. The extended accounts are to be found in Wood, K. S., *Income and Product Accounts of Nova Scotia*, Institute of Public Affairs, Dalhousie University, *Nova Scotia*, Institute of Public Affairs, Dalhousie University, 1970.
7. For a detailed discussion of the problems involved see Czamanski: *Regional Income and Product Accounts of North-Eastern Nova Scotia*.
8. For a discussion of problems involved in the construction of aggregates at the national level see, for example, Rosen, *op. cit.*; Ruggles, *op. cit.*; and Schultze, Charles L., *National Income Analysis*, Prentice-Hall, 1964, pp. 18–39.

9. For some problems involved see Czamanski: *Regional Income and Product Accounts of North-Eastern Nova Scotia.*

10. See, for example, Leven, *Theory and Methods of Income and Product Accounts for Metropolitan Areas.*

11. D.B.S., *National Accounts, Income and Expenditure, 1964*, (Catalogue No. 13-201), annual, p. 39, gives dividends paid to Nova Scotia residents as part of interest, dividends, and rental income of persons. This includes dividends from corporations located outside the province.

12. For more detail see Leven, Charles L.: "Regional Income and Product Accounts: Construction and Applications," in Werner Hochwald (ed.), *Design of Regional Accounts*, Johns Hopkins Press, 1961, p. 160, and the ensuing discussion at the meeting of the Committee on Regional Accounts.

13. Canada, Department of National Revenue: *Taxation Statistics*, annual.

14. For more details see Czamanski, S., *Structure of the Nova Scotia Economy: Analysis of Income and Product Accounts*, Institute of Public Affairs, Dalhousie University, 1971.

15. For details concerning this type of multiplier, often described as Foreign Trade Multiplier or Interregional Trade Multiplier, and differences existing between these concepts, see Chipman, J. S., *The Theory of Intersectoral Money Flows and Income Formation*, Johns Hopkins Press, 1950, pp. 13-15; Isard, *Methods of Regional Analysis*, pp. 205-8; Peterson, *op. cit.*, pp. 174-5, 225-6, and 301-3; and Metzler, Lloyd A., "A Multiple Region Theory of Income and Trade," *Econometrica*, XVIII, 4, 1950, pp. 329-54.

Chapter 4

1. Fisher, Allan G. B., "Production: Primary, Secondary and Tertiary," *The Economic Record*, June 1939, pp. 24-38. See also Clark, Colin, *The Economics of 1960*, Macmillan Co., 1942, p. 22.

2. Florence, P. Sargant: *Investment, Location and Size of Plant*, Cambridge University Press, 1948, pp. 162-163.

3. Weber, Alfred: *Theory of the Location of Industries*, translated by Carl J. Friedrich, University of Chicago Press, 1929, p. 219.

4. For a detailed discussion see Isard, *et al., Methods of Regional Analysis*, pp. 270-73.

5. For a discussion of factors influencing the iron and steel industry see: Isard, Walter, "Some Locational Factors in the Iron and Steel Industry Since the Early Nineteenth Century," *Journal of Political Economy*, LVI, June 1948; Isard, Walter and John Cumberland, "New England as a Possible Location for an Integrated Iron and Steel Works," *Economic Geography*, XXVI, October 1950; Isard, Walter, *Location and Space-Economy: A General Theory Relating to Industrial Location, Market Areas, Land Use, Trade, and Urban Structure*, M.I.T. Press and John Wiley & Sons, 1956; Isard, Walter and Robert E. Kuenne, "The Impact of Steel Upon the Greater New York-Philadelphia Industrial Region," *The Review of Economics and Statistics*,

XXXV, 4, November 1953; Atlantic Development Board, Planning Division, *A Study of New Manufacturing Establishments and Expansions in Canada and in the Atlantic Region, 1956–1965*, August 1967; Atlantic Development Board, Planning Division: *Derivation of Capital Stock and Capital Output Ratios for Industries in the Atlantic Provinces*, Draft report, July 1968; and United Nations, Economic Commission for Europe: *Criteria for Location of Industrial Plants* (Changes and Problems), New York, 1967.

6. Stone, Leroy O., *Urban Development in Canada*, Dominion Bureau of Statistics, 1967; Pred, Allan R., *The Spatial Dynamics of U.S. Urban-Industrial Growth:* 1800–1914, The M.I.T. Press, 1966; and Isard, *Location and Space-Economy*.

7. Perroux, François, "Note sur la notion de 'Pole de croissance'," *Economié appliquée*, January-June, 1955, pp. 307–320.

8. Nichols, Vida, "Growth Poles: An Investigation of Their Potential as a Tool for Regional Economic Development," *Regional Science Research Institute*, Discussion Paper No. 30, May 1969, mimeo.

9. Nova Scotia Voluntary Planning Board, *First Plan for Economic Development to 1968*, Nova Scotia Department of Finance and Economics, February, 1966.

10. Christaller, Walter, *Die zentralen Orte in Sueddeutschland*, translated by Carlisle W. Baskin as *Central Places in Southern Germany*, Prentice-Hall, 1966.

11. Airov, Joseph, *The Location of the Synthetic Fiber Industry: A Study in Regional Analysis*, The M.I.T. Press and John Wiley, 1959; and Karaska, Gerald J. and David F. Bramhall, *Locational Analysis for Manufacturing: A Selection of Readings*, The M.I.T. Press, 1969.

12. This classification is similar to the one introduced by Hoover, Edgar M., xn Jr., "Integration of Processes in Plant, Concern and Production Center," in National Resources Planning Board, *Industrial Location and National Resources*, U.S. Government Printing Office, 1943.

13. Scitowsky, Tibor, "Two Concepts of External Economies," *The Journal of Economy*, April, 1954, p. 149.

14. Czamanski, S., "A Model of Urban Growth," *Papers, Regional Science Association*, XIII, 1965; and Czamanski, S., "Industrial Location and Urban Growth," *The Town Planning Review*, Liverpool, XXXVI, 3, October 1965.

15. Bogue, Donald J., *The Structure of the Metropolitan Community: A Study in Dominance and Subdominance*, University of Michigan Press, 1949.

16. Christaller, *op. cit.*

17. Loesch, August, *The Economies of Location*, translated by William H. Woglom, with the assistance of Wolfgang F. Stolper, Yale University Press, 1954.

18. Myrdal, Gunnar, *Economic Theory and Underdeveloped Regions*, G. Duckworth, 1957.

19. Hirschman, Albert O., *The Strategy of Economic Development*, Yale University Press, 1960.

20. Friedmann, John, "Regional Economic Policy for Developing Areas," *Papers, Regional Science Association*, XI, 1963, pp. 41–61.

21. Bachi, Roberto, "Standard Distance Measures and Related Methods for Spatial Analysis," *Papers, Regional Science Association*, X, 1963, pp. 83–132; and Bachi, Roberto, *Graphical Rational Methods*, Israel University Press, 1960. See, also, Duncan, Otis Dudley, Ray P. Cuzzart, and Beverley Duncan, *Statistical Geography*, The Free Press of Glencoe, 1961.

22. For detailed calculations see Appendix E.

23. Bachi, Robert, *Standard Distance Measures*, pp. 96–97.

24. The feasibility of planning to have Halifax achieve a population of 350,000 or 500,000 by 1986 was examined by Robert Lewis and Andrew A. Dzurik during a workshop organized by the Voluntary Economic Branch of the Nova Scotia Department of Finance and Economics and directed by this author in January–February 1969.

25. Ullman, Edward L. and Michael F. Dacey, "The Minimum Requirements Approach in the Urban Economic Base," in the Royal University of Lund, Sweden, *Proceedings of the I.G.U. Symposium in Urban Geography*, Lund, 1960, C.W.K. Gleerup, 1962.

26. This technique was first developed and reported by Creamer, Daniel in *Industrial Location and Natural Resources*, National Resources Planning Board, 1942. Later progress was due to Dunn, Edgar S. Jr., "A Statistical and Analytical Technique for Regional Analysis," *Papers, Regional Science Association*, VI, 1960, pp. 97–112. More recent contributions are due to Ashby, Lowell D., "Regional Change in a National Setting," United States Department of Commerce, Office of Business Economies (undated), mimeographed; and Perloff, Harvey S., Edgar S. Dunn, Jr., Eric E. Lampard, and Richard F. Muth, *Regions, Resources, and Economic Growth*, Johns Hopkins Press, 1960. For a different, interesting application to regional growth theory see Isard *et al, Methods of Regional Analysis*, pp. 544–563. For the methodology used in Nova Scotia see Appendix F.

27. Canada, Dominion Bureau of Statistics, *Fixed Capital Flows and Stocks, Manufacturing, Canada, 1926-1960: Methodology*, Cat. No. 13–522.

28. George, Roy E., *A Leader and a Laggard: Manufacturing Industry in Nova Scotia, Quebec and Ontario*, University of Toronto Press, 1970.

29. Howland, R. D., "Some Regional Aspects of Canada's Economic Development," *Royal Commission on Canada's Economic Prospects*, November 1957, Appendix D.

30. The Economist Intelligence Unit, *Atlantic Provinces Transportation Study, Shipping Report*, Part III, 1962.

31. George, *op. cit.*, pp. 88–90.

32. Harris, Chauncy D., "The Market as a Factor in the Localization of Industry in the United States," *Annals of the Association of American Geographers*, XLIV, December 1954; Dunn, Edgar S., "The Market Potential Concept and the Analysis of Location," *Papers and Proceedings of the Regional Science Association*, II, 1956; and Isard, *et al., Methods of Regional Analysis*, pp. 516–525.

Chapter 5

1. For problems involved in construction and regional applications see
    Chenery, Hollis B., and Paul G. Clark, *Interindustry Economics*, John
    Wiley & Sons, 1959; Dorfman, Robert, Paul A. Samuelson, and Robert M.
    Solow, *Linear Programming and Economic Analysis*, McGraw-Hill, 1958,
    pp. 204–264; Isard, Walter, "Interregional and Regional Input-Output
    Analysis: A Model of a Space-Economy," *Review of Economics and
    Statistics*, XXXIII, November 1951; Isard, Walter, and Thomas W. Langford,
    Jr., *Regional Input-Output Study: Recollections, Reflections and Diverse
    Notes on the Philadelphia Experience*, The M.I.T. Press, 1971; Isard, *et al.,
    Methods of Regional Analysis*, pp. 309–371; Leontief, Wassily W., *Input-
    Output Economics*, Oxford University Press, 1966; Miernyk, William H.,
    The Elements of Input-Output Analysis, Random House (1957), 1965;
    Stone, Richard, *Input-Output and National Accounts*, Organization for
    Economic Co-operation and Development, 1961; United Nations, Depart-
    ment of Economic and Social Affairs, *Problems in Input-Output Tables
    and Analysis*, New York, 1966; Carter, A. P., and A. Brody (eds.), *Con-
    tributions to Input-Output Analysis*, 2 volumes, North Holland Publishing
    Company, 1970; Isard, Walter, and Stanislaw Czamanski, "Techniques
    for Estimating Local and regional Multiplier Effects of Changes in the
    Level of Major Governmental Programs," *Papers, Peace Research Society
    (International)*, III, 1965, pp. 19–45; Isard and Kuenne, "The Impact of
    Steel upon the Greater New York-Philadelphia Industrial Region"; and
    Malinvaud, E., and M.O.L. Bacharach, *Activity Analysis in the Theory of
    Growth and Planning*, Macmillan, 1967.
2. Levitt, Kari, "A Macro Economic Analysis of the Structure of the Economy
    of the Atlantic Provinces, 1960." Paper presented at a meeting of the
    Canadian Economics Association, June 1969, mimeographed.
3. Bhalla, G. S., "Sectoral Income Multipliers in the Atlantic Provinces," and
    "Sectoral Employment Multipliers in the Atlantic Provinces," two unpub-
    lished reports, Planning Division, Department of Regional Economic
    Expansion, July 1968 and May 1969.
4. For a discussion of differences between various multipliers see Isard and
    Czamanski, "Techniques for Estimating Local and Regional Multiplier
    Effects . . ."
5. Williamson, J. G., "Regional Inequality and the Process of National
    Development," *Economic Development and Cultural Change*, XIII, 1965,
    pp. 3–45.
6. Chenery and Clark, *op. cit.*
7. Ibid. See Also, Chenery, Hollis B., "Development Policies for Southern
    Italy," *Quarterly Journal of Economics*, LXXVI, November 1962, pp.
    515–547.
8. Lyall, Katherine, *Regional Investment Allocation: Equity and Efficiency
    in Yugoslav Development Planning*, unpublished Ph.D. dissertation,
    Cornell University, 1969.

9. Casetti, Emilio, "Optimal Interregional Investment Transfers," *Journal of Regional Science*, VIII, 1, 1968, pp. 101–107.

10. Hooker, Owen T.: "Input-output Analysis in Development Planning for Nova Scotia," manuscript, 1969.

11. Czamanski, Stan, "Some Empirical Evidence of the Strengths of Linkages between Groups of Related Industries in Urban-Regional Complexes," *Papers, Regional Science Association*, XXVII, 1971.

12. U.S. Department of Commerce, Office of Business Economics, *Survey of Current Business*, XLV, 9, September 1965, pp. 33–49.

13. U.S. Department of Commerce, Office of Business Economics, *Survey of Current Business*, XLI, 4, April 1966, pp. 14–17.

14. U.S. Department of Commerce, Office of Business Economics, *Survey of Current Business*, XLIX, 11, November 1969, pp. 16–35.

15. Isard, Walter, Thomas W. Langford, Jr., and Eli Romanoff, *Philadelphia Region Input-Output Study*, Department of Regional Science, University of Pennsylvania, and Regional Science Research Institute, 1966.

16. Bourque, Phillip J., Edward J. Chambers, J. S. Chin, F. L. Derman, Barney Dowdle, Guy G. Gordon, Morgan Thomas, Charles M. Tiebout, and Eldon E. Weeks, *The Washington Interindustry Study for 1963*, Center for Urban and Regional Studies, University of Washington, Seattle, Washington, 1966.

17. The differences, and problems involved in making the table comparable to the United States table were discussed in Czamanski, S., with the assistance of Emil E. Malizia: "Applicability and Limitations in the Use of National Input-Output Tables for Regional Studies," *Papers, Regional Science Association*, XXIII, 1969, pp. 65–77.

18. The table will form part of a forthcoming publication by Miernyk, William H. *et al.*: *An Interindustry Analysis of the West Virginia Economy*. A prepublication copy has been graciously made available by the West Virginia University Foundation.

19. Levitt, *op. cit.*

20. For details see Czamanski, "A Model of Urban Growth"; and Czamanski, "Industrial Location and Urban Growth."

21. Streit, M. E., "Spatial Associations and Economic Linkages between Industries," *Journal of Regional Science*, IX, 2, 1969, pp. 177–188; and Isard, Walter, Eugene W. Schooler, and Thomas Vietorisz, *Industrial Complex Analysis and Regional Development*, The M.I.T. Press and John Wiley, 1959.

Chapter 6

1. Barna, Tibor, "On Measuring Capital," in F. A. Lutz, Chairman, D. C. Hague (ed.) *The Theory of Capital*, Macmillan, 1963, pp. 76–77.

2. The first approach has been used by Barna at the National Institute of Economic and Social Research in London, the second by the Harvard

Research Project and by the Rand Corporation, the third by Creamer and Bernstein at the National Bureau of Economic Research, and the fourth by Goldsmith in the United States, Redfern in England and Krengel in Germany. The perpetual inventory method has been explained in detail in Goldsmith, "Measuring National Wealth in a System of Social Accounting"; Goldsmith, Raymond W., "A Perpetual Inventory of National Wealth," *Studies in Income and Wealth*, XIV, National Bureau of Economics Research, 1951; Goldsmith, Raymond W., *A Study of Saving in the United States*, Princeton University Press, 1955; Goldsmith, Raymond W., "The Growth of Reproducible Wealth of the United States: Trends and Structure," *Income and Wealth*, International Association for Research in Income and Wealth 1961; Goldsmith, Raymond W., *The National Wealth of the United States in the Postwar Period*, Princeton University Press for National Bureau of Economic Research, 1962; Goldsmith, Raymond W. with Robert E. Lipsey, *Studies in the National Balance Sheet of the United States*, Princeton University Press for National Bureau of Economic Research 1963; Redfern, Philip, "Net Investment in Fixed Assets in the United Kingdom, 1938–1953," *Journal of the Royal Statistical Society*, CXVIII, Part II, 1955, pp. 141–192; Hood, Wm. C. and Anthony Scott, *Output, Labour and Capital in the Canadian Economy*, Report of the Royal Commission on Canada's Economic Prospects, 1957; and the work of T. K. Rymes in D.B.S., *Fixed Capital Flows and Stocks, Manufacturing. Canada, 1926–1960: Methodology* (Catalogue No. 13–522), 1967.

3. The estimates of Kuznets go back to 1869. Kuznets, Simon, "On the Measurement of National Wealth," Conference on Research in Income and Wealth, *Studies in Income and Wealth*, II, National Bureau of Economic Research, 1938.

4. D.B.S., *Fixed Capital Flows and Stocks . . .*

5. Canada, Department of Trade and Commerce, *Private and Public Investment in Canada: Outlook*, annual, 1950 to 1960; Canada, Department of Trade and Commerce, *Private and Public Investment in Canada: Outlook and Estimates*, annual, 1961 to 1963; and unpublished tables for Nova Scotia.

6. Canada, Department of Trade and Commerce, *Private and Public Investment in Canada, 1947.*

7. Canada, Dominion-Provincial Conference on Reconstruction, *Public Investment and Capital Formulation: A Study of Public and Private Investment Outlays, Canada 1926–1941*, Queen's Printer, 1943.

8. Urquhart and Buckley, *op. cit.*, p. 507.

9. D.B.S., *1961 Census of Canada: Housing: Dwelling Characteristics by Type of Household* (Catalogue No. 93–521), Table 89, p. 89–4.

10. Baumol, William J., "Macroeconomics of Unbalanced Growth: The Anatomy of Urban Crisis," *American Economic Review*, LVII, 3, June 1967, pp. 514 ff.

11. For a recent exhaustive treatment of the subject see Isard, Walter, in association with Tony E. Smith and Peter Isard, Tze Hsuing Tung, and Michael Dacey, *General Theory, Social, Political, Economic, and Regional*, The M.I.T. Press, 1969.

12. Musgrave, Richard A.: *Fiscal Systems*, Yale University Press, 1969, pp. 4ff.

13. Czamanski, Stan, "Direction of Land Absorption and Development Patterns of Urban Areas," Institute of Public Affairs, Dalhousie University, under a grant from the Canadian Council for Urban and regional Research, in progress.

14. For earlier work along these lines see Czamanski, S., "The Effects of Public Investments on Urban Land Values," *Journal of the American Institute of Planners*, XXXII, 4, July 1966; and Isard, Walter and Stanislaw Czamanski, "A Model for the Projection of Regional Industrial Structure, Land Use Patterns and Conversion Potentialities," *Papers, Peace Research Society (international)*, V, 1966.

15. For details and some empirical results see: Czamanski, "The Effects of Public Investments on Urban Land Values."

Chapter 7

1. This classification has been adopted from Tingergen. See Tingergen, Jan, *Economic Policy: Principles and Design*, North Holland Publishing Co., 1956, pp. 3ff; and Fox, Karl A. and Erik Thorbercke, "Specification of Structures and Data Requirements in Policy Models, in B. G. Hickman (ed.), *Quantitative Planning of Economic Policy*, The Brookings Institution, 1965, pp. 43–44.

2. For an example see Appendix I.

3. The model of Nova Scotia was commissioned by the Nova Scotia Voluntary Planning Board and developed by the author during two summers 1967 and 1968, with the assistance of Manas Chatterji, Andrew A. Dzurik, Glen Alexandrin and Janet Wykes. It was published as Stanislaw Czamanski, with the assistance of Glen Alexandrin, Andrew Dzurik, Janet Wykes: *An Econometric Model of Nova Scotia*, Institute of Public Affairs, Dalhousie University, 1968; more recently it has been reprinted by the Center for Housing and Environmental Studies, Cornell University, Ithaca, N.Y., and and abridged version appeared in Czamanski Stanislaw, "Regional Econometric Models: A case Study of Nova Scotia," in Allen J. Scott (ed): *Studies in Regional Science*, Pion, London, 1969.

4. For sources of data concerning all variables see Czamanski *et al., An Econometric Model of Nova Scotia*.

5. Based on the system presented by Bentzer, R. and B. Hansen, "On Recursiveness and Interdependency in Econometric Models," *The Review of Economic Studies*, XXII, 3, 1954–55, 153–168.

6. Malinvaud, E., Statistical Methods of Econometrics, Rand McNally & Co., 1966, p. 60.

7. Ibid., p. 512.

8. Goldberger, A. S., *Econometric Theory*, John Wiley & Sons, 1964, p. 355.

9. Klein, L. R., *Textbook of Econometrics*, Row-Peterson & Co., 1953, p. 92; Malinvaud E., *op. cit.*, p. 542ff; Goldberger, A. S., *op. cit.*, p. 306;

Tintner, G., *Econometrics*, John Wiley & Sons, 1952, p. 155ff; and Johnston, J., *Econometric Methods*, McGraw-Hill, 1963, p. 263ff.

10. Christ, C. F., Econometric Models and Methods, John Wiley & Sons, 1966.
11. For the use of this important device, see Appendix J.
12. For details see Czamanski, *Regional Income and Product Accounts of of North-Eastern Nova Scotia*, pp. 54–56.
13. Christ, *op. cit.*, p. 484.
14. For details and full results of sensitivity tests for all variables, see Czamanski, *et al., op. cit.*
15. A complete set of Figures for 1954 to 1961 can be found in Czamanski, *et al., op. cit.*
16. A complete set of figures for 1954 to 1961 can be found in Czamanski, *et al., op. cit.*
17. The actual tests were performed by Mr. Robert E. Geraghty and Miss Kaye Fisher of the staff of Voluntary Economic Planning, Nova Scotia Department of Finance and Economics.

Chapter 8

1. Williamson, *op. cit.*
2. See in this connection Hirsch, Werner Z., "The Supply of Urban Public Services," in Harvey S. Perloff and Lowdon Wingo, Jr. (eds.), *Issues in Urban Economics*, Johns Hopkins Press, 1968, pp. 477–524.
3. Based on data derived from Hildebrand, G., and T. C. Liu, *Manufacturing Production Functions in the United States, 1957*, New York State School of Industrial and Labor Relations, Ithaca, 1965, pp. 60–70; and U.S. Department of Commerce, Business and Defense Services Administration, *Industry Profiles, 1958–1966*, Washington, D.C., 1968.
4. See Chapter 5, especially Section 5.
5. Atlantic Development Council, *A Strategy for the Economic Development of the Atlantic Region*, 1971–1981, 1971.

Appendix J

1. Pearson, K., "On Lines and Planes of Closest Fit to Systems of Points in Space," *Philosophical Magazine*, II (1901), pp. 559–572.
2. Hotelling, H., "Simplified Calculation of Principal Components," *Psychometrika*, I (1936), pp. 27–35.
3. See, for example, Morrison, D. F., *Multivariate Statistical Methods*, McGraw-Hill, 1967, Chapter 7; and Tintner, *op. cit.*, Chapter 6.

Index

About the Author

Stan Czamanski was born in 1918 in Poland. He studied textile engineering and business administration at the College for Foreign Trade in Vienna, economics at the University of Geneva, philosophy at the Hebrew University in Jerusalem, and regional science at the University of Pennsylvania. He earned the Lic. ès Sc. Comm. degree from the University of Geneva and the Ph.D. from the University of Pennsylvania.

After teaching for some years at the University of Pennsylvania he joined Cornell University in 1966, where he is Professor of City and Regional Planning. At various times he held visiting appointments at the University of Pittsburgh, the University of Puerto Rico, Harvard University, Technion-Israel Institute of Technology, the Florida State University, and Tel-Aviv University.

In 1966 Professor Czamanski organized a Regional Studies Group at the Institute of Public Affairs, Dalhousie University, Halifax, Nova Scotia, which he has directed since. Among his numerous research and planning activities over the past twenty years his work in Nova Scotia, in Hawaii, and in Baltimore has led to the development of several new and improved techniques of regional analysis.

He has published over forty papers, articles, and research reports ranging over a wide variety of topics.